DRAGON RISES, RED BIRD FLIES

Dragon Rises, Red Bird Flies

Psychology & Chinese Medicine

REVISED EDITION

Leon Hammer, M.D.

FOREWORD BY TED KAPTCHUK

EASTLAND PRESS ≈ SEATTLE

First edition published in 1990 by Station Hill Press, Barrytown, New York.
Revised edition published in 2005, additional material in 2010,
by Eastland Press, Incorporated
P.O. Box 99749, Seattle, WA 98139 USA
www.eastlandpress.com

Library of Congress Control Number: 2005923289
ISBN-10: 0-939616-47-5
ISBN-13: 978-0-939616-47-3
Printed in the United States of America

6   8   10   9   7

Grateful acknowledgement is due to the National Endowment for
the Arts, a federal agency in Washington, D.C., and the New York
State Council on the Arts, a state agency in New York City, for
partial financial support of the first edition of this book.

Book design by Gary Niemeier

To those who are
teaching me how to love —
especially to my wife, Ewa,
my children, Paul and Kirin,
my grandson Andres and
those who loved me first,
my mother and father.

Contents

CONTENTS

Map of Contents

FOREWORD

A medical system always takes a patient on a journey that is at least partly self-discovery. Contemporary biomedicine tells a person about abnormalities in the endocrine system; Chinese medicine describes 'dampness in the Spleen'; and psychology uncovers repressed emotions. The more dimensions of the human personality contained in a medical conceptual model, the greater its potential for self-recognition. The more 'humanness' in the system, the more capacity to reveal, encounter, and transform.

The Chinese medical language is intensely metaphoric and has the potential to describe any aspect of human being. Historically, its metaphoric language has been used to contain different aspects of humanness with no self-imposed restraints. The physical, mental, emotional, intellectual, behavioral, social, existential, and spiritual domains all have, to one extent or another, depending on circumstances, been included or excluded from its inner dialogue and the doctor-patient exchange. Whether it has or is currently fulfilling its "holistic" potential is a complex historical and cultural question that all practitioners of Oriental medicine need to consider and constantly reconsider, both theoretically and in their daily clinical work.

The utilization of Chinese medicine's broad potential has depended at least partly on patient expectations and partly on the practitioner's own concerns and inner capacities. A medical encounter is always limited by how far the practitioner-guide can take the patient. No matter what the strength of a system, if the practitioner is only comfortable addressing the physical or the psychological or the behavioral or the existential, the healing transformation is likely to be confined to that single dimension. Also the less the intervention is focused on the physical, the more crucial becomes the self-understanding, insight, and inner resources of the healer.

Dr. Leon Hammer, one of the deans and elder statesmen of Chinese medicine in the United States, is a courageous practitioner who insists that Chinese medicine be a vehicle for all aspects of the human personality. He is aware, both from training and experience, of Chinese medicine's inherent possibilities and insists that its conceptual categories embrace the "entire" human being. He is a Western psychiatrist who studied with such notables as Fritz Perls, Eric Fromm, and Alexander Lowen, and a practitioner of Chinese medicine who bore the rigors of apprenticeship under idiosyncratic elderly "masters." Dr. Hammer is a healer who has plunged into the depths of his patients and himself. By using the insights of modern Western psychology, the energetic definitions of Chinese medicine, and the teachings of insightful Chinese healers, Dr. Hammer has taken Chinese medicine on a journey to seek a new sense of its own terrain. Using his inner powers, meticulous training, and rich experience, Dr. Hammer has brought new light to the depths of Chinese medicine. While readers, such as myself, may not agree with all of Dr. Hammer's informants, nor with all his sources, nor even at times with Dr. Hammer himself, every reader cannot but be pushed to probe into their own depths to discover anew what Chinese medicine means. *Dragon Rises, Red Bird Flies* forces practitioners of Chinese medicine in the West to further consider some of the inherent possibilities of the Chinese approach and advances us in our own scholarly, clinical, historical, linguistic, and cross-cultural explorations of the vast medical system of the East. *Dragon Rises, Red Bird Flies* is an important self-examination and exploration of Chinese medicine by one of its most dedicated, informed, and distinguished practitioners.

TED KAPTCHUK

Pain and Stress Relief Clinic
Lemuel Shattuck Hospital
Boston, Massachusetts

PREFACE TO REVISED EDITION

Fifteen years have passed since the publication of *Dragon Rises, Red Bird Flies*. The book was an attempt most of all to demonstrate natural functions of the energetic phases of Daoist (Taoist) Chinese medicine, and the parallel ontological development of the human psyche with the concurrent evolution of these phases, within the template of the human condition.

Illustrations of the distortions of these natural functions by life trauma and heritage were necessary to highlight the natural functions, and were not meant as a text on psychopathology, as I tried to explain in a note to the reader that preceded the chapters on the phases (elements). There I emphasized my abhorrence of typology of any kind.

Shortly after the publication of this book, several things occurred. First was the surprising acceptance of the book as a contribution to the understanding of our humanity and its appreciation by the informed reader as evidenced by its appearance in popular bookstores for many years.

Second was the awareness of many errors in the book that are finally being corrected in this revised edition, and of the omission of aspects of these natural functions and their vicissitudes, especially of the Earth phase, that is advanced in this new edition. I am grateful to the editors of Eastland Press, and in particular to John O'Connor, a witty, respectful and capable partner in the difficult and precarious endeavor to re-shape words and ideas, with whom I have worked most closely during the past five years, and to Gary Niemeier, a book designer and gentleman *par excellence*.

Another alteration is the substitution of the word 'phase' for 'element'. Phase is a more accurate translation and is commensurate with emphasis in the book on the evolution of qi and the psyche that pass through precise yet overlapping developmental stages.

After I had finished the first edition, it was my intention to write a sequel involving diagnosis and treatment of psychological conditions, and especially to focus on the general principles of growth and development and on the therapeutic relationship, especially for practitioners of Chinese medicine.

Instead my attention was drawn away by what I believed to be a short project of collating my notes regarding Dr. John Shen's pulse practice. What was to be a six-month diversion became a twelve-year odyssey and obsession resulting in the publication, in 2001, of *Chinese Pulse Diagnosis: A Contemporary Approach*. Writing this book sharpened my understanding of many of the issues discussed in Chapter 14 of *Dragon Rises, Red Bird Flies*, which is entitled "The Systems Model of Dr. Shen." That chapter has been revised accordingly here.

I wish at this time to correct a common misconception regarding the source of *Dragon Rises, Red Bird Flies*. The concepts developed here began their formulation around 1974, prior to my encounter and apprenticeship with Dr. Shen, and developed over the following years completely independent of this esteemed Chinese physician, who knew nothing of its contents except for the chapter devoted to his 'systems model.' Apart from Chapter 14, nothing in this book was drawn from my work with Dr. Shen, and even that chapter is a melding of his teaching and my own experience, as explained in the introduction to that chapter.

At this time I am engaged in developing a program at the Dragon Rises College of Oriental Medicine in Florida, which is known as Contemporary Oriental Medicine. This is based on the thesis that a medicine grounded in an advanced, sophisticated Chinese medical diagnostic methodology leads to more comprehensive management of an individual than a symptom-disease-pattern driven methodology, and on the premise that Chinese medicine must grow and change with the industrial and communications revolutions of the past three-hundred years. This program will include the sequel to this book mentioned above, evolving into an as yet to be determined body of written work.

The reader will find here a more correct and complete rendition of *Dragon Rises, Red Bird Flies*, whose thesis is evolution and which is itself a work in continuous progress.

ACKNOWLEDGEMENTS

I am indebted to many people who have assisted me from the beginning of my mid-life transition from psychiatry and Western medicine to Oriental medicine. Leslie Kenton gave me the encouragement, love, and opportunity to begin this work. The exceeding kindness and patience of Dr. and Mrs. Van Buren, and the great clinical skill which Dr. Van Buren shared with me so generously, can scarcely be fully acknowledged. My principal teacher for 27 years until his passing in 2001, Dr. John Shen, has given me a deeper insight into the endless ramifications of this medicine, especially in terms of diagnosis. His brilliant rational mind and capacity for experiment and originality have been for me a model of innovation in the context of orderly thinking. Sidney Zerinsky has been an inspiration and friend from the beginning of my journey. I have met many people along the way who have given me their friendship and support, especially the late Rosalind Roberts, Edward Roberts, and my former secretary and friend, Rita Scholl.

I am of course forever grateful to the William A. White Institute where I received my essential psychoanalytic training, and to my teachers and analysts, including Clara Thompson, M.D., Gerard Chernowski, M.D., Eric Fromm, Ph.D., Ernst Schactel, Ph.D., Harry Bone, Ph.D., Anina Brandt, Ph.D., Anna Gourevich, Ph.D., Ralph Crowley, M.D., Louis English, M.D., and Benjamin Wolstein, Ph.D. I also wish to thank Julia Ludmer, who has always encouraged me to write.

Others have shared their knowledge as well as their good will: Giovanni Maciocia and Alan Papier in England; Drs. Li and Ye and Mme. So in Beijing; Dr. Timothy Mar, Dr. Jerry Deutch, Dr. Al Lowen, and Dr. John Pierrakos in New York; and my valued friends Joanne Ehret, C.A., Dipl. Ac., Jason Eli as, C.A., Dipl. Ac., Elaine Stern, C.A., Dipl. Ac., and Phyllis Bloom, C.A., Dipl. Ac.

ACKNOWLEDGEMENTS

Those who so generously gave of their valuable time and thought to this book have my unlimited respect and gratitude. Peter Eckman, M.D., Ph.D., proffered a wise balance and made me reexamine statements which might have appeared excessive and therefore inaccurate. I am indebted to Bob Felt. He has read the manuscript, given me valuable advice and encouragement, and directed me to George Quasha, whose enthusiastic good nature, wide experience with, and genuine dedication to, the Daoist (Taoist) path has made him a perfect publisher with whom to collaborate. Ted Kaptchuk has kindly read the manuscript and offered his valuable input and dissent. His thoughtful Foreward is a valuable addition to this book.

I am especially indebted to Robert Duggan, M.A., M.Ac., Director of the Traditional Acupuncture Institute in Maryland, for the opportunity to know him and study with him during the 1980s. Mr. Duggan has been successfully training students in the Five Element Worsley School of acupuncture for many years. He has persuasively expounded the core concepts of this school of Chinese medicine, which was the first in the West to place the psychological and spiritual condition as a primary consideration in illness and in healing. His willingness to give not only his own time and effort but also that of his staff has resulted in valuable comments and suggestions, which have benefited this manuscript. I deeply appreciate his contribution.

I am grateful to Dr. Mark Seem, Director of the Tri-State Institute of Traditional Chinese Acupuncture, for the opportunity to present my ideas to his students. Dr. Seem has been a pioneer in presenting the case for the relevance of Western psychology to Chinese medical practice, about which he has written eloquently in a book entitled *Bodymind Energetics*. I wish to extend my special gratitude to him for giving this book a remarkable amount of detailed and worthwhile comment, which has been reflected in improvements of the text.

I am endlessly grateful to Joan Kaplan for her sensitive and exhaustive "developmental editing" of my manuscript. She has transformed this work into a more readable and useful text, fulfilling its basic purpose, to communicate. All authors need Joan Kaplan.

Megan Hastie's careful reading has contributed to virtually every page of the book. My thanks to her, and to Charles Stein, for their close collaboration with George Quasha. Michele Widrick's labors are also deeply appreciated.

My current secretary and friend, Phyllis Wilsey, is a dedicated, resourceful person whose wisdom and patience have been surpassed only by her caring and concern. She has given her heart as well as her skills to this book. Having her with us on this enterprise is deeply appreciated.

I want to thank the editor of the *American Journal of Acupuncture*, Mr.

John Nawratil, for giving me the opportunity to share my ideas with the world, and Richard Grossman, author and former publisher, who was the first person to encourage me to write. And not least, I am indebted to Tom Tunney for the gentle and unassuming instruction in meditation and Chinese exercise, which has shown me the path to my self, and to his wife Patty whose life embodies what the path itself seems to offer.

{*xxvii*}

I cannot leave these acknowledgements without a long overdue recognition of my teachers in Junior High School P.S. 125 in Queens, New York, and Stuyvesant High School, who, along with a family friend, Sam Kellner, and peer, Norman Kretchmer, M.D., rescued me fifty years ago and set me on a productive life path. Norman pointed me in the direction in which I found my best educational experiences at Stuyvesant High School and Cornell University.

In a category by herself is Augusta Schlesinger, deceased in 1952, who by the touch of her hand and the shape of her character, renewed me. Equally revered is Mary Duhig, a former nun, who I have described as the "wind and the anchor" of my soul.

Most of all, I want to thank my wife, Ewa, for her endless love, support, and constructive criticism, with which almost anything is possible. She has untiringly and without complaint devoted the past two years to editing this book, to the point of exhaustion and to the exclusion of her own work and relaxation. Without her this book would never have reached publication. My son Paul has never ceased pressing me to write, and through him and Kirin (he will not believe me), as well as Ewa, I have learned most of what is important to being human.

Preliminary Distinctions

PART I

The purpose of this book is to explore the energy concepts of Chinese medicine as they pertain to both the most mundane and the most esoteric aspects of the psychology of man. It is meant to serve as a springboard for continuing investigation by those who share my commitment to healing physically, mentally, and spiritually. It will speak most directly to those who sense that genuine healing is a unified activity that encompasses all three domains.

Chinese medicine has been for me the fulfillment of a search for a congenial system of healing that embodies the inseparability of body and mind, spirit and matter, nature and man, philosophy and reality. It is a personal, subtle, gentle, yet highly technical medical system, which allows me to be close to essence—to the life force—both my own and that of others.

The reasons for using it, teaching it, and discussing it are two-fold. First, it works. Second, it is a masterpiece of harmony, intricacy, and movement, which never ceases to engage me, fascinate me, and intrigue me. It surrounds me like nature, or a great work of art. I am consumed and renewed at one time.

I am a physician trained in psychiatry and psychoanalysis, and my medical odyssey from Western to Chinese medicine unfolds in the pages below. Based on 34 years of direct experience, this book examines the natural energy functions of the human organism as it differentiates into mental, emotional, and spiritual manifestations. The emotional correspondences of the energy organ systems, presently identified with negative pathological states, are re-examined here in such positive terms as directed assertion (Liver-Wood), creative awareness and expression (Heart-Fire), divine power, love and faith, the transcendental identity of man (Kidneys-Water), bonding and boundaries (Spleen-Earth), separation and the transformation of bonds (Lungs-Metal).

These are viewed in a framework of both human energy and psychological development and further examined in terms of interferences with their normal evolution and expression. Pathological responses (energy transformations), arising as restorative adaptive strategies to maintain *contact* and stay *intact*, are examined as deviations from these natural functions, rather than as defense-resistance maneuvers of an immature personality. The distortions in the natural functions of energies during different life periods leave us with general personality configurations which may be among the earliest indicators of energy pathology. I stress emphatically at the beginning that the reader should focus on the natural functions of these energies and that the clinician attend to variations from the norm only in the context of his individual patient and not in conformity with the examples of disharmony which I have included for illustration. The latter are not intended to be taken and followed literally.

It would be appropriate at the beginning to define some of our recurrent concepts and themes. By 'Chinese medicine' I mean the myriad and complex array of diagnostic, therapeutic, and philosophical information developed in China since the dawn of time, studied and applied to human and other animals, apparently originating in the Daoist (Taoist) concepts of a universal cosmic energy as the determining factor in life and health.

I wish also to identify my use of the term 'Western medicine' with that practice and accumulated body of knowledge known as allopathic medicine, and to be clear from the start that I fully recognize that other allopathically-related or unrelated medical practices exist in the West. We refer to these as 'alternative,' 'complementary,' and 'holistic.' Some of them share with Chinese medicine the theory and practice of energy; others have an energetic impact on health, yet do so without a conscious theory or practice of energetics. An abbreviated list of alternative practices would include Homeopathy, Naturopathy, Osteopathy, Chiropractic, Anthroposophy, Cranial Osteopathy, Orgonomy, and Ericksonian Hypnosis. More recent disciplines include Alexander Technique, Feldenkrais Functional Integration, Bioenergetics, Trager Psychophysical Integration and Mentastics, Craniosacral Therapy, Rolfing, many forms of therapeutic massage, and related body/mind practices. These approaches use a variety of different models of health and body/mind functions. It is not my interest in this book to draw any sort of comparisons between them and Chinese medicine; they are occasionally used below as reference points.

The areas referred to below as Bioenergetics are my own extrapolations of basic concepts laid out by Alexander Lowen and John Pierrakos (deriving to different degrees from Reich) during our years of association and are in no way an attempt to reproduce these concepts exactly as they were or are conceived by these gentlemen in their writings or other teachings.

The following is a personal history of my movement from Western to Eastern medicine. Prior to entering medical school I studied chemistry. I found that, upon being asked why I wished to be a doctor, I answered unconvincingly to myself and to others that it was a means of pursuing an interest in science. I realized even then that my interest was more personal and that, in fact, my need to be a physician would be better satisfied in psychiatry.

In medical school I became aware of disparate forces at work. Most impressive was a burgeoning body of technical knowledge that was not cohesive, was rarely integrated, and which contradicted itself year in and year out. Investigation was limited by a statistical verification system, which threw away information simply because it might have occurred by 'chance.' The entire system of study and acquisition of knowledge was accepted religiously, without question. Yet it was only in rare cases that research findings were verifiable, or usefully applicable, with the certainty which this faith implied. The data from most research rarely raised questions about basic physiological assumptions. Instead, it was used to reinforce these assumptions.

If thought remains only within specific conceptual parameters, whatever it addresses will be limited to the effective range of these concepts—that is, unless the underlying premises are actively questioned. I came to realize that in medicine this would be tantamount to treason. If, for example, back pain is conceived as due to arthritis of the spine, an x-ray search will almost always reveal a structural deformity, such as 'spurring,' confirming this assessment. Yet, beyond a certain age, spurring is ubiquitous, causing no problems for the majority of people who have it. Maslow once suggested that "If the only tool you have is a hammer, you will always be looking for a nail."

An important disparity of which I became aware was the one that existed between this lofty research and the way medicine was actually practiced. What took place was an often desperate, indiscriminate exploitation of any tool (usually discovered accidentally, outside the scientific method), primarily chemical, which mainly alleviated symptoms. Little consideration was given to how a procedure affected the rest of a person's body and life. Frankly, the carnage I witnessed through the wanton application of penicillin, cortisone, ACTH, psychotropic medications, lobotomies, electric and insulin shock, radiation treatments, and anesthetics—not to mention the debilitating use of dangerous, painful diagnostic procedures—was terrible.

As the profession thus became specialized, technologically oriented, and alienating, there developed increasing depersonalization between doctor and patient. The art of care disappeared before my eyes. Throughout the medical profession, including nursing, sincere dedication was too often replaced by cynicism, coldness, and barely disguised contempt represented by an order for TLC (tender, loving care) in a patient's chart. It strains the imagination that a doctor should have to write an order for tenderness. An even greater contempt crept into medicine through the door of psychosomatic medicine. Any illness that could not be pigeon-holed as 'organic' was branded as 'functional', the implication being that the patient was 'mental', a crock or a malingerer. Little consideration was given to the possibility that the problem might be with the medicine or beyond the range of the physician's diagnostic tools.

After medical school I found not much room in our medicine for the average patient with a minor complaint. Apart from offering a placebo—or worse, a tranquilizer—the doctor had no recourse but to instruct the patient to come back when there was a disease that the Western diagnostic armamentarium could decipher. Often, this was at an already advanced point in the disease process. Western medicine became a medicine of heroics. If one qualified for the intensive care ward, one could depend upon remarkable care. This emphasis on extreme pathology precluded the study of the disease process from its inception in the 'normal' person. Rather than defining health, we could only roughly approximate the absence of gross debilitating pathology. Nothing more than lip-service could be paid to 'preventive medicine'.

I found no integrated concept and practice of psychosomatic medicine. I was forced to make a choice between body or mind, and I chose the mind. Since psychiatry at that time was a relatively humane practice, one could continue to practice without surrendering one's being. Or so it seemed.

My training in psychiatry included a three-year residency and seven years at a psychoanalytic institute. Though the psychoanalytic school I chose was interpersonal in its orientation, it was heavily influenced by Freudian concepts, and its method was characterized by an artificially detached relationship between patient and doctor. I questioned the emphasis placed on the concept of 'resistance', which I reconceptualized as 'restorative contact'. I will elaborate this idea throughout the text. Psychiatry proper strove to become a technological stronghold, to become more and more like the rest of medicine, which it envied for its 'objectivity'. If only the workings of the human psyche could be as experimentally verifiable as the rat's liver!

I discovered in my practice that psychotics who had nothing to lose frequently became 'well' faster and more completely than neurotics, for whom change was a threat to the known and proven misery-ridden roads to power. Paradoxically, 'failure' was a great opportunity and 'success' an obstacle to growth. I learned that the availability of dissociated material made change possible, provided that one could construct a 'new life experience' with that material, significantly different from the original. I realized that transference was simply the opportunity for that experience and that 'resistance' was restorative behavior, to be noted and respected as an attempt at survival—an attempt, to be sure, that had later become fixed and, therefore, a handicap. All 'restorative behavior' was, however, an attempt to maintain *contact,* while staying *intact.* I came to feel that the resolution of this polarization of energies was the main issue in therapy and life, rather than the psychoanalytic preoccupation with 'resistance,' which is the *real resistance to growth, perpetrated by the therapy.*

My focus on 'contact' led me back to the body, to touch, to the work of Reich, Bioenergetics, massage, Rolfing, Gestalt, and LSD for new opportunities to contact dissociated selves. The body and mind were coming back together for me at last. And the meaning of 'energy' was emerging.

Simultaneously, I became actively involved with conservation (1961-71) and increasingly influenced by the field of ecology and the concepts of the interrelatedness of all phenomena, balance, and the universal tendency toward a dynamic harmony. I experienced a growing cognizance of our compulsion to master and control nature for profit, rather than join with it in partnership. I witnessed the consequent destruction of ecological balance, harmony, and life. My awe of 'creation' increased, as did my sadness at our loss of reverence and humility. Without these fast-disappearing attributes, man is unequal to his Biblical task as the earth's steward.

In my search for a healing art in concert with these concepts of energy, ecology, and balance, I discovered Chinese medicine quite by accident. During the past 34 years, it has fulfilled my need for a successful practice in which my patients and I are increasingly concordant beings. I wish to record my views of this medicine from the perspectives I have just outlined.

These remarks are not intended to be a condemnation of the Western medical model. This model is valid and necessary. It has saved countless lives, including my own. The emphasis I have placed here on its limitations and abuses is only a response to its disproportionate influence on the daily routine of medical care in the Occident. Nor is this book meant to be total approbation of Chinese medicine as the alchemist's stone: the one, only, and final statement on the subject of healing and health.

{ *xxxiv* } Chinese medicine has been fashioned, over the centuries, for a society vastly different from our own, particularly with regard to emphasis placed on individuality. The astounding honesty and insight of the works of Lu Xun[1] and Bo Yang[2] should be read by anyone who wishes to place this medicine in the not altogether flattering context of Chinese character and culture. Joseph Campbell should be consulted for his remarkable account of the countervailing philosophies of hate emerging in concrete book form in the fifth century B.C., which have influenced the mainstream of Chinese life to the present and which are historically hidden by the superficial layers of ethical Confucianism and beautiful, spiritual Daoism (Taoism).[3]

Life is a paradox. The very special attributes of precision, predictability, exactness, and systematization which characterize Chinese medicine are also its greatest drawbacks. From the time of Confucius to the present, these attributes have been exaggerated, creating a rigidity which, in my opinion, has hurt the development of the medicine. Intellectual disciplines require new questions and new answers, as well as the immutable wisdom of the old. My own teacher, Dr. John H.F. Shen, has often pointed out that Chinese medicine evolved from the work of men like himself, who, while sometimes having great insight into reality, must, because they are human, always find perfection beyond their reach. In its contact with the West, Chinese medicine has begun to change, for the first time in hundreds of years, in a direction which will ultimately speak more cogently to the issue of a personal, rather than a mass, psychology. The reservations and revisions that I make, and that others have made, in no way challenge its fundamental truth and worth.

PART II

In the *Yellow Emperor's Inner Classic (Huang di nei jing)*, Chi Po, minister to the Yellow Emperor, states that "In order to make all acupuncture thorough, one must first cure the spirit."[4] Some modest advancement toward a broader realization of this profound insight is all I hope to achieve in the service of our ultimate objective: a unified healing instrument for a unified being.

For me this inquiry is part of an ongoing process, which I hope will deepen and widen my understanding of the relationship of the traditional Chinese organ systems to both natural personality functions and emotional disharmony states. The chapters below on disharmony are offered only as food for thought, and not as a final word on the subject. The material is being reported at this stage of its evolution, not because it is complete or entirely accurate, but because some arbitrary time, neither premature nor excessively delayed, had to be chosen for its exposure. I have permitted my age to be one determining factor in the timing of this book, in the hope of allowing enough opportunity in my own life to share the intellectual fruits that these concepts may inspire in others.

Each individual approaches the problem of psyche and soma according to his or her own training. One whose emphasis is on the actions of the acupuncture points will begin there to find correspondences between energy 'spheres of influence' and emotion. Another whose training is with the 'phases' (or 'elements') and 'officials' will have a perspective from which to approach these relationships between body and mind. Those with a background emphasizing the concepts of the Japanese *hara* and the Chinese *dan tian* (tan-t'ien) will proceed from these precepts.

My own training began with the Five Phase (or Element) system, including some use of the 'officials,' and the shifting of energy as taught by Dr. Van Buren. After studying this for four years, I spent the next eight years studying diagnosis with Dr. Shen, relying on his unique interpretation of the pulse, tongue, face, and eyes. Part of that training included using these modalities to identify the emotional factors in the pathogenesis of disease. In China I became better acquainted with the Eight Principles system of diagnosis, as it is more conventionally understood. In recent years I have turned back to the Five Phase system as taught by Worsley, and to the Japanese system of the *hara,* as taught by Matsumoto. Gestalt, Bioenergetics, and Applied Kinesiology, along with Oriental meditative practices, both quiet and active, have affected my position.

The greatest influence on this book has come from my seven years of training as a psychoanalyst, 25 years of working with children, and years of developing significant deviations from established thought and practice before I encountered Chinese medicine. My early training prepared and prejudiced me to examine energy in terms of psycho-social development. My own viewpoint liberated me to approach energy and human behavior from the standpoint of health (natural functions) rather than pathology, to emphasize the 'positive,' and to understand the 'negative' as its shadow—as the positive at an impasse. This is the perspective from which this work has been written.

The inspiration for this book began with Lawson-Wood's book, *The Five Elements and Chinese Massage,* which I first read in 1973. By 1974 1 was working on an evolutionary concept of energy, expressed in a series of speeches at the William A. White Institute in New York City and the Finca La Falenca in Spain; then, later, in Toowoomba, Australia in 1982; and elsewhere. During my eight years with Dr. Shen, beginning in 1974, I set this material aside, and then resumed work after my return from China and partial retirement in 1982.

Chapter 14, on the 'systems model,' was built around a series of lectures at the Tri-State Institute of Traditional Chinese Acupuncture during 1985 and 1986. Dr. Shen's ideas have been widely elaborated here in terms of Western psychology, with which he is naturally unfamiliar, so that much here is also based on my own extrapolations and experience.

I have knowingly taken no one else's material without direct acknowledgement. My exposure to the Worsley school came long after these ideas were conceived. Recently, I have been drawn to that school, as well as to the Japanese system of the *hara* and *Toyahari*, as a part of returning to a way of working with energy that accentuates balance and a more sensitive, delicate, and respectful use of energetics. To them I am deeply grateful for this opportunity.

PART III

What follows here is a collection of observations intended to help the reader frame the material in this book. Certain terms and particulars may need clarification.

Working with Patients

My first contact with each person lasts from two to three hours, and each subsequent visit involves up to one hour of private consultation in the office before I begin treatment with acupuncture. Visits vary from once a week in the beginning to once a month or less during the later part of treatment. I inform each person that I am available seven days a week to talk by phone about any aspect of his or her life or therapy.

Before any information is shared, I give a careful explanation of the differences between Chinese and Western medicine. The energetic, functional aspects of the former are sharply differentiated from the morphological aspects of the latter, partially by contrasting the functions of the organs in the two systems. An emphasis is placed on the absence of pathology from a Western perspective, unless, in rare instances, I feel that an evaluation from that perspective is advisable. I have been greeted with appreciation for the referrals I have made, which have given my patients the feeling that I genuinely care about their well-being rather than about pressing my kind of medicine over another. I have found, after 53 years of clinical experience, that in the main it is not what one says that matters, but rather how one says it.

Some concern has been voiced about sharing with the patient potentially upsetting information gleaned from the Chinese diagnostic methods about his deep-seated emotional and/or physical problems. Such disclosure has been critically referred to as "shock" therapy. Over the last 34 years of active practice I have come across only one person, examined in a teaching situation, who, I am told, was either offended or adversely affected by my sharing this information. There will be occasions when strong emotional feelings are evoked. Time for working through these feelings should always be allowed, and no therapeutic relationships should be ended until these feelings have been incorporated into some positive growth process.

Anthropomorphizing Energy

Objections have been made to the 'anthropomorphizing' of energy, as it has been passed down in the *Nei Jing*, for instance in the designation 'officials,' by the same people who say simultaneously that the Liver 'attacks the Spleen,' or that the qi is 'rebellious' or 'wild', or that the blood is 'reckless.' If anger, joy, compassion, fear, and sadness are acceptable analogues of energy transformations, why not judgment, planning, will, warmth, and precision? Why not pretense, denial, projection, repression, reaction-formation, reversal, and sublimation? We can and must consider the entire range of behavior, personality, and intention as a province of energetics.

Judgment is an energy function no less than digestion. If energy is differentiated for every function, how can it be less so for a mental construct than for a purely physical one? If one energy repels pathogens and another holds the organs in their place, how can we deny an energy which drives the will, creates consciousness, bonds people to one another, asserts that will, and transforms that bond? Rationally speaking, a system that is by definition a unified statement of the cosmos cannot rationally be applied piecemeal. If we experience energy as a reality, we must acknowledge it in its totality.

Fragmentation of Western Practice

I wish to register my regret at the divisions in Western acupuncture which are appearing more frequently and with greater vehemence with each passing year. Each approach to this subject came to the West by way of a person who had available to him or her the translation of only one fragment of the total picture of a medicine as vast and variegated as China itself. Even if we had the sense to recognize this and accept each fragment as legitimate, it would take centuries of research to capture the entire fabric of this rich and valuable heritage.

This is especially true because so much of it has been suppressed in China during our era. With all due respect to the remarkable achievement of the People's Republic of China for reviving the medicine which had been outlawed during the rule of the Kuomintang, what is called 'Traditional Chinese Medicine' does not comprise a single body of knowledge, contrary to the impression given by the books now emerging from that country.

On my way to the Beijing airport at the end of a three-month stay, a Chinese doctor explained to me that in the early 1960s, responding to a drive by the World Health Organization to encourage the use and spread of indigenous health systems, the Chinese government brought together a group of acceptable Chinese physicians and ordered them to create 'Traditional Chinese Medicine' so that, under the auspices of that organization, it could be taught to the Chinese people and to foreigners. Thus ended the practice of 'following a master' for many years in relative servitude, and the thousands of blossoms on the tree of this medicine fell away until only one was left. Anyone in the West who believes they alone have the 'real' Chinese medicine is living in a dangerous world of fantasy.

THE NERVOUS SYSTEM

The 'nervous system' is a term that arises occasionally in this book and is the principal subject of Chapter 13. I use it in lieu of a Chinese word to which we could attribute the phenomena we commonly associate with this system. The term covers those pathways, both central and peripheral, that control our musculoskeletal system, control smooth muscle wherever it appears in the body (autonomic), and mediate all kinesthetic information and those functions of the brain ordinarily called 'mind.' It is a term that also refers to states of tension or lack of tension when qualified by the terms 'stressed' or 'calm.'

For Dr. Shen, the 'nervous system' is associated with the lightest and quickest energy, which by the very nature of Chinese thinking would be closest to the surface of the body and nearest to the lighter energies of the atmosphere. For this reason, he calls the 'nervous system' the Tai Yang (greater yang), using the term for energies associated in Chinese medicine with the surface. His choice to view these lighter surface energies as analogous to the nervous system is due to the relative functional rapidity of both compared to the speed of other physiologic operations noticed in either Chinese energetic or Western bioelectrochemical medicine. It is worth mentioning here that most of the outer acupuncture points of the Bladder channel, one of the two Tai Yang pathways, are among the most useful for psychological problems.

The peripheral and central nervous systems of Western science are conceptualized in Chinese medicine as one of the five 'singular organs.' (Other 'singular organs' are the Uterus, blood, bone marrow, and Gallbladder.) The term 'singular' is used to separate these energy functions from those of the five Zang organs (Heart, Lungs, Liver, Kidneys, and Spleen). The 'nervous system' or 'brain' is called the 'sea of marrow,' which is filled by the fundamental prenatal energy of the body called Kidney *jing*, or essence.

'Mental energy,' on the other hand, is one of the five 'functional energies' emanating from the 'five tastes,' which are the energies left over from metabolism and stored in the Spleen. This energy is directed to the Heart, which controls the mind, according to Chinese medical classics. Here we have the higher levels of mental activity such as memory, concentration, abstract thinking, and communication, as well as Spirit *(shen)*. In the medical context the latter refers more immediately to the general vitality of a person and liveliness of his or her mind than to esoteric levels. In the *Spiritual Pivot (Ling shu)*, for instance, it is said: "The origin of Life is in the Life Essence (male and female sperm/egg). When these two unite to make one, that is called the Spirit"; and: "Basically the Spirit is the Life Essence Qi derived from food and water." The word for heart and mind *(xin)* is the same in the Chinese language. According to another authority on Chinese medicine, the Liver yang energies are said to nourish the 'nervous system,' and Spleen energies are involved because they store the 'mental energy' and because rising Spleen qi is said to nourish the 'brain' and the 'mind.'

Regarding the 'nervous system,' we are dealing therefore on the most concrete level with the Kidney essence *(jing)* and the Sea of Marrow as the material foundation, as well perhaps as unconscious mental activity of phylogenetic origin (collective unconscious). On the most ephemeral level we have Heart spirit *(shen)* 'mental energies' which subsume the functions mentioned above connected with the 'mind.' And at another level we are concerned with those lighter energies which control the activity of the 'nervous system.' These are the Bladder and Small Intestine energies of the superficial Tai Yang, as well as those other energies also mentioned above, which nourish this system. Thus, when we use the expression 'nervous system,' please keep these distinctions in mind.

SPECIAL TERMS: USAGE AND SPELLING

References to the vital organs are to be interpreted only in energetic terms as defined in this book and in other sources listed in the references and the bibliography. Conceptually, the Heart, Liver, Spleen, Kidneys, and Lungs are to be clearly distinguished from the material organs of the same name in Western medicine. In reality, they are in a continuous dynamic exchange, and at the point where 'energy' solidifies into 'mass,' these concepts merge and the distinction is clinically obscure. While Chinese medicine is equipped to address both energy and mass, it clearly speaks most eloquently to the former. For purposes of clarity, we will capitalize the energetic organ systems to distinguish them from the material organs in Western terminology. We have also capitalized the names of the Five Phases, and the qualities of the pulse.

I have avoided the use of the term 'pathological' because of the common association with a relatively rigid Western morphology, although I consider this association prejudicial against a fully legitimate term. The term existed before the now dominant Western morphology and before practitioners of energy medicines (such as myself) discovered our resentment to the prevailing medicine for its intolerance of our work. Here I have acceded to the word 'disharmony' as a replacement in order to adhere more closely to the language of Chinese medicine and to its implications of a dynamic rather than a fixed process.

Throughout this text, I often use masculine pronouns for the human. I wish to state that with each exercise of that choice I experience a sharp twinge of regret that we have evolved without an unencumbered reference to both sexes simultaneously. Should I have a second chance to write a book, I will try to balance the female-male scale by using the female gender throughout.

With few exceptions, Chinese terms have been Latinized according to the widely used pinyin system. The formerly used Wade-Giles system is no longer in use in the People's Republic of China and is rapidly disappearing elsewhere in the world. However, in a few cases, both forms are provided.

ILLUSTRATIONS

Charts of the acupuncture channels (meridians) and points are not included because they are not necessary to the understanding of the substance of this book and because they are readily available in other books. In the best of all possible books, everything could have its image (worth ten thousand words).

POINT OF VIEW

Over the years I have watched the shifting tides of man's preoccupation with ideas wash up one point of view or another as the 'truth,' and just as quickly wash it away. Each leaves some trace, to be collected by beachcombers such as myself, and added to the inner decor of our being. I believe it is necessary that some individuals focus narrowly and intensely on one fragment of the truth. These are the scholars. Their in-depth contributions to knowledge are indispensable to the growth of our meaningful awareness. But I also believe in the beachcomber, and his or her creative place in the 'great order.'

This book is the work of the beachcomber, picking the sands of his own mind. It is the precipitate of a lifetime and has no academic pretensions. Its potential value is in being gloriously free of the tyranny of academia and of the oppression and tunnel vision of the 'double-blind' illusion. Its limitations are those of the writer, who would like to have been all things to himself and to others, but is no longer disappointed in being just himself.

I have little patience with those who examine the beachcomber only through the eyes of one or another philosophical prism and, focusing only on the difference of perspective, miss the whole message. Some years ago I debated for six hours with a prominent 'thinker' of our time whose frustration at the end of this most heated discussion was, he claimed, due to his inability to place me in an ideological cubbyhole. I have no objections to the criticisms of those who have the humility to identify their prisms and acknowledge their use. They are helpful and constructive. I do object to mere dogmatism, however brilliant the mind behind it, and regard it as dangerous to our mental and spiritual health.

THE TITLE AND RELATED HIGHER ISSUES

The dragon is the symbol of force and power. He is the energy of the cosmos, which is inevitably the central theme of this book. The red bird, or phoenix, arises from the ashes of immolation, only to return again to ashes, repeating its cycle endlessly. This too is the subject of the book, the tale of an emerging soul, its spiral growth within the shell of a developing ego, which reaches its apogee by consuming its material self and freeing its contents to the spirit world. There it will once again begin the process of choosing an ego structure within which to grow towards a oneness with God, the Tao, All That Is, shedding again and again its inescapable integument. One is the power, the other the rhythm of the universe, and both together the energic 'evolution of a being.'

I have used the expression 'evolution of being' to mean the unfolding of the life-force in continuous increments of increasingly complex organization, function, and performance, as an organism progresses from a single cell to a mature adult and finally to death and beyond. (The expression is in the spirit of 'becoming,' as eloquently expounded by Gordon Allport.)

My use of the terms 'soul' and 'spirit' come from my readings of Rudolf Steiner, who roughly defined spirit as the eternal aspect of our being and the soul as spirit incarnate, within the being in its material sojourn on earth. I am not a follower of Steiner, or for that matter of any institutionalized religion, and my references to the spiritual are eclectic. I recognize that soul and spirit may have other meanings to those of the various religious persuasions.

There is no way that we can consider the continuum of human concerns or the spectrum of the evolution of human energies without at some point coming to the interface between what we conceive of as reality and the great unknown. For even if we could explain in biochemical terms how life came to be, and even if we could explain in biophysical terms how the universe came to be, we would still be no closer to answering the question, What is this all about? What was here before the universe, and before that? Einstein said that life is a mystery, and that it will always be a mystery, and furthermore that this is a good and beautiful phenomenon. All of our strivings bring us to this mystery, to this great interface. It is healthy for those who choose to enter and experience it. Therefore I do not in any way apologize for those parts of the book that lead me into a realm where there is no science, where all we have is not what we believe but what we 'know.' Entering those spaces we need only remember to respect what others know as much as we hope for their respect of our unique experience. Therefore, by qualifying such phenomena as 'love' and 'power' with the attribute of 'divine,' I am moving the thrust of our inquiry into those places where no one goes except as a hero of his or her own experience, with no prejudice toward where one goes or the 'truth' one encounters.

My use of the word 'God' is without reference to any established recognizable theological instrument. I am referring only to the ineffable, mysterious forces that unify all phenomena of the universe, most succinctly verbalized in book one of the *Tao Te Ching*:

> *The way that can be spoken of*
> *Is not the constant way;*
> *The name that can be named*
> *Is not the constant name.*
> *The nameless was the beginning of heaven and earth.*
> *The named was the mother of the myriad creatures.*
> *Hence always rid yourself of desires in order to observe its secrets,*
> *But always allow yourself to have desires in order to observe its*
>   *manifestations.*
> *These two are the same*
> *But diverge in name as they issue forth.*
> *Being the same they are called mysteries,*
> *Mystery upon mystery —*
> *The gateway of the manifold secrets.*

1

CHINESE MEDICINE AND PSYCHOLOGY: CONGENIAL THERAPEUTIC PARTNERS

Psychology and Chinese medicine are congenial therapeutic partners. They are closer in concept and practice to each other than either is to the principles of Western science and medicine (except to Western science in the realm of theoretical physics). Together they function in the patient's interest better than either alone. It is my purpose first to examine the essential ingredients of this congeniality. I shall begin by defining the terms.

Psychology in this text refers to that study and treatment of the human condition where respect for the individual is the unifying concept and practice. The object of psychological study has been to understand the basic issues of human existence, the enduring qualities characterizing all human beings, and those fundamental attributes as they exist and evolve in the changing environments to which human beings are endlessly exposed during phylogeny and ontology. The term includes all those disciplines of the mind and spirit which have been grounded in respect for the individual, intending that the individual's growth and self-realization be relatively free of anxiety, crippling pain, guilt, disorganization, compulsion, obsession, fear, and depression. Whatever the theory or method, including the many psychotherapeutic traditions (Freud, Jung, Adler, Will, Sullivan), energy-based therapy (Reich, Lowen), Existential Psychology (Boss, May, Binswanger, Laing), Object Relations (Fairbairn, Gendlin, Guntrip), Humanistic Psychology (Maslow, Rogers, Fromm, Fromm-Reichman, Allport, Buhler, Horney), Reality Therapy (Glasser), Rational Emotive Therapy (Ellis), Logotherapy (Frankl), and even Behavior Therapy, respect is the thread that binds them to the use of the term 'psychology' in this book.

The term 'Chinese medicine' in this book includes all of the claims to the "true" Chinese medicine, including the terms classical, Traditional Chinese Medicine, Traditional Acupuncture, Five Phase (Element) Acupuncture, Core Energetics, Hara Acupuncture, Eight Principle Chinese Medicine, and Six Division Chinese Medicine. While I appreciate the distinctions made among these different disciplines, and have studied them all to one extent or another, they are, in reality, each only a part of the whole entity of an endless body of knowledge. The current claims of knowledge of the "true" picture of what this medicine encompasses remind me of the well-known story of the blind men who were asked to describe an elephant, and each portrayed the elephant as that part with which he was in contact. During seventeen years of work in this field, I have come across entire diagnostic and therapeutic modalities about which I have learned only from practitioners. Every village and every clan in China, Japan, Korea, Vietnam. Laos, and Cambodia evolved a Chinese medicine distinctly different from those even nearby. Those Jesuit priests who translated texts from one place in China or another had no way of knowing that what they were bringing back to the West was one small segment of a massive tradition. Therefore I choose to use the term Chinese medicine to include all of the rich, illimitable medical information which is the heritage of at least three thousand years of continuous Chinese culture.

Chinese medicine classifies the etiology of disease into three main categories. Foremost of these is the emotions, the Internal Demons:[1] anger, grief, fear, joy, compassion, anxiety, and worry. In the Chinese system, these Internal Demons are responsible for alterations in the energy system of a person, affecting to one extent or another the mind, the body, and the spirit. A review of Felix Mann's book, *The Treatment of Disease by Acupuncture*, Part 1, "Function of Acupuncture Points," reveals that 135 of the original 365 acupuncture points are used to treat mental, emotional, and spiritual disharmony, and many of the 'new' and 'strange' points are appropriately designated for this purpose. I agree completely with Peter Eckman, whom I quote from a personal communication, that "all therapeutically active points have an effect on the mind and spirit as a direct corollary of the denial of the Cartesian split" between body and the mind-spirit. At this early stage of the study and practice of Chinese medicine in the West, we rely still upon translations, such as those by Mann, of works which cite some points as being more relevant than others.

DIAGNOSING THE WHOLE PERSON

In contradistinction to most Western medicine, in which we classify and diagnose disease and not the person, Chinese medicine, like most psycho-therapies, is concerned with an individual's unique physical and emotional state. Chinese medicine and psychology also have systematic classifications of disease; however, the diagnostic and treatment modes of these practices emphasize the distinguishing intrinsic attributes of each individual. The human organism has a limited repertoire of signs and symptoms with which to signal alterations in natural functions. Treating those signs and symptoms without reading in them the story of the person is a denial of the role which the patient plays in his or her own disharmony. Two patients who recently came to me complaining of joint pains had each previously been treated with medicinals in exactly the same way by different doctors. From a combined Chinese medical and Western psychological perspective, one was a large woman in her fifties, whose pulse was Full and Bounding. She was red in the face and her tongue was heavily coated. Even more important was her lifelong history of self-abuse with alcohol, tobacco, excessive and poor food, overwork, accidents, and four hours of sleep a night. She was driven to sacrifice her 'self' to her 'ego', which had dreams and plans of glory. These had suddenly crumbled, when all the good she seemed to have achieved was undone by her business enemies, whom, in her grandiosity, she had offended with impunity over the years. She had been treated with exactly the same arthritis medicine by her physician as the second patient, a thin, pale father of several children, with a family history of debilitating arthritis. This man had a Deep, Thin, Tight pulse and a pale tongue with a red tip. He had experienced enormous emotional stress through a divorce, and he had a history of alcohol and drug abuse as a very young man fifteen years before, from which depths he had slowly risen with new wisdom. He was presently remarried and gainfully employed, enjoying a relatively happy and productive life except for his illness.

{3}

The similarity of their symptoms, which we call arthritis, is almost irrelevant to the essence of their illnesses, which are as different as their beings. For the man my treatment was a matter of undoing some of the damage of the past, sharing with him the dilemmas of this stage of his growth, and adding what my experience could to the upward spiral of his self-knowledge. The herbs, the acupuncture, the conversation, and the course of his treatment were almost diametrically opposed to that of the woman. From a Chinese medical perspective, their pulses, tongues, and other signs and symptoms indicated two very different disharmonies, just as their psychological profiles were very different. Yet they had received the same Western medicine for joint pain.

Both Chinese medicine and psychology anticipated Roger Williams' model of Biochemical Individuality.[2] In this model, there are no minimal daily requirements or recommended daily allowances. Each person is regarded as having a unique and separate biochemical system. According to his research at the University of Texas, where he synthesized vitamin B-6, one individual may require one gram a day of vitamin C, for example, and another might require 13 for the viability of their distinctive enzyme systems.

Symptoms as Messages

Both Chinese medicine and psychology focus primarily on the root sources of imbalance. The relief of symptoms alone is not the first consideration of the 'superior Chinese physician' and never supercedes the goal of balancing internal function. Symptoms must, of course, be alleviated for several reasons, apart from humanitarian ones: initially, to allow the patient's energy to be free for healing, and later, to give access to a more accurate diagnostic reading, especially on the pulse as understood by Chinese medicine. However, the alleviation of symptoms is only the beginning. We are concerned with the inner state and the causes for that inner energy state. Two patients having what Western medicine considers identical disease pictures may actually have two entirely different etiologies and therefore require two entirely different treatment plans. We have, in this analysis, as many 'diseases' as we have people.

Early in its development, psychology distinguished the symptom from the character structure in which it appeared, and recognized the necessity of dealing with the underlying character in the effort to achieve a meaningful healing. Thousands of years ago the Chinese described character structure and placed it squarely in the etiology of disease. The 'superior physician' concerned himself with behavior, with values, with relationship to family and to society, and consequently treated his patient as a total person. Chinese medicine is a 'medicine philosophy,' which is understated as the 'philosophy of the mean,' calling for moderation in all things and harmony with nature. Thus guided, the superior Chinese doctor counseled his patient to alter his lifestyle so as to minimize disharmony and maximize health. The underlying 'cause,' as expressed by character and behavior patterns, and not by the 'symptom,' is the focus of both disciplines. The 'cause,' as we use the term, is not an outside invading force, a virus or bacterium; rather, it is intrinsic to the individual and the lifestyle he or she generates.

Both psychology and Chinese medicine regard a symptom as a signal of unattended, underlying issues and not as a disagreeable phenomenon to be eliminated. Symptoms are opportunities to examine one's life, to reconsider one's values and habits, to re-evaluate one's personality and relationships, to expand awareness, and to change. The goal of a humanistic psychology is growth; and the goal of Chinese medicine is prevention of illness through the knowledge of natural law, which includes altering oneself so as to live in greater harmony with that law. Each in its own way is less concerned with extirpating a symptom and more concerned with utilizing its meaning.

DESCENT INTO HELL

Another area of coincidence between the two disciplines, in contradistinction to Western medicine, is the mutual realization that growth and healing frequently involve a 'healing crisis.' Change involves discomfort, or, in Chinese terms, 'aggravation.' At the beginning of acupuncture therapy, in a minority of instances, the illness for which the patient has come to be treated may temporarily worsen, or symptoms of previous illnesses may temporarily return. This is a positive sign that the suppressive measures to which he or she has been exposed are now being eliminated. Healing crises such as these are short-lived (a few hours to a few days) and are strongly favorable signs, especially for those beginning to withdraw from lifestyles characterized by abuse of drugs or food.

The 'pain' associated with growth and change in the practice of Western psychotherapies has long been understood and accepted as a positive experience. The 'descent into hell'[3] that the patient makes with the therapist is necessary for substantial regeneration. It is also an integral part of mythology that 'metanoia', the change of mind, is the result of a dangerous journey into the 'inner' self. This odyssey is identified with cultural heroes and is one of the rites of passage[4] into adulthood in many societies. Progress in healing is measured, in Chinese medicine, primarily by the patient's mental state. If the patient is physically better but mentally worse, the treatment is considered a failure. As long as the mental state is improving (except for the healing crisis), the course of treatment is considered favorable. Western psychology and psychosomatic medicine have long espoused this viewpoint.

HEAVENLY POINTS

In Chinese medicine all illness has spiritual implications. Such implications are not admissible within the Western model, except in the confines of 'humanistic' psychology, where, for instance, Assagioli's psychosynthesis[5] has expanded the spiritual dimension of psychology. This work of course derives from that of Carl Jung[6] in the early part of the 20th century. Rarely in recent Western science or medicine have 'spirit' and 'soul' remained integral to practice. The use of these terms here and throughout this book is based on my understanding of Rudolf Steiner's usage.

[6]   In Chinese medicine-philosophy, concepts of the spirit are an integral part of diagnosis and treatment. There are acupuncture points, all of which begin with the word *tian* (meaning heaven or heavenly), that are specifically used to open a person to spiritual awareness. The *shen* (spirit) is derived from the pure yang of the universe, also known on the human level as *hun* (spirit-soul). The *jing* is derived from the pure yin of the universe, also known as *po* (body-essence). Essence refers to the material aspects of existence and spirit to the nonmaterial. Within the Chinese medicine-philosophy model, the fusion of the spirit *(shen)* with the essence *(jing)* is the ineluctable event that creates life, *yuan qi* (ancestral qi), the functioning energy of the human animal. (There are points on the back that are specifically for the animal-soul and spirit-soul, as well as other spiritual and mental functions.)

The combined *shen qi* is the 'spirit' of the individual, which is said to live in the Heart by day, and in the Liver by night. During the day it may be assessed through the pupils of the eyes. In health it will be expressed as a shining light. In disease it may be dull, withdrawn, or out of control (wild). At night, it rests in the Liver and may be assessed by a person's dreams. According to the Chinese clock, which attributes specific times of day to the peak activity of each organ system, the combined Liver-Gallbladder time is between 11 at night and three in the morning. Some authorities on Chinese medicine believe that a contented spirit does not dream.

Others believe that the *shen* or spirit in its corporal life (in humans) differentiates into the animal spirit, which lives in the Lungs *(po)* and directs physical energies, and the soul, which lives in the Liver *(hun)* and controls conscious and unconscious thinking. The Heart is the pure spirit and divine consciousness, the Kidneys are pure animal will. *Yi* (pronounced "-ee") resides in the Spleen and controls reflection. My own observations and experience, which are developed later in this book, find exceptions to this scheme. The spiritual condition of an individual is closely related to each of the major organ systems, and each of these systems is related to particular human attributes.

The concepts of the *hun* (spirit/soul) and the *po* (animal soul) are subtle. The spirit that is attached to the form, substance, or *jing yin* of things is *po*, and the spirit that is attached to the moving energy or qi of things is called *hun*. The spirit that is related to *po* is also referred to as *ling*, meaning 'magic' and 'miraculous.' The spirit which is related to *hun* is also referred to as *shen*, meaning divine or god. *Shen* is the 'active impulse' (yang),[7] and *ling* is the active, enabling mover (yin), the material acting out of the impulse.[8]

For practical spiritual guidance, the Chinese physician and patient had available the *I Ching: The Book of Changes.*[9] This body of knowledge emerged over thousands of years, beginning with the observation that there were eight fundamental states in the universe that are symbolic of the cosmic physical world as well as the spiritual, emotional, and mental world of man. It was understood that the majority of spiritual, ethical, and philosophical dilemmas in which human beings might find themselves could be expressed by various combinations of the eight basic units or trigrams *(ba gua).* While they are by no means exhaustive, the sixty-four hexagrams (eight times eight) are remarkable in the extent to which they capture the human condition.

An important section of ancient Chinese medicine integrates energy cycles with the eight *ba gua.* Formulae are associated with each of the sixty-four hexagrams which arise from the combinations of the trigrams. Acupuncture points thus derived ('timing points') are valuable for all treatment, especially of circulatory disturbances. They are also meant to assist the supplicant of the *I Ching* to comprehend and follow successfully the message of the hexagrams in the interest of harmonious mental health.

Miles Roberts, C.A., a Kanpo physician (Japanese herbal medicine) who has taught me much about Chinese medicine, states that there are five levels of practitioners in the Japanese medical tradition. What is relevant to the theme of this book is that even in a society such as Japan's, which does not encourage individual introspection as we know it in the West, the highest of these levels is the physician who counsels.

The Chinese physician had and has available a system of spiritual-physical movements intimately corresponding to the unifying principle of energy, and the biorhythmic laws of yin and yang. This system manifests in many forms of tai ji (T'ai Chi Chuan), qi gong (Ch'i Kung), or gong fu (Kung Fu). These exercises are an expression of the principle in nature of a rhythmic, alternating series of the 'firm and yielding' movements. They correspond in principle to the trigrams of the *I Ching*, in which yang is a firm, solid line, and yin is a yielding, broken line. In that book it is said that on the spiritual level there is the 'firm' and the 'yielding,' and on the correspondingly human level, there is 'rectitude' and 'love.' Health at any level of existence is said to be a function of the dynamic balance of these apparent polarities.

Though Chinese medicine is today a long way from its Daoist roots, meditation is still recommended by Chinese doctors. In the People's Republic of China, Daoist exercises such as tai ji and qi gong are recommended for the entire population, especially the sick and elderly; and qi gong is part of a large-scale movement in the successful treatment of cancer. Even in modern China, the 'energy' that traditional Chinese medicine utilizes in diagnosis and treatment is understood to be one with the larger energy of the universe.

THE ROLE OF THE HEALER

Another similarity between psychology and Chinese medicine, as opposed to established Western medical thought, is the importance of the healer to the healing process in both a real and a symbolic sense. The symbolic meaning of needles and of authority (the physician) is given a place in Chinese medicine and is of greater significance for some people than for others. Dynamic psychotherapy is a discipline in which the healer has always been a recognized part of the healing process, even in the limited sense of working through the transference.[10] In fact, psychology and psychiatry have contributed proportionately more practitioners to 'alternative medicines' (where the healer's central role is viewed as essential) than has any other branch of Western medicine.

In the Western tradition, if the personal presence or activity of the healer is of direct consequence to the course of the disease, the patient, by definition, is considered never to have been 'sick.' The patient's illness is 'imaginary,' and the patient who is not 'really sick' is viewed with condescension and subtle contempt as someone 'highly suggestible,' mentally unstable, and undesirable as a patient. The doctor who treats him may even be viewed as a quack, exploiting the infirm.

In those instances where emotional or spiritual considerations play no part in the initiation of the disease process, the mere presence of disease is nevertheless an emotional distress and a spiritual drain. Throughout history, every culture has recognized the need to provide a ritual for the delivery of its medical care, and has judged any absence of the approved ritual to be inferior therapeutics. Ritual reduces the cumulative burden of stress, alleviating, through culturally supported activities, the emotional and spiritual strain, either directly or indirectly associated with the disease process. Any real reduction in stress by nondestructive means gives an organism a better chance for recovery.

Western medicine today continues to provide medical care through rituals which are foreign to our cultural heritage. X-rays administered by technicians in sterile white coats, on tables with cold surfaces, in rooms which resemble the inside of a spacecraft are generally not stress-relieving.

Suggestion continues to be an important constituent of the healing process, for, although our environments have become drastically altered, human beings have not. Along with others in this country who have had success in treating chronically ill people otherwise considered untreatable by the health care system, I have been accused of using a powerful form of hypnotic suggestion. Ironically, the accusations have come from those most adamant in their rejection of the notion that emotion can cause 'real disease.' (If suggestion can cure disease, it can certainly cause it.) They have inadvertently acknowledged that suggestion is a powerful weapon but remain unwilling to examine how it could be used for the general welfare.

There is a basic conflict between technology and art in the healing process. Technology insists that, as a test of the validity of the healing modality, the healer must not be essential to the healing process. However, in a healing system in which the movement and balance of energy is the critical factor in sickness and health, the energy of the healer always enters significantly into the system as a positive or negative force. In such a system, the healer is a significant factor in the healing process. His intention and his life force influence the energy of the patient.

No attempt is made in psychology or in Chinese medicine to separate the tool from the artisan. They are one. Both the conscious and the unconscious intention of the practitioner are energies capable of profoundly interacting with the energies of the client for better or worse. For this reason, since Freud used his own dreams to analyze himself, psychology has advocated that the practitioner consistently monitor his or her intentions, preferably with a relatively objective participant-observer. "Know thyself" is equally appropriate for the practitioners of all the healing arts.

THE ACT OF OBSERVATION

Both bodies of knowledge, Chinese medicine and psychology, are experiential rather than experimental, and both embrace the importance of the unique healer to healing. Consequently, both have been widely criticized in the West as unscientific. Such a judgment ignores the fact that science began as the art of observation (as opposed to speculation). Art implies that the data is not completely objective since idiosyncratic influences of individual propensity and perception are not excluded from the final product. From Pythagoras to Einstein, the greatest advances in science have consistently arisen from the creative vision of idiosyncratic individualists. Observation without art leads to a sterile, uninspiring accumulation of inert details. The finest contributions of the humanistic psychological tradition and the Chinese tradition continue to emanate from the honest recording of personal, human, non-technological experience and observation combined with intuition and the wisdom of accumulated living. Repeated success is the criterion of truth. Emerson warned us over a hundred years ago of the danger of dismissing the knowledge gained from experience.[11] A personal communication from Miles Roberts, notes that Japanese herbal medicine is basically experiential, based on the shamanistic tradition. Theoretical rationalization based on Chinese medical principles was used to explain the actions of the herbs. This rationalization was imposed at a later time and only partially accounts for all of the applications of these formulae. The spirit of man, the energy of nature, and the knowledge of nature's ways are the healing powers of Oriental medicine.

The modern scientific institution will test and apply only that which is verifiable by reproducible and statistically significant experimentation. Statistical significance means the elimination of chance as a factor in the success of a procedure. Eliminating the element of chance is unthinkable to the Oriental mind, for whom unpredictable forces outside our control (loosely defined as fate) and constitution are two of the three fundamental factors determining the course of a person's life. The third factor is individual will.

In various ways in Hindu and Buddhist tradition, the purpose of earthly existence centers around the karmic struggle to give each person an opportunity to rise to a higher spiritual plane by correcting in this life the mistakes of the past. Seen in this light, disease takes on an entirely different relationship to each person's life. The double blind, statistically significant experiment becomes ludicrous when viewed from this point of view.

Militating even further against statistical significance as a test of the truth is the traditional role of the guru-healer in the resolution of the karmic dilemma of his disciples. Great Oriental healers take on the karma of their followers and often become profoundly ill, just as in the Christian faith Christ suffered for all mankind so that forgiveness might heal their original sin. In smaller ways, the dedicated psychotherapist expends his own energies in the therapeutic exchange of transference, and the Chinese doctor trained by meditation and gong fu utilizes his energies on behalf of his patients. Both traditional Oriental and Western psychotherapeutic healing practices are far closer in concept to the widely accepted Field Theory of Alfred North Whitehead and Kurt Lewin[12] than to the experimental mode of Western medicine. This theory states that there can be no truly objective experiment, since the mere presence of the observer changes the 'field' in which the experiment takes place. The psychologist and the practitioner of Chinese medicine accept the field as inevitable and attempt to use it. Western medicine regards the field as a contaminant which can and should be eliminated.

PHILOSOPHY OF THE MEAN

For both disciplines, health and disease are ultimately the responsibility of the patient. Values and behavior, as well as the honest confrontation with self, are basic to health in both the Chinese and the psychoanalytic tradition. The doctor helps, nature cures, and each person is responsible for his relationship to nature and to himself. [11]

The Yellow Emperor's Inner Classic, Simple Questions (Huang di nei jing su wen) has this to say:

> In ancient times when the Yellow Emperor was born he was endowed with divine talents; while yet in early infancy he could speak; while still very young he was quick of apprehension and penetrating; when he was grown up he was sincere and comprehending; when he became perfect he ascended to Heaven. The Yellow Emperor once addressed T'ien Shih, the divinely inspired teacher: "I have heard that in ancient times the people lived to be over one hundred years, and yet they remained active and did not become decrepit in their activities. But nowadays people reach only one-half of that age, and yet become decrepit and failing. Is it because the world changes from generation to generation? Or is it that mankind is becoming negligent [of the laws of nature]?"
>
> Chi'i Po answered: "There was temperance in eating and drinking. Their hours of rising and retiring were regular and not disorderly and wild. By these means the ancients kept their bodies united with their souls, so as to fulfill their allotted span completely, measuring unto a hundred years before they passed away."
>
> "In most ancient times the teachings of the sages were followed by those beneath them; they said that weakness and noxious influences and injurious winds should be avoided at specific times. They [the sages] were tranquilly content in nothingness, and the true vital force accompanied them always; their vital [original] spirit was preserved within; thus, how could illness come to them? They exercised restraint of their wills and reduced their desires; their hearts were at peace and without any fear; their bodies toiled and yet did not become weary. Their spirit followed in harmony and obedience; everything was satisfactory to their wishes, and they could achieve whatever they wished. Any kind of clothing was satisfactory. They felt happy under any condition. To them it did not matter whether a man held a high or a low position in life. These men can be called pure at heart. No kind of desire can tempt the eyes of those pure people, and their minds cannot be misled by excessiveness and evil. [In such a society] no matter whether men are wise or foolish, virtuous or bad, they are without fear of anything, they are in harmony with Dao [Tao], the Right Way. Thus they could live more than one hundred years and remain active without becoming decrepit, because their virtue was perfect and never imperiled."[13]

Each discipline in its own way acknowledges the relationship of mind and emotion to physical disharmony. While modern psychology and Western science have struggled for a century to formulate this connection, classical Chinese medicine has precise correspondences between the two. This is a subject which requires, and will subsequently receive, its own separate elaboration.

A principle of Chinese medicine holds that symptomatic illness is always the product of multiple etiology. This is in keeping with the work of

Hans Selye,[14] a well-known researcher in the biological consequences of stress, who has shown that disease is a consequence of the maladaption of an organism to multiple stressors. The sources of stress may be physical, chemical, mental, emotional, or spiritual. His work has been quite influential in the fields of psychology and psychosomatic medicine, but less so in mainstream medicine. Chinese medicine agrees that stress is the principal issue in disease and that more than one stressor is usually necessary to produce signs and symptoms. There is a Chinese saying, "You cannot make a sound with one ball."[15]

THE LIFE FORCE OR E=MC²

The Chinese see all phenomena as manifestations of one unifying principle of energy, the life force, or Dao (Tao). All form and substance in the universe is the materialization of energy (E=MC²).[16] The Chinese observed and recorded in intricate detail the rhythmic movement of this energy in the most cosmic and most minute structures of the universe within their sphere of scrutiny. Out of this study and observation came the Laws of Nature.[17] Only man, among all the manifestations of energy in the universe, collectively and consistently has a choice to follow or defy these laws. All other manifestations of this energy, from rocks to apes, follow their inner rhythms and biological clocks. Whatever the rationalizations, disease will follow significant deviations from the laws governing values, eating habits, work, and exercise patterns. The patient is responsible for his illness. With knowledge and awareness he can also prevent it.

Energy concepts in the Western medical world have appeared only in the psychoanalytic literature. Freud, in his concept of the libido,[18] postulated an energy whose vicissitudes in the unconscious mind played an integral role in mental and physical health and illness. The accurate translation of what is now recorded as 'instinct' is energy drive, which denotes a totally different meaning. Jung conceived of the 'collective unconscious' as a sea of psychic energy, as the soul of man.[19] While Freud's 'libido' gradually disappeared from the writings of his successors, one man, Wilhelm Reich, expanded the libido theory into a practical therapeutic modality called Orgone Therapy,[20] later developed by Lowen and Pierrakos into Bioenergetics.[21] The latter have expanded the theory of Orgone from its original sexual meaning into the realm of cosmic, spiritual, and psychic forces. Harry Stack Sullivan, founder of the interpersonal school of psychiatry, wrote about "enduring energy transformations" and "dynamisms of energy"[22] in order to describe the development of character (the self-system) in interpersonal terms. With the exception of this work in psychology (and that of theoretical physics),

Western science has been unable to entertain within its conceptual frame-work the existence of forces which are not available for measurement by our chemical and electronic technology. {13}

SYNTHESIS OF EAST AND WEST

On the other hand, Chinese medicine lacks a synthesis of its highly developed energy constructs with Western psychological concepts. In order for it to be a most significant health vehicle in the modern Western world, where individualism and individuation is so highly valued, it must investigate these associations and discover the correct correlations. Individual psychology is new territory for Chinese consciousness, where the proscription against individualism has been the bedrock of Chinese society at least since Confucius, when one of his interpreters stated: "A ruler should not listen to those who believe in people having opinions of their own and in the importance of the individual. Such teachings cause people to withdraw to quiet places and hide away in caves or on mountains, there to rail at the prevailing government, sneer at those in authority, belittle the importance of rank and emoluments and despise all who hold official posts."[23] In the Occident, individualistic psychology has long been in ascendance, and the West has constructed a psychology of the individual which cannot be ignored by those who seek to introduce the concepts and practices of Chinese medicine into the West.[24]

Psychology has searched in vain for a physiology which could demonstrate a clear connection between somatic events and psychological concepts of the 'mind' and emotion and for a spiritual model into which it could extrapolate its concerns with 'will,' 'intention,' 'becoming,' 'love, and 'self-realization.' Western science and Western theology have been uneasy partners for modern psychology; the perambulations of the former into 'psychosomatic medicine' and of the latter into 'humanistic psychology' have been relatively unproductive. My hypothesis is that, in order to deal effectively with problems which we classify as 'mind,' it is necessary to deviate from the standard medical model in the direction of the core assumptions of Chinese medicine. Western psychology, as the study of the 'mind' rather than the 'brain,' is in fact closer in principle to the tenets of Chinese science and philosophy than to those of its own culture.

We will begin our examination of energy-based medicine with those experiences that attended the introduction of Chinese medicine into my clinical practice of psychiatry and psychoanalysis in 1973. We will follow with some consideration of where the Chinese medical model stands in relation to the Western picture of health and disease and then with some of the postulates of Chinese medicine in the areas of mind-body-spirit currently available in recent Chinese texts from the People's Republic of China.

Then we will embark on the important work of this book to redefine the negative implications of the 'Seven Devils' or 'Seven Emotions'— anger, fear, sadness, worry, rumination, excess joy, and apprehension — in terms of positive natural energy functions. These natural functions include all of those mental, emotional, and spiritual qualities by which we define ourselves as human. Each will be examined within the context of the Five Phase system and as part of an evolutionary schema. The Fire energies will be seen, for example, serving conscious awareness, intelligible communication, interpersonal contact, creativity, and the 'yes' stage of development. The Heart yin enhances spontaneous conscious awareness of creativity, symbol formation, joyous divine inspiration, mutuality, and the celebration of the self and others. Heart yang concerns itself with the organization and systematization of expression, the word or logos, articulation, inspiration into understanding, and the circulation of ideas.

Using these natural functions as a base, we will examine the personality disharmonies that follow when these functions are deficient or excessive. The characterological configurations that evolve are to be experienced only as guideposts and are in no way meant to be the basis for a diagnostic typology.

Dr. Shen's 'systems model' will be explored, especially with regard to what he refers to as the 'nervous system.' An attempt will be made to distinguish his basic ideas from my own elaborations, based on my background as a psychiatrist and psychoanalyst since the mid-1950s. In this chapter, we will examine Dr. Shen's view of the relationship of development and emotional function, as well as the effects of organ energy system dysfunction on mental and emotional stability, and of emotion on organ energy systems.

A chapter on Chinese medicine as a medicine-philosophy will be followed by a recapitulation of some of the major conceptual thrusts of this work. This book is only the beginning of the reshaping of my own comprehension of energy and psychology, a springboard toward a meaningful guide for living, and a useful intervention in disharmony.

2

First Encounters and Empirical Implications

Mental and Muscular States

Beginning with my own treatment by Dr. Van Buren in England in 1971 and with my first patient in 1973, it was clear to me that Chinese medicine had a profound effect on emotion, mental states, cognition, and personality. By that time I had read Lawson-Wood who states: "All thought processes and mental states coexist with related muscular activity and tension. If a therapist is able to affect muscle tension activities, he will, ipso facto, affect the same degree of thought processes and mental states." Later he added, "Rigidities on the level of the psyche will tend to externalize corresponding rigidities on the level of the soma. Fixed ideas are all too often the precursors of fixed or stiff joints. Even if articular or muscular rigidities are not yet present, one would select and treat points as if they were. Rigid narrow minds, obstinacy, and stubbornness that refuses to re-evaluate prejudices etc., would be treated for arthritis, muscular rheumatism and fibrocytis."[1] Lawson-Wood goes on to talk about yin types of fear where the person becomes "limp with fear," in which case he would treat with points for "extreme weakness," and the yang types of fear where the person becomes "stiff with fear," in which case he would treat with points for "spasm and muscle tension in general, or even convulsions."[2] This expresses the concept of treating by similitude, using the vastly more available information about physical illness and applying it analogously. In 1975 I reported to the First World Congress of Acupuncture in New York that I had treated approximately 120 patients during the previous one-and-a-half years in the setting of a general psychiatric practice in a rural community.

The problems I had encountered covered the entire range of psychiatric disabilities, including borderline states, anxiety states, depression, manic-depressive illness, psychophysiological disorders, schizophrenia, addiction, and personality disorders. I had previously treated these disorders for 20 years in a standard psychiatric practice with psychoanalysis, Gestalt, Bioenergetics, group therapy, family therapy, play therapy, encounter workshops, and occasionally psychotropic drugs.

ACUPUNCTURE ENGENDERS AWARENESS

Acupuncture clearly demonstrated its ability to shorten the period of time required for significant change to occur, and to engender major alterations in patterns of behavior and thought well beyond what the other modalities of treatment could contribute. Prior to using acupuncture, I enjoyed a reasonable success, particularly treating the population of psychiatric patients who were the most ill and who had the least evidence of a 'self.' (In passing, I will say that these people were the easiest to help, and usually made rapid progress because they had the least success with their current behavior patterns and had the least to lose in changing.)

I was clearly introducing a new dimension to my work. Acupuncture fit well into the framework of a humanistic psychotherapeutic tradition, and many patients, especially those coming only for physical problems, frequently opened up to their deepest, unexpressed and even unknown feelings and thoughts. My personal experience of the "descent into hell"[3] and that of my patients during the years of my psychoanalytic practice enhanced the working through of these insights.

The accepted goal of therapy, to achieve a change in character in the ways in which a person characteristically avoids living life, was more readily achieved with the introduction of the needles. The depressed person who avoids both joy and responsibility for negative feelings; the obsessional person who avoids feeling by means of rigidity and orderliness; the oral person who avoids standing on the earth with his own two feet by demanding to be held and nourished; the schizoid person who avoids feeling through detachment; the schizophrenic person who avoids terror through fragmentation; or the paranoid person who avoids the unknown through projection: all of these desperate, maladaptive restorative maneuvers represent the best that a person could do at the time, and with what was available, to stay in contact while staying intact. And any such individual might be helped toward a constructive restoration by the needles.

Perhaps the most important consequence of the introduction of acupuncture into my practice was the flowering of *awareness* in my patients and my own appreciation of its significance to growth and development.

People became aware of the tensions in their body, and how they were creating them through thought and action; of their resistance to feeling good and how they made themselves feel bad. Their sensitivity to food, sound, air, and emotional ambiance made them more alive and better able to care for themselves and self-heal. There were abreactions and cathartic events. Repressed emotions, thoughts, memories, dreams, images, and dissociated material (including that of childhood, the birth experience, and even perhaps old incarnations) came into awareness.

{17}

With even momentary relief of tension, anxiety, depression, and pain there came, often for the first time, the knowledge that it was possible to be free of the commonplace and accepted misery. Hope of renewal, accompanied by fear of the unknown, emerged from the shadow of the past. Perhaps most remarkable to me were changes in body awareness, balance, centering, groundedness, esteem, and even amazing changes in physiognomy. Psychophysiological conditions were profoundly affected. My first patient, a Frenchwoman who had received acupuncture in France, not only recovered quickly from a manic-depressive illness, but also, within a matter of months, from a lifelong asthmatic and allergic condition. I recall one patient saying to me, "Now that you have relieved my physical pain, I must face my mental pain."

Patients have reported feeling more alive and balanced, with an increase in energy to cope with problems of survival, communication, relating, working, and other stresses. Ego functions often improved, accompanied by expression of overall satisfaction with life. Even spiritual growth has been included by some as one of the benefits of acupuncture in this setting. Strangely, acupuncture has seemed to have the most dramatic results with people who showed the strongest denial mechanisms, the least insight, acute debilitating emotional states such as panic, drug, and alcohol dependent conditions, and the most severe psychiatric disorders. Even the draining, 'toxic' personality became more nurturing.

REFLECTIONS OF AN ACUPUNCTURE PATIENT

One patient with whom I worked during this early period reported the following:

> I first came to see Dr. Leon Hammer when I was 29. My wife of nine years had just delivered our first child. I had graduated college three years previous to this and was employed as ——. Because of deep set feelings of inadequacy and an accompanying high anxiety level, I felt a need to drink heavily and take large amounts of Valium to keep functioning in my job, my social life, and my marriage. I also abused certain other drugs, especially marijuana.

I lost time from my job because of hangovers. I performed my job in a uniformly mediocre fashion, often avoiding the more difficult tasks because I couldn't cope with the anxiety those situations would produce.

I found friendships hard to handle and often insulted others and carried on in such a way that they would not come back for more. This destructive behavior carried over into my marriage.

After my daughter was born, certain feelings developed in me that I could neither identify nor handle. I felt dizzy and horribly insecure, often experiencing a slipping sensation, as if I were going to fall down. I could not sleep at night and frequently awoke sweating and choking on something that was caught in my throat. I never knew when I would have an anxiety attack. I thought I was going insane.

I saw Dr. Hammer in therapy about seven months initially. We worked with Bioenergetics. After I was grounded, we worked to unravel some of my feelings. It took a long time before I would trust him. He helped me to work through and resolve many feelings. I stopped taking Valium after three months of therapy and never took it again. The same with other drugs. However, I continued to drink, but not as heavily. Feeling much better, we terminated therapy after seven months by mutual agreement. I continued to go to group therapy (which I started some four months after beginning individual therapy). I finally dropped group because it did not work for me. I started another group nine months later which I still attend.

After Christmas of 1973 I became profoundly depressed. Some of the old symptoms began to return. I began to drink heavily again. I felt like I was coming apart again after almost a year. During that year I had struggled to maintain myself and put to use what I had learned in therapy, and now it seemed as if I was going crazy again.

I went back to Dr. Hammer. After about ten sessions of psychotherapy he began to use acupuncture. Almost immediately I felt changes happening. After about seven treatments I felt like a whole person. I no longer drink. (I tried to get drunk a couple of times, but didn't like it anymore). The craving for alcohol has disappeared. I no longer get depressed. I seem able to deal with difficult situations without wanting to withdraw or become defensive or aggressive. I can get appropriately angry, deal with it, and get it out of my system. Anger is directed now, not dispersed. I seem able to feel a whole lot more and act on that feeling. I have about twice as much energy as before. I feel good about myself. I exercise regularly now and work out every morning at seven with weights. My job has become routine and easily handled. The group tells me I am closer to them than ever before.

Acupuncture has worked, and I feel the change will be lasting because of inner knowledge gained through some 35 psychotherapy sessions. Acupuncture seems to be the vehicle by which this inner knowledge is integrated within me. I don't know if the acupuncture results would be as dramatic without psychotherapy. I feel that without certain tools and insights given me in therapy, the acupuncture treatments would probably provide only temporary relief. I am getting stronger with each treatment.

I continued to have personal contact with this client until 1982, and his con-

dition and life constantly improved without therapy during this period of
time. His response was typical of those given by patients asked to describe
their experiences with acupuncture, many of whom did not have concomitant or previous psychotherapy.

THE DIAGNOSTIC PROCESS AS THERAPEUTIC

The diagnostic process has in itself been particularly therapeutic. Especially
after mastering Dr. Shen's work with the pulse and face reading, I was often
able to tell people things about themselves and their lives which seemed to
by-pass the usual resistance encountered in the psychotherapeutic process.
Somehow, presenting hard and painful facts to the patient based on objective data, rather than trying to evoke them in a searching and provocative
interview, eliminates the gamesmanship which inevitably occurs when one
person is trying to get another to reveal him or herself. The material is, of
course, presented to the client in a rough and incomplete form, which then
becomes a springboard for a usually much-needed catharsis during which
the details become available. Progress on the basic issues moves more rapidly, and the defensive, restorative maneuvers fall by the wayside with much
less of the endless struggle which characterizes most psychotherapeutic
relationships. This struggle has always seemed to me to replicate the worst
of what made the patient sick in the first place and to reinforce the negative
rather than release it from the patient's life.

The diagnostic process is therapeutic in another way. People have been
tortured since childhood and have consequently tortured themselves for
their inadequacies. I have had many patients who expected themselves to
perform in ways which were constitutionally impossible. We were not created equal, except for the respect which we may demand for who we are.
Sorting out the possible from the impossible empowers these people to
give their energies to the things they can do, and to leave to others those
for which they are inherently unprepared. I refer the reader to the photo on
the following page which I feel speaks more eloquently to the issue than any
case history.

The diagnosis as practiced by Dr. Shen can also help to distinguish the
important issues in one's life from the unimportant. As pointed out several
times in case histories in the text, these diagnostic skills can highlight emotions and events originating at ages no longer in the patient's awareness,
yet which may have played a much more important role in who they are,
and how they feel, than other events or emotions whose importance was
exaggerated. This clarification opens the way to insight and growth by re-
channeling therapeutic energies in more productive directions. Using the

diagnosis in these ways also helps to deepen the working bond and enhance the faith and trust between patient and therapist.

RIGID ENERGY TRANSFORMATIONS

The maladaptive patterns of thought, behavior, and feeling which we identify as pathology are characterized by a high degree of rigidity. Harry Stack Sullivan captured this in his introductory discussion of what he called "dynamisms":

> When I speak of dynamisms of difficulty, I mean those processes which, although they are a part of every personality, are at the same time the particular parts of the personal equipment that are often misused. In other words, these dynamisms go into action in situations or in fashions that do not achieve a goal, or that, at best, achieve only an unsatisfactory goal. As a result they tend to go on and on. Their frequent recurrence or their tendency to occupy long stretches of time characterizes the mentally sick as distinguished from the comparatively well. It is the extraordinary dependence of a personality on a particular dynamism that is, I suppose, the fundamental conception to have in mind in thinking of mental disorder.[4]

Sullivan referred to one aspect of experience as "energy transformations," both "overt and covert." These rigid "energy transformations,"[5] which appear as reverberating circuits, are uniformly projected on both soma and psyche, perpetually feeding back on and reinforcing themselves. It is these circuits which acupuncture has the capability of interrupting and opening to new feelings, thoughts and behavior, to new experience and new energy transformations. The outcome depends, to some extent, upon the skill of the therapist to exploit this opportunity for new experience. In a dynamic exchange the patient can live through vital life issues in a positive way, substantially different from the original. Often, however, this encounter is unintentional and subliminal, going almost unnoticed by both parties, or worked through in meaningful encounters outside of the therapeutic relationship.

THE CASE OF H.

The following story, which I have reported elsewhere,[6] illustrates how illness is a vicious cycle where emotions and attitudes affect organ systems which in turn affect emotion and thought. This is the only detailed case history in this book, and though lengthy and complex, it is presented early to give the reader a flavor of how one may usefully merge concepts of Chinese medicine and Western psychology.

> H. was an attractive 19-year-old, white, red-haired girl of athletic build. She was somewhat overweight and on the masculine side, with wide shoulders and narrow hips. She was referred by her mother who had previously been a patient. The presenting problem was pain in the left knee, with swelling and tenderness. Seven or eight years previously the patient had an accident with her left leg at which time the knee became swollen. From that time on it had always been slightly painful, and the pain was exacerbated upon other falls. Approximately six months prior to the first visit, the patient had another fall in which her knee and leg were again bruised. Two months before the first visit her knee again began to be painful, swollen, and tender. At the time of the first treatment, she was barely able to walk.
>
> Pertinent facts of her medical history included a chronic recurring ear infection on the left side with simultaneous gastrointestinal discomfort. Both were associated with anxiety. There had been a tonsillectomy at an unspecified age.
>
> At the initial examination her pulse rate was 68. There was some Change in the Rate at Rest and some Change in the Intensity. There was Tension in the Liver and Gallbladder pulse and stagnation between the Liver and the Heart. Her tongue was swollen and dry with mucus and a tremor. Her eyes showed no abnormalities. The palms of her hands had a blue color and blue lines. The left knee was swollen and tender. My initial impression, apart from the knee problem, was that the patient was a moody and perhaps somewhat depressed person with a consider-

able amount of repressed anger. Changes in pulse rate at rest, especially in a rate that is not particularly fast, are indicative of a person who is somewhat moody and depressed and who is probably very worried and unstable emotionally. In this case, these emotional problems affected the Liver, which in turn was affecting the rest of the gastrointestinal system. Later examinations tended to confirm this instability of mood since the rate would actually change considerably from one time to another, being at some points as low as 58 and others as high as 84 with rates in between of 70, 74, 60, and 68. In addition, there were changes in intensity, which indicated two things. First, that the condition of her body was in a state of flux; the pathology was not yet fixed. Second, that there was evidence of emotional disturbance.

In subsequent readings there was Pounding over the entire pulse, especially on the left side. This pounding reflected her inner tension and its effect on the nervous system. Pounding can also come from poor body condition. A poor body condition is usually accompanied by 'heat' in the eyes and tongue. In her case the eyes revealed little or no heat from deficiency, and the tongue showed no heat in its deeper parts. In Chinese medicine, heat from deficiency (weak heat), in contrast to heat from excess (strong heat), refers to heat in the body due to a chronic disease process in which the traditional organ systems are worked beyond their energy capacity. Like an engine in a car which is working beyond its ability, the body with a chronic disease process will tend to overheat. Both require fluid. In humans this is provided by the Kidneys. Initially, the Kidneys can keep up with a rising demand, but as a person becomes older and time passes, the energy of the Kidneys weakens, the heat is not balanced by the water, and signs of heat are manifested in the eyes and tongue. The patient H. was only 19 years old. Apparently this condition had not yet set in, though it would be predictable.

Muscular and Emotional Tension

Let us examine the problem for which H. presented in light of her overall body condition. I noted Tension on the Liver-Gallbladder pulse. The Liver and the Gallbladder, in Chinese medicine, are organs related to the Wood phase, which controls ligaments and tendons. Their functions are intimately interrelated. If the Liver and the Gallbladder are tense, the ligaments, tendons, and muscles also become tense. This creates a negative feedback situation because the tense muscular condition reinforces the original emotional tension.

This is why so many autogenic or biogenic exercises are directed toward the relaxation of muscles, ligaments, and tendons. If you relax the body, you relax the mind. In this case we have a situation where there is an organ system of the body which is constantly feeding tension into the body. This is an extremely important point to which we will return for further consideration. In addition, the Liver recovers the qi or energy. In Western medicine it is also considered the detoxifier, the cleanser. If the Liver is not working properly, there will be noxious energy. According to Chinese medicine, the noxious energy will escape from the normal energy pathways to those paths of the body which are weak or stagnant either due to constitutional weakness, unhealthy living, or trauma, and it will cause pain. Tension, according to Chinese medicine, will also generally inhibit circulation. When this occurs, those vulnerable areas will experience further impairment and pain. We see that the patient's overall condition plays a part in the difficulty she experiences in recovering from musculoskeletal trauma. Fortunately, many of the important points treated around the knee are Gallbladder points, which were helpful in the strengthening of her overall condition, and one in particular, GB-34 *(yang ling quan)*, is the master point for tendons and ligaments in the entire body.

GB-34 is also a *he* point. According to a branch of Chinese medicine based on the functions of the five *yuan* points, the *he* point of a channel, when needled, will directly affect its related organ. Needling the Gallbladder points around the knee indirectly affects the Liver since the Gallbladder and the Liver energies are closely integrated. I needled other Gallbladder and Liver points as well during the first treatment. Using these points and two special knee points made the knee completely asymptomatic after three treatments.

At this time the patient began to experience a sore throat, and shortly after that her ear began to hurt. In the ensuing weeks the ear began to run, she experienced severe stomach pain and indigestion, followed by a cold with congestion and a considerable amount of discharge.

These developments follow the principle of Chinese medicine that if the treatment is successful, the patient will temporarily re-experience old illnesses which have not been completely resolved. Infections in the throat and ear from which she had suffered over the years had been treated primarily with antibiotics, which tended to suppress the symptoms, kill the bacteria involved, but of course did nothing to the terrain on which the bacteria thrived.

Tongue Diagnosis

H. gave as part of her history that when she had ear problems she also had stomach problems. I initially described the tongue as being swollen, with dry mucus, and having a definite tremor. The first two signs suggested a problem with digestion. When digestion is poor, the Stomach, which normally produces mucus, will increase the rate of production. Using the energy of the Spleen, the mucus will rise to the Lungs which 'digest' it into saliva. If too much is produced, or if the Lungs are weak, there will be an excess of mucus and a lack of saliva. This will show itself on the tongue, usually through a thickening of the top layer and dryness, which may sometimes take the form of a 'furry' (coated) tongue. According to Chinese medicine, the swelling may be due to the inability of the Spleen to perform its normal task of moving and directing fluid. If this function is impaired, we have a tendency toward non-pitting edema. The tremor was indicative of some problem with the nervous system, most likely emotional in origin, meaning that nervous components rather than the parenchyma (the essential or functional tissue) of the organs were involved. The palm of the hand showed blue coloration, indicating involvement of the Liver (also emotional), as well as blue lines, indicating emotional shock.

During the second examination I noted that the tongue had become coated white. Though initially the eyes were normal, there was now some heat from deficiency. The former indicated to me that the patient had been invaded by cold, through her Lungs. This was borne out on the third visit, when she came with a sore throat. At this time, we did the *gua sha* (a scraping massage) and cupping (suction cups on the skin), both techniques for removing cold from the blood and body. The response was strongly positive. At this session the pulse rate change was somewhat less, though the rate itself was a little faster. The left side of the pulse was more balanced, and the right side (Lung, Stomach, and Bladder) was Pounding. The Lung pulse was a little Floating, and there was some Vibration on the Stomach, indicating that the cold had got into the Lungs and that the Stomach was distressed. If the gastrointestinal tract were in order, the Lungs, if not weak in their own right, would ordinarily be able to handle the cold and dissipate it; but, with the Stomach overloading the Lungs with mucus, the Lungs are hard put to function normally and exercise their normal ability to handle the cold. The cold creates further stagnation of circulation and allows the ever-present bacteria digesting the mucus to accumulate waste products. They cannot be eliminated, and the elements of the immune system which deal with infection cannot perform adequately when circulation is impaired. The body will discharge these toxins. Involvement of the ear in this accumulation may be the result of weakness and impaired circulation due to a constitutional deficit from early trauma, such as the use of forceps in delivery. The forceps theory is a good one in this case, inasmuch as her infections started at a very early age.

It should also be pointed out that there are gastrointestinal points all around the ear: Small Intestine, Gallbladder, and particularly the Triple Burner. This last channel is responsible for the movement of energy from one area of the body to the other, and especially from the different parts of the Stomach to other organs such as the Lungs, Heart, Kidneys, Spleen, and Pancreas. The Triple Burner channel is extremely important to all ear functions, especially through the points TB-3 *(zhong zhu)*, TB-17 *(yi feng)*, and TB-21 *(er men)*. It is noteworthy that the gastrointestinal channels (Stomach, Small Intestine, and Large Intestine) all pass from the thorax to the face through the neck, with the Stomach channel being most anterior, the Large Intestine lateral, and the Small Intestine channel most posterior, so that symptoms of sore throat are not surprising in view of the gastrointestinal difficulties. The relationship between digestion and infections of the upper respiratory tract, in particular the ear, is not apparent in Western medicine. If, however, we think in Chinese and naturopathic terms, we realize that there are significant relationships.

Acupuncture for Emotional Tensions

During the second visit I began to treat H. with the needles for emotional tension as well as for her knees. The third session evoked a very powerful emotional reaction. The patient trembled and cried, and there seemed to be a considerable amount of grief and much release of tension. Points used on this occasion were on the back, the *shu* or associated points, which go directly to their associated organ. The points used went to the Lungs, to the diaphragm, Liver, and Stomach. In addition I used LI-4 *(he gu)*, Triple Burner points TB-3 *(zhong zhu)*, TB-17 *(yi feng)*, and two points which particularly help the throat when used in conjunction with each other: LI-7 *(wen liu)*, and K-6 *(zhao hai)*. The throat grew immediately worse and then recovered rather quickly the next day. The patient also recovered emotionally by the next day.

The gastrointestinal and ear problems coincided, as they had done many times in the past. As soon as the ear cleared up, the stomach became worse. H. was given nutritional counseling after a review of her eating habits. She was given sweet rice, ginger, red date, Wei Shen, and a Chinese proprietary herb called Weisen-Yu, all of which are medicinal to the gastrointestinal tract. The cleansing diet primarily consisted of the sweet rice, the herbs mentioned, and the elimination of all toxic foods. There was an immediate period of discharge and then an increased feeling of well-being, despite H.'s tendency to mistreat herself through inadequate rest or excessive work. LI-4 *(he gu)* and Liv-3 *(tai chong)* were particularly important at this stage. LI-4 is the great eliminator of both mental and physical toxicity. It is the source point of the Large Intestine. Liv-3 is the Liver source and Earth point and is very effective for relaxing the Liver and eliminating heat, especially if the needle is passed through toward K-1 *(yong quan)* at the bottom of the foot. By themselves, these two points are generally very relaxing and act as an anti-depressant when the needles are left in for a considerable period of time.

Pulse Diagnosis

The eighth, ninth, and tenth sessions showed increasing Vibration over the entire pulse, which indicated that the patient was feeling guilty, afraid, and worried. She had just returned from a visit to her home. By reading her pulse I presented this impression of her emotional state, and, for the first time, she began to talk about herself. Up to this time there had been very little verbal exchange on a psychological level or personal level. The one outburst of emotion following the third treatment was not followed by any verbal cathexis. For the last five sessions we were able to discuss some of her problems, particularly low self-esteem and her relationship with members of the opposite sex. This is an extremely important thesis. From the pulse and face reading one can tell a great deal about a person's emotional state, past, present, and future. Somehow the experience of being presented with this material derived directly from the pulse seems to bypass the long struggle people experience in revealing themselves to a psychotherapist. The personal resistances almost universally encountered in psychotherapy do not emerge, and material which might take months or years to work through may sometimes be resolved in days or weeks. This is most true for the patient who comes initially with a physical problem and has been least exposed to previous psychotherapy.

Altogether, there were thirteen sessions, and from the tenth session on, the patient reported no problems of any sort. The pulse tended to stabilize in terms of Changes in Rate and Intensity, and Vibration, although at the end it was a little Rapid and a little Pounding, since she had taken a job as a lifeguard and was clearly overworking and over-exposing herself to the sun. This was creating heat in her blood. Her tongue had considerably less mucus. All the white had disappeared, although it was still a little dry. The small amount of heat from deficiency in the eyes had diminished considerably. The blue lines in her hands, however, remained. Under the mucus, one discovered on the tongue a thin line, running longitudinally. The tongue itself appeared somewhat pale as the yellow coating disappeared. This, together with the line, was indicative of an underlying constitutional weakness in the energy of the Heart.

Thus, evidence emerged that she had started out life with some weakness in the energy of her Heart. Since the Heart is considered to be the emperor and the spirit of the body, such weakness in its energy would leave her somewhat weakened and most certainly over sensitive to anything affecting the spirit. (We also know from Chinese medicine that the Heart tends to control the throat and tongue. As a child H. experienced a good deal of difficulty in terms of sore throats, tonsillitis, and later, ear infections coinciding with her Stomach problems). Diagnostically we begin with a person who is physically and emotionally vulnerable because one of her organ systems is constitutionally weak. However, it is a principle in Chinese medicine that vulnerability manifests in disease only as a result of the combination of more than one problem, and not from simply one source. Constitutional vulnerability is not enough.

With an extremely Tense Liver and Gallbladder pulse, and stagnation between the Liver and Heart, we can, from Chinese medicine, assume that the patient had lived her tender years under conditions which forced her to control and maintain many of her emotions, in particular, anger.

Repression of Anger

To begin with, weakness in the Heart system has a tendency to make the child easily afraid. Therefore, traumatic events as well as the personalities of parents and other people would have a greater impact. If there is a good deal of anger-inspiring behavior in the family and social situation, the child would be less inclined to express hostility openly and therefore more inclined toward developing the Liver-Gallbladder tension to which we are referring. It is, of course, not anger itself but the repression of anger that affects the Liver and the Gallbladder system. Why is this so? We know from Bioenergetics and other disciplines that when anger is repressed the musculoskeletal system, muscles, ligaments, and tendons are brought into play in the exercise of its control. We know that under these conditions toxic substances, which the Chinese call noxious energy, are accumulated. It is the responsibility of the Liver to deal with body energy, and excessive build-up of this noxious energy may create an overload for that organ system. The Liver-Gallbladder system is also said to control the nerves. An increase in heat in the Liver and Gallbladder heightens tension in the nervous system. We see again a vicious cycle between an organ system and an emotional state.

If we were to project the course this condition might follow should no treatment occur, another problem might be expected to arise. The Liver is said to store the blood. If it is overworked and heat is created, the blood itself becomes hot. Since heat rises, the tendency, in terms of energy flow, is for the heat to go toward the head. At first headaches may occur. Later, as the heat affects the elasticity of the blood vessel walls, hypertension and, ultimately, stroke may occur. This contingency is further enhanced by the underlying issue of the constitutional Heart energy problem. If we look on the other side of repressed anger — if we look upon the natural function that is distorted in order to achieve repressed anger — we see functions of assertiveness and the endless discharge of impure energy. The antithesis of stored anger, hate, or rage is assertion and discharge. Translated into more existential terms, one might say that these natural functions of the Wood phase enhance a state of being. In Chinese cosmology Wood is the phase related to spring, the time when things begin to grow and come into being.

When one's being is frustrated and unable to assert itself, we have impotent rage and all the self-destructive behavior that follows: guilt, passive-aggressive behavior, negativity, and self-deprecation. We have an ego function problem. Inasmuch as the Liver is considered the planner, and the Gallbladder the decision maker, the entire body is affected. As the Chinese would put it, "The other officials [there being an official for each organ system] become angry if they have no plan." Planning and decision-making take place primarily at night during sleep from 11 P.M. to 3 A.M., the time on the Chinese clock associated with the Liver and Gallbladder. Depending on other aspects of the personality, impotent rage leads to either depression and passive-aggressive behavior or to violence. Biorhythms are affected.

Other organ systems become involved as the patient becomes

older. The Kidneys exhaust themself in attempting to provide fluid to deal with the increasing heat in the body from the tension in the Liver and the heat in the blood. With the breakdown of these systems, further psychological problems occur. The Kidneys, in terms of emotional disharmony, are related to fear. Their natural functions are related to will power, resolve, and the balance between courage and awareness; to reverence for, and awe of, the transcendental; and to the acceptance of real limitations in the awareness of cosmic considerations. The Stomach, strongly related to both Liver and Kidneys, is part of the Earth phase, which, when impaired, may cause overconcern, worry, and a variety of thinking disorders. In H.'s pulse we could begin to read the frustration of her being.

THE RELATIONSHIP OF PART TO THE WHOLE

This case demonstrates rather clearly the relationship of one part of the body to another in terms of the normal functioning and development of illness. It shows that what happens in one part of a complex organism may have a profound effect on what happens in another, and that we cannot separate the systems and view them in an isolated fashion. This principle gives us some sense of what is meant when people say that the mind and the body are essentially one. No matter how much work this person puts into solving her emotional problems, some attention must be given to these energy systems or else the continued dysfunction of her Liver and Gallbladder systems will recreate the very same problems, and she will find herself resolving them over and over again. Imbalance in these systems (Heart, Liver, and Gallbladder) will continue to generate underlying fear, negativity, ambivalence, guilt, impotent rage, the inability to plan and make decisions, a passive-aggressive approach to life, and the inability simply to be and grow. A successful therapy has to be an integrated one. There have been a number of instances in my experience where people have come with physical symptoms and worked through powerful emotional problems with extraordinary rapidity as the energetic, physical side of the problem was resolved. Often there is, as in the case just presented, a tremendous cathexis of emotion, followed by a rather rapid integration through insight and understanding. It is as if a self-fulfilling negative feedback circuit between perception, interpretation, and behavior is broken so that new experiences, and new ideas of a corrective nature, may enter into the system.

My principal purpose in presenting this case is to give a practical presentation of what is popularly referred to as holistic medicine, and in particular to illustrate the necessity of dealing with both body and mind in searching for the solution to a problem either one may be presenting.

I feel it is important that we give a considerable amount of thought, energy, and effort to the development of integrated systems which recognize in a practical sense the essential relationships between the various functions of the body, especially between, on the one hand, those of the mind and spirit, and on the other hand, those of ingestion, digestion, assimilation, circulation, metabolism, and excretion. I have tried to give a practical illustration of how Chinese medicine embodies this principle of oneness.

The previous chapter elaborated on the various congruities of Chinese medicine and Western humanistic psychology, which this case history is meant to illustrate. In the following chapter, we will examine some of the underlying concepts of an energy-based medicine, both generally and specifically. We will look at how these concepts shape a medical model that both complements and balances some of our misgivings with the allopathic model.

3

THE FUNDAMENTAL ENERGY
CONSTRUCTS OF CHINESE MEDICINE

Disease is the process which begins, at the health and life end of a spectrum, with subtle signs and vague symptoms, and stops, at the other end, with gross pathology and death. For reasons that are unclear to us thousands of years after the fact, the Chinese ancients concentrated their intellectual and spiritual energies on those insubstantial, natural, and pathological phenomena occurring at the beginning of the disease process.

This took place even while they described and were well acquainted with the circulation of blood, with gross anatomy as revealed by dissection, and with gross pathology at the disease and death side of the spectrum. Prohibition of dissection and surgery by the emperors of the Han Dynasty may have been a factor in determining the emphasis placed on the more subtle conditions rather than on the more concrete pathological symptoms.

Dedicating themselves to what we would consider the ineffable, they seemed, from this perspective, to have been primarily concerned with illuminating those aspects of reality which defy, to this day, assessment, description, or measurement by any mechanical instrument. Seeking a practical way to assess health and disease, they chose first to define and characterize life in terms applicable to such an assessment. The sages fulfilled the promise of this quest by looking for the essential difference between life and death, between a living and a dead person. This quintessential difference they identified as movement. Simply stated, where there is life, there is movement; and where there is death, there is no movement. Those of us who frequently have been in the position of pronouncing death may best appreciate this elegant formulation: cessation of movement and utter stillness dramatically differ from life.

According to the written record, it became the preoccupation of the ancient scientists to study the phenomenon of movement, which, they found, represented the life of the universe (macrocosm), the earth (mesocosm), and man (microcosm). Observing movement in the heavens, they became good astronomers, and in the seasons, good farmers. Seeing it in man, they became good physicians. At some point, their science required them to account for this remarkably ordered and constant movement and change in the universe; they postulated that in the universe there was a force that obeyed observable laws and that was responsible for the systematic passage of their cosmos.[1]

PREDICTABILITY AND PARADOX

The 'force', in its primordial form, was considered to be pure potential, symbolized by a single point. This point of potentiality evolves into a completed circle. The entire circle symbolizes the force's fundamental characteristics of unity (harmony), continuity (no beginning and no end), strength and dynamic fluidity, centeredness, intuition, expansion, and contraction. Of course there is no more powerful or universal symbol than the circle, which seems always to have meant the totality and essence of life, the self, the cosmos. It shows up as Mandala and as the benzene molecule, the basis of organic chemical life.[2] For the American Indian, it stands for strength and for woman, the life giver and taker since the beginning of time. To the extent that Chinese medicine is a blend of intuition and deductive reasoning, and because it can embrace paradox, it is itself thought of as being round.

This potential energy or force, symbolized by the circle, becomes kinetic through an event that divides the circle into two parts and creates polarity necessary for the movement of life. Everywhere they observed that movement created change, and they believed that man must constantly deal with it. If one has acted in accordance with nature, one adjusts to change; if not, one becomes ill. But even more than the ubiquitousness of change in the universe, the Chinese were impressed by its predictable order, which calculation could discover in phenomena.

The Chinese were a practical people who did not question the existence of this force but were content to observe and harness it in their own interest. Just as the Jews were content to accept God as He revealed to Moses his name, Yahweh, "I Am who I Am," the Chinese accepted the force "to be what it was." Their concern was only for its soundness. Force was considered sound when it was sufficient in quantity; when it moved in a predictable, patterned rhythm; and when it was balanced. When any one of these parameters was compromised to any extent, this soundness, or health, gave way to disease. While the astronomer studied this force in the living heavens, the physician studied it in the living person. Both considered this force to be the same in man as it is in the cosmos. Its unity and soundness form the real base of Chinese medicine, in which all functioning constituents interconnect as parts of the cosmic whole. This holistic attitude stands in marked contrast to Western medicine.

ELEVEN SYSTEMS PLUS ONE

In the West we have studied the following systems, more or less independently of each other:

1. The cardiovascular and haemopoetic system, responsible for circulation and for supplying and nourishing all the organs and tissues of the body.
2. The gastrointestinal system, which makes food available to us through the process of digestion and assimilation.
3. The musculoskeletal system, which provides support, mobility, and haemopoesis.
4. The neurohumeral system, a bio-computer providing rapid regulation and coordination.
5. The immune lymphatic system, the protector.
6. The genital system, for reproduction.
7. The urinary system, for electrolyte balance.
8. The respiratory system, for oxygen, electrolyte balance and Ph stability.
9. The sensory system, for perception.
10. The metabolic system, involving the liver and the pancreas, which is the sustainer.
11. The endocrinological system, which, in contrast to the neurohumeral, is a relatively slower regulatory system.

The Chinese and other ancient cultures recognized many of these systems in a more sophisticated way than Western medicine has done until recently. The vascular haemopoetic system and circulation of blood was described in *The Yellow Emperor's Inner Clasic (Huang di nei jing)* about 2,000 years ago. Yang, arterial blood is described as light in color, and ying, venous blood is described as being dark in color. Pathology of systems such as the neurohumeral, endocrinological, and metabolic, which were not within the lexicon of Chinese medicine, were and are nevertheless being treated successfully by this medicine. In addition, the Chinese included one more system which has never been among those studied in modern Western medicine.

This system they considered to subsume all of the others, providing the force just described, which: 1) gives organized life to what would otherwise be a collection of inert materials; 2) provides the force-field matrix within which the developing embryo and future organism take shape; 3) provides the force-field matrix that shapes all future function and functional relationships which we describe as life.

QI (CH'I): THE LIFE FORCE

For the Chinese ancients, the integrity and operation of all of the body's systems depend entirely upon the vicissitudes of this force. For this reason the observation, assessment, and use of this life force became the core of ancient medicines, including Chinese medicine, and remained, almost up to our time, their primary concern in the pursuit of health. The relevant dictum is: "The energy that causes disease cures it." Sickness is only a variation of, and not a state separate from, health. The force, known in the Chinese tradition as qi (ch'i), has not been totally unknown in the West, where it is referred to somewhat ambiguously as 'energy.'

In the West, we have gradually come to measure many forces in the world around us which we also classify generally as energy. Sound energy is measured in decibels; light energy is measured in foot candles. To the best of my knowledge, there have been no 'objective' measurements of the life force. However unmeasurable, we are obligated to consider it a reality, since our existence as living entities is an unavoidable fact. The Bible says, "By their fruits ye shall know them."[3] The Chinese said: Qi shall be known only as it manifests itself, as it materializes either physiologically or pathologically.

The Chinese ancients believed that the way of life is based on qi; everything in the universe relies on it. When the qi is outside heaven and earth it embraces them. When the qi is inside heaven and earth, it circulates through and sustains them. Stars depend on it for their brightness. Weather is formed by it. The seasons are caused by it. Man cannot stand outside of qi. It supports him and permeates him. It is the unifying, synthesizing concept, which emphasizes the single tie that binds us, rather than the less significant issues that tend to divide and scatter us.

PRISONERS OF PATHOLOGY

On the continuum from health to disease, from life to death, we find the concerns of Western medicine situated mostly at the disease end of the spectrum. The focus, for instance, is on laboratory tests capable of detecting objective, concrete, measurable, organ tissue damage. The patients whose electrocardiograms, G.I. series, or brain scans are clearly positive justify this focus. The doctor who makes the diagnosis has fulfilled his genuine desire to be helpful and has vindicated his long, arduous, and expensive training. Presently, however, such patients account for only about one percent of all people who seek medical assistance in the consultation rooms of Western medical practitioners. The other ninety-nine percent come with complaints that cannot be quantified even by our most sophisticated, expensive laboratory equipment. The vast majority of patients actually belong somewhere toward the health end of the spectrum, where our measurements reveal nothing!

[35]

What is the reason for this state of affairs, so frustrating to both patient and practitioner? It is that Western medicine has a theory of disease but no theory of health. We are thus prisoners of pathology, and in thinking about health we must always start with serious disease or death as our subject. In recent times, concerned with the early diagnosis of disease, Western medicine seems to be attempting to move toward the health end of the spectrum. We begin with gross pathology and move via computer technology to master the measurements of ever more minute fragments of matter. Having started with a corpse, we are engaged now with molecules. We are searching for a method of early diagnosis by refining our ability to scrutinize smaller and smaller particles, hoping to pick up the process of disease at the molecular level. Whereas, without a doubt, this is proving to be an extraordinarily interesting development in the history of knowledge, it has thus far proven to be an expensive and futile exercise in the quest for early diagnosis and prevention. Preventive medicine in the West is, at best, an early warning system of an already existing morphological, identifiable lesion.[4] The truth is that at the health end of the spectrum, material changes are not yet manifest even at the level of small particle physics. The idea that we can reach these changes through increasingly fine instrumentation is untenable. It is this concept and experience of energy that essentially divides the East from the West.

Since the life force may never yield itself to instrumentation, it may never be acceptable to the Western scientific mind whose knowledge of reality reposes entirely within its instruments. The ancient Chinese observed that qi is unlimited and that movement, regardless of how small or large, how brief or long, how quick or slow, is caused by qi. When qi concentrates, it is called matter; and when it spreads, it is called space. When qi gathers together, it is called life; and when it separates, it is called death. When qi flows in a living entity, it is called health; and when qi is blocked, there is sickness. Energy and matter are, therefore, interchangeable. And $E=MC^2$,

the famous formula of Einstein, has this unexpected metaphorical confirmation.

FROM THE INEFFABLE TO THE MATERIAL AND BACK

All of this is not to say that Chinese medicine is irrational, unempirical, or
opposed to science's deepest purposes. According to the Oxford Twentieth
Century Dictionary, science is defined as "knowledge, most severely tested,
coordinated, and systematized, especially regarding those wide generaliza-
tions called the laws of nature." Chinese medicine clearly fits this definition.
Science, in its inception in modern Western times, originated in the attempt to return — and I emphasize return — to an ethic that elevated the art
of observation above the art of speculation.

Chinese medicine is science in its original and most creative form. It
has perfected the art of observation, the superb refinement of our senses,
blended it with rigorous logic, and enriched it with the intuitive gifts and
varied experience and personality of the observer. The trained Chinese
doctor, like the trained Western physician of yesteryear, is a keen observer
of phenomena. Whereas in Western medicine we are now alienated from
the power and value of our senses, in Chinese medicine the training and
value of the senses is retained. Chinese medicine is far more faithful to the
basic tenets of science, in the primary sense of its meaning, than is modern
Western medicine, where science has become identified with statistical significance and with the 'double blind' study.

Chinese medicine may seem strange to us, not because it is any less
scientific than our medicine, but rather because its science was applied to a
different part of reality than the one to which we have addressed ourselves
since the beginning of the Industrial Revolution. We have, in Chinese medicine, a mature science "observing, massing, severely testing, coordinating,
and systematizing the laws of nature" at the health and life end of the spectrum of the disease process, where Western medicine is still in its infancy.
We in the West are experts at one end of the spectrum; in the East they are
equally expert at the other end. To be complete, we must in fact consider
disease as a process that begins with the ineffable and ends with the material fact of organ disease; and we must ponder both ends of this process
simultaneously.

Although Chinese medicine is, in the best sense, a science, the importance of the healer's role makes us think of it also as an art. As an art it
stands in contrast to modern science and its criteria of validity. There will
be, for instance, little of the verifiable data required by current versions of
the 'scientific' method. This method also insists that the healer must not

be important to the healing process. The irrelevance of the healer even becomes a test of the validity of the healing system. But in a healing system where the movement and balance of energy is the critical factor in sickness and health, the energy of the healer enters significantly into the system as a positive or negative force. Lawson-Wood says, "What is going on in the practitioner's mind is therapeutically significant. In other words, the practitioner's intention has great influence upon the quality and polarity of the treatment he will, in fact, administer."[5]

ANCIENT INTERNAL MEDICINE

What, then, does ancient Chinese medicine consist of and how does it serve the patient by attending to the processes of health? Chinese medicine is not only a holistic system but, according to its oldest written record, *The Yellow Emperor's Inner Classic, Simple Questions (Huang di nei jing su wen)*, possibly dating from as early as 200 B.C., it is a total system of internal medicine. This medicine has an anatomy, physiology, pathology, diagnostic system based on signs and symptoms, as well as a treatment system that includes diet, massage, heat, exercise, needle puncture, herbal preparation, meditation, guidance, and counseling.

It addresses itself to the basic issues of life and death, health and disease, without the massive but disjunctive biochemical and bioelectrical data accumulated by Western science. It achieves a practical understanding of, and solutions to, a bewildering array of medical enigmas, without this astounding and impressive knowledge. Its overriding concern is with the individual and with the cause of disease, not with the suppression of symptoms. The fundamental philosophy is two-fold. First, the physician counsels the patient regarding the relationship between particular behavioral patterns (including diet, exercise, sex, etc.) and the illness in question, and then treatment assists and supports the body's own healing forces. A physician's job is to return physiology to normal. His effectiveness depends entirely on the accuracy of the diagnosis, on the wisdom of the counseling, on the patient's willingness to change, and on the correct choice of treatment modalities for the rebalancing of the body's physiology.

In my clinical experience, barring gross mismanagement, this medicine can do far less harm than Western medicine. I have observed few of the powerful side effects that are so common in the course of Western medical treatment. It is, of course, correct that any energy alteration can lead to greater balance or to greater imbalance. And surely no one is so wise as to always correctly manage all of the complex human beings encountered. Even the capacity of an individual to transform positive to negative is part of the equation which a wise physician must understand. He must also know that there are some people he should not treat. Certainly this wisdom is hard to come by, and few of us can avoid mistakes on any level of practice.

The thrust of Chinese medicine is cohesive, avoiding the anarchy created by the endless proliferation and compilation of disjointed facts. Health is, therefore, a welcome return to, not an endless struggle against, nature. In this system, man is not the ego-oriented master and controller of the universe. He is simply part of it: one who must obey its laws and not make them.

Chinese medicine, like Ayurvedic medicine, its Indian counterpart, is the science of life. This science is dedicated to grasping the laws of the life force, which includes: its flow, or movement; its balance, or harmony; its change, or transmutation *(qi hua)*; its rhythms, or cycles; its origin, supply, assimilation, transformation, storage, release, and excretion; its pathways; its correspondences; and its functions. All of these are susceptible to a precisely refined and sophisticated diagnostic methodology.

AN INFUSION OF ORIENTAL MEDICINE

It is my strong conviction that Western medicine, even in the face of its enormous technological accomplishments, requires an infusion of Oriental medicine. By Oriental medicine I mean the three great systems of ancient medicine that survive in the modern world: the Indian or Ayurvedic, the Tibetan, and of course the Chinese. Let me review the reasons why I believe these systems must be studied to complement Western medicine.

First, the increasing fragmentation of medicine into specialties, without an appreciation of the relationships between these fragments, will render Western medicine more and more ineffective. Western medicine has no unifying matrix. In the West, some token homage is paid to the unity of man with the universe by academic theologians, theoretical physicists, and a few science fiction writers. But Western medicine is an uncoordinated accumulation of anatomical, physiological, pathological, and biochemical information about the human life system, coalescing in dramatic, technologically superb, heroic life-saving procedures. The Ayurvedic, Tibetan, and Chinese systems emphasize the relationships and unity not only between different aspects of bodily function, but also between body and mind, between body and spirit, and between the human being and the universe at large. Oriental medicine can provide a matrix on which Western medicine can place its endless accumulation of facts, in order to create a unified system.

Second, as we have seen, Western medicine has no concept of health. Its approach reflects the culture's general emphasis on conflict, and its basic aim is to destroy alien forces regarded as responsible for disease. This struggle is played out chiefly between the medical technology and the offending agent. The field of battle is the patient's body. Whereas there is an increasing number of physicians who appreciate the dangers of this approach, who place greater reliance on the capacity of people to heal, and who approach the use of drugs and other devices more conservatively, most of the Western doctors with whom I have contact are still operating within this mindset. It is, of course, a fact that the quality of the practitioner varies with the individual, regardless of the approach to healing.

Though Western medicine is familiar with, and acknowledges, mechanisms that exist in the human body for its own protection, it does not see disease merely as an alteration in those defenses, but rather sees those defenses as being overwhelmed by an alien, external force. A consequence of conceptualizing sickness as the result of an extraneous force is the emphasis placed on synthesizing drugs foreign to our life system to combat the invader. The thrust is to detach ourselves from the struggle. The price for this detachment is incalculable, measured only very partially by the remarkable list of adverse and often fatal side effects of allopathic medicines. In Oriental medicine, transient reactions are part of the process of cure, not a new illness.

Western medicine is heir to Cartesian thinking and the industrial revolution, aimed at controlling, even defeating, nature and the universe. Its methods reflect the resentment of Western man toward anything affecting his fate other than his own ego. I believe this is the deepest source of his impressive compensatory, obsessional, and, therefore, never-ending struggle for power as well as his escalating alienation and loneliness. In Oriental medicine, man helps and nature cures.

The patient as the primary factor in the development of the disease and as the agent who needs to be strengthened to cope with disease is an Oriental approach deeply needed in Western practice. Chinese medicine views illness as an expression of a personal violation of nature. It calls upon the person to become aware of how he is interfering with the flow of his own nature. He is encouraged, then, to examine how he lives, how he thinks, how he feels, his habits, and his values, in order to understand why he is ill. The focus is on an inner, rather than an outer, alien cause; one is ill because of something innate in oneself or in one's way of life.

CHINESE MEDICINE: UNITY OF MEDICINE AND LIFE

Chinese medicine is fundamentally a preventive medicine. Since the cause of disease is within us and can be known and understood, disease becomes a more rational proposition as a personal crisis in life. By studying the pulse, tongue, eye, and physiognomy, imbalance can be corrected prior to overt disease. The attention of the patient may be brought to focus on how he is living, eating, thinking, drinking, sleeping, and believing before his life is further encumbered by debilitating physical and mental illness. Medicine and life are one.

In Chinese medicine, one studies and treats the person and not the disease, whereas in the West, we treat the disease and not the person. The physician using a diagnosis made by means of the Chinese pulses or other parameters is taking account of the inner state of the individual in terms of energy balance in the body. Each individual is treated for his own special imbalance, notwithstanding the nature of the symptoms, though for specific kinds of symptoms there are special points and point formulas. In general, treatment is of the unique and total person, not of alien signs and symptoms.

Another significant manifestation of Chinese medicine in the unity of medicine and life is the relative lack of distinction between body and mind. They are one and part of the same system. An imbalance of energy may show itself as a disturbance in the highest functions or a disturbance in the so-called lower functions, or both. Corrective medicine concerns itself with a disturbance in the balance of energy, not with whether the symptom be emotional or physical. For this reason, if an emotional catharsis is what is called for, one may treat the Large Intestine channel, the great eliminator of the body.

The Large Intestine symbolizes 'elimination' in all of its many senses, including the elimination of bad thoughts as well as bad energy (feces). Likewise, the Stomach digests food and it also controls, and is involved with, the digestion of thoughts and feeling. While the Small Intestine separates the pure from the impure in food, it is also responsible for separating out pure from impure thought, reabsorbing the pure, and passing on the impure to the Large Intestine. The implications for the treatment of thought disorders will be elucidated.

There is a similar confluence of functions on a musculoskeletal level. Chronic anger is blocked in the muscles of the upper back that control the movement of the upper extremities, as well as in the lower back (holding back). This anger can be released by treating the spasm in these areas. As it is released, it is worked through by its own momentum on the levels of past, present, future, character, and total personality. This aspect of the work has been most impressive.

Another example would be the treatment of one kind of depression. In the Chinese system, the purifier of the spirit-soul in the body is the Wood phase, of which the Liver is one of the organ systems. Allopathic medicine tells us that the Liver metabolizes and separates what the body considers toxic from what it considers safe, excreting that which it deems unsafe. (The Chinese knew this thousands of years ago, prior to Western laboratory science.) Thus, in a situation in which one's spirit is agitated and depressed simultaneously, one would look to the Wood phase for imbalance. One might treat depression by draining or supplying the Liver channel. In the theory and practice of Chinese medicine, the mind and body are one.

A Case of Early Shock

I would like to illustrate briefly what we have discussed by studying the case of a thirteen-year-old boy. As our guide we will use Chinese diagnosis, which consists of *looking, listening, asking,* and *touching.* My object here, using three of these, is to capture the conceptual style of this energy medicine by commenting on my observations of a patient as I go through his examination. The purpose is not to teach Chinese medicine, but to convey its particular flavor.

I will begin with *looking.* Looking involves observing the total physiognomy of a person, as well as noting individual details. In the case of this boy, a slightly bent posture indicated that the energy of his Lungs was compromised and that his spirit was sagging. In his eyes there was a lost look and excessive brightness, which indicated that the energy of his spirit was damaged and out of control. The dark blue-green color under his eyes indicated that the Kidney yin (water) and *jing* (inherited essence) energies were overtaxed. These energies are responsible for the passage of genetic energy from one generation to another, for providing the 'water of life' to the tissues of the body, and for the development of the nervous system, among other tasks. The blue color indicated overwork and fluid deficiency. The hair of his eyebrows crossed above his nose, indicating a tendency to easily lose his temper, sometimes an inherited or congenital 'nervous system' problem. The light blue-green color around his mouth meant that he had also suffered some kind of 'shock,' probably early in life. Because the color did not appear around his nose as well, the likelihood is that the shock came after birth. The mottled color of his face indicated gastrointestinal disturbance. The relative redness of his face and whiteness of his hands showed a problem with circulation, and the spots on his fingernails suggested a recent illness (and/or zinc deficiency). His lips were dry and cracked, indicating heat in the Stomach. Relatively large ear lobes and a long, full philtrum showed that his general inherited energy store was good and could be relied on as a source for healing; and it showed that the Kidney deficiency was congenital, or occurred after birth, and was not genetic.

The tongue was swollen, which told us that he was not moving fluid in his body and probably had interstitial or cellular edema (electrolyte imbalance). The tongue was slightly pale, which indicated that this edema was from poor Kidney and/or Spleen energy function. There was a line down the center, which indicated that his Heart energy was also not strong, and, at his age, this may have been constitutional. However, the evidence (on his face) of 'shock' since birth indicated that the line on his tongue (Heart energy) might be related to that shock. Shock tends to affect the Heart energy more than any other. Red spots at the end of the tongue indicate heat from deficiency in the Heart. This type of heat is analogous to the heat of friction in an inefficient machine, and here it means that the Heart is overworking, working beyond its energy. It may have been weakened by the severe shock to which I am alluding. My original impression that his spirits were flagging may be relevant here. The spirit is housed in the Heart and can be seen in the eyes, which, as previously noted, appeared lost and overly bright. The red on the sides of the tongue meant heat in the Liver, probably due, at his young age, to repressed emotion, and was a sign of a system working beyond its capacity.

Passing over *listening,* next I made use of *asking.* Asking revealed that the immediate problem was cramps in the stomach, under the right costal margin, "like being stabbed with many needles." These attacks lasted for 15 to 20 minutes, were relieved by drinking milk, and had occurred for two years. There was prodromal discomfort, which made him restless. He wanted to "punch" the pain. All this was accompanied by nausea, hiccoughs, and a sensation of pain rising with a stuck feeling in his throat. These episodes occurred at 1 P.M. and anywhere from a half to one-and-a-half hours after lunch. Bowel movements were normal, urine sometimes light. He had dull frontal headaches. There was a history of hyperactivity, insecurity, and, currently, severe nightmares. What is implied here is inflammation in the Small Intestine (a half hour to one-and-a-half hours after eating), caused by the heat from deficiency of the Liver-Gallbladder, which tends to "wander" to vulnerable areas. Likewise the symptoms of rising pain, pain under the right costal margin, nausea, hiccoughs, and the stuck feeling in his throat are all related, in Chinese medicine, to stagnant Liver energy, causing 'bad' energy (heat from deficiency) to 'attack' the digestive system. The redness on the side of the tongue supports this thesis.

The dull frontal headaches are usually related to digestion, which, together with the stuck feeling in the throat, may indicate some phlegm from the poor digestion (Spleen dampness). The severe and terrifying nightmares are frequently the result of a combination of a 'weak' Heart (referring only to energy and the *shen,* or spirit) and poor Gallbladder function. According to Chinese medicine, the Gallbladder is the decision maker in the pantheon of cognitive functions. The boy had to decide between living with his mother or father, who were divorced and vying for his loyalty. The weakened Heart energy I have already mentioned in relation to 'shock.' According to Chinese medicine, the Heart controls the mind. The history is much more extensive than recorded here and includes a very detailed psychological history and family history, all of which is pertinent.

Finally, *touching* involves taking the pulse and palpating various points and areas of the body for tenderness or nodules, both of which ascertain in different ways the energy integrity of the inner organs.

The pulse is the most important and most difficult diagnostic tool to develop. It requires a lifetime of refinement and for this reason is a gradually dying art and science. I have spent eight years studying the pulse with a Chinese doctor who himself has studied it for fifty-six years. Some of this knowledge has been passed down and should continue to be taught and kept alive.

The boy's pulse rate was 66 beats per minute, which, according to the Chinese, is very slow for a child of 13 and indicates Heart-circulatory problems, confirming my past suspicions. The entire pulse was Pounding, meaning heat or overwork, in this instance, of a 'nervous system' that is stressed by the emotional turmoil associated with the divorce. (The concept of the 'nervous system' will be explained in Chapter 14, which describes the systems model of Dr. Shen, my teacher). The pulse wave on the Heart and Lung areas was Flat, indicating severe disappointment, probably long ago, since circulation has been so profoundly affected. This may be the shock to which the signs are constantly pointing.

The Liver pulse was Full and like a Bowstring, which is indicative of stagnation, as I already suspected. The source is usually emotional stress beyond the capacity of the person to successfully cope. The Stomach pulse was very Tight, indicating inflammation, also from working beyond its energy by overeating or eating too quickly. The latter is often related to emotional stress and to the concomitant Liver qi stagnation. One of the Kidney pulses related to the Kidney yin (water) was Deep, Thin, and Wiry, indicating overwork and approaching exhaustion of body fluids. The other Kidney pulse, related to general metabolism (*ming men*) and water movement (Kidney yang), was very Weak.

In conclusion, my diagnosis takes into account both the long range issues of this boy's life and the short range issues currently concerning him. The immediate problem is stagnant Liver qi 'attacking' the digestive system, combined with a dietary change for the worse two years previously. The cause of the stagnant Liver qi is severe emotional stress, due to long-term conflicts between his divorced parents and his profound sense of inadequacy and frustration because of long-term learning disabilities, which kept him in special classes all his life. He is reaching puberty, a time of great change and pressure for everyone, without the basic skills for survival and with little hope inside himself for a normal life in the future. He has chosen to live with his father (for the past two years), seeking for some answers by being close to a man. However, he is torn by this decision, which has further affected his Liver-Gallbladder function. Together with weakness of the Heart, the Gallbladder weakness has led to severe nightmares and night terrors.

All of this exists in a setting of weakness in his 'nervous system,' which is possibly congenital. His mother used drugs recreationally during her pregnancy with him. Kidney yin, as we have seen, is stressed. The Kidney yin and Kidney essence (*jing*) are related and slightly differentiated energies. When one is weak the other is also frequently compromised. Kidney essence is responsible for, among many other things, the development of the central nervous system. Its weakness in so young a person must be from an early insult and must be related to his 'soft' neurological signs, including severe learning disabilities and hyperactivity. Since the Kidneys are the 'mother' of the Liver, which is under duress, the Kidneys are also called upon to expend their precious energy to support the Liver, causing it to neglect its other responsibilities, especially to the 'nervous system.'

Furthermore, his Heart and Lung energies have been stifled by disappointment (shock), as evidenced by the blue-green color around his mouth and the Flat wave on the pulse, adding to his many problems, especially of the mind (his nightmares).

For treatment, this model has at its disposal the 'eight limbs' of classical Chinese medicine. These include herbology, acupuncture, nutrition, moxibustion, cupping, exercise, massage, and meditation. The first three are generally understood to mean the use of herbs, needles, and food as treatment, following the principles of Chinese physiology and pathology. Moxibustion is the burning of a specific herbal preparation on acupuncture points, causing little if any discomfort to the patient. Exercise is either tai ji quan or qi gong, or some other variation of the Daoist manipulation of energy through movement, such as gong fu. Massage, called tui-na, is energy-centered and differs markedly from Swedish massage, which is concerned with blood circulation. Meditations are non-specific and will vary by prescription from one problem or person to another. These modalities may be used alone or together, following the treatment plan which evolves from the diagnosis.

With regard to my patient, treatment was limited to herbs and some advice about diet and eating habits, because he lived at a great distance. Herbs were prescribed to relax and remove the stagnation from his Liver, to remove heat from his digestive system and move the energy downward, to open and relax his Heart and calm his spirit. Since he was seen only once, the more fundamental treatment of his Kidney energies was never attempted.

Within a few days he was feeling considerably better; and when his father became ill, he recommended me to him because "he helps and doesn't hurt." The long-range issues are, of course, quite complex and will require a great deal of management.

The purpose of this presentation is to communicate the flavor of an energetic medicine as it is used to diagnose and treat physical, mental, and spiritual deviations from the natural functions of a person's organ systems. It is not meant to be an exhaustive teaching exercise.

With a sense of the congeniality between Western psychology and Chinese medicine, both abstract and clinical, and with a sense of an energy-based medicine and the medical model it engenders, we can examine in the next two chapters the formulations of mind-body-spirit in the current Chinese medical model. We will then be prepared, I hope, to explore certain revisions to these formulations. These revisions constitute the principal thrust of this book.

4

PSYCHOSOMATIC MEDICINE: WEST AND EAST

PRELIMINARY CONSIDERATIONS OF MIND-BODY

The simplest definition of psychosomatic medicine comes from *Stedman's Medical Dictionary* where it is understood as "refer-ring to the relationship between mind and body." The *Psychiatric Diction-ary* greatly elaborates this definition and concludes that, "more commonly, however, the term is used in a nosological or classificatory sense to refer to a group of disorders whose etiology, at least in part, is believed to be related to emotional factors."[1]

In the 1952 revision of *Psychiatric Nomenclature (Diagnostic Statistical Manual II* [DSM-II]) such psychosomatic disorders are called 'Psychophys-iologic, autonomic, and visceral disorders.' DSM-II states:

> This term is used in preference to psychosomatic disorders, since the latter term refers to a point of view on the discipline of medicine as a whole rather than to a certain specified condition. It is preferred to the term 'somatization reactions,' which term implies that these disorders are simply another form of psychoneu-rotic reaction. These disorders are here given a more separate grouping between psychotic and psychoneurotic reactions to allow more accurate accumulation of data and etiology, cause and relation to other mental disorders.
>
> These reactions represent the visceral expression of affect which may be thereby largely prevented from being conscious. The symptoms are due to a chronic and exaggerated state of the normal physiological expression of emotion with the feeling or subjective part repressed. Such long, continued visceral states may eventually lead to structural changes.

However, by the time DSM-III was formulated in the late 1970s, psycho-physiologic, autonomic, and visceral disorders gave way to the term 'somatoform disorders,' and the description went from two pages to ten. At this point they were defined as follows:

> The essential features of this group of disorders are physical symptoms suggesting physical disorder for which there are no demonstrable organic findings or known physiological mechanisms and for which there is positive evidence or strong presumption that the symptoms are linked to psychological factors or conflicts.

WESTERN MEDICINE GRAPPLES WITH PSYCHOSOMATICS

Two groups of illnesses were implied by the earlier definition of psychosomatic. First, conditions that were symptomatic. They consisted of the patient's subjective complaints (including headache, palpitations, dizziness and fainting, restlessness, fatigue, nausea, pain, even conversion reactions such as hysterical paralysis) and showed no discernible *signs.* (Signs, in contradistinction to symptoms, are observable to a second person as well as to the patient. Examples of signs are bulging eyes, a red tongue, facial pallor, a tense and tender abdomen, wheezing, and tremor). The second class included illnesses with distinct signs as well as symptoms which were unexplainable by Western pathology and therefore were ascribed to an emotional etiology. These included gastric and duodenal ulcers, asthma, colitis, mononucleosis, unexplained fevers, thyroid disease, obesity, anorexia nervosa, coronary heart disease, eczema, speech disorders, sleep disorders, cancer, and tuberculosis. Both groups had earlier come under the scrutiny of psychoanalytic theoreticians and psychophysiological researchers and had also become the object of study, observation, and speculation by such well-known physicians as Groddeck.[2] (Groddeck was a medical doctor who originally studied with the naturopathic physician and professor of anatomy Ernst Schweninger, who cured the apparently dying Bismarck with deep massage, diet, and hot water applications at the height of Bismarck's power, when other physicians had failed. Groddeck at first attacked Freud in writing, but, after establishing the most famous sanatorium in Europe in Baden-Baden and treating most of the rich and famous of his time, he came through his work to realize that he was dealing primarily with the "will to be ill" or to die. He corresponded with Freud, who insisted on calling him a psychoanalyst, to the horror of some of Freud's followers. Groddeck came to be known as the "wild analyst" because his unorthodox methods included holding and touching his patients. He died of a broken heart, unable to accept the Nazi transformation of Germany and the persecution of many of his patients, including Eric Fromm, despite his personal efforts to intervene with Hitler.

The important work of early psychoanalytic investigators such as Franz Alexander[3] in Chicago and Otto Fennichel[4] in Europe engendered a lineage of innovative psychophysiological research, notably among those who worked with them. Others involved in neuro-physiological research were Stewart Wolf and Harold G. Wolff[5] at New York Hospital, whose studies focused mainly on migraine headaches and gastric function. Utilizing an opening (stoma) in the stomach of a patient who had had an accident, they observed his gastric mucosa in relation to emotional stimuli. Alexander based a great deal of his work on the differentiation of symptoms into parasympathetic and sympathetic responses, believing that the key to understanding the psychosomatic mechanism lay in the autonomic nervous system. Fennichel's work leaned more toward the symbolic. For example, he equated asthma with separation anxiety and gastrointestinal disorders of the lower intestine with fixations in the anal stage of development.

Recently the field of psychoneuro-immunology has emerged. Here attempts are being made to link the central nervous system centers, such as the hypothalamus and pituitary glands, to the autonomic nervous system, the hormonal system, visceral organs, and, most recently, to the immune system. This work is summarized in the volume *Psychoneuro-Immunology.*[6] Its thrust is to reaffirm the ancient conviction that "mind and body are inseparable"[7] and the wisdom of Sir William Osler who said, "The care of tuberculosis depends more on what the patient has in his head than in his chest."[8] Increasingly, the relation of emotional stress to physical disease is being studied. The emerging data only confirms, by scientifically acceptable experimental models, what has already been proposed by many. Nevertheless, this perspective has been largely rejected by the medical establishment.

If viewed from the perspective of the health-to-disease spectrum, conditions that show only symptoms would fall towards the health end of the spectrum, where there are no signs of disease by Western standards. The second group, where signs are already discernible, would tend to fall more toward the disease end of the spectrum, although still well within the domain of energy considerations. At the health end we have disorders of function, and at the disease end, disorders of morphology.

There is a gradual progression from functional disorders, or distorted energy states, to detectable organ tissue damage. However, Western medicine has remained completely unaware of, and unaffected by, the energy-based physiology and pathology of Oriental medicine and is thus unable to detect or classify disease in its incipient and developing stages. Despite the new research, whatever escapes the dragnet of morphologically oriented

Western diagnosis or pathological theory currently finds itself subsumed under the category of psychosomatic medicine.

I have chosen not to elaborate on the history of psychosomatic medicine in the West. While immersed in it during my training in psychiatry and psychoanalysis during the 1950s, I witnessed its demise as a useful pursuit because of its inefficacy as a therapeutic tool. Nothing postulated during the preceding decades proved clinically sound. It was, correctly, abandoned as a medical discipline within the framework of Western science because it had no way within Western physiology to explain how an emotion affected an organ or the reverse. The concept of "organ inferiority" was too vague a concept to test. (I recommend *Bodymind Energetics* by Mark Seem[9] on this subject, which recently I have been privileged to read, and have found both comprehensive and illuminating.)

CLASSIC ANCIENT CHINESE MEDICINE IS PSYCHOSOMATICS

Chinese medical physiology does provide us with the tools to explain the relationships between the psyche and the soma. Let us resume our examination of the psychosoma within the Chinese medical model. Working from the health end of the spectrum, any act by man or nature which interferes with the quantity, circulation, or rhythmic balance of the life force, or energy, will lead in the direction of disease and toward the death end of the spectrum. The active factors may include constitution, eating habits, work habits, environmental stress (e.g., chemical pollution), weather and climate, sexual habits, social milieu (including drugs, poisons, epidemiological diseases), and, perhaps most central to the Chinese medical system, emotion, or the 'seven passions.' Using the modalities of Chinese diagnosis, particularly the pulse, the tongue, the eyes, and facial color, one can measure how these different aspects of daily life may be adversely affecting the integrity of the energy systems even before the development of symptoms, and, more certainly, after early symptoms develop. The focus is on health, on the patient in everyday life, and on prevention.

A concentration of these signs at the health end of the spectrum may encompass and explain most of the early signs and symptoms of the disease process which do not fall within the purview of Western diagnostic techniques at the disease-death end of the spectrum. It is possible to identify and treat, through early diagnosis, much of what has been confusingly alluded to in the latest definitions as 'somatoform disorders.' Those are defined as "Physical symptoms suggesting physical disorder for which there are no demonstrable organic findings or no physiological mechanisms."[10] At this point, very real physiological changes are taking place, and pathology does exist. However, these are physiological alterations of the life force, of energy rather than morphology, and the disharmony is limited to the energy system. It is disclosed by the color, sound, pulse, and tongue of the individual. Depending on one's definition of reality, observable and measurable changes do occur. Some, but by no means all, of these changes may be due to emotional stress, and at this early stage they can be differentiated from the other etiological factors mentioned above. Disease, from this point of view, is a progression from 'energy' to 'mass.'

The fact is that this process is both psychological and somatic at all stages. Changes in color, sound, odor, pulse, tongue, and eyes are there from the beginning, and the psychological factors are there until death (*see* CHART 1, page 58).

Another misunderstood theme in psychosomatic medicine is the assumption that the emergence of a physical illness in the presence of a psychological stress is a sign of psychological weakness. Nothing could be further from the truth. Physical symptoms may develop, in fact, when a person is psychologically sound. In terms of survival, keeping one's wits is worth the sacrifice of developing a physical symptom; a gastro-intestinal disturbance is a small price to pay for one's sanity. Ideally one should be sufficiently competent to deal with most stress without developing either physical or mental aberrations. Since most important problems begin early in life before the 'nervous system' (Kidney essence/*jing)* is fully developed, this ideal is permanently elusive. If a child develops a chronic headache rather than a psychosis in reaction to living with an alcoholic parent, he is in possession of a more than adequate mental-emotional apparatus.

Incorporating this fact into the consciousness of our culture is of great importance. Notwithstanding the efforts of medical education to orient health care professionals to increasing respect for their patients, those who are tainted by the brush of an emotional-mental deficit are still an underclass in medicine and in a society which esteems the 'strong silent type.' Patients with problems thought to be psychosomatic are often viewed with condescension. In the face of this unrelenting bias, I must emphasize as often and as strongly as possible that the person who develops physical symptoms when confronted with emotional stress is demonstrating both an admirably resilient mental and emotional apparatus and the capability to choose the less disorganizing option of a physical disease rather than the massively disorganizing one of a mental breakdown.

Health, by definition, is a condition in which all systems within the microorganism are harmoniously interlocked with each other and in dynamic consonance with nature. Focusing on health and engaging the concept of energy as the basic issue of health, disease, life, and death means viewing these phenomena as part of a single universal substrate in which all phenomena are but diverse expressions of its infinity and its unity. Because Chinese medicine is grounded in unity, it is oriented toward finding relationships and correspondences in nature.

THE INTERNAL DRAGONS AND THE FIVE PHASES: AN INTRODUCTION

I have set out broadly the basic tenets of Chinese medicine before which the issues of 'psycho' and 'somatic,' of mind and body as dichotomies, begin to fade.

Let me now, and in the following chapters, address myself to the reversible energy transformations and to the physiology and pathology of these transformations between the materially undefinable, which we call 'emotion,' and the materially definable, which we call 'body.' I will do this first according to the tenets of Chinese medicine, and later, according to variations that I and others have observed and defined.

THE FIVE INTERNAL AGENTS OF DISEASE

Before we begin, let me repeat that Chinese medicine developed along a myriad of paths during the course of its existence. Each clan, each hamlet and village, each city and state, and each dynasty had its own tradition. The recent synthesis, which is known in the People's Republic of China as Traditional Chinese Medicine (TCM), is an attempt on the part of a modern Marxist state to present Chinese medicine as a discipline in keeping with the materialistic tenets of that state and to make it more acceptable to the scientific community of the West. Elements of this multitude of disappearing traditions have nevertheless seeped into the West, and from these much may also be learned about our subject.

According to Chinese medicine the etiology of disease is systematized according to internal agents and external agents.[11] The internal causes are the ones which are germane to our discourse. Most texts list these inner causes of disease as the 'seven sentiments,' the 'seven psychic or mental phases,' the 'seven demons or seven dragons,' the 'seven passions,' and, more recently, as the 'five emotions.'[12] They are joy, anger, anguish (or grief), reflection (meditation or thinking), sadness (or melancholy), fear (or panic), and apprehension (fright and shock). There are many variations on this theme. Some reduce the inner agents of disease to just five—joy, anger, reflection, sadness, and fear—in order to fit the Five Phase theory.

With regard to the traditional organ system, there is overall agreement within Chinese medicine that, when excessive, anger injures the Liver, joy injures the Heart, reflection injures the Spleen, sadness injures the Lungs, and fear injures the Kidneys.

As already noted, allusion to these vital organs is to be interpreted only in energy terms, as defined in this book and in other sources, where conceptually the Heart, Liver, Spleen, Kidneys, and Lungs are clearly distinguished from the material organs. In reality, they are in a continuous dynamic exchange, and, at the point where 'energy' solidifies into 'mass,' these concepts merge and the distinction is clinically obscure. While Chinese medicine is equipped to address both energy and mass, it clearly speaks most eloquently to the former.

Joy affects the Heart, which is said to be the home of the spirit. The spirit is equated with energy on the 'mental' plane; thus, the Heart controls the mind. Excessive joy (shock) injures the mind by creating too much fire, causing excitement or overtaxing of mental energy. This may lead to palpitations, anxiety, insomnia, irritability, and/or shortness of breath, depending on whether the deficiency is one of qi (kinetic energy), blood, or yin (water). This is known as a disturbance of the *shen* or spirit. Conversely, an energically weak Heart can make one vulnerable to shock.

Unreleased anger damages the Liver, and a diseased Liver gives rise to easy anger. The classics say that the Liver corresponds to the phase Wood. In Wood, the sap must flow. Anything that inhibits the flow of this material (yin) aspect of the energy will cause a greater output by the functional (yang) energy. The result is a nonproductive 'heat of friction,' known in Chinese medicine as 'heat from deficiency' (emptiness, weakness). As the heat from deficiency increases, the entire organism undergoes a subtle rise in temperature, experienced as tension and ultimately pain. The Liver stores the blood, which becomes hot, as the heat from deficiency accumulates in the Liver. The increased Liver heat has many manifestations on a physical level, and on an emotional level this 'slow burn' or 'fast burn' is expressed, respectively, as smoldering or as explosive irritability and anger. One might say that the person has become "hot-blooded," an expression corresponding exactly to the heating process occurring in the stagnant stored blood in the Liver. These basic concepts will be developed further below.

Reflection (thinking) is the process of attention and concentration in the service of problem solving. For reasons to be explained later, the Spleen, which controls the process of digestion, separation, absorption, and elimination, as well as distribution of metabolites, is primarily affected by excessive rumination, which slows the digestive process. Symptoms of anorexia, fullness, diarrhea, and weakness may result. Any injury to the Spleen system will lead to a disorder in thought process.

Sadness concerns an unresolved, and most often unconscious, early experience of grief. Because grief is usually expressed by crying and sobbing, the breathing apparatus at the physiological level is heavily involved in the reaction of sadness. To control the outward expression of sadness, one has to suppress the breathing mechanism. For this reason, sadness at first affects the Lungs. We will elaborate on this at another point. Likewise, Lung disease can lead to unexplained sadness.

Since fear descends to the lower part of the body, it affects the Kidney system, which controls this terrain. As explained elsewhere, the Kidney system in Chinese medicine includes the hormonal function of the adrenal glands, which are the endocrine organs most intimately associated with stress. Prolonged, fearful stress or 'frozen panic' affects the Kidney system, whereas sudden fear most often affects the Heart. These factors will be elaborated at another place in our discussion.

Concerning their effect on overall energy, it is said that anger makes the energy climb to the top of the body; joy renders it harmonious; sadness disperses it; reflection concentrates it (in the brain); fear makes it descend; and apprehension troubles the energy. In some instances, emotion will first affect one organ and later affect the entire balance of energy as that organ deteriorates. In other situations, emotion will have a more general effect on the entire organism; to a lesser extent, or later, it may affect the specific organ systems.

Traditionally, the emotions are regarded as dangerous only when they are extreme. The other factor is the relative integrity of the organ system. Emotional distress originating from organ system dysfunction may produce distinctly different emotional states, depending on whether the organ system is in a state of excess (strong-active) or deficiency (weak-passive). Syndromes of excess (hot, yang, strong) tend to produce conditions of excitement; syndromes of deficiency (cold, yin, weak) result in conditions of a more muted description, such as depression.

BALANCE, CIRCULATION, AND ENERGY

I have said that these internal elements create disharmony when they interfere with the energy function of the specific organs (Zang-Fu) or with the general circulation of energy, qi, blood, and fluids, and the overall balance of yin and yang.

In addition, two underlying principles of Oriental medicine, independent of etiology, must always be applied in considerations of disharmony.

One principle acknowledges the *a priori* weakness of an organ before it can be injured by a pathogenic factor, emotional or otherwise, unless the factor is cataclysmic, such as a massive accident or the plague. The other is that symptomatology always involves at least two or more causes.

The principal functional considerations of Chinese medicine are rhythmic balance, circulation, and quantity of energy. Disturbances in any one, alone or in combination, may lead to emotional disorder. Conversely, emotional disorder may disturb the integrity of any one or all of these. 'Unbalanced' is a term universally associated with mental distress. Of the three basic differentiations of energy, which include qi, blood (and fluids), and organ systems, the qi is the immaterial expression of energy. It is, therefore, most labile, susceptible to even the smallest stresses, and most closely related to the shifting moods and states of emotional distress. (The hierarchy of these energies, from superficial to deep, is expressed in the concept of the 'four levels' of *wei*, qi, *ying* (fluid), and blood, as described by the warm disease school).

The potential for balance is expressed by the concept of yin and yang, which is a summation of many factors, including: the Eight Principles of hot/cold, interior/exterior, excess/deficiency. Combinations of the aforementioned result in either yin or yang, which constitute the seventh and eighth principle. The balance of yin and yang is also a function of left and right, in the law of 'husband-wife'; back and front (*shu* and *mu*); upper, middle, and lower (the three 'burners' or 'warmers'). Balance exists between the Zang (solid interior organ) and the Fu (hollow exterior organ) of a phase; likewise, within the Chen and Ko cycle of the Five Phases (elements) and the channels of the Six Divisions, expressed through the pulse, tongue, eyes, color, and symptoms. For a complete discussion of the Eight Principles, the reader is referred to *The Web That Has No Weaver,* by Ted Kaptchuk, O.M.D.; and for a thorough exposition of the Five Phase system, to Dianne Connelly's book *Traditional Acupuncture: The Law of the Five Elements.*

Circulation involves the qi, the blood, the body fluids in the channels, the organ systems, and the five 'special organs.' The Lungs, Spleen, and Heart are the organs principally involved with the physiology of circulation, though any organ, especially the Liver, can also be involved in the disruption of circulation. Stagnation of the qi can be due to an accident, weather, or emotional shock.

Energy involves strength or weakness. Constitutional energy comes from the Kidneys, which store the inherited (as well as acquired) essence. Sources of energy during life are the Lungs (air-qi), and the Stomach-Spleen (food and fluid). Problems with any one or all three of these organ systems will mean a deficiency in overall essential energy. Excesses of general energy are rare. Localized excess in an acute disease, when the body is putting additional energy into one area to overcome a disease process, is sometimes confused with a true condition of actual excess. Energy depletion is usually the result of a long period of overwork, chronic illness, chronic emotional problems, old age, and/or excessive exercise.

There are a number of ways to conceptualize energy in Chinese medicine: yin-yang, the Five Phases (elements), the Six Divisions, the Chinese clock, the qi, blood, and organs, the Ying and the Wei, the Stems and Branches, the *I Ching,* Astrology, Hun and Po, *shen* and qi, and the Antique Points. In addition, there is the channel (channel) system, among which are the twelve main, eight homeostatic (ancestral or extraordinary), fifteen (or sixteen) connecting, and twelve divergent channels.

All of these are relevant to our subject. However, I will focus for the moment on the Five Phase system, which provides the richest organization of correspondences between mind and body, and I will attempt to coordinate it with all of the other significant aspects of Chinese medicine. The Five Phase system must be examined within the larger context of the medicine. Chapter 14, entitled "The Systems Model of Dr. Shen," will address those aspects of Chinese medicine which, in the face of the complexity of the subject, could not be completely integrated in those parts of the book containing the fullest exploration of the Five Phases.

CHEN AND KO CYCLES

The phases of energy between yin and yang of the Five Phase system have been observed to be related to each other in an orderly, organized, and predictable cycle of generation and control, known respectively as the Chen (generation/production/creation) and the Ko (control) cycles. These follow the movements of the seasons and the deeper flow of body energies. Beginning with the spring, we have the Wood phase (Liver and Gallbladder), which generates, or is 'mother' to, the summer or Fire phase (Heart, Small Intestine, Triple Burner, and Pericardium), which in turn gives rise to the late summer or Earth phase (Spleen-Pancreas and Stomach), which then produces the autumn or Metal phase (Lungs and Large Intestine). The Metal phase creates the winter, or Water phase (Kidneys and Bladder), which completes the Chen or generation cycle and begets again the spring and Wood phase. Balancing this cycle of generation is a cycle of control (Ko) in which the Wood 'covers' the Earth, the Fire 'melts' the Metal, the Earth 'contains' the Water, the Metal 'cuts' the Wood, and the Water puts out the Fire. (See Charts II and III.) Function is a variable of this continuous, uninterrupted circulation.

The Five Phase system describes the deeper physiological relationship of the organ systems, just as the Chinese clock describes the superficial energy cycles. In order to understand the disease process within the Chinese medical model, we must first understand these relationships and then continue to explore other physiological factors which complicate these patterns.

Theoretically, when an emotion affects an organ system such as the Liver (Wood phase), the other organ in the phase system would be the next to be affected — in this instance, the Gallbladder. The son, then the mother, the controlled, and finally the controlling systems would be most likely to be affected in that order, according to Five Phase theory.

It follows that at some point in the course of correction, homeostasis or treatment might, in this context, consist of strengthening the controlling phase. "Anger injures the Liver, and sadness controls the anger. Excess joy hurts the Heart, and fear controls the joy (Water over Fire). Sadness affects the Lungs, and joy controls the sadness (Fire over Metal). Fear may injure the Kidneys, and thinking controls fear (Earth controls the Water)."[13]

Centuries before Freud's formulation in the late 19th century, the concept of "reaction formation"[14] was clearly outlined in the law of the Five Phases as a natural homeostatic mechanism: the establishment of a trait or regular pattern of behavior that is opposed to a strong unconscious trend.

THE HEALTH–DISEASE CONTINUUM

HEALTH → **DISEASE**

PHYSICAL SYMPTOMS	Minor changes in stool consistency and frequency (hard to soft)	More marked changes in stool consistency and frequency; occasional diarrhea; some cramps	Presence of mucus in addition to increase in previous symptoms	Previous symptoms continue, pain increases, and blood and debilitation present	Neuropathies, edema, depression, blood dyscrosias, headache, nausea, vomiting, oligospermia, skin rash, bone marrow suppression, death
WESTERN MEDICAL DIAGNOSIS	Spastic colon	Irritable bowel	Mucous colitis	Ulcerative colitis	Iatrogenic medication side effects
WESTERN PSYCHOLOGICAL DIAGNOSIS	Neurotic	Psychosomatic	Somatopsychic	Somatic	Major depressive episode; psychoses; suicide
WESTERN TREATMENT	Counseling; medication: Lomofil	Counseling; medication: Paragoric	Medication: Imodium	Medication: Sulfasalazine, Metronidazale, Corticosteroids, 6Mercaptopurine, Cyclosporine; surgery	Medication to control the iatrogenic disease
STAGES OF DISEASE IN CHINESE MEDICINE[1]	**QI STAGE** Shao Yang (Lesser Yang)		**NUTRITIVE STAGE** Tai Yin (Greater Yin)		**BLOOD STAGE** Shao Yin (Lesser Yin) Jue Yin (Absolute Yin)

[1] In *Chinese medicine* these stages are integrally interrelated theoretically and clinically. Disease may evolve through these stages and/or appear clinically in any one stage without ostensibly moving through those preceding stages when there is exceptional vulnerability or an overwhelming pathogenic factor. In *Western medicine* there is no established theoretical or clinical connection between these syndromes or stages.

5

THE TRADITIONAL FIVE PHASE SYSTEM: EMOTION AND THE DISEASE PROCESS

FIRST LINE OF EMOTIONAL DEFENSE

Using the Liver organ system as a starting point, and the Five Phase (or Element) system as a guide, let us explore the disease process. The Liver is the organ system occupying the first line of emotional defense for the entire body. This energy system is the organism's first choice in coping with any noxious emotional stimulus,[1] especially if it is chronic. It is endowed by nature in several ways to do this. Constitutionally, it is the strongest system. Considering the abuse it has taken just from the consumption of alcohol throughout the ages, it has remained a dependable defender of our physical and mental survival. Perhaps in our time it will succumb to the enormous increase in the use of drugs and other toxic substances, especially by women throughout pregnancy, and to the onslaught of tensions and toxic substances throughout our lives.

Functionally, the Liver is especially endowed in that, according to Chinese medicine, it "stores the blood."[2] Rich in blood, the Liver is more capable of restoring itself than any other organ system. In fact, one of its most important functions for the entire body lies in recovering all the energy when the body is depleted. The Liver organ system is also responsible for what the Chinese call the "free going condition of the qi."[3] This means that the Liver energies, based on their advantageous blood supply, play a major part in the movement and circulation of qi and the prevention of stagnation. Its rich blood supply also enables the Liver to nourish ligaments and tendons[4] and make the body a supple and lithe machine for work and defense. Liver yin controls the ligaments and tendons, including the muscular innervation of the eyes; and Liver yang controls, in the same fashion, the nervous system.

Let us examine the reversible pathway in which tension, anger, frustration, suppression, repression, and stress in general interplay with the Liver organ system and the functions we have just described. 'Reversible pathway' refers to a principle of Chinese medicine in which the energy condition of an organ system may influence the mental and emotional condition of a person, while at the same time, or at any time, the latter may be either stimulating or suppressing the energy function of an organ. Classical Chinese medicine asserts that a particular emotion and a particular energy organ system are inextricably linked in this manner so that whatever happens, for example, in the Earth phase's sphere of influence will affect only the emotions of sympathy and compassion, while these emotions in turn will affect only the Earth phase's sphere of influence. Thus it is with joy and the Fire phase, anger and the Wood phase, fear and the Water phase, sadness and the Metal phase. In subsequent chapters we shall amend this law with certain qualifications. (We are using organ system and 'sphere of influence' interchangeably, both of which are related to Porkert's concept of 'orbisiconography.'[5])

Emotion immediately contacts the nervous system and several events are set into motion. To begin with, the Liver nourishes the nervous system and is called upon to increase the amount of blood in the circulation to meet its obligation. The increased tension in the nervous system may, under normal circumstances, be released through verbal expression or physical activity, thus restoring homeostasis. If speech is used, the Heart organ system will be engaged. If physical activity solves the problem, the Liver itself, as 'controller' of the ligaments and tendons, the Lungs as the receiver of the qi, and the Heart organ system (circulation) will all make a contribution.

What is the fate of these emotions when discharge and rebalance are not available? How does the Liver function when emotions are not discharged into adaptive pathways? Let me now examine this process which, in psychiatry, is known as repression.

Unreleased Emotion and the Liver Organ System

If the tension or energy that initially creates hyperactivity of the nervous system is not released, the latter will continue to call upon the Liver for added nourishment. The musculoskeletal system, which is unable to respond to the call for release, will hold the tension and gradually also require more nourishment. Both of these systems will call upon the Liver to empty its stored blood for their use. The Liver will slowly find that it has inadequate supplies left for its own recovery and for its many other functions. In such a situation, the energy that the Liver cannot recycle and renew becomes noxious energy; and, because the Liver is associated with wind and the 'free-flowing' of the qi, this noxious energy will affect many parts of the body. Inhibition of the flow of qi will create stagnation and pain in vulnerable areas.

At the same time, the circulatory system is constricted peripherally by the mechanical tension in the muscles. Internally, the noxious qi (or lactic acid and its metabolites, such as acetaldehyde) stimulates circulatory centers, such as the carotid sinus, and the autonomic nervous system centers, such as the sino-auricular node. The result is increasing blood pressure, which, in addition to affecting the Heart, causes the blood to be pushed too quickly through the Liver. This rapid passage of blood, as well as general overwork, first causes the Liver to develop heat from excess, and, over a period of time, heat from deficiency. The latter is analogous to the heat of friction in an engine that is working beyond its capacity. The heat from excess causes the blood vessels to expand and the blood pressure to rise. At this point, we find on the pulse that quality for which the Liver is so famous in Chinese medicine, the 'string-taut' pulse (Tense, Pounding, a little Overflowing, all of which indicate heat).

In referring to Western medical concepts, I wish to make it clear that, to my knowledge, there have been no established physiological connections between the two medicines. My references are purely speculative and quite unavoidable, due to the 12 years I have spent studying Western science. Though I thoroughly subscribe to keeping the two medicines separate, I shall not refuse myself the pleasure of indulging an occasional lapse.

CONDITIONS OF HEAT

The heat is now part of a vicious cycle: created by tension in the nervous system, it continues to feed that tension. It is for this reason that, in addition to psycho-therapeutic efforts to deal with the origin of these tensions on the emotional level, we must assist the Liver by reducing the heat, removing the stagnation, and giving it support. Although the original emotional cause may long since have been resolved through time or therapeutic intervention, the Liver organ system will continue to generate tension until we restore it to normal physiology.

This odyssey leads us to a depleted Liver no longer capable of storing the blood. The complex glucose buffering action of the liver is disturbed, leading to hypoglycemia and many allergies, when metabolites cannot be detoxified. All of this compounds the initial psychological picture.

Some of the consequences of Liver organ system disharmony, according to Chinese medicine, are mental irritation, depression, and anger,[6] which diminishes the 'free-flow' of the qi in the Liver and the qi in other vulnerable parts of the body. The gastrointestinal tract is often most immediately affected by this stagnation. Along with the Liver-Gallbladder, it occupies the middle burner. Some of the symptoms are pain and distention of the hypochondrium (which is referred to the chest, back, or scapula), stiffness of the chest, sighing, sensation of a foreign body in the throat, anorexia, belching, sour regurgitation, and hiccoughs.[7] Sudden, explosive diarrhea is another expression of Liver qi attacking the Spleen-Pancreas constellation of functions — in this case the Large Intestine. (Whereas the Large Intestine is related to the Metal phase in the Five Phase system, during my study in Beijing in 1981 I was taught that, for all practical purposes, within the Eight Principle system the Large Intestine energies can be subsumed under the aegis of the Spleen energy system. Furthermore, Metal-yang [the Large Intestine] and Wood-yin [the Liver] have a direct connection, according to the 'Ten Celestial Stems Controlling Cycle Balance,' as described by Kiiko Matsumoto and Stephen Birch in their book *Five Elements and Ten Stems.*)

This stagnation of the qi, or noxious energy, also affects the urogenital system in a similar fashion. The symptoms are irregular menstruation, abdominal pain before menstruation, headache, distended sensation of the breasts, and easy irritability.[8] The Liver energies are further involved in menstruation because of their function of storing the blood. When stagnation of the qi in the Liver has occurred for a prolonged period, the Liver, as explained above, will weaken. It will not be at all able to store or hold the blood, and this loss of control will result in menorrhagia (uncontrolled bleeding). Later, when the Liver is exhausted, there will be less blood available for menstruation, and oligemia (decreased bleeding) or amenorrhea (no period) may result.

As the disease process progresses, the yin of the Liver is depleted first. This will be accompanied over a period of time by a depletion of the yin of the Kidneys, which is the mother of the Liver and supplies yin to the body generally. The result is hyperactivity of the yang of the Liver and the following syndrome: headache, distention of the head, vertigo, tinnitus, deafness, insomnia, amnesia, numbness and tremors of the extremities, red dry tongue, and String Taut pulse.[9] Diseases included in this condition are hypertension, neurosis, vertigo, hyperthyroidism, and climacteric syndromes.

A more severe condition of heat is called 'flaring up of Liver fire.' The diseases in this category of Liver imbalance are caused by heat in the Liver channel; indulgence in drinking and smoking, as well as long-term depression of the qi of the Liver, can turn heat to fire. This is seen in hypertension, hemorrhage of the upper gastro-intestinal tract, acute conjunctivitis, and vertigo. Symptoms include headache, tinnitus, hypertension, red eyes, dry mouth, hematemasis, epistaxis.

Severe Conditions of Heat

The final syndrome in this progression from mild to severe is called 'stirring of wind.' The three sub-syndromes may be expressed as follows: 'utmost heat may produce wind'; 'deficiency of yin and hyperactivity of yang, which may turn to fire and produce wind'; and 'deficiency of the blood of the Liver may produce wind.' When the 'utmost heat produces wind,' the principal symptoms are delirium, with high fever, tic, upward-staring of the eyes, opisthotonos (a spasm of the entire spine), mental confusion, red tongue with yellow coating, and a String Taut and Rapid pulse. The sub-syndrome, deficiency of yin and hyperactivity of yang turns into fire and produces wind,' results in stroke with sudden syncope, deviated mouth and eyes, hemiplegia (paralysis of one side of the body), red tongue, and a String Taut and Thready pulse. Insufficiency of Liver blood and deficiency of blood producing wind leads to epilepsy, with numbness of the extremities, shaking head, tremor, spasm of the extremities, convulsion of the extremities, pale tongue, and a String Taut and Thready pulse.

Wind produced by the 'utmost heat' may be seen in febrile diseases. As the pathogenic heat factor becomes excessive, the Liver channel may be injured. Since the tendons and vessels are short of nourishment, tic and opisthotonos may occur. Insufficiency of the yin of the Liver may cause hyperactivity of the Liver yang, which turns into fire and ascends to the top or invades the channels and collaterals, causing mental confusion and hemiplegia. With deficiency of the blood of the Liver, the tendons can no longer be nourished; and with the stirring of Liver wind comes numbness of the extremities, tremor, and convulsions. Stirring of Liver wind can lead to many other less severe syndromes, including migrating joint pain and facial paralysis.

We have been discussing the effect of emotion on the Liver organ system and the consequences of that effect when the coping mechanism is confined to that system. (Other causes following the same pathways may be excessive use of heat-producing, water-depleting substances such as alcohol, nicotine, and other drugs.) Let us explore some ways in which homeostatic energy mechanisms can assist the Liver in the context of the Five Phase system as well as some undesirable consequences of these interactions.

The Homeostatic Process

We have outlined the orderly sequence of reinforcement and control within the Five Phase system. After the Liver, help would be expected from its yang partner, the Fu (hollow organ), the Gallbladder. Assistance could then come from the mother, the Kidneys; from the son, the Heart; from the Lungs, which control the Liver; and from the Earth, which the Liver controls.

Whereas this is the ideal sequence of events, many factors influence the course of the homeostatic process. For the moment, assuming that all else is equal, we will proceed with the ideal.

The Gallbladder: Fu (Hollow Organ) Partner

A brief glance at the symptomatology we have just reviewed reveals that the Fu organ partner, the Gallbladder, obviously plays a significant part in the early stages of the homeostatic process. Stagnation in the Liver will, of course, reduce the production and flow of bile to the Gallbladder, whose function is primarily to store and discharge bile. A reduction in the flow to the Gallbladder will require it to discharge more frequently, unless eating habits change; and I believe that anorexia, in some situations, is a restorative maneuver by the body intelligence to spare the overworking system. This intelligence will function more effectively in those for whom it has not been destroyed by chronic, excessive medications or a harmful environment.

The Fu (hollow) organs in general operate primarily to relieve the parent Zang (solid) organs of the toxic energies and wastes, which accumulate more quickly when these organs are forced to overwork for any reason. For example, if there is excess heat in the Heart, it can be discharged through the Small Intestine, which is its partner, and, in the extreme, may appear as hematuria. A similar relationship may occur with the Lungs and the Large Intestine. Naturally, the outcome also depends on the integrity of the Fu organ.

In addition to serving a beleaguered Liver as an outlet for accumulated toxicity, the Gallbladder, in my experience, plays the largest part in the disease process when decision making is an important part of the picture. According to the energy cycle of the Chinese clock, the Gallbladder is at its energic height from the hours of 11 P.M. to 1 A.M., preceding the ascendancy of the Liver from the hours of 1 A.M. to 3 A.M.. The ego function of the Gallbladder is decision making and that of the Liver is planning. Common sense and logic dictate that intelligent planning is predicated on thoughtful decisions. Thus the Gallbladder, the decision maker, reaches its energy peak just before the Liver, which is the planner; they are a complementary pair of the same phase, Wood.

If the emotional situation which is adversely affecting the Liver involves decisions about which there is significant ambivalence, the Gallbladder will, in consequence, be burdened. If the Gallbladder is strong and can lend its energy to resolving the dilemma, the Liver will be concomitantly relieved. Many functions will improve, including planning, which will become more reliable.

Should the Liver and the Gallbladder require other homeostatic apparatus to cope with the effects of prolonged emotional stress, all or any one of the other phases could be of assistance.

With the exception of the Spleen, all organ systems that begin in a relative state of health will produce heat from excess in the early stages of distress as they attempt to overcome stagnation. The intermediate and late stages of distress develop what we have described as heat from deficiency. The yin fluid of that organ system will be required to balance that heat, to put out the fire, so to speak. As the yin of an organ system is depleted, it will require reinforcements, which are supplied by the Water phase, the Kidney organ system. This system performs this function continuously for all organ systems, and especially for the Wood, because Wood requires Water for growth. Thus, the Water creates, or nourishes, its son, and, in this fashion, assists the Liver organ system in coping when it is burdened. It too, as we have seen, may eventually be depleted, leading to the symptoms described as the syndrome hyperactivity of Liver yang.

WATER: MOTHER OF THE WOOD PHASE

Kidney yang energies may also assist the Liver organ system. The Kidney yang is the source of will-power for the entire organism. In those circumstances where the Liver is under stress due to the repression of anger or other feelings, Kidney yang may contribute its energies by reinforcing the will to express those feelings and to overcome the fear which has caused the repression. Should the conflict between fear of expression and the will to assert oneself become chronic, the Kidney yang will suffer, leading to syndromes involving deficiency of Kidney yang.

The Kidney organ system in its traditional role has a psychological vulnerability to fear (and, some authorities believe, to grief, with a groaning sound). The repression of feeling, leading to stagnation of qi, is often founded on fear; this implies, consistent with the reversibility of our formula equating mind and body, that the Kidneys are imbalanced to begin with. Kidney yin (fear, actually awe) predominates over Kidney yang (the 'will' to overcome fear), engendering, in our hypothetical person, a base-line fear which would, of course, most immediately affect its 'son' in the Five Phase system. If the Kidney yang was initially weak, the person who represses assertion and/or anger, a Liver activity, may have been unable to assert that anger or other feeling, thought, or action, due to a lack of will-power.

On the other hand, any depletion of Kidney yin will lead to a concomitant rise in Kidney yang. Thus fear may be compensated for by a show of will, which itself may be ultimately exhausted, leading to one form of depression. Likewise, a loss of Kidney yin, which leads to a decrease in Liver yin and a simultaneous increase in Liver yang, may end in more explosive anger, with which we are all too familiar, as a way of dealing with fear.

Our exploration of the Liver organ system inundated by tension and anger beyond its ability to cope has taken us first to the mother in the Five Phase system, the Kidneys, where we see some of the interchange between assertion, anger, fear, and will-power.

FIRE: SON OF THE WOOD PHASE

Next in line is the Fire phase, son of the Wood in the Five Phase cycle, and its most important organ system, the Heart. If this organ system is strong, it can drain the excess anger or other pent-up emotion from the Liver organ system with which the latter cannot cope (the Fire will burn the Wood). As long as its energy holds up, it can transmute this stifled feeling into activity and excitement, usually of the communicative variety (the Heart controls the tongue). The person will talk away the anger and/or simultaneously appear overly cheerful, perhaps slightly agitated, or hypomanic. Denial, a restorative mechanism of the Pericardium, is fully operative here; and conversion hysteria symptoms are possible, depending on other factors. (Conversion hysteria is a reaction in which an underlying psychic conflict is transformed into a sensory or motor symptom such as functional anesthesia, deafness, blindness, or paralysis. Denial is the first step in this direction.)

Should the Fire phase's energy begin to fail or the restrained feelings become overwhelming and Liver heat rise, first anxiety and then a full-scale agitated manic state (scattering of the spirit) may occur, bringing in its wake a state of exhaustion and depression. Palpitations, tachycardia, and chest pain are some of the familiar accompanying physical symptoms.

Even if the Heart organ system is not called upon to be a major participant in absorbing the inhibited emotion, it may still be affected. At the stage of stagnation of the qi, the Liver energies (Wood) are blocked and are not feeding the Fire (Heart and Pericardium). This will lead to a functional deficiency of the Heart and to a dampening of joy, which we will call sadness. Certainly we have observed sadness, and especially depression, in connection with repressed anger; the latter is classically associated with depression in psychiatric and psychoanalytic writings.

Depending on which aspect of the Fire phase is vulnerable — the Heart, Pericardium, Triple Burner, or Small Intestine — one can get a variety of emotional and physical disturbances, either as an outlet for the overflow of muted emotion or as a consequence of Liver organ system disharmony. For example, at the stage of hyperactive Liver yang, the Kidney yin is diminished and is not available to balance Heart fire (yang). This is one of the critical balances of energies in human beings. An imbalance will lead to insomnia, irritability, problems with the absorption of ideas, and confusion when the Small Intestine energies are affected. A reduced flow and imbalance of ideas, as well as social withdrawal, will occur when it affects the Triple Burner energies. Should this 'fire' combine with phlegm from Spleen dysfunction and go to the Heart, one form of schizophrenia is possible, as well as a form of epilepsy. These subjects will receive greater attention in Chapter 14.

METAL: CONTROLLER OF THE WOOD PHASE

The controlling phase of the Wood phase is Metal. If this phase is strong, it may attempt to control the stifled feelings that the Liver cannot manage within its own system. In my experience it accomplishes this through obsessive-compulsive characterological mechanisms and stagnation of the lower bowel, creating such problems as constipation, diverticulosis, and hemorrhoids. If, on the other hand, it is weak, separation anxiety, phobias of places, respiratory (asthma) problems, and/or deficiency-type lower bowel symptoms (colitis) may develop.

Imbalances may occur in the Metal phase even if the problem with repressed assertion is contained within the Liver organ system. Among the early symptoms of stagnation of Liver qi is hypochondriac (beneath rib) pain referred to the chest, especially upon reclining, when the 'noxious qi' rises to attack the chest area. In addition to pain, there will be breathing difficulty, stiffness of the chest, sighing, and the sensation of a foreign body in the throat. In the syndrome flaring-up of Liver fire, hemoptysis and epistaxis are possible.

EARTH: CONTROLLED BY THE WOOD PHASE

Finally, we come to the controlled phase, the Earth. Here we are primarily concerned with the gastro-intestinal system, vascular integrity, anti-gravity support for the Zang-Fu (solid and hollow) organs, and cognition, controlled by the Spleen organ system. Some of the curbed emotion uncontainable within the Liver organ system can be absorbed by the Spleen as excessive worry and rumination, which, over a period of time, will slow the digestion and lead to gastro-intestinal discomfort. If the Earth phase energy is less substantial, excessive 'sweetness' may be the 'reaction formation.'

Earth may ultimately be overwhelmed by the quelled emotion. Subsequent decompensation (disorganization of the personality under stress) can produce an obsessive-compulsive neurosis, which can further decompensate into schizophreniform states with serious thinking disorders. Liver qi helps the Spleen qi move up and the Stomach qi move down. The physical manifestations could be any range of gastro-intestinal problems related to the various Spleen-Stomach syndromes, including symptoms specifically related to the stagnation of Liver qi in the form of anorexia, belching, sour regurgitation, subcostal pain, and hiccoughs. In the syndrome flaring-up of Liver fire, even hematemasis is possible.

Since the Spleen, whose energy rises, is responsible for the maintenance of the internal organs in their normal positions, gastroptosis may be a consequence of severe weakness. A more serious consequence is the breakdown in its ability to 'control the blood,' which might lead to hemorrhage of the portal vein, in the event of significant Liver pathology, and to portal hypertension.

In summary, the involved organ, the Liver, will try to contain or express energy until it fails and faces damage (qi stagnation → irritability). The Fu partner (Gallbladder) will draw off excesses until overburdened and then show heat signs (cholelithiasis → poor judgment); the 'son' (Heart) will do the same and face overloading (manic-depressive illness). The mother (Kidneys) will try to feed and nourish the involved organ to help it cope and will become exhausted (yin deficiency → fear, and yang deficiency → loss of will). The controlling organ (Lungs) will tend to exaggerate its natural tendencies and become fixed (rigidity), and the controlled organ (Spleen) will attempt to protect itself by overreacting (sweetness). Generally, in deficiency the 'mother' is most important, and in excess the 'controlling' phase may play a larger role.

Thus far we have explored the implications for psychosomatic medicine of diagnosis at the health end of the spectrum; the unifying influence of energy concepts in terms of body-soul-mind continuity; and the correspondences between body and mind (using the Liver as an example within the framework of the Five Phase system, and including interrelationships between the Liver organ system and other organ systems).

EMOTIONS AND THE ORGAN SYSTEMS

Let us examine more casually the physiological mechanisms by which emotion impinges on the other systems, as described by Chinese medicine and amended by experience. These are subjects to which we will be returning again and again in the course of this book.

Thinking Affects the Spleen

This refers to constant and endless rumination, especially during meal time. The thoughts may vary in form and content from preoccupation (with ideas and work) to worry. The result is nearly the same. There are several factors involved in the relationship between thinking and digestion. One involves activity: the subtle movements associated with mental alertness and awareness that are prerequisite to fluent circulation and that in rumination are quiescent. Often the eyes of a ruminative person are focused on the ceiling, as if the answer were written there, and usually he or she is seated and lost in reverie. The proclivity to a depression in circulation is compounded by this sedentary position, which cuts off circulation in the middle burner, just when digestion requires vigorous circulation in order to function normally.

A second factor is the relationship between the enjoyment of a meal and the excellence of the circulation in the gastrointestinal tract. Chinese tradition, in which eating is a highly-regarded art, states that if one is preoccupied with thoughts one is not likely to be enjoying one's meal or the benefits of good circulation. The diminishment in the latter must, over a period of time, cause gastrointestinal dysfunction, slowing of the digestion. Translated into Western terms, we might see the same event as competition between the brain and the gastrointestinal system for circulation, the latter losing to the former during meal time, with the result described above.

Since the Spleen qi rises, it carries energy (glucose) to the brain. Some aspects of consciousness, such as complaints of cloudy thinking, poor memory, and difficulty with concentration and attention, are related to Spleen qi deficiency. Cognition, as it relates to the excesses and deficiencies of the yin and yang of each organ system, will be examined in turn and will be explored more fully in Chapters 8 through 12. Briefly, conscious thought is controlled by Heart energies, unconscious thoughts by Kidney and Liver, and the boundaries between the two, balanced thinking, by the Spleen-Stomach, Large Intestine, Small Intestine, and Triple Burner energies. These are my own observations.

Joy Affects the Heart

According to Chinese medicine, the Heart organ system corresponds to the emotion joy. Joy is a positive emotion which will be explored more completely in the section on the Fire phase. English translations of textbooks and documents of Chinese medicine are remarkably obscure on the subject of the emotional distress caused by joy. My own work with experienced clinical practitioners reveals one generally accepted aspect of this distress to be conceptually synonymous with the experience of 'shock.' Whereas the

Liver is the organ system most often affected by chronic emotional distress, the Heart is the organ system most vulnerable to sudden emotions of any kind, both positive (joy) and negative (fear). Sudden, powerful emotional experiences have a potent impact on the nervous system, especially the autonomic nervous system. The most immediate autonomic nervous system response to sudden overwhelming excitement (danger, as our organism experiences it) is a massive increase in circulation, placing upon the heart an enormous, often cataclysmic, demand for pumping action, which may overwhelm its own blood supply if that supply is already compromised or the emotional experience is too powerful. We are all too familiar with the scenario of people dying of fright or even unexpected good news (winning the sweepstakes). The nervous system is equated with the Tai Yang, the Small Intestine and the Bladder. Rapid excitation, I believe, is mediated by way of the Small Intestine to the Heart from outside (Fu organ) to inside (Zang organ). (See Chapter 14 for elaboration.)

In my opinion, each of the acute emotions has a different effect upon the Heart. Sudden sadness will cause stagnation, a dampening of the circulation of blood and energy. Joy and anger will cause a sudden filling of the Heart (trapped qi), when these emotions are not revealed when experienced. The Heart, therefore, will hold the qi and blood and become 'full'. Most serious is fright, which will cause an emptying of the Heart in its attempt to maintain the circulation, resulting in a state of shock and an inability of the body to get blood into and through the Heart. Apparently this drains Heart yin. According to Chinese medicine, once a state of shock has occurred (especially if the person is very young or very old), circulation is, to some extent, permanently altered until adequately treated. If the yin and blood supply to the nerves of the Heart is permanently reduced, it will result in some degree of nervous instability of the Heart throughout life, or until some form of therapy intervenes.

According to Dr. Shen, if the condition of the Heart is constitutionally sound, the residue of the shock will be only a fast pulse. If the Heart is weak, variations will occur in the rate. These conditions are known in mild form as 'Heart nervous' and in more severe form as 'Heart weak,' which is reflected on the pulse as a large Change in Rate on Movement. In 'Heart nervous,' the pulse may be a little Rapid. In 'Heart weak,' it may be a little Slow because the circulation is more affected.

Persistent stagnation over time can generate the condition known as 'Heart closed' in the less severe form, or 'Heart small' in the more severe condition. The fullness of the Heart can lead to various degrees of heart enlargement over a period of time, and 'Heart small' to coronary insufficiency.

(See Chapter 14 for a fuller discussion of Heart disorders.)

Dr. Shen also states that the Heart is most likely to be affected in acute situations if the person is active at the time of shock. This is true for sudden anger. If the shock occurs during eating, the Liver and Stomach pulse may become stagnant, with a Flat wave and a little Tightness; the pulse rate will be a little Rapid. If it occurs while urinating, the Bladder will be affected. This occurs mostly in children, especially when they are yelled at or whisked off to a "potty" while being toilet trained. Dr. Shen says that if the shock occurs at rest, the Liver will bear the consequences of stagnation. The Heart is also, of course, affected by chronic emotional stress, as we saw in our discussion of the Liver. In fact, since the Heart controls the mind, ultimately all mental distress, which involves problems with consciousness, must be mediated through the Heart.

FEAR AND SADNESS AFFECT THE KIDNEYS

There are two schools of thought about emotion and the Kidneys. One describes chronic fear as the emotion that damages the Kidneys; the other considers a very profound sadness as the emotion which impairs Kidney function. Let us examine each in its turn, since it is most likely that both are true.

Fear, the Chinese say, is an emotion which "descends." Sudden fear, we saw, affected the Heart. Deep-seated fear that develops gradually and remains for a long time has a different effect on the nervous system. My own experience shows that sudden fright affects the Small Intestine part of that system and goes to the Heart. Chronic fear moves from superficial to deep, affecting first the Bladder part of the Tai Yang and then going to the Kidneys, the organ with which the Bladder is most closely related within the Five Phase system, as well as a complementary organ in the Water phase. It will travel through the Lo and Divergent channels as well as the deep pathway of the main channels of both organs. (Apparently these latter pathways are not well known even to acupuncturists and are mentioned here only for completeness. They are discussed at some length in Felix Mann's book, *The Channels of Acupuncture,* for those who wish to explore the subject further.)

Considered in terms of Western physiology, a sudden shock would require a rapid response by both the nervous system and the circulatory system. On the other hand, chronic emotional stress would call more upon the slower adaptational mechanisms associated with the endocrine system, especially the adrenals, according to a theory advanced by Hans Selye in his *General Adaptational Syndrome.* The adrenal glands are of course in close proximity to the Kidneys and, in my opinion, should be included in the broad purview of the Kidney organ sphere of influence. In fact, adrenal medullary gland functions and those of Kidney yang, the Ming Men, or Kidney fire are quite similar; each in its way is ascribed the task of providing the rest of the organism with the drive and push necessary for each of the other systems to fulfill their special energy function. The adrenal cortex resembles in some ways the actions of Kidney yin, as anti-inflammatory and water regulating. Likewise, the Kidney yin is associated with pituitary, and Kidney yang with thyroid, function.

According to Dr. Shen, long-standing, deep-seated sadness or anguish is the other emotion that affects the Kidneys. This sadness is expressed only by little sounds or groans, with no tears. Most charts of the correspondences in the Five Phase system associate groaning with the Kidneys. Since this sadness is so deep, tears are repressed, the entire water control mechanism is suppressed, and the Kidney yin which supplies that system is depleted, causing both the Kidney and then other organ systems to become dry. Dryness will turn eventually into fire, and the latter will make the nervous system tight. Without too great a stretch of the imagination, one could see electrolyte balance impaired and the neuro-humoral system depleted by such a sequence of events.

Chronic fear will damage the Kidney yang, and chronic deep-seated anguish will damage the Kidney yin. Ultimately, both yin and yang will be depleted.

GRIEF AFFECTS THE LUNGS

Chronic, unexpressed grief depresses the circulation of qi and blood in the upper burner, especially the Lungs. The posture of the sad person is common knowledge: head down, eyes focused on the ground, the back bent forward, and chest depressed: this bearing gradually 'kills' the circulation of qi in the chest. Since the Lungs make the qi, which is the driving force of the energy and the blood circulation throughout the body, it has to work harder and is slowly weakened. The Lung pulse at first has a Flat wave, indicating stagnation. Later, the Lung pulse will be Deep and Hidden; the special Lung pulse a little Full; the pulses a little Rapid; and the chest uncomfortable. One almost always finds stagnation and then weakness on the Heart pulse as well, for reasons explained in the section on the Triple Burner. The Lungs and Heart share the upper burner.

Sudden, profound grief, like any sudden emotion, will affect the weakest part of the body — weak either constitutionally or from abuse. Suddenness also always impinges on the Heart, whether it is weak or strong. Generally, the effect will be stagnation. I have observed this effect on the Liver pulse several times in people who had used drugs when they were young and then had a sudden, great disappointment. The clinical result was hepatitis on two occasions and mononucleosis on several others.

A seemingly unrelated complication of Lung weakness from chronic unexpressed grief may show up as a form of epilepsy. The Lungs, in Chinese medicine, are actually a part of the digestive system; they digest the excess mucus produced by the Stomach and Small Intestine, especially when the Spleen is weak or when the person has poor eating habits. If the Lungs are weak and cannot digest the mucus, it may go to the Heart, which controls the mind, or to the Pericardium. If other unfavorable conditions (described later) exist simultaneously with the excess mucus, an epileptic condition or dysphagia in stroke may be precipitated.

Anger Affects the Liver

We have already studied in depth the pathways by which chronic anger affects the Liver organ system. Sudden anger has the effect of speeding up the circulation of blood. The increased speed creates a rapid heating effect on the blood stored in the Liver. It expands faster than it can circulate and so becomes blocked in the Liver, leading to the condition on the pulse known as Liver Full.

There is a variety of other emotional states that are not ordinarily considered separately by Chinese medicine within the framework of the Five Phase system. One of these is worry, another is guilt, and still another is the 'spaced-out' condition which we see so often in young people.

Worry and Guilty Fear Affect the Heart Pulse

Dr. Shen contends that worry is detectable on the pulse by Intermittent Superficial Vibration on the Heart pulse, which will also be Tight. The entire pulse will be a little Rapid, and there may be Changes in Rate. The tongue will be red at the end. If the condition is mild, the Change in Rate will come about only with movement. The greater the rate of change, the more serious the problem, especially when a great Change of Rate occurs while a person is at rest. One can have these changes without the Vibration, which would indicate only instability and fear. The Vibration on the Heart pulse is the indicator of worry.

Guilty fear is indicated when the entire pulse has a superficial Vibration, especially the Liver and the Heart. Generally the individual has done something serious and is afraid of being discovered. One must be careful to distinguish these conditions from those in which the Vibration occurs deeply and consistently at one position on the pulse. This means that the organ in question is in great danger. For example, if this were found on the Stomach position of the pulse, then imminent, severe ulceration could be expected; or if on the Heart pulse, possibly a heart attack. The Heart pulse Vibration that we mentioned as being due to worry is more superficial and coarse. The Vibration associated with an organ that is about to collapse is Deep, very Fine, and Rapid.

A crucial tenet of this medicine is the reversibility of etiology. Disaffections of energy, qi, blood, fluid, or any of the organs can create emotional disorders. Therefore Liver disharmony can engender anger; the Heart or Pericardium invites disharmony, excessive apprehension (anxiety), or excessive joy (mania); Spleen disharmony can affect thinking; Lung dysfunction creates sadness or anxiety; and Kidney weakness elicits fear. The reversibility of these correspondences renders Chinese medicine a precise, dynamic, psychosomatic, somatopsychic medical system that is especially well suited to the modern health sciences. In the ways described here, Chinese medicine is a comprehensive mind/body science and, in this and many other senses, fully holistic.

CHART 2

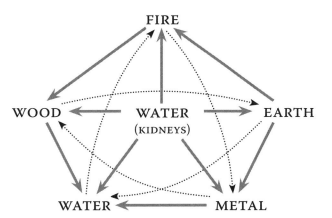

BEFORE BIRTH — Early Heaven of the *I Ching*

CHART 3

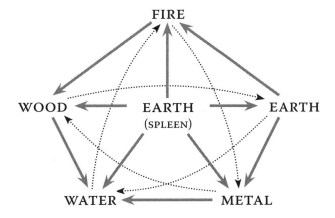

AFTER BIRTH — Later Heaven of the *I Ching*

——— *Chen (generation) cycle*

·············· *Ko (control) cycle*

6

A Revision of The Traditional Concepts of Emotion in the Context of the Five Phase System

I should like to present a way of looking at emotions that is more compatible with my life experience as a psychiatrist than is the conventional concepts of emotions within the Five Phase (element) system described in Chapters 4 and 5. In formulating this point of view, I have been inspired by the work of Lawson-Wood. Stated as briefly as possible, the convictions arising from my experience may be summarized as follows:

1. Except for joy, all the emotions described in the preceding chapters have negative implications.
2. Negative emotions are always a secondary expression of some failure in the realization of a primary positive emotional force or need.
3. Thirty-five years of intensive work with people has convinced me that the basic issue in life is *contact*. People will make contact in any way available that will keep them *intact*.
4. Except in instances of 'possession' (control by external forces), human beings strive to contact others within a context of positive emotion.
5. Human experience may not always allow the positive emotions to flourish; in many circumstances, negative or hostile contact may be all that is possible and, paradoxically, may be life-sustaining. If life requires this as an enduring condition, negativity becomes a way of life.
6. Negativity is maladaptive and it ultimately fails. Negativity is annoying, and our understandable response is to destroy or contain it.

This is a natural reaction but is rarely therapeutic, except under very special circumstances (in a context of proven love). The therapeutic community, since the dawn of our era, has experienced this negativity as 'resistance' and has reacted to it with professionally rationalized and distilled hostility, known in the literature as 'analyzing the resistance,' 'shock treatment,' or 'chemical restraints.'

7. As health practitioners we are of value to the people who consult us only if we can offer them something significantly different from the usual response. Of course, we recognize and acknowledge the negative in all its destructiveness. However:

8. We are needed for our ability to recognize the positive quest for contact beneath the negative emotions and behavior; this need is especially great for those who have already come to disdain themselves.

9. This is the beginning of a 'new experience' with someone who is reliably more concerned with finding, and responding to, the positive rather than the negative in them; with someone nourishing rather than condemning; with someone capable of putting, at least temporarily, another person's needs ahead of his or her own.

10. Only as we allow a 'new experience' and provide a new model can our contact with our patients be a truly healing, growing, therapeutic experience.[1]

Given these convictions and my understanding of the theory of the Five Phases as an affirmation of the positive thrust of nature towards life and renewal (and one which interprets even death positively as an immutable part of life), I could not be reconciled to the negative role assigned to the emotions in Chinese medical literature. It was with relief and great satisfaction that I discovered Lawson-Wood's *Five Elements of Acupuncture*. He states: "The Primary Emotions are those given in Ilsa Veith's translation of the *Nei Ching*. With all due respect to the scholarly work of Ilsa Veith, I am not satisfied that these words cover what is traditionally meant. The Chinese written language uses a symbol to convey an idea practically impossible to translate by one word only." [2] Lawson-Woods goes on to expand his point with each of the Five Emotions: anger, for example, "tends in the West to have derogatory implications. Traditionally, Anger is the emotion of the Soul or Spiritual faculties in self-urge or birth and growth of the Ego. This represents the healthy urge to become something, to live, to expand, combating restrictive environment as much as a plant pushes itself upwards through the soil towards light..."[3]

The Five Phase system is the life cycle of the creation and control of 'being.' I mean by 'being' the essential qualities of the individual, evolved, through the process of individuation and differentiation, from our common racial unconscious and spiritual heritage. From conception through death, the Five Phase system embodies and expresses the growth and development of potential 'being'; experience, throughout the significant stages of life, may enhance or destroy this development. The life stages are paralleled in their complexity by each of the phases in progression.

If the Chen and Ko cycles are the cycles of life and human development, and if we regard life as inherently positive, we are obligated to describe the natural functions of that cycle in exclusively positive terms. The negative emotions which are customarily associated with these phases are artifacts of a distortion of that process, not the process itself. They will occur only as that life cycle is disrupted. That disruptive experience will alter the balance, circulation, and supply of energy. Order is indispensable to life. Disorder, as we shall see, is necessary to and compatible with life only for short periods of the growth cycle, accompanying major reorganizations of the self. The organism whose life cycle is threatened by prolonged disorder must, above all, restore order to its system with the homeostatic means available to it. Depending on the maturity of the organism and the strength and chronicity of the threat, the restorative mechanisms brought to bear will prove to be adaptive or maladaptive. The 'seven dragons' or 'demons,' the 'seven emotions,' are such restorative measures. While they may be linked through the law of correspondences to the Five Phases, they must be understood primarily as an expression of disharmony in the cycle, not as its essence.

In synchrony with Lawson-Wood's assertion that the 'seven demons' (he lists five) are a distorted and negative interpretation of the psychology of the Five Phase system, it is my intention to re-examine this system as an expression of the entire range of the human development of 'being.' I will explore the positive natural functions of each phase and their unique contribution to 'becoming.' I shall then study and catalogue in detail the complex restorative maneuvers, both physical and emotional, that we call disharmony and that are engendered by the inhibition of the appropriate, controlled evolution of human 'being.'

I wish to state at the beginning that restoration, though a drain on the energies necessary for growth and development, is itself a natural function. We will examine disharmony for diagnostic purposes, always keeping in mind that restoration is in fact a person's creative effort to cope with adversity, from which, over time, emerge the finest, as well as the worst, aspects of character.

NOURISHING ENERGY

In the West, some body therapies associated with psychology are committed to the concept of energy. The concept of energy, as well as the related technique, however, is often limited to the surface, to the muscles and fascia. Modern psychological therapies, both verbal and nonverbal, tend to emphasize breaking through this surface, through the 'defenses' (or 'dynamisms of difficulty') and the resistance that they represent. In part, this emphasis is due to an incomplete knowledge of overall body energy and in part it is due to Western psychology's preoccupation with resistance, which has spilled over into its somatic therapies. Perhaps this preoccupation arises in part from a fear in Western cultures of acknowledging the need for nourishment, a need which adults associate with weakness, with the infantile helplessness we seem to abhor in ourselves and in others. In some respects, the expression of this need, and especially meeting it, is regarded as subversive to our values, sinful, and reprehensible.

Even in bioenergetics, one of our most energy-conscious therapies, the focus, except for the occasional hug at the end of a session, is on getting the patient to breathe for himself in order to provide his own nourishment. This statement assumes that air is a complete or adequate source of energy for human life. It further assumes that a person may find his psychological way to significantly alter a lifetime of stagnation, imbalance, disharmony, and disintegration by simply improving breathing and grounding and by relaxing muscular blocks.

However valuable such therapies have been they have led us in the West to ignore the importance of other nourishing energies necessary to psychological as well as to physiological well-being. (Obvious exceptions occur indirectly in the alternative medical practices that emphasize nutrition.) Western psychology too often assumes that if it can reduce defensiveness, nourishment will take care of itself. This has not been borne out in the almost one-hundred years since Freud and Breuer ushered in the modern psychological era with the idea that, if you break the resistance and undo repression, growth will occur automatically.[4] In my opinion, the relative inefficiency of psychotherapy is due in large part to its inability and unwillingness to deal adequately with the nurturing aspects of growth and development. The life-giving succor to which I refer is not only reassurance, warmth, friendship, or love — though each of these is often missing and should be restored. Rather, it is the basic ground material and energy that sustains all levels of existence. Nourishment is not readily available as a Western therapeutic modality.

It is, however, much needed. Whereas most healing occurs without outside intervention, the damage of 'wrong living' is sometimes too great and too prolonged. It is fundamentally wrong to deprive a patient of requisite nourishment on the premise that the need is a strategy on the part of the patient to resist therapy and to avoid helping him or herself. This ignores the requirement of the body and mind to be strengthened, or re-strengthened, after periods of living in ways that are destructive to 'self' and 'ego.' Except for fatigue, people are, after all, limited to only a few recognizable longings that register what is missing.

One requires strength to face life, especially to change oneself and the condition of one's existence. For any form of deficit, including inherited ones, Chinese medicine has much to offer. Systems that have been destroyed beyond the person's own ability to heal them can be assisted to regain sufficient energy to enable the person to correct 'wrong living' and sustain him or herself. The latter step is, of course, always the final and indispensable one. Nobody denies that assuming responsibility for oneself is the ultimate issue in growth and development. The physician must identify the energy leaks, and the patient must seal them by changing his lifestyle. It is, however, only one step and cannot be taken until the organism and person are strong enough. This strengthening is a collaborative process and must often begin with help from an outside source. Chinese medicine provides this outside source in many ways.

Chinese medicine is concerned with a balance between defensive energies known as *wei*, and nourishing energies known as *ying*. *Wei* refers to energy that flows near the surface of the body just under the skin and through muscle and connective tissue. This energy flows through the *jing luo* system of channels (meridians) which cover the entire body surface, and not just through the twelve major or eight 'extra' channels on which appear the acupuncture points. It has its own cycle, circulating, it is said, 25 times through the night and 25 times during the day. *Wei* energy is considered the protective energy of the body. In psychological terms I would consider it to be identical with the defensive energy of Reichian orgone energy.[5] (To his credit, Reich saw this energy as one with cosmic energy.)

Ying is the nourishing energy of the body which flows in the organs and with the blood and along the major channels of energy mentioned above. It is the fuel which sustains, supports, integrates, and renews all of the life functions of an organism, including the mind and the spirit. Oriental medicine has achieved a balance between these two energies, the protective and the nourishing. It is thoroughly capable of dealing with defense, resistance, and negative emotion. It is equally capable of the more important positive task of coping with the problems of nourishment for human change and development. It is said that "man helps and nature cures." Unfortunately, nature is unable to assume the burden entirely; man must help.

7

Introduction to the Natural Functions and Disharmony States of the Five Phase System

Developmental Stages in the 'Evolution of Being'

It is my intention to expand upon the traditional theory of the laws of the Five Phases as an expression of the 'evolution of being.' The developmental stages of human life chronicle a growing capacity for 'self' and 'self expression,' for introspection, and for interpersonal communication. Attachments to one's 'self' and contact with other beings occur at all levels, involving a wide range of touch and powerful channels of energy. Few people are aware of the substantial but invisible energy links that exist within themselves and others. Examined through the illuminating energy concepts of Chinese medicine, these connections tell us something of the contributions to human development made by the natural functions of the Five Phases.

'Contact' through these bonding avenues of the life force is the essential issue for human survival. People instinctively put their creative capacities in the service of preserving the integrity of these energy threads. This is true even when their tactics are detrimental to development of 'self' in a broader sense. We call these tactics disharmonious when they are maladaptive. I shall discuss and catalogue, in energy terms, these complex restorative maneuvers, both physical and emotional, which constitute a response to any inhibition of appropriate, controlled growth and development of 'being' from conception to death.

The conceptual system that I am about to explore views the Five Phases as developmental stages in the 'evolution of being.' In anticipation of the detailed statements to follow, I wish to outline briefly the natural functions and disharmonies of the energies of the five organ systems or spheres of influence:

1. *The Water phase* energies supervise the genetic and intrauterine developmental phases of evolution. A faltering of these energies is associated with both pervasive and subtle neurological disorders and a predisposition to the most severe psychological disturbances (schizophrenia).

   Water energies are the repository of all phylogony as well as ontology. These energies encompass the unconscious reservoir of innate and intuitive intelligence, intelligent will, and the life force which drives them to fruition. They are concerned with the identity of people individually and collectively, with the human race and with the transpersonal, with a balance between awe and wonder and the banal and prosaic, with the best and the worst. In the larger view, Water energies relate to divine love, power, and spirit and to all that we are potentially capable of as children of the universe.

2. *The Wood phase* is responsible for the primeval rebirth, the assertion and direction of being, the free and easy flight of the 'red bird.' The repression of any of these leads to passive-aggressive personality disturbances. Perplexing life problems hinging on the question of when to advance and when to retreat are Wood energy issues, the same ones so eloquently addressed by the *I Ching.*

3. *The Fire phase* generates and controls, protects and integrates, sorts and harmonizes energies for the joyful and loving expression of being. Deficiency or repression of these functions leads to problems of creativity, both of the right brain (yin) and left brain (yang), and to many of the interpersonal disasters that beset our race.

4. *The Earth phase* is responsible for bonding and boundaries, including the first bond with a mothering figure. This bond begins in utero in the latter part of pregnancy, continues through the early years of childhood and later expands, with the assistance of Metal energies, to include surrogate parents (teachers) and surrogate siblings (friends). Earth energies are more relevant to the quality and maturation of bonds rather than merely to their formation and expansion. Certain schizophrenic, schizoid, borderline, oral dependent, and narcissistic disabilities emanate from a failure of Earth energies during these developmental stages.

5. *The Metal phase's* jurisdiction is the expansion and transformation of this bond to significant others and to society at large. The tenuous or

consuming nature of the bond, both in its making and its keeping, depends on the excess or deficiency of these energies. Lung energies afford us our most immediate give and take with the environment and are especially important during preadolescence and adolescence, as well as during the initial incorporation of authority into ourselves.

{85}

6. Although there are only five phases, there is a sixth stage in the cycle of being. The Water phase, where this cycle begins, sets also the final scene on this planet. It is responsible for moving the bond beyond society to a oneness with all creation and the life force—in Western terms, a union with God. Here we find problems concerning power.

The maturation of all these energies in the growing person depends on their integrity in the parent and the quantity and quality of appropriate investment of power in the relationship. The opportunities for abuse are legion.

In short, concerning the evolution of the life force or the 'dragon rising': the power is Water, the direction is Wood, the bonding is Earth, the expression is Fire, and the expansion/transformation is Metal.

BONDS, RHYTHMS, IDENTITY, MIND, SPIRIT

The energy for letting go of the old bonds and taking in the new comes from the Metal phase. The force for holding and maturing the bond (loyalty, dependability, faithfulness, commitment) is from Earth, with Fire giving passion (union). The direction (assertion) is from Wood, and the power (will and courage), as ever, is from Water.

With regard to the *natural rhythms,* Water is generation, Wood is renewal and cleansing, Fire is rapid expansion and contraction, Earth is fruition, and Metal is slower expansion and contraction.

Concerning *identity,* Water is constitution, "I exist"; Earth, the boundaries of "I am"; Wood, the negative assertion, "no, I am not"; Fire the positive assertion or "yes, I am"; Metal, the incorporation of authority into "I am"; and finally Water again, "I am one with God or the life force."

As for the *mind,* Kidney yin is the substance, and Kidney yang the drive for its development. Heart yin brings that substance into awareness, and Heart yang gives form to the creative idea. The Pericardium gives it protection and appropriateness, the Small Intestine clarity, and Metal the refreshing and cleansing spirit for renewed inspiration. Wood gives it the direction, and the Spleen feeds it. Water delivers the *spirit,* the racial and individual unconscious, from generation to generation. Wood is the soul spirit which encounters the world during the day and grows through living, while at night it 'stores' the spirit which comes to us in dreams. Fire stores and distributes the spirit by day and brings it to awareness. The Earth nourishes the incarnate being that stores the spirit, and Metal renews and refines the spirit with meditation on and through the breath.

EARLY HEAVEN AND LATER HEAVEN

My concept of the Chen (generation) cycle of the Five Phase system is two-fold. One system predominates before birth, and the other system predominates after birth. (See Charts 2 and 3, page 75.)

The two schemes are in dynamic interplay with each other. Even after birth, the former scheme (Early Heaven), at appropriate times, will supersede the latter when, for example, the need for essence and divine love, will, and spirit (the natural functions of the Kidneys) are in special demand. Though not schematized here, the Ko (control) cycle continues to operate in both.

In either version, the cycle begins and ends with Water, the phase of winter. Water is the phase which transmits the life-energy from one generation to another, controlling the genetic apparatus. It ushers us into this realm of existence at conception, when the 'dragon rises' and the 'red bird flies.' It conveys us to another realm at death. Water energies channel us from the winter of inception to the winter of completion (which we call death), when the red bird self-immolates and the dragon rests.

This life energy or spirit is conveyed from lifetime to lifetime by Water energies. During life, the spirit is housed by the Heart, transformed by Fire into the 'spirit-mind,' and made manifest by Fire's 'reason' into language, the Word or Logos. During this life the spirit-mind exchanges energies with other spirit-minds through the medium of the Fire energies, the 'spirit-mind.' The Wood (spirit-soul) feeds the Heart (spirit-mind) so that by the time we pass on, our Water energies are rendering a developed spirit to eternity. This, in fact, is the only justification I can make for the very act of our suffering existence on this magnificent planet.

PHASE WITHIN A PHASE

All the phase (or elemental) energies are operational at all times, either on their own, or as a 'phase within a phase.' One or more play a crucial role in any particular stage in the evolution of being. According to J.R. Worsley (founder and director of the Traditional Acupuncture Institute in England), each phase contains energy from each of the others as a necessary part of its own evolution. It is the 'phase within the phase,' the Wood within the Earth, which individuates the Earth at every step of its transition. At the same time, the Wood could do nothing without the nourishment it is receiving from its seemingly opposing force in the Ko (control) cycle.

In light of a 'phase within a phase,' let us examine the disharmony of anger. According to Worsley's school of Traditional Acupuncture, if the anger is a cold one in which the person gives the 'cold shoulder,' this is 'Metal in the Wood.' If the anger is fiery, it is 'Fire in the Wood'; and if the anger dissolves into tears, it is 'Earth in the Wood.' If the anger sputters and shakes with fear, then there is too much 'Water in the Wood.' Shouting is simply 'Wood within the Wood.'[1]

Keeping in mind that the natural function of the Wood energies is to 'assert,' we observe that the impetus and direction of assertion is 'Wood in the Wood,' the power to assert is 'Water in the Wood,' its nourishment is 'Earth in the Wood,' the risk or 'Heart' to assert is the 'Fire in the Wood,' and the precision and expansiveness of assertion is 'Metal in the Wood.'

This concept is most useful in understanding the energy aspects of evolution. Each of the phases dominates a major aspect of the evolution of personality, yet, from conception onward, all of the energies are operational at all times, to different degrees, inside each other. In any particular developmental stage, one is dominant and one or two others may be significant.

AN AMENDED SYSTEM OF CORRESPONDENCES

As human beings, we function as a unit but we try to think and communicate in an analytic (Cartesian) sequence in which global knowledge is broken down into small, manageable pieces of information. We 'are' as 'one,' but we think in fragments, which in turn we are forever trying to link together and inflate into an orderly 'concept.' We seem innately limited to formulating concepts that we must forever strive to convert again to reality. However artificial the distinctions we make between 'spheres of influence,' they are nevertheless real and necessary. They are indispensable to discussion and invaluable for therapeutic intervention. They are not, however, meant to be used rigidly.

That having been said, I shall proceed to describe initially the *natural functions* of each phase as a whole. The separate aspects of these natural functions, which we allude to as yin and yang, will then be elucidated. The natural functions of the organ energy systems can be examined on at least three levels. They are the old, familiar, and by now almost worn out concepts of body, mind, and spirit. The natural functions which we are about to explore go far beyond those found in the modern texts, where excellent descriptions of the physiology and pathology of the Zang-Fu (solid and hollow organs) are set forth. They differ from those in the Worsley school by my emphasis on development, though some overlap is hopefully inevitable if both views have some validity.

The distortions of the natural functions of each energy system that result in the disorders of character and behavior to be described are the direct result of a constitutional deficiency or excess or a significant inhibition or repression of those natural functions and their underlying energies. At the level of energy, we are dealing with its emptiness or stagnation.

Stagnation itself may be the result of a blockage of energy or of weakness. The blockage may occur suddenly or gradually over a long period of time. Weakness can be constitutional or the result of prolonged stagnation. Except where indicated, the principal etiology with which we are dealing involves a melding of constitutional configurations with enduring patterns of inhibition of natural functions. The result is the relative absence or distortion of those experiences necessary to the development of a complete human being.

Until a state of exhaustion is reached, the stagnant energy is capable of being tapped by either acupuncture or psychotherapy or by both, to be developed and realized through new experience. When a state of exhaustion is finally reached, due to the constant attempts on the part of nature to restore itself, we then find levels of imbalance which are threatening to mind and to life.

The restorative distortions of each of these natural functions by the vicissitudes of life, in the process of 'becoming,'[2] will be discussed in terms of personality and behavior, anxiety and depression, cognition and psychosis, love and sex, and bioenergetics. Mental and emotional disorders will be discussed in detail, based on my personal experience and extrapolations. Specific phenomena of emotional disharmony that I have not studied in detail, primarily dream material, will be stated according to classical material from available sources. I shall pass on the traditional material on dreams in Chinese medicine as I understand it. Bioenergetic considerations are based largely on the work of Alexander Lowen and John Pierrakos.[3]

The result will be an amended system of correspondences between organ system and personality. This, I hope, will broaden and enrich the scope of the human psyche within the Chinese medical framework, augment the other well-documented and long-used criteria for diagnosis and treatment of mental and emotional disorders within the Chinese medical system, and broaden the interface between Chinese medicine and Western psychology.

PERSONALITY ATTRIBUTES

It is extremely important to realize at the outset of this discussion that, for better or worse, the natural functions which characterize each of the organ system energies, as well as their distortions in the form of characterological disorders, are qualities found in all human beings without exception. Each of us is capable of the best and the worst. Whereas we are "more alike than otherwise,"[4] we are nevertheless concerned here with certain unique qualities of being that consistently distinguish us from others and thus serve as clues to deficiencies or excesses of the major energy systems.

Many of the qualities of personality defined here may be influenced in their unfolding by factors other than those associated with a given phase system. We will discuss these qualifying considerations in Chapter 14, "The Systems Model of Dr. Shen." Life is too complex to file any one part neatly in a cubbyhole.

The character attributes that will be delineated are offered, at this point in the evolution of my ideas, as guides in the diagnostic process, as 'food for thought.' They are meant to be used 'in conjunction with,' not 'instead of.' As with all diagnostic modalities, these characteristics may sometimes be as misleading and false as the clues provided by diagnosis of the tongue, the pulse, and the physical symptoms. They are therefore most useful when considered as part of the whole.

Characterological signs of disharmony are among the earliest possible indications that the natural function of the phase is being disrupted. Generally, they precede by a considerable period of time the signs and symptoms usually associated with disease of these systems and may be thought of as early warning indicators. In relation to the spectrum of the disease process described earlier, it will be seen that: the psychological states appear early in the process; the familiar changes in pulse, tongue, eyes, and color come to the surface in the middle states; and the diagnostic criteria for Western medicine appear toward the end of that process. Should the classical signs and symptoms conflict with the personality indicators, the latter will, in my opinion, give the more enduring information about the true energy dilemma, and the former will suggest the more immediate energy imbalance. Both must be dealt with in their own good time. The Chinese tend to treat the more obvious first and the more subtle later. The Japanese do exactly the opposite. Both systems work.

Specific personality attributes, however, should point toward a particular system as the one to be seriously investigated within the context of the total diagnostic picture. This assertion is based on my own observations of the children with whom I have worked, whose characteristic adaptational patterns were relatively stable almost from birth. If a large group of children were to be followed from birth, observing all diagnostic parameters, it is certainly possible that the other indicators would present as consistent a picture from the beginning as do personality traits.

YIN AND YANG

In most texts, yin and yang are discussed only as complementary, dynamically interdependent and interconsuming, yet opposite, aspects of the total reality or Dao (Tao). The yang symbolizes those phenomena that have the properties of Fire, including warmth, brightness, expansion, upward movement, and agitation, while yin symbolizes coolness, darkness, contraction, downward movement, and quiescence. According to this view of yin and yang, each is a condition of the other's existence. They are also interconsuming, meaning that if one is consumed, the other gains. Our use of these terms will add to this commonly and correctly held view.

We shall refer to yin and yang primarily as nouns rather than adjectives. They exist as qualities and quantities inherently independent of each other and apart from the issues of balance and homeostasis, though always subject to their influence. These autonomous entities may develop from life experience, from genetics, or from a combination of both. In any one phase, both yin and yang may be deficient *(xu)* or excessive *(shi)*, to one extent or another, in the same person, at the same time. The precedent for this exists within the traditional Zang-Fu organ syndromes. On the purely material level, practitioners frequently encounter deficiencies of both yin and yang within the same phase, such as Stomach yin deficiency and Spleen yang deficiency; or within the same organ, such as a simultaneous condition of Kidney yin and yang deficiency. Lung yin and qi deficiencies may exist concurrently in such conditions as tuberculosis; and I have observed many patients over the years who have used both marijuana and alcohol intemperately and shown both Liver yang deficiency and yin deficiency simultaneously.

Turning to the Six Division methodology of classifying the stages of disease, we find in the first three stages a strong yang reaction, while yin is relatively stable. In the last three 'deeper' stages of the disease process, we have a weak yang and ever-increasing weak yin with false yang (heat from deficiency) symptoms. Nevertheless, yin and yang in the homeostatic sense are germane to this discussion inasmuch as whenever there is a real excess or deficiency of either yin or yang, even simultaneously, there will be forces set in motion to compensate and restore equilibrium. These forces are energy, but they may take any form, either mental, somatic, or spiritual.

BALANCE

This leads us to the doorstep of the controversial subject of 'balance' in Chinese medicine. Balance as a value may, like all human concepts, be used for good or evil. No doubt the Confucian 'doctrine of the mean' was used throughout Chinese history to suppress the excesses necessary to creativity, to change, and to revolution. This doctrine, which provided history with a social system of unprecedented stability, was a great leveling force, leading to remarkable rigidity and mediocrity in many areas of Chinese life throughout the past 2,500 years.

According to the more ancient conceivers of the yin-yang construct, balance was never something to be 'achieved.' Daoist cosmology states that the universe was a single point whose first differentiation was into lighter energy (yang) and heavier energy (yin). The former rose, and the latter fell, eventually forming a circle of potential energy, the Daoist symbol of unity. A 'ridgepole' came into the picture, dividing the circle in two, cleaving the unity into the opposite energy properties of yin and yang, and setting into motion for the first time the kinetic dynamic energy of the universe. Here imbalance was the source of the movement, from yin to yang, which is the very essence of life.

We have, therefore, two conflicting constructs around the issue of balance: one which extols it, the other which abhors it, and both of which are necessary. It is the opinion of some that extremes of energy imbalance are necessary to greatness. I have come to no conclusion about this point, because I have no way to test it. Some have expressed the view, for example, that Einstein could not have "sat for twelve years" waiting for the inspiration which led him to the theory of relativity had he not had a massive excess of Kidney yin and a massive deficiency of Kidney yang. Certainly the enormous puffiness under his eyes supports this theory. I believe that each of the phases and their resident organs could be profitably approached from this point of view. I would rush, however, to point out that many people "sit for twelve years" and accomplish absolutely nothing, and, while the capacity to wait is essential to creativity, so too are imagination, intelligence, a coherent and organized ego, a capacity for awe, and profound grounding.

Disharmony, in my opinion, is an extreme of a normal function. Human beings have a limited repertoire of behavior, so that even the most abnormal and bizarre conduct and cognition are recognizable in the most ordinary person. Hallucinations and ordinary fantasies or daydreams are of the same fabric. The former, however, lack the essential ingredients of strong and clearly controlled boundaries that characterize the latter as healthy creative activities. The extremes that accompany a loss of clearly controlled boundaries are sometimes necessary in life and in history, for brief, dramatic moments, in order to initiate or complete a desired change. I know that there are those who disagree, but in my experience, extremes as a way of life are always destructive.

DEFICIENCY AND EXCESS

Distortions in the phase systems, reflected in disorders of personality and the other behavioral markers mentioned above, are considered as resulting from excess or deficiency. Although these are quantitative terms, they carry with them qualitative implications. Distinctions may be made between degrees of excess and deficiency which produce significant variations in personality development.

The words excess and deficiency are used to describe intrinsic, enduring energy states of the natural functions of the organ systems we are studying. Despite the persistence of the characteristics associated with these terms, there are situations when the very nature of the phase, for example, Fire, precludes durability, and where the qualities of excess and deficiency may occur in the same person at different times.

The diagnostic concepts from the Eight Principles of *xu* (weak, empty, deficient) and *shi* (strong, full, excessive) are not interchangeable with those of deficiency and excess as presented here. Excess in the sense of *shi* implies that a pathological process is occurring in an organ that is sufficiently healthy to be actively fighting that process. A clinical picture of excess is produced because energy is being strenuously focused in one area, concentrating it in time and space. This is known as a 'strong *(shi)* disease' and is characterized by severe, acute symptoms, such as severe pain and high fever. By contrast, a 'weak *(xu)* disease' is one in which the symptoms are less powerful and tend to be more chronic and associated with energy depletion, such as dizziness, shortness of breath, palpitations, and easy fatigue.

The concept of excess in the Eight Principle model also refers to accumulations, which may in fact be the result of deficiency. Excess is a misleading word, because the implication is that, since energy is good, excess is more of a good thing. Phlegm-dampness (excess mucus) is, in fact, due to a weakness or deficiency of Spleen qi or yang. In Chinese medicine, chronic serious disease is associated with states of deficiency.

Excluding the views mentioned above with regard to Einstein, in Chinese medicine, balance is critical. Even the excess of something positive is not a healthy situation for more than a short time. Homeostatic mechanisms are there to constantly sustain that balance in the face of the potent, perpetual, and ineluctable dynamisms which define life. If Einstein's Kidney yang deficiency was in fact an asset, it must have functioned as such because of the many excesses of intelligence, wisdom, and compassion that counterbalanced the deficient condition.

I wish, however, to make it clear that I am adopting an extreme position with regard to 'balance' primarily for purposes of emphasis and discussion. I am perfectly aware — and have conducted my personal and professional life on this premise — that no real person is totally 'in balance.' Nor for that matter would the world be the interesting and fascinating place it is, were we all so terribly balanced. Furthermore, I consider that in most circumstances in life judging 'normality' and 'abnormality' is a dangerous and often repugnant exercise. Considering the obstacles to survival and growth that most of us have encountered during our lives, we all deserve the largest benefit of the doubt.

I shall use the terms excess and deficiency quite differently: as exaggerations and extremes of the natural functions of the organ systems that we have selected to study. I am confining myself to extremes, which may be extrapolated towards the mean to capture imbalanced states of lesser severity. Excess or deficiency is always and explicitly understood as disharmonious in the context of the ensuing pages.

For purposes of exposition, the natural function in balance represents the only healthy expression of these attributes. For example, a person with beneficial Kidney qi may tend toward a strong spiritual faith and appear moderately fanatical by some standards. Yet this person will have his 'feet on the ground.' His zeal and strict religious principles will be balanced by a flexible consideration of, and respect for, other people's needs and beliefs. (The argument that many tyrants have had strong Kidney qi is correctly asserted only according to current accepted usage and within the confines of the physical parameters of these energies. It is made without consideration of the concepts of these energies on a mental, emotional, and spiritual basis such as I am about to present in the following chapters).

The principal character descriptions within each phase will be those which are the result of the diminution or amplification of the natural yin and yang functions of that phase within the total picture of the 'evolution of being.' The deficient characterological states are, in a sense, reflections of a depletion or inhibition of the yin or yang function associated with that phase. The depletion may be either constitutional or the result of living (acquired).

Excesses exist within every phase pair, both yin and yang, as absolute constitutional plethoras of energy or as compensatory mechanisms or as both. True constitutional excesses may, as mentioned above, occur in any phase. They are especially clear-cut clinical entities within the Water phase, because this phase is the one most affected by genetic and intrauterine influences. The other phases are more affected by life and less by genetics. Therefore, excesses within these phases are rooted more in life experience than is the case with the Water phase, though the final picture, of course, includes both. There may be some objection to the implication that in the Water phase there can be an excess not met with on the material level, except in those who abstain from sex. On the mental and spiritual level it cannot be denied that the natural functions of the Water phase — courage, drive, power, and will — do appear excessive in people as an innate and real expression of themselves, apart from any restorative or compensatory function.

COMPENSATORY ATTRIBUTES

The natural response to any suppression is restoration — an attempt by an organism to provide, as best it can, substitutes for the missing attribute. Most often, this will be done within the phase itself, so that if either yin or yang is in trouble, the other will attempt to compensate. For example, if the yin function is undeveloped, the yang function will tend to try to balance it and vice versa. Thus, if Heart yin is troubled and the creative and tender emotions are relatively absent, Heart yang — the energy of the organized expression of this emotional creativity — will compensate, and the person may talk, sing, paint, write, compose, plant, or sculpt a great deal more than 'normal.' The expression will lack real creativity and warmth of authentic Heart yin, although perhaps simulating it. This is one of the 'as if' situations.

The natural function of Wood yin is the ability to retreat when strategically appropriate. The Wood yin deficient person can never retreat gracefully as an adaptation acceptable to his ego. When retreat is essential to survival, he may find it acceptable to withdraw on the surface and nourish his wounded ego with hate and rage. This state of affairs strongly resembles the personality characteristics of the Wood yang deficient person, except that it is not as enduring and comes and goes only as needed. On the other hand, the Wood yin deficient person may assume some of the characteristics of a Wood yang excessive person by becoming unremittingly aggressive and advancing, in order to discourage a would-be aggressor and to avoid a confrontation. Protective coloring or inner restorations may assume any form and confuse the picture temporarily. Diagnostically, the distinction can be made by the durability of the character trait and the time of onset. Constitutional traits are more consistent and more durable, often obvious even from infancy.[5] Compensatory attributes are less consistent and less enduring, appearing at a later time in life. The compensatory aggressiveness of the Wood yin deficient person will be seen, with experience, to be primarily defensive, rather than the cardinal attribute of a personality and trademark of behavior.

Although the tendency is for the natural, compensatory restorative mechanism to come from within the same phase, as just described, life and the human psyche are too complicated to be so conveniently predictable. Both natural and compensatory characteristics may be borrowed from any-where and everywhere, to insure the survival of the individual. The more intelligent the person, the more complicated the weave.

The personality profiles that follow are stereotypes and are not to be taken literally. Classifications are regrettable and dangerous conveniences. While they are meant only as illustrations, they tend to develop a life of their own and become reified and institutionalized. The danger lies in the potential to dehumanize, which is the unfortunate result of a tendency in all of us to grasp at simple certainties. In reality, no one completely fits into any of the personality profiles I am describing in this book. They are presented merely to illustrate the projected pathological extreme of each excessive and deficient state.

Examination of the dynamic interplay of organ system function, life experience, constitution, and restoration finds one or the other playing the major etiological role, depending on the developmental period under consideration. Events prior to birth are mediated through the Water phase, which in turn may register the impact of events such as radiation on chromosomes or drugs on fetal metabolism. Events in the early years will be determined by the adequacy of the adult care-givers and the integrity of the dominant Earth phase both in them and in the child. It is the total energy system of the parent, bearing on the needs of the child's emerging and in-choate energy system, that shapes the personality of the dependent child. In any one developmental period, there will be a dominant organ system for both the parent and the child. The condition of the mother's nourishing Earth energies will be more important than her directional Wood energies during the child's first year of life.

However, it must be kept in mind at all times that a 'new person' is not a *tabula rasa*[6] on whom life experience simply inscribes its message. A child is born with a life force bearing patterns of 'being in the world' that distin-guish it clearly from any other child. The ability to generate from within the organization necessary to interact at a particular level with the environment is as important to personal development as the readiness of the environ-ment to respond. If the energy template for the development of the child's Earth energies is compromised by problems in the earlier period of Water energy dominance, leaving him incapable of bonding, then even what the best mother has to offer may not be enough.

In any given instance, therefore, the outcome will depend on the innate potential of the significant energy system, the strength of the other energy systems (especially the preceding), and the opportunity for positive growth experience in the environment all along the way. For example, the behavior and character of a Kidney yang deficient person, who has little sustaining motivational energy, will be greatly affected by his internalization of the attitudes of significant people, those who influence his self-image. (We become, to perhaps an unfortunate extent, what we are perceived to be by significant others.) Should these people be tolerant and accepting of the Kidney yang deficient person, his character and behavior will be far more benign than if he is greeted at every turn with pressure, criticism, and hostility for his inability to sustain effort. Furthermore, relationships beyond those with our original family may make a difference throughout life. Teachers, friends, and even counselors may improve or worsen the situation. In this text, I shall emphasize the worst possible outcomes, urging the reader to keep all of the above qualifications ever in mind.

The enduring patterns of character and behavior are imprinted on energy organ systems, and the organism will resist the best intentioned efforts to change those patterns, unless the energic systems themselves are included in the therapeutic program. Oriental medicine provides us with the opportunity to do just that. What follows is a guide to the correspondences between personality and energy, which will hopefully demystify, to some extent, the ambiguous relationship of 'psyche' to 'soma.'

A Note to the Reader

The most efficient use of the following material on the mental, emotional, and spiritual disharmonies of the organ system energies can be made by keeping in mind a clear picture of the natural functions of that division of the energy system (yin, yang, or qi). The disharmony will emerge more distinctly. The yin aspect is the solid (Zang) organ and the yang aspect is the hollow (Fu) organ.

A brief word about the use of yin and yang in the following chapters about the phases. Yin here means the passive aspect of the phases, such as the yin aspect of Wood being the ability to retreat, while yang refers to the active aspect of the phases, such as the yang aspect of Wood being the ability to advance, both when it is appropriate to do so. Thus here we are not referring to the aspect of yin and yang that represents substances, balance (dark and light sides of a mountain), or as a weak (yin) or strong (yang) person. Again, yin and yang in this context refer only to their passive (yin) or active (yang) aspect.

Thus Wood yin is the Liver and Wood yang is the Gallbladder. This is not spelled out with each phase but must be kept in mind throughout the book. Heart yin is the Heart and Heart yang is the Small Intestine. Pericardium yin is the Pericardium and Pericardium yang is the Triple Burner, Kidney yin is the Kidneys and Kidney yang is the Bladder, and Lung yin is the Lung and Lung yang is the Large Intestine.

It must be emphasized that the pictures of the stagnation or deficiency of energy systems that follow are extremes of these conditions. I have chosen to present the material in this fashion for didactic purposes. One rarely encounters such drastic personality defects as I have illustrated in my case histories. My intention is to make a dramatic presentation and allow the reader to imagine for him or herself the myriad less severe, therefore more common, clinical pictures that might arise from conditions of stagnation or deficiency.

The combinations and permutations of influences that shape personality are too intricate to allow us to consider all of the possibilities in one book or even in one lifetime. Though the actual picture in life is a complex interplay of excesses, deficiencies, and balances, together with all of the factors extrinsic to the Five Phases, we can and indeed must consider each energy in isolation.

Typecasting people is an abhorrent oversimplification; yet it is an unavoidable hazard in any attempt to define ideas in relation to people. Each picture of psychodisharmony described in these pages is, of course, a stereotype, which cannot be found in its pure form in life. I acknowledge these categories as artificial and recognize the inherent danger of reductionism and overstatement. In the pursuit of internal cohesion, we are never far from imposing external rigidities on a reality that is never completely within our grasp. Nevertheless, there are dominant traits that may be readily followed and understood within human analytic capabilities. These descriptions are heuristic models.

Accordingly, the case histories I am presenting in the following chapters are possible outcomes of the distortions of the 'natural functions' of a given energy on an emotional, mental, and spiritual level. They are not an attempt to classify people into Wood, Water, Fire, or any other type. The emphasis is on the 'natural function,' which is the positive statement of these energies. The consequences of their misdirection are not positive, except in the sense that their misdirection constitutes restorative measures. From the latter perspective, even in their most negative form they represent an attempt to endure against great odds and involve the forging of one's greatest talents and most creative energies. Therefore, in no way are these 'negative' outcomes to be considered simply bad or regarded as hard and fast states of being. As long as we live, we all do our best to flow with the life force. We leave its path only under protest and only when the alternative route is imperative to survival. Our being never ceases to seek its way back to the unimpeded unfolding of the inherent self.

The presented case histories are illustrations only of the distortions of natural function to which I have just referred. They are not proffered as examples of approaches to treatment, and include no material for this purpose. They should be regarded only as concrete examples of the enduring patterns of personality I have described more abstractly in the particular section of the book.

8

The Water Phase

Natural Functions of the Kidney Energy System

Kidney energies are the inherited energies that unite past, present, and future and bind all three, in the individual person, to cosmic forces, to the secrets and mysteries of the universe. In the narrative of this chapter, the terms Kidney and Water are interchangeable.

Kidney Yin

Material Being

Kidney yin (including Kidney essence or *jing*) stores the genetic essence that produces the 'marrow' that fills the brain. "The brain," it is said, "is the sea of marrow." Parenchymal and functional integrity, on all levels of the central nervous system, depend upon the ability of the Kidney essence to create and maintain it. An endless variation of cerebral insults may occur from conception to death anywhere that Kidney essence does not produce sufficient 'marrow.' (Cerebral palsies, retardation, neuropathies such as multiple sclerosis and amyotrophic lateral sclerosis, and mental disorders such as schizophrenia or depression, may result from tissue damage or chemical imbalance.) The genetic essence is responsible also for the bone marrow, upon which the hemopoetic and immune systems depend.

Kidney yin also controls the storage of acquired essence, the energies that are acquired after birth from food and air and that are in excess of those used immediately by the body in the course of its daily functions. They represent a backup system which the body may call upon at times of strain. The acquired energy is added to the inherited genetic essence for maintenance of those body functions that depend on essence, such as the central nervous system, immunological functions, and hemopoetic functions. (Aspects of this 'stored energy' may include the corticosteroid endocrine functions of the adrenal cortex, calling forth glycogen from muscles and liver in times of crisis, and the varied epinephrine effects on heart, circulation, and brain function, mediated by the adrenal medulla. The adrenal gland is undoubtedly included in what the Chinese regard as the Kidney organ system.)

The combined stored essence controls fertility in men and women by mixing with the blood (which is stored in the Liver) to make semen in the testes and ova in the ovaries. The stored essence dominates the growth, development, and hardness of bones, including the teeth. This latter function is transferred, in part, to Kidney qi, which becomes the active controlling mechanism of all reproduction, growth, and development.

Whereas the heat of Kidney yang controls Water by 'misting' it to other parts of the body, Kidney yin is the Water itself. Since we are over eighty percent water, and since water is an essential part of every metabolic process, the importance of Kidney yin to every aspect of the organism is obvious. The working of all body systems always involves the Kidneys, especially when any system is overworking. As a consequence, Kidney yin energies are among the first to give way with age.

On a cognitive level, the healthy development of the central nervous system (CNS) implies a balance between right and left brain functions. The balanced person would have available the logical, rational thinking afforded by the left brain, as well as the intuitive, psychic, extra-sensory powers contributed by the right brain. Though one might be dominant, the other would contribute complementary functions for the complete solution of a problem.

The question of balance might lead us to certain conjectures. Interestingly, there seems to be a gradual shift in the West from one historical period to the next in the dominance of one side or the other, with variations evident from the Middle Ages through the increasing complexities of the Renaissance, the Age of Reason and Science, the Romantic Age, and into the present. We are now well into a period during which the logical, rational dominance of Newtonian physics is giving way to a broader view of reality. Here it becomes recognized that reality can only be approximated, that matter and energy are interchangeable in various states of vibratory frequency. Thus, theoretical small particle physics, Oriental philosophy, psychology, and spiritual science will be roughly overlapping each other in the coming era.

In addition to cognitive functions of the CNS, these energies superintend the development and sustain the *modus operandi* of the modalities of sensory awareness. Each of the Five Phases is responsible for one type of sensation. In practice, the relationship of the organ systems to the organs of sensation is far more complex than indicated by textbooks. Tinnitus, for example, may represent a problem in one of three systems, depending on the quality of the sound. A high-pitched sound is pathognomonic with respect to the Liver; the sound of running water indicates the Kidneys; and a sound that has the quality of being stuffed and muffled is associated with the Lungs. Apart from these specific correspondences between organ system and sensory mode, the Kidney yin is always the foundation of functional integrity for all sensory awareness.

Kidney yin *(jing)* energies provide the individual with a profound but balanced perspective on the past. At least a part of the capacity for a through-time experience of life is made possible by these energies. The entire process by which the past is a part of learning, growth, and cultural development is mediated by Kidney yin. The broad range of the meaning of 'roots' in our lives is a function of this organ system. Interests in history, archaeology, anthropology, genealogy, and paleontology depend on the integrity of Kidney yin. However, over-involvement with the past may ultimately weaken these energies.

Spiritual Being

Kidney yin transmits the genetic material of the life force from one generation to another. This is our past in the deepest sense, the water that has provided the milieu for the existence of all living things. At this level of abstraction, the role of Kidney yin calls for theological speculation, seeing it, for instance, as the water of life that baptizes and cleanses the spirit and as the essence of divine love. The Western approach states the case this way: Love is the capacity for forgiveness in the spirit of the Lord's Prayer, "forgive my trespasses as I forgive those who trespass against me."[1] It is, therefore, unconditional. Kidney yin, as divine love, is the capacity for such forgiveness. This capacity is a potential love transmitted from generation to generation by Kidney yin energies and underlies the bonding love of the Earth energies and the creative love of the Fire energies. Without the divine love of the Kidney yin energies, the others could not begin.

Inasmuch as Kidney yin energies transmit man's humanity from generation to generation, these energies are the foundation for man's realistic identity of himself as *Homo Sapiens,* as distinguished from all other phenomena, material or ethereal.[2] There is a tendency in man to identify either with the animal world or the 'higher' worlds. A desirable, healthy balance depends on our ability to recognize and accept our earthbound, limited assets. The capacity to appreciate these limits (without repression) is a gift of Kidney yin energies.

Kidney yin energies are related to the balanced understanding of human limitations. The principal limitation with which we must cope is the dangerous expansion of 'ego,' which leads to the illimitable destructive states of megalomania. We cannot know the nature, reason, or purpose of God and of the infinite. With our intelligence we may learn much about 'how' things work, but never 'why,' except in rudimentary, meditative insights. When, for any reason, we begin to imagine ourselves as being able to expand beyond the limited parameters of humanity, we endanger all of it.

Man seeks the outer limit of his identity by idealizing his own image, with a set of standards based on the ideal of the moment. These shared measures of ideal conduct and internal attitude are values which unite nations, and provide individuals with motivation and drive. Kidney yin people in balance may be those who are realistic and rational, yet passionate in their quest for internal and external perfection. This pursuit is founded on the slowly evolving love of men for one another and on the quest for their common good. This love emerged socially in the eighteenth, nineteenth, and twentieth centuries as one man's respect for another's autonomy, freedom, and liberty and as the giving up of some power to the powerless. It did not happen without a struggle, and nothing was given away charitably.

Many of our mid to late eighteenth century and nineteenth century heroes were trying to free their fellow man from one kind of bondage or another: Lincoln and slavery in America, Marx and alienation in Europe, and Freud, who fought internal repression. Spiritual leaders of our time, such as Gandhi and King, have all been engaged in the struggle for freedom and equality, in the realization of our current idealized image. In our time, the idealist has been the ideal and has been eulogized and dramatically characterized in all of his impotent rage in the book *The Last Angry Man.*[3] The "last angry man" is dead, and the idealized image for which he died is now obscured by political rhetoric. Our ideal of perfection is in a state of active transition. The Aquarians are claiming possession. So also are the Moral Majority. For every idealized image there is its reactive partner, which accompanies it everywhere and completes it. We on earth cannot escape from this duality, since it is duality which has given us life. And so, whatever we aspire to will perpetually be wed to its opposite: love to hate, freedom to oppression, wellness to illness, and life to death.

Kidney yin energies are critical as well to coping with the anxiety associated with all meaningful separations, of which death is of course the most profound. Kidney yin energies give us strength to appreciate that we are not limited by mortality and allow us to face the inevitable without catastrophic panic. Furthermore, these energies (essence) are responsible for a competent central nervous system (brain-mind) with which we rationalize a variety of philosophical and theological reconciliations to corporal death. Some envision a return to the womb, to a oneness with Mother Earth, and some await a union with God the Father on another plane. In either instance, Kidney yin energies would be indispensable to a productive transition to the hereafter.

KIDNEY YANG

Material Being

Kidney yin and Kidney yang give, respectively, the 'life' and 'force' to the life-force. The 'force' induces the movement that distinguishes that which is living from that which is not, and it is coincident with the concept of the qi. If 'energy,' to which all organ systems contribute, is the total capability of the organism to survive, then qi is the working agent or the power provided partly by the Spleen, Lungs, Kidneys, and Liver. Qi moves that energy over a specific distance in a specific time, generating power, work, movement, and circulation. Energy is potential, qi is kinetic. Kidney yang, the Kidney's contribution to qi, is the kinetic component of the Water phase. (For a more exhaustive discussion of 'structive energies' and 'active energies,' I refer the reader to Manfred Porkert's book, *The Theoretical Foundations of Chinese Medicine*.[4]) Kidney yang (also known as Kidney fire, or the fire at the gate of vitality [*ming men*]) is, therefore, the functional energy that provides 'drive' to all the organ systems and circulation. The heat energy, required for the physical and mental digestive functions of the Earth phase, comes from the *ming men* ('gate of vitality'). The bonding and separation of the Earth phase depend on the motivating force of Kidney fire. Without this drive, the body will function sluggishly. On the mental level, this drive is motivation and will-power. The assertive role of the Wood phase in the 'evolution of being' requires the will power provided by the fire of *ming men*. Kidney fire provides the metabolic heat to transform what would otherwise be a relatively inert organism into a dynamic, goal-oriented, aggressive being. From the beginning, it provides the 'force' to the life-force and the 'will' to the will to live.

One component of this forward motion, mediated through Kidney yang energies, is an appropriate involvement with the future. Kidney yang energies provide the prospective aspect of the 'through time' phenomenon, just as Kidney yin energies afford us the retrospective, historical view. With the former energies, we become capable of collating all of the current available information, in combinations of possibilities; these we can test against our concept of reality in order to produce a reasonable approximation of the future. Those in whom this talent is more highly developed are the visionaries and prophets, almost always unsung in their own time and canonized in retrospect. Poet/artist William Blake saw this function as belonging to the imaginative and creative faculties of people, and Ezra Pound called poets "the antennae of the race." In our time the prophetic impulse is strong among science fiction writers, who have fared generally better in the scientific age than their counterparts did in other times.[5]

The propensity to see ahead involves a 'gift' for projection, which permits us to move outside ourselves to other places and times, both past and future. This may be realized in esoteric ways (such as out-of-body experience) or, as with all natural functions, it might become a defense, in this case a rehearsal in preparation for future 'insults', which we call 'paranoia.' The 'clear vision' capacity of the Wood phase as expostulated by Worsley is the focused use of this gift of the Water energies for a specific purpose.

Kidney yin provides the 'water of life,'[6] the medium of nutrient substances necessary to material being. Kidney yang provides the fire that fuels the biochemical processes and stabilizes the balance of these substances through the control of glomerulal filtration. Between the Lungs and the Kidney yang, homeostasis of anions and cations in the body is maintained. Electrolytes are one of three bodily systems in which there is little tolerance for any major imbalance without a threat to life itself. Any compromise in the performance of Kidney yang carries serious potential implications. Though Chinese medicine itself does not make references to Western biochemical science, I feel there is no harm in speculating on the possible correlations.

Spiritual Being

Where Kidney yin transmits the genetic essence (material life) from one generation to another, Kidney yang transmits the genetic force (the fire of *ming men).* This inherited, surging force impels men beyond their material essence and sensory awareness to divine awareness, to intuitive wisdom that transcends the obvious, to knowledge beyond the power of our senses, and to divine power. In the theological perspective, divine power gives man the strength to exercise his creative intelligence (Heart energies), to wisely assess and exploit all of his life-enhancing divine will, and to infuse divine love with passion, excitement, and direction. Divine power may be said to mandate a rational self-appreciation, a proportioned egocentricity, a stable center of gravity, and the centered focus inherent to the meditative phrase, "I am purpose itself." Only from this center can humankind enjoy its unique talent to 'know' God, in a rudimentary sense, through its own creativity, and to identify with Him as the ultimate stage in one's becoming a 'whole person.'

On the spiritual plane, the final step and ultimate freedom stimulated
by Kidney yang and mediated by Kidney qi energies in the 'evolution of being' is the internal search for God's will and the surrender of our inherited
will to the will of God. It is the paradoxical function of the Kidney energies
to supervise the endless transmission of the ego from generation to generation, always directing it to its conclusive destruction, to the death of the
ego.

KIDNEY QI

Material Being

Kidney qi is the dynamic kinetic discharge of energies at the interface
of Kidney yin and Kidney yang. Kidney qi energies direct growth, development, and reproduction throughout life. They are most influential during
the periods of greatest growth, particularly during that early part of the life
cycle in utero and in the first three years after birth, which are dominated
by Earth energies. These energies are especially susceptible to trauma during early years, as well as to any excess or distortion of basic functions, such
as nutrition, work, and sex.

Kidney qi assists the Metal phase, or Lungs, in the 'reception of the qi.'
This involves the inhalation of air and qi from the atmosphere for the entire
body, which it provides in a form known as *zhong* qi. (*Zhong* qi combines
with the energy from digestion, *gu* qi, and constitutional energy, *yuan* qi, to
form the working energy of the body.) A breakdown in this contribution to
respiration may result in asthma.

Poised between an attraction to the past and a fascination with the
future, we are constantly called upon to confront the present. Kidney qi
energies help us to anchor ourselves in the gestalt of the 'here and now,' to
achieve authenticity of feelings and thoughts and to communicate these
feelings and thoughts as the present demands.

Fritz Perls made a major contribution to modern psychotherapy with
his emphasis on directness.[7] We may envision the healthy balance between
the past, present, and future in the form of the 'normal curve,' with the main
area dominated by the present. Kidney qi energies are necessary in order
for us to achieve the dynamically stable construct that we conceptualize as
the 'imminent present,' and they enable us to encounter the immediate challenges of daily life.

Again as a balance between the Kidney yin and yang, Kidney qi brings
together on a cognitive level the power of the 'force' (the yang fire at the
gate of vitality, or *ming men*) and the strength of the 'material' structure

(yin essence) to forge our 'intelligent will.' Intelligence implies memory, concentration, attention, abstract thinking, association, judgment, insight, and communication, all essential characteristics of *Homo Sapiens.* Kinetic conscious intelligence is the domain of Fire. Potential unconscious intelligence is the realm of Water. The 'will,' or functional drive, involves the active exercise of all these potential facilities toward a productive goal. They are equally requisite to personal fulfillment.

The balanced evolution of our incarnate being as healthy ego is governed by Kidney qi energies. In the spiritual perspective, a clear and realistic awareness of the ineluctable boundaries between man and God is indispensable to the safe and satisfactory explorations of "Man in God and God in Man," to which all people apparently have been drawn since the dawn of awareness. Kidney qi energies afford man a realistic view of himself in the cosmos, with his "feet on the ground and his head in the clouds."

Spiritual Being

Kidney qi energies achieve some semblance of this equilibrium, which we could call 'creative sanity,' by their critical influence on certain human attributes:

– *Awe,* the astonished awareness of the breadth and depth of creation.

– *Reverence,* the assimilation of awe into a quieter, less dramatic, and enduring attribute of self.

– *Humility,* the direct consequence of the wonder a sensitized person experiences upon contemplating the enormous complexity of life, e.g., the spectacle of a single cell extrapolated to the intricacy of an entire person, or to the ecosystem of the earth and the universe.

– *Meditation,* of which the varieties are endless, uniting conscious man, by way of unconscious divine potential, to superior orders of being and to a mature bond between creative man and the larger creation.

– *Universal values,* awareness of apparent laws governing our relationship with nature, ourselves, and others, which put the expansive human ego in a rational perspective.

– *Acceptance* of the incomprehensibility of the entire 'will of God' (or the 'life-force'), that crucial surrender of ego to paradox wherein existence always appears to be beyond the limited capacity of our intelligence.

– *Faith* in some positive framework, e.g., that life has a meaning, though we may never know it, or that life is worth living even if 'being' is absurd is the ultimate paradox.

In this perspective, the conclusive triumph of Kidney energies is the crowning stage of the 'evolution of being.' Man is moved by his divine spirit to abandon the struggle for security and to a total and cheerful acceptance of inevitable and endless insecurity. In this condition of truth, man may find 'salvation' (nirvana).

Water and Fire: Inherited Spirit and Developed Spirit

On earth the Water phase is the carrier of the 'inherited spirit,' and the Fire phase is the expression of the 'developed spirit.' Each needs and balances the other. All too often we encounter each in extreme. Of the first sort are those who lay claim to a degree of divine spirit which they do not possess and to which they do not have access. The more persuasive among this sort can, as Abraham Lincoln said, "fool some of the people all of the time and all of the people some of the time." Of the other sort are the deeply endowed ones, whose Fire phase lacks the capacity for expression and who live in a state of deep frustration with no creative outlet. Clearly there is no perfect balance on the human plane.

The Water is the potential mystery expressed in both human love and, in the realm of the spiritual, in divine love (and in the non-discriminating 'knowledge of God'). The Fire is the kinetic, higher intellectual manifestation of the mystery or cognitive knowledge of God (the 'Word,' the 'Logos').

General Mental, Emotional and Spiritual Disharmonies of the Kidney Energy System

The deficiencies and excesses of the Kidney energy system are intrinsic factors that, for the most part, represent either constitutional conditions based on genetic dispositions or congenital abnormalities induced during pregnancy or delivery. A possible exception to this rule would be those extreme conditions of deprivation in infancy or early childhood that compromise the entire organ energy system and thereby affect the energies of the Water phase. Some of the obvious and many of the more subtle central nervous system dysfunctions subsumed under the heading of minimal brain damage are, I believe, the result of intra-uterine and parturition insults to the fetus. I came to this conclusion after eight years of experience as the medical director of a community child guidance center and thirty years of work with children, adolescents, young adults, and their families. Most of these insults affect either the Kidney energies that are responsible for the orderly development of the central nervous system throughout pregnancy, or, through trauma, the already-developed central nervous system at delivery. The spectrum of disabilities, ranging from personality disorder to the grossest neurological disease, depends upon the location and extent of the damage to these energies and to the central nervous system. (A study from Cornell Medical Center demonstrates a statistical correlation between adolescent suicide and respiratory distress at birth.[8] My section on depression further elaborates this issue.)

Kidney energy problems that are the result of abuse in later life, such as excessive sex in adolescence (including masturbation), will tend to produce similar though less severe disorders if all other considerations are equal.

PERSONALITY: EXPANSIVE EGO

The disharmonies with which we will concern ourselves are primarily those of spiritual development, which are superintended and guided by Kidney energies. I am assuming for the sake of the following discussion that the material aspects of Kidney energy physiology are optimal and equip the subjects of our discourse with the highest potential mental capacity.

The principal problems center around the expansive ego, which presses toward a central position in its own universe and, ultimately, in the larger universe of others. It does this to the exclusion of any deference to a higher power except as it perceives itself as a special representative of that power. The critical issue here is the inability to deal with the 'fear of the unknown.' This mandates an ego-centered personality organization which, through projection of its own thoughts and feelings, leaves little out there that any longer feels like the threatening unknown. Compensatory attributes may also develop as a 'reaction formation,' an attempt to cope with one's ever-burgeoning ego by going to the opposite extreme and becoming overly restricted or self-effacing.

Projection is the principal mode of restoration (defense). With the ego problems outlined above, 'self-blame' is too serious a threat to the personality organization to be a conscious option. Provided the central nervous system is intact, placing the 'blame' on others is a sophisticated maneuver and more challenging to intelligence than the relatively naive strategy of 'denial.'

OTHER ATTRIBUTES OF KIDNEY ENERGY DISHARMONY

- *Psychotic* episodes will tend, therefore, to fall under the umbrella of paranoia in all of its variegated shades and hues, depending on the usual variables of intactness of boundary structure, grounding, bonding, and the special variables of energy polarity, deficiency, and excess. Jealousy, envy, hate, and vengeance are common themes.

- *Cognition* is strongly dominated by ideas of reference. The person whose Kidney organ system is malfunctioning experiences himself as the center of the world. All cognitive processes are influenced and distorted by this premise. Such a person is propelled by a need to feel important, which can escalate into a megalomaniacal state. While this egocentricity at first is experienced as extremely gratifying, later it falls prey to the inevitable, terrifying, hostile transmutation of all ego-gratifying delusions. The person who has held himself in sufficiently low esteem as to require a delusion of grandeur soon becomes the tortured victim of self-hatred, as the projected material inevitably returns upon the self-proclaimed center of the universe. Self-delusive projection, as an attempt to empty the self, is an ongoing necessity to this character structure, leading also to problems with the storage of cognitive material.

– *Phobias* likewise function in the service of the paranoid delusional system. Other people are perceived as the ultimate cause of low self-esteem and so are identified as the enemy. Sufferers who have defects in the Water energy complex are especially prone to a problem that besets us all, the fear of the unknown. For it is these energies we must rely upon to help us cope with death, the greatest of all unknowns. The unknown has ever new terrors for those whose Kidney organ system energies are impaired. The most immediately dangerous and least predictable unknown is other people. Projecting familiar thoughts and feelings from our own psyche onto them may make them seem less menacing at first. In the long run, as we have seen above, these thoughts and feelings turn our erstwhile enemies into horrendous, unmanageable tormentors, as our projected self-hatred comes back to haunt and taunt us. Phobias in this case are of people, not places or things.

– The *depressions* associated with Kidney energies vary from one subgroup of yin, yang, or qi energies to another. All of these depressions tend to have in common both a chronicity and a seemingly inexplicable cause at their time of occurrence. This places them in the diagnostic category of 'endogenous' depression. This lifelong tendency to depression, for which theories continue to be offered by psychiatry, is rooted in the genetic and intra-uterine stage of development, controlled by Kidney energies (through the *chong mai*, or Penetrating vessel). Any interference in the natural evolution of these energies ('to be'), will lead to depression, as it would in any developmental stage. The significant difference is that interference at this earliest stage leaves a larger, more profound, and enigmatically arcane emotional legacy than at any other period of growth. Perhaps this is because Kidney essence, in its role as the material source of the central nervous system, is probably the closest of all the energies to the amine chemical compounds and equations such as acetylcholine, epinephrine, and dopamine now associated by Western medicine with the transmission of nerve impulses.

Chinese medicine declares that deficiency of qi in the Kidneys will produce dreams of shipwrecks and drowning. It also alleges that a 'flourishing' of yin, which is largely associated in a substantive way with Water in Chinese medicine, evokes dreams of floods, wading through great waters, and being weary with anguish and fears. An excess of qi in the Kidneys is said to elicit dreams of worms and wounds. A condition of excess is reported to evoke dreams of the spine being detached from the body. Excess of the Bladder is associated with dreams of swimming, and deficiency with dreams of voyaging. As previously mentioned, I have made no attempt to test these correlations.

According to the tradition of symbolization that makes use of 'ministers' and 'officials,' the Kidneys are the Minister of Energy, supervising the storehouse of pure energy and "doing energetic work"; it is the official "from whom the strength of the body is derived." The Bladder is the Minister of Education who supervises the "archives," is responsible for memory storage, and functions psychologically to prevent one from drowning in emotions. Together they are responsible for power, drive, and will.

According to Chinese medicine, the energy of the Kidney energy system should normally flow downward. The imbalanced states of this system have, in all instances, a reversed, upward flow for each of the polarities, excess and deficiency. This will be discussed below, under the heading of "Bioenergetics."

KIDNEY YIN DISHARMONY

Since Kidney yin (Essence) energies supervise the development of the central nervous system, we shall consider separately those conditions in which, by present standards, the central nervous system has developed normally and those which demonstrate both hard and soft neurological deficits.

KIDNEY YIN DEFICIENCY WITH CENTRAL NERVOUS SYSTEM INTACT

Personality: Brutal Competitor

The person whose Kidney yin energies are genetically deficient does not identify with human values and ethics and, in the extreme, will be identified as crude and savage among his fellow men. He will have little use, possibly even a strong defensive contempt, for the accouterments of culture and civilization and indeed for the sources of his culture and its historical perspective. He is generally indifferent to aesthetics and all the refinements of the senses. He is a brutal, egoistic competitor with no code of honor, whose behavior is built on the premise that the world is inherently hostile and threatening. Self-serving, he has no compassion for those who seem to stand in the way. His philosophy is to kill, literally or figuratively, before he is killed. All of the developed sensibilities of life are dangerous distractions from the primary issue of destroying before one is destroyed. He will be the ruthless, senseless developer who levels his environment, who has never actually experienced nature as anything except an obstacle to his ambition. Without a sense of his limitations as a human being in a larger order of things, his own order will take precedence. This new order, removed as it is from the endless variegated nuances of nature, is unimaginative, repetitive, and endlessly boring. This order is perpetuated by those who succumb to it as their daily aesthetic fare and who, in turn, become as prosaic and uninteresting as what they see, hear, touch, and smell.

Egoistic impulses dominate this behavior, limited only by what society will bear. Intellect and awareness are used to test the limits, not to set them internally in synchrony with considerations of the greater good and the cosmic order.

Man, it follows, is the brute beast who preys on his fellow man without compassion. "Every man for himself." "Let the buyer beware." The world beyond self is intrinsically "the enemy." Life is cheap and is given or taken thoughtlessly. The chase is everything. These people may be the professional soldiers and killers and bullies. Impulse is accorded an inflated value as a guide to living. "If it feels good, it must be good." The person with deficient Kidney yin energies is a sub-human hunter who has no respect for the hunter's sacred needs for renewal. (Such awareness and respect is, by contrast, a pervasive spiritual guide in primitive hunting societies.) Love for his fellow man is limited, at best, to family, clan, club, or small social group, within which the same principles of intimidation of the weak by the strong still determine the quality of relationships. For those outside the small group there is even less compassion. The tendency is to mandate the larger social authority to the smaller group and to move to extremes (as, for example, in the case of Charles Manson). There is little intellectual rationale, although where relative sanity prevails, there may be references to rugged individualism, survival of the fittest, and *laissez-faire*. Where sanity begins to slip, an idiosyncratic rationale may prevail, as it did with Manson's cult—an exaggerated example of the megalomania that may occur to varying degrees in yin deficient individuals and groups.

Kidney Yin Deficient Attributes: Born or Bred

The emphasis, in this discussion, is on genetic yin deficiency. However, people of similar character tend to come together to form families, clans, and communities. The characteristics become increasingly formalized and rationalized into organized patterns of living and child rearing, so that even those born with less of the basic yin deficiency will emerge with similar character structures. If one searches, however, one finds differences between those born with, and those bred into, these attributes. Mitigations of the hard line occur in the latter group, whose members are constitutionally endowed with other strong, positive energy qualities and often grow and develop away from the group standard. This may bring them into conflict with or sometimes, paradoxically, even into antithetical leadership of the community for a limited period of time. These people may become the conscience of their clan, with whom they remain identified (Gandhi) until destroyed by its more enduring qualities. From time to time we even find people born into these relatively 'primitive' situations who break away entirely and who distinguish themselves in life by becoming highly advanced intellectually and spiritually.

We must distinguish between those people born as yin deficient with the tendencies described above, and those who acquire the deficiency over a lifetime, for a variety of reasons (such as excessive sexual activity). These character traits are far less pronounced or predictable in the latter group. The results depend on the extent to which the individual is able to assume responsibility for the changes that take place. Some will grow as individuals, despite a tendency to become increasingly egocentric.

It is common knowledge in Chinese medicine that the genetic Kidney yin essence diminishes with age. And it is also common knowledge that with advancing age there is an increased tendency to lose the functions of the higher centers of the central nervous system. Along with both diminutions come changes in personality, some of which can be traced in less dramatic forms to earlier life, and others of which were previously unsuspected. Generally, these characteristics fit our description of Kidney yin deficiency (accompanied by Kidney yang deficiency in old age), including, most notably, increasing irritability, egocentricity, paranoia, and depression. Those with innate Kidney yin deficiency will not gracefully assimilate these changes (for example, decreasing sexual abilities and memory losses) or show a growing acceptance of the fairness of nature, which says, "If you draw too much from the bank, you must eventually face the consequences of being overdrawn." Those whose egos cannot permit this spiritual acceptance will grow increasingly bitter and defensive, blaming others for their limitations or denying them.

Other Attributes of Kidney Yin Deficiency

Although *fear* is the inevitable concomitant of this existential posture, it is often masked by an aggressive pose, which may cause people in the environment to feel uncomfortably intimidated. This exaggerated show of will and drive is the yang excess compensatory factor for the yin deficiency. Another quality is relative cheerlessness, a lack of spontaneous gaiety. Though they may often be impulsive, spontaneous cheerfulness would place them in the untenable position of being off guard against the inevitable hostility and danger in the world around them.

In the constitutionally Kidney yin deficient group, any felt need for the friendship, tenderness, and softer feelings of another person will provoke *anxiety*. Anxiety is provoked by friendliness, which is experienced as an attempt to disarm. The personality is organized around the expectation of attack. The principal phobia in this group is one against any intimacy which involves tenderness.

In contrast to friendliness, danger provokes little anxiety but, instead, a considerable, and apparently desirable, feeling of excitement. This excitement may be the only relatively pleasant emotion allowable. There will always be a tendency for an agitated *depression*—the depression due to the constitutionally determined Water deficiency, and the agitation due to heat from deficiency associated with a yin deficiency. Any prolonged situation that renders the person less than perfectly defended against the world—less than the invulnerable center of his own universe and chronically dependent on the compassion of others—will provoke severe depression. (Ernest Hemingway is an example of this.)

There is a tendency toward concreteness as a defense against the subtle, clandestine threats hidden in abstractions. Concreteness leaves little room for deception. *Cognition* is also dominated by ideas of reference and projection, which are characteristic, defensive restorative maneuvers by all people with defects in the Kidney energy systems. Provoked by feelings of total isolation and unrelenting danger, there can be a paranoid *psychosis*, with delusional threats from the outside world, a projection of their own brutal life view.

Love is confined mostly to the clan, family, dynasty, or organization and is equated, to a great extent, with loyalty. The Mafia 'family' is a typical example of a clan in which the members exclude the outside world from their concept of love. The person, male or female, with Kidney yin deficiency is basically insensitive to his or her partner who, as I mentioned, is loved primarily as part of a defensive or offensive system. In contrast to the qi deficiency where the pact involves two, in this case it is the larger group (clan, gang) against the world.

Sex is basically a release of tension, which is associated with the person's existential position in which he sees the world as an ever-present threat and danger. A larger involvement would be too distracting and too dangerous, so the sexual act tends to be quick, with little concern for the partner. It is experienced within the context of the family, organization, or clan as a duty and part of the expected loyalty. In the male, there may be premature ejaculation at a later stage of Kidney yin deficiency. Preference here is in the direction of sado-masochistic sexual behavior only if it is freely obtained. These people tend to use and cast people away and do not appreciate paying for the privilege. They may, in fact, tend toward being pimps or 'madams.'

Bioenergetically there is a tendency for displacement upwards, creating a moderately heavy muscle condition in the upper part of the body and a relatively weaker one in the lower part. There are blocks at the base of the skull that dissociate the functions of consciousness from those of feeling and emotion. There is a block at the rim of the pelvis, cutting the genitals and legs from the rest of the body. Despite the appearance of strength this person will be quite weak inside, and not truly able to sustain a prolonged effort, especially after the age of 50 in men and 45 in women.

Kidney energies are the foundation of the organism in all of its manifestations. They are both in great demand and constitutionally limited in supply; for this reason, their replenishment is slow and more difficult than is the case with the other energies. More than any other energy, the treatment of Kidney energy is enhanced by tai qi quan (t'ai chi ch'uan) and qi gong (ch'i kung), the Daoist exercises increasingly practiced today as a health measure in the People's Republic of China.

Signs of Kidney yin deficiency may also appear, as already mentioned, in people after their basic personality has formed in directions quite different from the one outlined above. These people may already have a variety of subtle and complex supports that compensate for this development. Nevertheless, a tendency in the directions I have mentioned will occur and should be kept in mind, however well it is balanced by existing personality strengths.

A Case of Aggression

Few people with the above personal qualities seek psychological help, but some do require other medical attention. One such person was a young man of 28 who had been in an automobile accident that left him with a whiplash injury and severe subluxations of the cervical vertebrae. I came to know him even better by treating his wife, whose characterization of this man was corroborated by the physician who had referred him. His view of the world was strictly exploitative, giving him a large advantage in the small, slow-paced, rural town in which he lived. His father was known in a nearby, larger town as a ruthless businessman who had rejected his son as not terribly useful to the advancement of his own fortunes. By the time I met the young man he had already far outstripped his father as an unremitting and savage competitor. His wife and her family were of a higher social standing, which he relentlessly exploited. He used her in their day-to-day life to further his domination of a world in which neither he nor anyone associated with him could rest for fear of some unknown threat to his survival. He and his wife were referred to marital therapy in a distant city, because working with a local therapist evoked his terror of having it known in his own town that he was vulnerable and needed help.

It could be argued correctly that this young man simply "identified with the aggressor," his father, whose personality was in sharp contrast to the remainder of this laid-back mountain family. However, many young people in similar situations reject this option and choose to embrace alternative life postures. His choice, and his father's as well, should be examined with an understanding of the disposition of energy as well as the conventional psychological viewpoints. In such situations the two approaches together yield far more than either alone, and the energy-centered strategy is one which such people find more easily acceptable.

Kidney Yin Deficiency with Central Nervous System Deficiency

Kidney yin deficiency sometimes creates palpable central nervous system deficits which may be either physical, such as cerebral palsy, or mental, such as mental retardation (e.g., Down's Syndrome), in which repetitive, stereotypical behavior is common. There may be personality problems that are the natural outcome of living with such a defect in a prejudiced and competitive society. The result will depend on many variables, including family, economic status, community resources and attitudes, catastrophic reactions to frustration, excess stimulation, unreal expectation, and other stresses that are exacerbated by increasing age.

Entire areas of human brain function have not yet been clearly mapped, leaving large gaps in our knowledge of the specific effects of genetic or congenital defects. It is my belief that the following problems have a significant constitutional component: learning disabilities, literalism, schizophrenia, discerning of boundaries and limits, autism, and retardation. These will be examined in the above order.

A Case of Learning Disability

Learning disabilities include perceptual and mixed dominance problems. Especially when unrecognized as such, they cause the child whose intelligence tests are good to be labeled 'difficult,' 'bad,' or 'defective.' The ensuing injury to the child's self-image may follow many damaging courses, depending again on the variables of family, school, and community attitudes.

> V. was a young man who came to my attention after he had committed a capital offense and become suicidal while in jail awaiting trial. Careful research into his past revealed V. met all of the requirements for the diagnosis in DSM-III of Attention Deficit Disorder, previously described also as Minimal Brain Dysfunction, or Psycho-neurological Learning Disability. He met all of the neuro-behavioral symptoms of left hemispheric learning disability.
>
> The following case history of V. is offered as a typical example of a Kidney yin deficiency CNS deficit. The salient historical and diagnostic features were:
>
> 1. Prolonged labor: mother was in difficult labor for two-and-a-half days
>
> 2. Umbilical cord wrapped around neck at birth
>
> 3. Hernia surgically corrected at two months
>
> 4. Rhythmic banging of head throughout childhood
>
> 5. Double or triple vision and gross defects of eyes, documented as astigmatism, amblyopia, congenital nystagmus, and exotropia, requiring glasses at the age of four
>
> 6. Lisping, poor articulation, and diminished auditory perception in early grades
>
> 7. Very short attention span, inability to concentrate for more than five minutes; constantly on the go, attention span worst in a group, best

in one-to-one with minimal stimuli; easily distracted, constantly shifting activities, great difficulty organizing and completing tasks

8. Constant restlessness, fidgeting, hyperactivity, and preoccupation with speed

9. Poor coordination, frequent accidents, inability to play games such as baseball

10. Startle response and decreased level of tolerance to anxiety; gross tremor observed

11. Poor impulse control and low frustration tolerance, with rapid loss of interest if success not immediate

12. Functioning in all areas unstable, unpredictable, and uneven

13. Drawn to younger or older children, not to peers

14. Perseveration; concrete thinking (the inability to move from the specific to the general); learning disability, with reversals, skipping words, resistance to reading, and preference for picture books

15. Testing revealed "difficulty with visual perceptual motor integration tasks and best response to concrete stimuli"

16. Soft neurological signs, including mixed dominance (left eye, right arm, right leg)

17. Secondary signs including clowning, withdrawal, negativism, and avoidance

The causes of this Kidney yin CNS deficiency were probably anoxia at birth and severe physical abuse, especially blows on the head with iron pans during childhood. The problem was exacerbated by an uninformed and largely indifferent school faculty, administration, and psychological service.

A Case of Literalism

Literalism is a specific loss in the area of abstract thinking, which is not classifiable with the schizophrenias. The child's interpretation of communication is either 'black or white'; and, because he misses the 'grays,' verbal and non-verbal behavior in the environment becomes confusing. The confusion leads to conflict and finally to a sense of isolation on the part of the individual, who then suspects the worst of everyone and becomes clinically paranoid. Affect is flat. This condition, in my experience, begins at birth and is highly resistant to any known intervention. The course is downhill toward paranoia, at differing rates, depending on degree of impairment.

Q. was referred to me at the age of 22 because he was convinced that his parents had been deliberately trying to destroy him since childhood. This perception was spreading to other relationships, and his entire life was dominated by signs and symbols of impending destruction. For this reason he was unable to function in college and had recently left, admitting himself briefly to a mental hospital.

The Department of Labor cited him for "refusal of employment without good cause." When he applied for social assistance, they offered him a temporary job with the county cutting grass and vegetation along highways. His refusal became the subject of a hearing in which his reply to a stunned judge was that since he was a vegetarian, he would kill plant life selectively for his survival but would not engage in "mass homicide" by mowing a lawn or cutting down a tree.

His thinking was very literal and concrete, in keeping with the definition given above. Not killing plants was just not killing any plant, no matter what the context. If there were a forest fire, he could not kill plants to make a fire break, even though it might save many more plants and trees as a consequence.

Q. was not able to integrate stimuli. Each was separate from the other, and any communication between them had to be sorted out one-by-one and then put together. The usual functions of automatic amalgamation and commingling of information into a context including past, present, and future were missing.

Schizophrenia

Schizophrenia requires no further elaboration on my part at this point, except to say that I consider it to be, in varying degrees, a defect in the establishment of boundaries between the inner and outer world and in the development of abstract thinking. It originates in the genetic and intra-uterine environment dominated by Kidney yin and is elaborated by the failure of Earth energies after birth. The character issues have been discussed exhaustively in hundreds of books from a variety of approaches. I will elaborate my views in the chapter on Earth energies.

Judgment Problems

There is a group of people in which one finds a significantly diminished sense of limits that seriously affects judgment. They would fall generally into the DSM-II categories of 'immature' or 'inadequate' personalities abolished in the newer DSM-III version. These people cannot clearly comprehend the limits set by society, with which, for this reason, they are often in difficulty. Furthermore, they are poorly organized and incapable of cleverly conceived, well-concealed, anti-social acts, which adds to their difficulties with the law.

A small but important sub-group of those with limit and judgment problems are the *sociopaths*, formerly classified as 'psychopathic personalities.' In addition to their poor judgment and inability to grasp the consequences of their acts, these people are extremely incapable of forming bonds with other people. Since many of them have relatively uneventful early childhood experiences in which the bonding aspects of the Earth energies seem relatively intact, we must seek another explanation for their inability to bond in love relationships. The failure of the Kidney yin energies to transmit the potential for love is, I believe, the area to explore for an explanation.

Another sub-group may include those generally described as *autistic*. The potential capacity for love and attachment carried by Kidney yin energy is somehow not realized by Earth energies. The connection between Water and Earth is not made in utero or shortly afterward. Likewise communication on a verbal level does not become initiated, suggesting a further breakdown in contact between Water and Fire. Some of these children do respond to heroic efforts, and the connections can be made with sufficient appropriate stimulation. The use of acupuncture and herbs to open these energy pathways might be a productive path to investigate.

Mental Retardation

Among the CNS deficiency symptom complexes there may be a wide range of affect, from placidity in the younger Down's Syndrome individual to apathy in some of the more profoundly retarded people. In the person with Down's Syndrome over the age of 40, especially where there may be significant stress, expectation, or frustration, a range of affects from irritability to catastrophic reaction is seen, similar to those encountered in people with Alzheimer's disease. Except for the younger Down's Syndrome person, the affect is generally labile in response to the immediate situation.

The pervasive vulnerability of these people leads mainly to confusion and *anxiety* in those sufficiently aware of their defects to feel endangered. As in Alzheimer's disease, those who are cognizant of diminished mental powers will experience profound depression. *Cognition* includes concrete thinking, stereotypic thinking, and agosognosia.

The other sub-categories are not especially distinguishable from those described under the section Kidney yin deficiency, central nervous system intact.

Kidney Yin: Excess

Personality: Pride in Superior Brain

The primary attributes of this person center around his over-weaning identification with 'man.' Men pride themselves on their superior 'brain.' Where Kidney yin is in excess this brain will be superior, and an inordinate emphasis will be placed on its capabilities as this person confronts the challenges of life. Depending on whether the right or left brain is dominant, disparate personalities will develop with, of course, some significant overlaps. While Kidney yin essence is responsible for the integrity and development of the central nervous system, the dominance of one side of the brain over the other will depend on the relative amounts of yin or yang within the Kidney yin. Should the yin predominate, the person will be right brain dominant. Should the yang ascend, the left brain will prevail. Through the competency of the *corpus collosum,* the two sides of the brain are in constant interplay. Under ideal circumstances, the relative imbalances in right-left brain dominance should be partially alleviated by the integrity of the *corpus collosum.* The result should be a less one-sided, more stable person than those extremes described in the following pages as right or left brain dominant.

Left Brain Dominant: This person glorifies logical, rational reasoning powers to the exclusion of all other modalities of knowing. The six senses and the deductive process are the touchstones of his reality. To these and to 'man' who possesses these attributes, he ascribes the ultimate cosmic authority. He is the atheist, the agnostic, the materialist, for whom the scientific experimental model is the universal religion. His logical mind is god; and to this analytic mind, to this god, all the mysteries of existence will succumb in time.

Relationships are grounded in clear-cut rules of conduct dictated by reason and logic. This person is legalistic, contract-oriented, lives by reason, and expects others to be reasonable with him. Illogical behavior is highly disorganizing to him. He tends to be law-abiding and loyal. Duty is a strong motivating force. He has a tendency to be stable.

For this person death is final. Our bodies decompose and are recycled, and we leave our property/material expressions of our love in the form of inheritances. The finality of death is either profoundly experienced or totally denied. Since nothing is beyond, death is to be avoided at any cost. Our heroic life-saving medicine and intensive care units are the final expression of the materialistic existential position.

From the Age of Reason came 19th century idealism. Man is his own master, can control his own environment, will die for a cause that is strictly for man's self-advancement, and will engage in revolutions for independence and material equality.

Right Brain Dominant: This person exalts the endowments of the right brain. Revelation through intuition or psychic forces is the single avenue to knowledge. Logical, rational thinking is relegated to the realm of misleading falsehood, 'materialism' to the work of the devil. In the extreme, these are the fanatic psychics and the zealous dogmatists.

More moderately, this may be the highly idealistic romantic who absolutely loves mankind and wishes to save, sacrifice, and give his life for it. Many of our 19th century heroes had something of this in them, to excess.

Since the principal guide to behavior is inspiration and the inner voice, which often is highly unpredictable and impulsive, relationships may be erratic and unstable. The Bohemian lifestyle is symbolized by the French painter Gauguin, who abandoned his wife and family quite impetuously in order to paint in the South Pacific. He had little meaningful concern for his contractual responsibilities and duties.

LEFT BRAIN AND RIGHT BRAIN

Affect:

- **Left brain:** Lacking in spontaneity, controlled, tends to be overly serious
- **Right brain:** Affect is labile and impulsive, excessively spontaneous, often explosive and eruptive

Anxiety:

- **Left brain:** Anxiety occurs whenever this person is confronted with issues that defy logic or finds himself in any situation in which unreasonableness seems to prevail as a modus vivendi. This person tends to be phobic of social situations in which there is any strong suggestion of spontaneity and the possible loss of emotional control.
- **Right brain:** Anxiety will be provoked in those situations where there is a strong requirement for reason and logic. This person will tend to be anxious in situations with people who require from them regularity and routine as a significant part of the relationship. This would be especially true in work situations between employer and employee, as well as in closer interpersonal situations such as marriage.

Depression:

– **Left brain:** Depression will occur later in life, towards the involutional period, due to the failure of logic and reason to bring its promised fulfillment. Somewhere in middle age the person will find himself to be a spiritual and creative desert filled with feelings of emptiness.

– **Right brain:** Depression, again somewhere in mid-life, results from the inability to sufficiently integrate logic and reasoning into the creative process of producing an integrated, balanced, and finished work of art.

Cognition:

– **Left brain:** Deductive thinking prevails, with a tendency toward rigidity and an attraction to inflexible, conceptual models.

– **Right brain:** Inductive thinking prevails, with a tendency toward inadequate structure and loose cognitive organization.

Psychosis: generally paranoid

– **Left brain:** There will be projections of unconscious, repressed primary process material, often of a sexual nature.

– **Right brain:** Paranoid psychosis prevails, which is primarily a projection of self-doubts about creativity onto a generally conservative world which, though realistically unfriendly, is experienced as more dangerously hostile and threatening to their idiosyncratic unconventional behavior, ideas, and creations than is actually true.

Love:

– **Left brain:** Feelings of love are not corrupted by passion and are justified by an appeal to reason and logic. Relationships are often governed by principle, by duty, and obligation. Though these may not always be the real reason for the attachment, they are a necessary rationale for behavior that could never be acceptable on a purely emotional level.

– **Right brain:** The vicissitudes of love are governed partly by other-worldly considerations. An astrological reading unfavorable to a relationship might end it.

Sex:

– **Left brain:** Sex takes place in a 'legitimate' relationship, generally stereotyped, according to conventional rules, relatively unimaginative, in which variations are reluctantly admitted. However, there may be the acting out of unacceptable sexual fantasies under controlled circumstances logically associated with them, as for example in a house of prostitution.

– **Right brain:** There are two possible courses here. One is sexual behavior which is highly unpredictable, spontaneous, polymorphous, and a response more to the call of 'inner voices' than to the fulfillment of a maturing intimacy or out of concern for the needs of another person. The second possibility would be complete renunciation of these inclinations, which for other reasons may prove to be unacceptable, in which case celibacy may be practiced to one extent or another, even as a lifetime commitment (as with a priest or nun, many of whom have severe repressed sexual conflicts).

Bioenergetics:

– For both **left and right brain** dominated people there is a general displacement upward to the head, resulting in a relatively large head with respect to the body.

A Case of Left Brain Domination

One typical left brain person is a 65-year-old scientist who came to me suffering from hypertension and a bad reaction to conventional medications that had made him impotent. Although he was skeptical of a modality whose efficacy was unsupported by double-blind studies, my Western medical training appeased him sufficiently that he followed his wife's recommendation to try Chinese medicine. He was endlessly fascinated by the faith I had in my work without any 'proof' of its value. The benefit his wife had already received from this approach was of no consequence in the face of my lack of scientific method. For him, knowledge was limited to statistically significant information, which was the only truth in the universe. His own improvement held no meaning since statistically it could have happened by chance; the better he felt, the greater was his resistance to the idea that Chinese medicine could help. Yet, at the same time he wanted to believe, and so set out to read what he could to convince himself. He was also drawn to those who lived by faith and were at home with spontaneity. He seemed envious of their capacity to exist apart from a total dependence on deductive reasoning. It was, however, a line in his life across which he could not venture. Despite his clear-cut improvement he chose to return to his former physicians, who convinced him that without his medications he would die, which he did about two years later, fully medicated, in his sleep.

One could speculate that he wanted to be impotent as a way of either avoiding or punishing his wife, with whom he had had a stormy relationship; that is, that he found the medication less offensive than his wife. Whatever the motivation may have been, he chose a Western medical method, one to which he had, as a scientist, dedicated his life. He was forced to follow the method which appealed to his reason rather than the one which appealed to his experience.

A Case of Right Brain Domination

His counterpart was a talented 25-year-old woman who practiced psychic healing and was completely at home with the intuitive aspects of Chinese medicine. She came with a common cold and a "pain in [her] heart." Her Kidney pulses were amazingly low in an otherwise Bounding pulse. My note at the time said that "there is a struggle between recognizing the need for limits and her will." In fact there was little struggle. Though this was already 1975, she lived by the '60s creed that "If it feels right, do it." And she did. Shortly after the first treatment she felt better. Soon we began to refer patients to one another. The acupuncture and her psychic healing was a most productive combination for the many patients with whom we worked over a six month period. Many were her friends and acquaintances, whom she reckoned by the dozens. However, it became apparent within a short time that this ideal situation would not last. On several occasions she did not appear for our work, leaving me to see as many as 15 people myself in one afternoon, when I ordinarily saw five. When I asked her to discuss this situation with me, she told me that she would not work when the mood was not with her. Commitment, responsibility, professionalism were totally subordinate to the impulse of the moment; if the moment wasn't right, it just wasn't, sick people notwithstanding. She became pregnant, married, and had a child. When we met again several years later, she had grown tired of the child.

KIDNEY YANG DISHARMONY

KIDNEY YANG DEFICIENCY

Personality: Lack of Power to Act

This person's entire life is dominated by the lack of power to act. It is as if he were performing at a lower metabolic rate, a lower motivational voltage. From birth the incentive is lacking; the body and mind seem to lack 'charge,' as if he were born with an impaired energy battery. He or she cannot assume tasks demanding either duration or rapidity, though there may be repeated efforts early in life, often prompted by others, before the Kidney yang deficient person gives up altogether.

Consequently, a picture of sloth, laziness, procrastination, and a low level of achievement follows this person everywhere. There is an inadequate vision of the future, and even where one may emerge there is little vigor to act meaningfully on these good intentions. There is no forward movement, either for self or for the species, and activists are greeted, if at all, with defensive skepticism. {125}

The result is a deep sense of impotence and frustration, without the inner strength to develop the concomitant rage. Instead, we find self-diminishment and a pervasive lack of confidence and faith in oneself and others. At best such a person will search endlessly for these missing attributes, without which he will live an unfocused life characterized by chaos, confusion, deep anxiety, and depression. If Kidney yin is adequate, there may be a compensatory intellectualization, which is more an affectation than real. This could be the person who takes courses all of his life, from which nothing productive ever ensues. The person with deficient Kidney yang who remains unaware of his deep-seated and omnipresent psychological impotence may express it by pervasive envy, by blaming others for his failures, by openly or covertly hoping for others to fail, or by a general hostility to enthusiasm and efforts to create or try something new. He or she may cling to petty despotism, afforded by chance or design, over spouse, children, or employees, though with little intensity or resolution. At worst, this person will drift toward some inadequate version of the 'easy life' or toward the lowest level of kinetic existence, either as a bum on skid-row or a chronically inadequate inhabitant of a state mental hospital.

These people will tend to be on the gloomy, cheerless, and possibly somewhat irritable side. The rhythm of their being seems restrained and, in the extreme, might be experienced by others as a somewhat stifling dormancy and stagnation.

Other Attributes of Kidney Yang Deficiency

Anxiety is provoked by any situation in which a strong, aggressive show of sustained energy or the assumption of responsibility might be expected. This person may be phobic of people who have achieved success or those who might provide an opportunity which would lead to his/her own success. There is a profound, though mostly hidden, awareness of the inability to follow through in any area of endeavor; the fear of failure that might be evoked by some small success is enough to provoke the anxiety which we have already discussed. This deep sense of inadequacy will be accompanied inevitably by endless, lifelong fear.

A quality of *depression* and stagnation pervades this person's ambiance and existence throughout life. Major depression will generally occur somewhere in mid or later life, at a point where projective rationalizations of failures break down and the full flood of realization of inadequacy descends. Depression may also occur whenever there is a successful rebellion by those whom they have dominated, such as children or spouses. The nature of the depression tends to be endogenous, occurring in the involutional period with considerable psychomotor retardation and little insight.

Where Kidney yin is sufficient, *cognition* and intelligence may be adequate for clear logical thinking and good planning, lacking only the spark and mental energy for sustained application to specific tasks in order to overcome the inevitable obstacles. 'Brightness' and 'sharpness' will be missing. Thinking may also be dominated by an inner sense of inadequacy, the 'projection' of which places the problem outside, obviating the development of insight and the hope of seeking help.

Psychosis is primarily paranoid with projection of feelings of inadequacy and impotence and may occur as part of a major depressive episode when control over their small domain collapses.

There is little energy to sustain the active pursuit of close *love* relationships. When relationships do occur, they will be neglected on the level of intimacy since the latter involves the sharing of all those feelings of weakness that the deficient Kidney yang person does not wish to face. Instead, these relationships will be used as a vehicle to dominate and diminish other people in order to make the person himself feel superior.

There is a diminished ability to follow through in the *sexual* act, despite a strong need for sex as a means of bolstering one's ego. Eventually, there occur all the signs of the same impotence that pervades all areas of life. Following the failure to succeed in the adult sexual act, there may be possible sexual abuse of children. These acts may carry some threats of retaliation in the event of resistance, but lower energy levels generally reduce the risk of violence.

Bioenergetically, there will be some displacement upward, especially in those in whom the deficiency is not extreme. This manifests in slightly excessive muscular development in the upper part of the body as a compensation for feelings of inadequacy. There is more of an inflation of muscle than true development and therefore very little strength. The four limbs also lack appropriate power.

A Case of Physical and Mental Fatigue

A young man was referred because of profound physical and mental fatigue. He complained of poor memory, mental confusion, difficulty concentrating, spaciness, an erratic sleep cycle, agitation, irritability, and depression. His digestion was poor, with severe bloating after almost any meal and delayed bowel movements of up to four days. If he exercised, his knees and legs would weaken quickly, and he spent most of his days watching television. He had been this way since childhood.

His symptoms indicated a severe Spleen qi and yang deficiency, meaning that his digestive energies were not performing their functions of digestion, assimilation, transportation, and storage. In addition, Spleen energy which normally rises to the brain (glucose and oxygen) was unable to do so sufficiently to provide adequate mental function. However, Spleen qi and yang energies are generated by the fire at the gate of vitality *(ming men)* of Kidney yang, which is the basic metabolic heat of all the chemical reactions in the body (ATP). The early onset, the weakness of his knees, lack of drive, as well as extremely sluggish lower bowel all point to Kidney yang as the critical constitutional factor at fault. There was no dynamic energy in the foundation; indeed, his brother had similar, though less severe, symptoms; and his father was a hospitalized psychotic. In Western terminology he might have fallen into the cracks between schizophrenia, severe neurasthenia, and pervasive developmental disorder. I prefer the last since it coincides with the Chinese medical diagnosis of Kidney yang deficiency. This diagnosis includes weakened Kidney qi energies, which, as a unique combination of Kidney yin and yang, control growth and development. There were no indications of hallucinations or delusions to suggest a diagnosis of schizophrenia.

KIDNEY YANG EXCESS

Personality: Will and Drive

The person with Kidney yang excess energies will live, to a great extent, on his will and drive. If the other energies are likewise good, this will and drive may last through a long lifetime. If, for example, Kidney yin is deficient, the material essence to sustain this drive will be unavailable, and the person may be one of the many who burn brightly early in life and then 'burn out' at a very early age. The latter may occur in many areas, including creative, emotional, mental, and physical. The death of a corporate genius from a sudden and unpredictable heart attack in his early 40s may be explained by many models, including Type A Cardiac, cholesterol, free-radicals, clumping of platelets, and the wrong kind of prostaglandins. The fact that many who fit these descriptions live long lives leaves the final explanation to some other model. Excess Kidney yang (excess will), without the essence to back it up or the Heart energies to sustain the creative drive, will lead to this kind of burn-out. That is why so much of the therapy in 'alternative' medicine and in the treatment or prevention of burn-out emphasizes meditation. The mitigation of the will (ego) is intuitively understood as the goal and as a pre-requisite for avoiding or ameliorating the burn-out syndrome.

In the extreme, this person is experienced as a human dynamo, whose enormous drive cannot be entirely quenched through his own activities. Others are soon drawn into the frenzy, and there is little patience with those who do not accede to the driven pace. Thomas Edison, who rarely slept, drew toward himself a coterie of workers whose entire lives were centered around his work. This illustrates the dimension and direction we are considering. Like Edison, yang excess people tend to have an enormous self-confidence. Unlike him, however, some of them move in the direction of omniscience, sweeping along with them many who live in the illusion of absorbing the demagogue's puissance.

Like the classical demigod, this person's identification "with God" be-comes an identification "as God," of "being God," rather than "being one with God," as Eric Fromm reported the surrender of 60 million German egos to the will of one (Hitler) and called it *Escape From Freedom.* Loss of the distinction between one's own identity and God's evolves into an exag-geration of one's own assets at the expense of others'. The result is an egotis-tical, self-centered, self-obsessed, insufferably overbearing person who sees himself as the center of the universe, and obliterates the centers of all other selves, especially those less well-endowed or unwilling to worship him in his domain. The Kidney yang deficient individual becomes a petty tyrant, a demagogue. The Kidney yang excess person is a tyrant on a grand scale, al-ways overstepping the bounds and exercising power beyond his jurisdiction, often leading to failure.

We may think of this process as the introjection of the power of God without the love. It may be carried further by those who claim exclusive ac-cess to divine knowledge. The person with Kidney yang excess energies is overly involved in and concerned with the consequences of today's behavior on the future, to a degree which we would classify as superstitious. There-fore he may, along with his claim to divine knowledge, claim for himself the singular privilege of making prognostications about future cosmic events and draw to himself people who will shape their entire lives around these predictions at enormous sacrifice. Hitler promised Germany hegemony for a thousand years.

Since the circumscribed human perspective of God is one of unending perfection, the person who introjects the power of God without his love also projects all his own imperfections onto others. The denouement is the seemingly endless paranoia of our existence, expressed *for* all by the 'leader' in words (propaganda) and *by* all for the leader in action (war).

{129}

In the presence of these people, one feels a sense of strong attraction, magnetism, and stimulation, which in the extreme may have a boundless, overpowering effect (charisma).

Other Attributes of Kidney Yang Excess

Anxiety will be provoked by any circumstance that would temporarily contain or stifle the strong drive for power, especially over others. Those with Kidney yang excess are phobic of any situation or people associated with it in which passivity, inactivity, or the necessity of fitting into the routine of others is expected or imposed. *Depression* will be evoked by any mental, physical, or sexual impairment of their own power and drive or by the loss of power over others for any length of time. Depression will frequently be of the agitated variety, and suicide is a realistic possibility because of the high energy thrust and low frustration tolerance.

Because of their high energy drive, these people may be capable of, and even require, several *cognitively* demanding tasks at one time. These are the businessmen who may begin many enterprises simultaneously and frequently handle them well. In some instances, however, where the drive surpasses the innate mental capability, the result may be failure, severe disappointment, and depression. Paranoid *psychosis* with manic features may follow, and the individual may project onto the world his own need to drive himself and others and consequently feel controlled and driven by that world.

Love is felt for those who accede to their will, enhance their power, and serve their drive. Their 'love' will be available only as long as the partners meet these requirements — for themselves, and also that with which they identify, such as family, tribe, dynasty, or race. Power rather than pleasure is the dominant concern in these people. They generally have a strong drive toward *sexual* relations which may, because of the power issue, dispose them to promiscuity, especially if it is backed up by strong Kidney essence. Sexual perversions will be determined primarily by the need to dominate, to have others bend to their will. The act may involve abuse if their mastery is challenged, but power, not pain, will be the more important feature.

Bioenergetically, there will again be a displacement upward, with a greatly expanded and developed chest and head compared to the lower part of the body. With these people in particular there will be a very strong muscular development, a very thick neck, and frequently powerful shoulders and arms. However, there is a tendency to burn out at an early age, particularly if the excessive drive is not matched by sufficient Kidney essence.

A Case of Overstepping the Bounds

Although I have met people with these qualities in my practice, the person who immediately springs to mind is a man whom I have not seen in 43 years. We met at a university where the Air Force was training pre-pre-cadets. These were 300 of the most eager people I have ever known, bursting to fly against the Germans and the Japanese, and willing to do anything in order to reach that goal. There were five groups of 60 men engaged in the most fierce competition with each other to be the best. They competed with each other to paint the best 'butt' cans, to win on the field and in the classroom. During my group's five month stay, our first cadet leader was a graduate of a southern military school, a 'professional' college football player who had gone from college to college for 10 years, and an alcoholic. He lasted about three weeks. Then came Y. He was about 5'10" and 185 pounds of solid muscle; his neck had become as wide as his head as a result of standing on his head for an hour a day. Y. came from the midwest to play football for, and to graduate from, a prestigious East Coast university. He derided his father, who had only succeeded in creating the largest chain of furniture stores in the midwest, as a small-time operator compared to where he was going.

Presenting himself as a democratic "man of the people," he soon showed his ugly colors when the butt cans were not painted according to his high expectations. He drove our group to win the weekly competition, the prize for which was a free weekend pass. The latter we did only once, that I recall, when my friend Bill, a very bright engineering student, pulled us ahead with some high test scores. Y. gradually assumed more and more power. He began to consistently supersede the authority of the real officers. Even they were dazzled with his credentials but were forced to reluctantly relieve him of his exalted position after several incidents blatantly embarrassing to their leadership (which he had publicly usurped). He became just another pre-pre-cadet, while my friend Bill assumed a more rational command.

Each and every man wanted to become either a pilot, navigator, or bombardier. Only one man in six made it. The role of pilot was generally first choice since it was the most glamorous, that of commander of the plane he flew. We all assumed, as did Y. himself, that he would be a pilot and ultimately fly high enough to become God. When we moved to San Antonio for six weeks of exhaustive testing to obtain eligibility as aviation cadets in one of the above categories, Y. pushed once again and rose quickly to become Cadet Colonel of the entire base. And once again he increasingly overstepped the bounds of his authority until he assumed powers that were accorded only to the actual Commander of the base and had to be replaced and demoted.

{ 131 }

Kidney Qi Disharmony

Kidney qi is a function of the interaction of Kidney yin and Kidney yang energies. It represents the balance of the natural functions of the yin and the yang of the Kidneys for the purpose of supervising the growth, development, and reproduction of the organism. In terms of the absolute endowments of Kidney yin and yang, imbalances of varying degrees are the rule, not the exception. Kidney qi disharmony is, therefore, commonly encountered. As a balance, it assumes its own identity, both in terms of its broader natural functions in the evolution of being and in terms of the deficiency and excess of those natural functions. At the same time, clinical considerations of these issues will find us always in close proximity to those of the yin and the yang, because the qi is only an intrinsic blending of these polarities. The indispositions of the yin and yang will intertwine with those of the qi, and in those situations where elaboration of the disharmony of excess and deficiency of the qi are redundant, these indispositions will be omitted. Therefore the discussion of the qi may appear less exhaustive than the examination of the yin and yang energies, because we will include only that which is not already accounted for by the inevitable overlap.

Kidney Qi: Deficiency

Personality: Lack of Faith

The Kidney qi deficient person is one who is characterized by a lack of faith and such appurtenances of faith as awe, humility, acceptance, and surrender. The antithesis of faith is fear and endless, enervating, lifelong maneuvers to avoid the honest acknowledgement of that fear. This is a person who is afraid — afraid to 'be' — who, lacking faith in the silent power within himself and others, avoids the present and the authentic confrontation of strong, immediate feelings. Confrontation in a non-destructive interchange both depends on and engenders closeness. Since one can never completely know the heart of the 'other,' one lives on faith in their good intentions and faith in one's own ability to survive misplaced faith.

The need for closeness, which characterizes all mammals in varying degrees, cannot be gratified for this person who lacks faith. Instead he lives with internal conflict between longing and fear, often accompanied by the feelings of deadness characteristic of those who cannot permit themselves to experience the awe that renders life everlastingly wondrous. The inspiration for personal growth is therefore forestalled and underdeveloped.

Faith becomes an integral part of a human being when in childhood the people responsible for his survival, happiness, and self-esteem keep faith with him. These energies can be compromised by physiological insults and by the events of a previous lifetime. However, the paramount source of this lack of faith is, in my opinion, more the outcome of unfortunate early life experience than an innate deficit of Kidney qi energies.

Other Attributes of Kidney Qi Deficiency

- *Affect:* In some cases, the lack of humility, spiritual principles, and values that characterize this person may pave the way for the unrealistic assessment of limitations and assets characteristic of the arrogant ego. When this is combined with the fear described above, an ominously explosive condition exists in which the Kidney qi deficient person, when pushed to the extreme, may become dangerous. More often, in my experience, fear is the dominant and determining force mitigating the outward expression of audacity. Often this person will come to fear his own conceit, which tends to draw negative and dangerous responses from peers. His reaction may be to appear quite self-effacing. Closed off and inaccessible, unwilling to confront people directly, unable to look people straight in the eye, this seemingly flat-mannered person is nevertheless highly changeable, with unpredictable moods and sudden, often frightening shifts to rage and hate if thwarted.

- *Anxiety* in the form of general uneasiness will be provoked by any interpersonal situation which requires faith, trust, authenticity, and face-to-face confrontation, especially if an exposure of real and intimate feelings is involved.

- A major *depressive* episode will be evoked by a prolonged impediment to an expanding ego and, at the end of life, by spiritual impoverishment when facing the reality of the 'great unknown' without faith.

- *Cognition* lacks the brilliance that accompanies the integration of intuitive intelligence and will and is dominated by one to the relative exclusion of the other. A lack of faith in their own intrinsic intellectual powers, as well as lack of trust in those of others, will stifle cognitive advancement. We therefore will have either intuition going nowhere or dullness burying everything in its path. On the surface, this person may cover the difficulty by feigning an air of superiority and an appearance of condescending boredom.

{133}

– As a member of the Water family of energies, the tendency is for a *psychosis* to be paranoid. This is accompanied by considerable grandiosity and projection of this individual's own lack of faith; that is, he unjustly assumes others also lack faith in him. There is also projection of his own proclivity toward ruthlessness, making this person always fear sudden, unprovoked attack. Violent acting out is always a risk with people who are innately fearful, lack balance and limits, and are dissociated from their 'dark side.'

– Due to problems with 'intuitive intelligent will,' this person often lacks the intuitive judgment to choose partners realistically, thus tending to endlessly reinforce his lack of faith. *Love* is limited to the relatively safe formation of a pact with one other person, often a child, who is given immunity from the entire projective system. That one person, who willingly serves his egoistic needs, is seen as the only ally; it is "us two against the world."

– *Sex*, unadulterated by intimacy, may be the only secure means by which this person can funnel all of his otherwise unexpressed emotions. It is one of the few ways of making meaningful 'contact,' outside the above mentioned *folie-à-deux*, with a chosen partner. The sexual act therefore becomes so overdetermined and so heavily laden with otherwise unrealized emotion that it frequently results in impotence or premature ejaculation, to which this person is already vulnerable due to Kidney yin or yang deficiency. Lacking the mitigating human qualities of humility and reverence, this ruthless person may act out with unpredictable violence, perform rape, and be potentially dangerous if resisted.

– *Bioenergetically* there is a displacement upwards that tends to be dispersed. The face is very taut, the energy is used basically to control any facial disclosure of inner feelings, especially fear. The eyes are spiritless and blank, again obscuring disclosure of inner emotional states.

A Case of a Loser in Life

Mr. F. was a tall, frightened-looking, depressed man who came to see me asking urgently for help. Our meeting took place during the period of the Vietnam war, which he opposed. He was employed in a hospital as an assistant to a famous physician. In passing the pharmacy one day at the hospital, he had overheard a conversation in which people were discussing the killing of four students at Kent State University by National Guardsmen. The people in the room, including the director of the hospital, vehemently expressed the opinion that more should have been killed. Mr. F became terrified that he would be put into a concentration camp for expressing an opposing point of view. He immediately applied for a leave of absence from the hospital, which he now experienced as a dangerous place for him to be.

F. described himself as a "loser" in life. He had been intimidated by an older brother who forced him into a homosexual relationship until he was eighteen. This brother later became psychotic and lived for years in a mental hospital. Throughout his childhood both parents were invalids who had him sleep on a cot in the kitchen and who denigrated him in other ways. When he left home he turned to heterosexual relationships and married a woman who he said would never have gotten married "if someone like me hadn't come along." She was frightened by him sexually when he felt "strong" and she comforted him sexually when he was down. He had a natural talent for his work, demonstrated inventive abilities, and achieved considerable success in a very large company despite the fact that he had no formal education.

F. felt constantly cheated even by his own children. He trusted no one, saw the world as endlessly dangerous, and regarded people as always attempting to swindle him. Each moment with people was judged as if it were the first and the last, and none of the good ones left any permanent, positive legacy. He felt more comfortable with machines and had no friends or acquaintances except for his therapist, who was his only safe port. God did not exist and therefore could not be appealed to for comfort or security. In his home, and to his family, he was god and operated as a petty tyrant and unceasing critic of his wife and children.

F. would be correctly diagnosed as a paranoid personality by Western psychiatry. The fear that underlay this paranoia is a profound absence of faith in the reality of grace and goodness in the hearts of men, and the will of the gods. Without faith and awe there can be no joy and no safe place for him in the universe.

KIDNEY QI: EXCESS

Personality: Rigid and Conformist

The person whose Kidney qi energies are in excess is an intelligent, motivated person who, for a variety of reasons, has become heavily involved in esoteric dogma, to the exclusion of other considerations in his life and the lives of those around him. This exclusiveness takes on shades of fanaticism and rigidity. So deeply focused is he in his spiritual pursuits that significant consideration of past associations or future consequences fades into the background. Rigidity is expressed by a value system of inflexible principles, which allows for no dissension, personal initiative, or creativity and requires absolute conformity.

There are two general types. The first, in which the yin predominates, tends to be the rigid 'follower.' The second, where the person is more yang and endowed with a highly-developed 'intelligent will,' may become the charismatic focus of a 'religious' movement of any proportion. If the 'will' dominates the intelligence, there may be greater impulsiveness and a higher level of direct manipulation of people and events. Should the 'intelligence' predominate, we may find the master mind who fashions the plans that others execute. (This calls to mind George Bernard Shaw's well-known comment: "He who can, does, he who cannot, teaches" — the classic pedant.[9])

Those whose lives are dedicated to meditation may be highly advanced spiritual beings with well-developed egos. In our time, we have had many, especially the young, who attempt to escape the hard, painful labor that is prerequisite to the formation of a strong ego by making a premature retreat into meditation, humility, and faith. Mystical preoccupation has been too often an escape from the responsibilities commensurate with that part of the world's work which human beings must realistically assume. Faith does not obviate the reality that God indeed "helps those who help themselves." One cannot lose an ego (through meditation or any other means) which one has never had. For those without an ego, who are afraid and lack confidence, a profusion of awe may be followed by a condition of mental and emotional paralysis. Without strong ego 'boundaries,' meditation may become a conduit to a loss of touch with the human condition of earthly material reality and to severe mental illness. This might be expressed in Chinese medicine in terms of "the qi is wild." In the 60s and early 70s I treated many young people who became psychotic while doing *za zen* for hours or days in Zen monasteries in this country.

Other Attributes of Kidney Qi Excess

− There are two basic *affective* states: one, more yin, will have an other-worldly, spaced-out look, associated these days with the 'Moonie-type'; and the second, more yang, has the zealous, fire-in-the-eye, burning, penetrating expression. The former tends to have an angelic, passive, accepting quality, where the latter tends to have a more determined, insistent expression.

– *Anxiety* is provoked by any person or situation who tends to challenge or contradict the precepts that underlie the dogma. This anxiety may be relieved by the group support system. There is a phobia of people who are closely related by family or marriage. These are more likely to evoke strongly negative emotional reactions, such as anger and fear — emotions incompatible with an obsessional dogma that requires endless "love." Those excessively yang people who are predisposed to fire, hell, and brimstone may find that such contact with "close ones" evokes compassionate feelings that are not in keeping with their draconian precepts. In either situation, spontaneous emotional contact with intimate relations will be avoided.

– *Depression* is usually associated either with the collapse of a belief system or with rejection by the system or its leader.

– *Cognition* is conditioned by dogmatic tunnel vision, a rigidity that would view all phenomena under one theme. There will be mental blinders to any reality that may contradict the essential idea. Abstract and speculative thinking is rare, whereas obsessively concrete thinking abounds.

– As with all Water phase disharmony, the associated *psychosis* gravitates to paranoia. The more yang type of person may experience himself as the persecuted prophet of God, as exemplified by Jim Jones; the more yin type is the persecuted proselyte of the afflicted prophet.

– *'Universal love,'* as only they define it, is usually an impersonal, obsessional prescription for all of man's ills. Personal love is too much of a challenge to the euphoria evoked by the universal love pursued by the group. It is, of course, impossible in extended intimacy to avoid the entire range of emotions, including those which would be described as adverse. Euphoria does not long endure contention. Long-term commitments are therefore discouraged or highly formalized.

– If *sex* is to be permitted, it is encouraged to be adventitious, impersonal, and promiscuous, so that no close tie is established that could threaten individual commitment to the system (unless it can become part of the system). In some instances, in the interest of one's spiritual development, one may be permitted to engage in specialized

sexual practices. Where promiscuity is allowed or encouraged, any
and all kinds of sexual practices may ensue. At the other extreme {137}
are those wedded to God. Sexual fantasies of such a union are not
unknown, although the content is rarely reported, outside the protection of the confessional.

— *Bioenergetics* involves displacement of energy away from the 'root'
upward to the eyes; in the yang type, the fiery, zealous expression;
and for the yin, the spaced-out, other-worldly, dazed expression and
soothing, monotonous voice.

A Case of Fanatical Worship

The patient who comes to mind is the first I treated with acupuncture. With proverbial 'beginners luck' the results were fantastic. She
was a foreign woman, married to a professor, and in love with another
professor with whom she studied. A local psychologist made an emer-
gency referral to me following one of his groups in which she went into
a manic psychosis for three weeks, during which time she did not sleep.
As she spoke to me in her native language uninterruptedly and rapidly
for two hours, I sank into near despair. Providentially, I asked in my
halting French, "Voulez vous acupuncture?" (Do you want acupuncture?) To my amazement she sprang off the couch and onto the table.
Acupuncture did wonders for the mania and all of her other symptoms.
She slept for five hours in my office after the treatment. The problem
was a Water-Fire imbalance.

Then began the real problems with her husband, her lover, and
her child. These were sorted through over a period of time in which it
became clear that in all activities this woman was guided by the frantic
and fanatical worship of something or somebody. During some 11 other sessions the central theme was her complete helplessness and sense
of inadequacy. She came to realize that her claim that her husband kept
her captive was only a way of blaming him for her dependency. Despite
this realization and ongoing problems in the marriage, she continued
to be unable to break with her husband for several years. When she
finally left him, she became a follower of an Indian guru. During her
years of devotion she surrendered her daughter to her husband. Someone in an exalted sphere of spiritual authority was willing to relieve her
of the burden of handling her own inner disarray.

The last few sessions we had together took place four years later,
after she had been dismissed from the *ashram* to seek help for a chronic bronchitis and had been told not to come back until she was better.

> The members had offered her no help and had literally thrown her out with no place to go. She had long since broken with her husband and child and no longer had any family abroad. She again responded well to treatment but was last seen going from one to another of the guru's followers' houses for shelter and food, still devoted to her "teacher."

For an account of the more yang type of Kidney qi excess person, whom I have never seen in my practice, I refer the reader to the media where they continue to dominate the lives and pocketbooks of their yin counterparts.

9

The Wood Phase

The Natural Functions of the Liver Energy system

The Five Phases are the cycles of both the seasons of the earth and the seasons of human life. Wood is the phase of Spring, the east, and the rising sun; it is the reality of the gigantic forces that reawaken within the planet after their winter rest, the marshalling and ordering of the life force. Wood is the symbol of primeval rebirth; it represents the directional movement of existence itself ('being').

The Wood phase is well suited to its kinetic role in the life cycle of being. The Liver's function of storing the blood enables it to control the nourishment of the tendons and ligaments, the nervous system and major muscle systems, and all of the physical blandishments (ingredients) of action. The Wood phase is responsible for the 'unrestrained' free flow of the qi. The Liver possesses its own qi and enables the qi of other Zang-Fu (solid and hollow) organs to flow easily and smoothly. In Needham's terms, it creates an "easily workable" organism. Movement of energy is the *sine qua non* of action. The sensory organ most necessary for effective activity is the eyes, which are the 'openings' of the Wood phase. The Wood phase oversees all of the metabolic processes necessary to the anabolism and catabolism (building and breakdown) of being, with utilization of the 'pure' and detoxification of the 'impure.'

However, the Wood not only moves the qi, it also contains the qi that is responsible for the capacity of people to live together with frustration without acting on it in destructive ways. One way of looking at this is to characterize Wood yang as the moving qi and Wood yin as containing it.[1]

Activity may be considered from two points of view. One is the ability and the decision to move forward and act (Wood yang). The other is the capacity and decision to retreat and wait (Wood yin). The perfect solution in any one person is a balance of the two: the wisdom to know when to move and when to be still. Nature has put them together in the same energy system for maximum survivability.

Asking a small child to make decisions about where to place his allegiances is expecting a great deal from him. Nevertheless, children do make these decisions in enduring relationships with adults and siblings who have the child's life in their hands. Over time, patterns of advance or retreat develop that may be difficult for a growing person to change later when environmental circumstances change. Perhaps the most we can hope for is the ability to gradually learn survival through appropriate advance and retreat, so that later we have the flexibility to adjust realistically to new circumstances. This is indeed asking a great deal from any one person, especially when the early environment has Wood energies.

With respect to an individual's ability to advance or retreat expediently, there is another dimension to consider. The work of Chess and Thomas[2] 'scientifically' establishes the presence from birth of enduring, inherited patterns of response to inner and outer stimuli; this corresponds basically to what we translate from the Chinese as 'personality.' Their work is a valuable contribution to the controversy between 'nature and nurture,' in support of the former position. This study took place at a time when the pendulum had swung heavily toward 'nurture,' and it offers a balance toward 'nature.' I have always considered that both factors are important and that each individual bears a unique combination of the two.

These two aspects of Wood—the ability to advance, which is a yang function, and to retreat, which is a yin function—depend on both nature and nurture to determine their final configuration in any single individual. One value of Chinese diagnosis is the ability to sort out (through the use of the pulse, tongue, face color, and other diagnostic tools) the role and importance of each factor.

In existential terms, the Wood phase mobilizes the rebirth of life, of our 'spirit' on an earthly level, which we call 'soul' (animal soul). Wood phase energies direct the unconscious self, spirit, and soul toward purposeful, focused manifestation. If the antithesis of being is death, the suppression of being is rage. The psychic and physical problems associated with suppression of being do not ensue from passing or fleeting emotions. A momentary anger, fully understood and expressed when someone misplaces a favorite possession, or the sadness one might experience when one sees a dead animal on the road, or the grief for the loss of a loved one are healthy energy dynamisms. These emotions are syntonic with being and the assertion of being. The disharmony of Wood energies concerns itself with major and enduring dislocations of natural law, with energy dynamisms which are dystonic to the evolution of the life force.

GENERAL DISHARMONY OF THE WOOD ENERGY SYSTEM

The destruction of Wood energies may occur constitutionally or congenitally, as well as during the process of living. The rare constitutional Wood problems are usually yang deficiency (weakness of yang) rather than weakness of yin; and either may be of congenital origin. A middle-aged patient I recently saw had a Liver pulse suggesting that she had a severe yin condition from very early in her life. Questioning revealed that her mother was an alcoholic and drank excessively during pregnancy. This person was unable all her life to 'surrender' and felt an unending resentment that always sought someone or something to which to attach itself. She was perpetually discontented and angry. Yang deficient people are, from birth, unable to assert themselves and are excessively compliant. They are often angry with themselves because they cannot stand up for themselves in a disagreement with another person, and, as a result, become depressed and suicidal. Another such patient learned, after detailed questioning of her parents, that her mother had severe, uncontrolled 'toxemia' during pregnancy.

The insults to the Wood in this age of refined foods, recreational drugs, pollution, and prescription drugs are incalculable. It is my feeling that, more than any other organ system, the Wood phase is increasingly constitutionally impaired by the abuse of these substances on the part of both sexes, especially by pregnant women.

In terms of disharmony, I will deal first with impediments to the yin functions of Wood (the ability to retreat) and then with impediments to the yang functions of Wood (the capacity to assert).

BIOENERGETICS AND WOOD PHASE DISHARMONY

Bioenergetics is being discussed in this introduction to Wood energies because the picture of disharmony from this point of view seems surprisingly uniform, considering the panorama of widely varying characterological states we find.

After the work of Reich, bioenergetics is the principal psychology to systematically demonstrate the inseparability of body and mind, and it is a Western medical discipline unique in integrating concepts of energy into its psychology and physiology. In these two ways, bioenergetics and Oriental medicine have a common bond and have much to contribute to each other.

Bioenergetically, the person who becomes 'stuck' in the Wood phase of energy and psychological development is described as the masochistic personality. According to Alexander Lowen, "Every true masochistic character shows the condition known as muscle bound ... like the crushing strength of the gorilla ... the aggressive drive is bent inward."[3] Lowen goes on to describe a parent-child relationship characterized by an emphasis on caring in the material sense, such as food and/or toilet training. "Attention to the material needs of the child with disregard for its tender feelings or spiritual needs creates a masochistic problem."[4] Lowen quite correctly portrays the parent-child relationship as one in which the parent has little respect for the child's individuality and privacy (physical and emotional), leading to deep feelings of humiliation. Though some children are too weak to offer any resistance, many become oppositional, rebellious, and spiteful towards authority, leading to the passive-aggressive personality. Lowen's 'masochistic personality' has many characterological features of what has more recently been referred to as the 'narcissistic personality.'[5] The issues of autonomy and assertion often overlap, which has created confusion with nosology. This 'narcissistic personality' is also quite different from the one that I describe in Chapter 11, "The Earth Phase."

The masochistic character is distinguished by suffering and unhappiness, expressed by complaining. The life force has turned inward upon itself, and the person is unable to let love in or out, which is the source of the suffering. Whining is a restorative gesture enabling the person to let something out which provokes some response, often a violent one, and to maintain contact and experience aggression. The life force asserts itself inwardly; self-aggression results in self-depreciation and self-damage.

Lowen has described the energic characteristics of the person whose being has been stifled by materialistic, rather than enhanced by spiritual, considerations of sensitivity to basic individual needs. The outer-defensive *wei* energy becomes turned against the inner-nourishing *ying* energy. The former expresses itself in the musculature and the latter in the tender emotions of love and affection. In the 'masochistic' passive-aggressive character, the musculature blocks the expression of tender emotions. The musculature over-develops, especially in the neck, where it represents spite, and in the legs and thighs, where it prevents the full expression of sexual pleasure. The entire body tends to become muscle-bound and contracted. The tender feelings, which are expressed on the front, soft underbelly, are crushed and unable to move or be expressed by the overdeveloped defensive mechanism of the back. All of this musculature in the back, neck, thighs, and legs is in a state of tension useful only for containing, crushing, and hiding being, not for the agile movement of the athlete. The entire body and psyche are in a state of contraction, heavily weighed on the bottom. (The heavier material energy, or *zhi qi*, is associated with the Water or Kidney organ system, in contrast to the lighter spiritual, or *hun* energy, which is associated with Fire or the Heart organ system). As a result, the tender feelings are "compressed between the arms of aggression and thus bound." A feature of this personality is the consistent attempt to break being out of this prison and the equally consistent failure, resulting in recurring collapse and despair. Beneath these renewed attempts is a feared sense of hopelessness. The place between the hope and the hopelessness, where the masochistic character finds himself, has been described as a "morass" of impotent rage, from which the person may find temporary release in the form of punishment, either emotional or physical. Pain may lead to crying as a momentary, but life-saving, release of the tension that builds between a drive 'to be' and a fear of 'being,' and that, for the masochistic personality, is also associated with a fear of rejection and humiliation.

[143]

Whereas the above picture is most often associated with the Wood yang deficient state, I have found it to describe equally well all of the other Wood energy conditions of disharmony, especially the Wood yin deficient state. The critical issue is movement and direction. The Wood yin deficient person is unable to retreat. The Wood yin excess person can move, but only in one direction, away. The Wood yang excess person can move, but only forward. The single underlying factor is flexibility (or, in Needham's terms, "workability"). The masochistic body seems either to reflect the lack of movement, as in Wood yin and yang deficiency, or an attempt to contain movement, to maintain homeostasis, as in Wood yin and yang excess.

DREAMS AND WOOD PHASE DISHARMONY

My information regarding *dreams* is insufficient to provide us with material for more than a general statement about the Wood phase. Most of it is from clinical experience, some from my various teachers, and is limited to dreams associated with the constriction of the assertion of being.

These dreams are usually classified as nightmares and contain a great deal of anger and violence. Frequently, the dreams are characterized by impotence as, for example, those — especially in men — where the dreamer attempts to shoot a gun at an approaching enemy and the shells drop out of the end of the barrel or bounce harmlessly off the intended target. In other instances, the person is unable to raise his arms for defense. In women, I have more often encountered dreams in which all of their teeth have fallen out, as in the instance of the young woman to be described under Wood yang deficiency, whose being had been massively invalidated by her family. The loss of teeth renders women defenseless and impotent, since they traditionally defend themselves with their nails and teeth. In some dreams, people try to call for help and cannot make a sound. This is another expression of the general feeling of impotent, ineffectual paralysis. In the healthy person, in whom 'becoming' is no problem, dreaming during the Gallbladder hours (described as 'delta sleep') often involves the unconscious process of problem-solving. Many people have had the experience of going to sleep with a decision to make, or plans to develop, and awakening with the answer. A classic example is Von Stradonitz's dream in which the configuration of the circular benzene molecule was revealed to him as an image where a series of snakes were entwined, forming a ring. Others have found that dreaming during these night hours will provide them with spiritually enhancing experiences that may be considered cleansing. These are the hours and the real organs of the life of the unconscious mind.

A distinction should be made between recurrent nightmares and those which occur sporadically, in clusters. The latter are, I believe, most often related to sudden, and relatively isolated, episodes of suppressed emotion, in which case the qi is trapped in the Liver, and the Liver is 'full.' Recurrent nightmares are engendered by chronic problems in other organ systems, as well as the Wood organ system. The other organ systems express their unconscious selves through the Wood system due to its prominence on the Chinese clock during the sleeping hours (11 P.M. to 3 A.M.), when the unconscious is supreme.

Deficiency in the qi of the Liver is said to result in dreams of "lying under a tree and being unable to rise." Forests, trees, "grass and sprouting wheat" are other common symbols in dreams related to the Liver organ system, which belongs to the Wood phase and the spring season. I have already referred to dreams containing impotent acts of assertiveness in people with passive-aggressive personalities and 'masochistic' character structure. Lying under a tree and being unable to move is representative of such impotence, as well as the entire spectrum of psychomotor retardation associated with depression, which is the principal affective component of suppressed being.

Deficiency of the qi of the Gallbladder is said to give rise to dreams of suicide. Perhaps this is related to the role of Gallbladder as decision-maker in the pantheon of ego functions assigned to the five organ systems. Those of us who have been involved with the care of the 'mentally ill' have observed the sudden lifting of mood in depressed people who shortly thereafter make serious suicide attempts. These decisions seem to arise spontaneously and may conceivably he made first on an unconscious level during the hours when the Gallbladder, the decision-maker, is in energic ascendancy. Sleep and dreaming are, of course, not confined to Liver-Gallbladder time. Nevertheless, the Liver-Gallbladder organ systems are the primary, if not exclusive, providers of access to the unconscious, through which much of what we refer to in that mode of experience is mediated.

The states of excess may be either of a constitutional or compensatory nature. These can be distinguished from one another primarily by history. The constitutional excess will be present consistently from birth. The compensatory excess will arise later and be less persistent and more intermittently reactive as a restorative response to the more primary deficiencies. For instance, a primarily Wood yin deficient person who is unable to retreat may draw upon Wood yang to bolster and camouflage this inability; with a show of assertiveness he will attempt to convince himself and others that, rather than being unable to retreat, he is actually able to be aggressive.

Wood Yin

A great deal has been written and said in the East about the ability to withdraw, especially as it relates to the surrender of the ego. Lao Tzu said "Bend, and ye need not break."[6] Little has been said in the West to this effect; Christ's admonition to "turn the other cheek"[7] stands alone as a related dictum in our world, a dictum which we have rarely practiced.

In the East, individuals, if not nations and social structures, have more often lived as well as talked this way. The voluntary surrender of the ego is perhaps man's most difficult task. An example which has always stayed with me is Tolstoy's depiction of Kutuzov, the Russian general in charge of the army during the Napoleonic invasion. The Tsar had invited many famous German generals to run his campaign. In their obsession with military maneuvers, they were always soundly beaten by Napoleon, who simply attacked while the others theorized. Kutuzov was the perfect opponent for Napoleon. He slept through all the planning, and, at the end of every conference, he ordered a retreat. His ego did not require a great military victory over Napoleon. He simply let Napoleon defeat himself, employing only passive resistance, such as burning crops and destroying livestock. "General Winter and General Hunger defeated Napoleon,"[8] and this was quite enough for the wise old Kutuzov. His Wood yin was free and strong.

WOOD YIN DEFICIENCY

Personality: Retreat is Impossible

We all know the yin deficient, or yin blocked, personality. His ego is always on the line, always the prime consideration, and, in any controversy, retreat is impossible. Retreat means defeat and humiliation. He has no choice but to stand, to meet force with force, to struggle and fight, even when such behavior is totally self-destructive. This does not mean that he is truly assertive or aggressive. He may not be actually looking for a fight, but he is nonetheless unable to back down from one. Every 'provocation' is the scene of an engagement. Acceptance, surrender, withdrawal, and strategic retreat are not options.

Throughout his life, this person is in endless difficulty with authority, as well as peers. He is considered to have a chip on his shoulder and is always contentious because he cannot let any issue rest.

Other Attributes of Wood Yin Deficiency

Anxiety is aroused by challenges made to his territorial ego. The remotest possibility that anyone would attempt to subjugate him arouses 'fight,' not 'flight.' As time goes on, this person remains in a constant state of readiness, anticipating domination in all relationships. This outlook may lead to various shades of feelings of persecution, though frank paranoid *psychosis* is rare, except in old age, with abject loss, or during a 'major depressive episode.' A profound retreat into catatonia could occur.

Affect will tend to be on the serious side, since being on guard is an ongoing necessity. There is no room for relaxation and lightness. Though innately capable of humor, which may reveal itself at rare times when he feels safe, it will not be easily evoked.

Depression manifests whenever he senses, or experiences, irrevocable defeat and humiliation. Denial cannot long put off the realization that neither he nor anyone can always, or even often, win. Since it is all or nothing at all, eventually a sense of total failure may emerge, especially in the form of a 'major depressive episode' during the 'involutional' period.

Depression may also be a welcome retreat from the incessant struggle. It is experienced as an outside force, a chemical imbalance, from which his ego is completely detached. Here depression is an acceptable retreat, difficult to approach with insight therapy but generally self-limiting, with the person emerging when he is rested from the wars. Medication is acceptable to this person as further proof that the depression is an exogenous force, a disease unrelated to his character and life. Even in retreat, these 'dysthymic' disorders are characterized by agitation. It is difficult for these people ever to relax and rest.

The rigidity of the entire character structure permeates all aspects of personality, including cognitive style or thought processes. The mind that cannot retreat is unable to rest and will never know the tranquility requisite to depth, clairvoyance, and creative awareness. This mind and its products will become old before its time and will lose its freshness and value to itself and to the world.

All relationships are poisoned by this inability to retreat, to give way, beginning in childhood with parents and surrogate authority. The person's *love* relations are stormy, including his relationships to children (especially adolescent children, with whom parents can no longer 'win'). Closeness always carries with it the threat of being 'swallowed' by the 'other' and must therefore always be avoided, often by creating bogus issues to assure distance.

Sex will also be extremely threatening for both male and female; the partner's assertion of his or her sexuality will feel like a threat that must be met or avoided. The Wood deficient person will feel comfortable in regular sexual relationships, as in life generally, only when he is in complete control. Perversions will tend therefore to center around situations of a sadomasochistic variety, probably masochistic, since the innate need to give in may find expression only in areas of life which tend to be hidden from view and linked to other forbidden fruits, such as sex. Extremes are rare. Since he is emotionally rigid, the normal expression of bioenergetic patterns will tend to be fixed in a forward or neutral position. Flexibility will be limited in all directions.

Bioenergetically, the Wood stagnant person falls into the masochistic group and is, in a sense, tortured by his own inability to break out of the muscular shell (see Lowen). Despite stubbornness, this person tends in the end to collapse, often in the form of a physical illness from which he can be thoroughly detached emotionally. Retreat (defeat) in this form may come as an acceptable and most welcome respite and is often periodic, as mentioned in the discussion of depression. Even in illness, this individual remains restless and often for this reason cannot accept the required rest. This is commonly seen in coronary patients, who often suffer an early recurrence because of their inability to retreat and repair.

Whereas he may appear strong on the surface, the underlying lack of nourishment to ligaments, tendons, and muscles due to Wood yin deficiency leaves him unable to sustain musculoskeletal exertion or to recover energy once he tires.

A Case of Constant Battle

M. was a woman with one child who, at the time I saw her, was teaching in an untenured position, despite having graduated with honors from a superb school. She had been separated from her wealthy husband some years before, at which time they had been engaged in a lucrative business which he suddenly destroyed when he left her for another woman. She had been the 'brains' of the organization and he the front man. She was left penniless and took the first job offered her in order to support her child and herself. This marked the beginning of years of court battles to obtain a divorce and support.

From the beginning, her husband rejected the child. During visits the child was abused and forced to sleep on the floor of his mansion. While the fight about money and custody dragged on for years, the child pleaded with his mother not to send him to his father, but she sent him over and over again because she was determined to force her ex-husband to act like a real father. Even years later when this man appeared in court and told the judge that "I resign from fatherhood," she continued forcing the child to call his father and ask for visits. No argument by lawyers, friends, family, or physician could convince her that she was sacrificing her child. She could not give up her mission to make the ex-husband into a real father.

Financially she wanted many times more than the amount her ex-husband offered as a settlement. After many years she had still received nothing, due to his ability to pay lawyers to delay court appearances and allocations. When a sizable offer was made, she refused and decided instead to continue the battle which had drained both her and her child. When last seen she was off to prepare more court papers, angry that I had caused her a five minute delay, even though the energy and time she had already put into this battle had cost her a career and the physical and mental health of both herself and her child.

Her final words to me were that she was going to continue the struggle and the sacrifice until she had succeeded in making her ex-husband a responsible man. That was her mission when she married him, and a strategic retreat in favor of a productive life for her and her child was unthinkable.

WOOD YIN EXCESS

Personality: Forever Withdrawing

The Wood yin excessive personality is forever withdrawing from the exigencies of life's battles and makes retreat a virtue. This may be the extremely pacifistic person who sees no value to struggle in any form, except perhaps to struggle against struggle. Turning to Jesus' admonition to "turn the other cheek,"[9] he embraces this message as a false rationalization for his entire life. Affect is characteristically placid, showing little variation, with a low, soft voice, great hesitation to show any strong emotion, and with a tendency toward obsequiousness.

I am not referring here to the Gandhis and Martin Luther Kings of the world who struggle non-violently. In contrast, our subjects are people who martyr themselves to the aggressions of any and all who pass their way, and either actively or inadvertently find this pacifism useful to their short or long-term needs.

The mythology which includes the story of Atlantis also tells of another great island empire that existed in the Pacific Ocean at about the same time. It was inhabited by people called the Lemurians, who lived underground and were extremely passive. The genetic remnants of that long-extinct civilization would contain personality attributes similar to those people whom I am here describing as Wood yin excessive.

Other types of personality, such as the schizoid, also have retreat as a prominent feature. However, the difference is that the Wood yin excessive person exhibits none of the cold aloofness and preference for 'splendid isolation' which characterizes the schizoid. He is naturally warm and friendly, giving and gentle. In this world he does not survive easily without support and protection, and he will often be found in those rare places in society that offer both, such as some monastic orders.

Other Attributes of Wood Yin Excess

Any situation that requires a struggle, aggression against another, or the need to show outward force will elicit *anxiety*. Aggression against self is acceptable if not desirable. Attempts may be made to avoid trouble at all costs, but the principal fear is of his own aggression. This fear may escalate to panic and beyond, into chronic phobic conditions involving the necessity for either verbal or physical aggression or assertion.

The necessity to injure even a fly might evoke a deep hurt and pain. If this were part of an ongoing, unavoidable situation, either with himself as the aggressor or someone else as the victim, it might evoke a strong emotional withdrawal. This kind of *depression* is a form of silent protest, a statement of not wishing to be part of something over which, however, he has no control. I observed this in medical school when course material required people to perform experiments on animals.

Cognitively, the tendency to withdraw one's thoughts from, rather than advance them into an interchange in the larger arena of other people's thinking will inhibit this person's development through loss of stimulation and render thinking stale and repetitive.

Psychosis would express itself in catatonic states of immobility, the ultimate state of retreat short of death. This would be the natural tendency on the part of Wood yin excessive people, when and if the threat to their existence seemed very real and the alternatives for resolution seemed impossible.

One aspect of *love* is the unconditional acceptance of another person even at times when one is engaged in an active interchange of sometimes necessarily unpleasant thoughts and feelings. To the extent that such an interchange is required, the Wood yin excessive person will experience great difficulties with intimate relationships.

Whereas the tendency to retreat may have some advantages in certain tantric/taoist *sexual practices* (where, in fact, it is not retreat but 'alertly relaxed retention'), retirement is generally not traditionally associated with successful sexual encounters. This quality militates against frequent and exciting sex. It is more acceptable and forgivable in women, who are associated with receptivity, and it may even be considered a desirable female trait by men who are afraid of sexually assertive women. In our time of sexual 'liberation,' however, passivity may be considered a desirable male trait particularly by those women who need the challenge of a passive man or by those who are afraid (often for good reason) of an assertive, aggressive, or insensitive male. As with Wood yin deficiency, the mode is sadomasochism, either as a victim or a tyrant or both. Since with perversions one tends to get the less dominant aspect of the personality than is generally encountered, one would probably uncover sadistic fantasies, if not activities.

As with all stagnation in the Wood phase, *bioenergetically* the inclination will be toward what Lowen has described as the masochistic body structure. The excess yin and surfeit of blood in the Liver will create an edematous condition (swelling) in the musculoskeletal system, which will make that system sluggish and less capable of acting quickly and effectively. For someone whose tendency is retreat, this is not extremely significant, though, as with all handicaps, it will take its psychological toll on some level.

This phlegmatic condition is somewhat ameliorated by the tendency of this group to eat sparingly as an inherent existential expression of their tendency toward prudence and non-aggression.

Children with Wood Yin Excess

The personality traits which have just been described are more obvious in children than in adults who may have learned that it is unwise to reveal themselves in this aggressive world. During the years that I worked as a child psychiatrist I encountered many children who were so constituted. They were described by their parents as "easy children," highly malleable, easy to "train." In the playground, or even with younger siblings, they characteristically gave way in any encounter involving territory or possessiveness. If attacked they simply lay down. I recall one child who, upon seeing another with whom he frequently played approach the playground, would lie down on the ground. When asked why, he replied, "Well when P. gets here I am going to be down anyway." At a younger age when these two children encountered each other in passing baby carriages, S. would allow P. to board his carriage and remove whatever items took his fancy. They were of equal size and only three days apart in age, from similar backgrounds, and with appropriately aggressive parents.

Many of these children were later a frustration to their parents because they required constant pressure to move ahead whenever they met obstacles in life. Usually they preferred activities that did not involve many people and gravitated toward other children with similar proclivities. Today computers have become the ideal retreat for the more active, and of course television for the more passive. Eventually, with parental or other guidance, these children may find a niche in life that requires little assertiveness and in which they perform tasks which remove them from the day to day strife of competitive life. In these positions they feel no frustration from lack of advancement. They are not, in Thoreau's words, the ones who are leading "lives of quiet desperation."[10] Without the good fortune of wise counseling, their families and spouses may, on the other hand, be endlessly vexed.

WOOD YANG

With regard to the evolution of being: the will to assert is Water yang, the nourishment to assert is Earth, and the means to assert is Wood. The function of Wood yang energy in this regard is to balance the Wood yin's capacity to retreat and wait with the ability to advance and act. The disharmony of Wood yang centers around the failure to perform this function at the appropriate time and place, with the appropriate person, and with appropriate execution.

The drive to be is characteristic of living things generally and in people reaches its zenith in the organism whose Wood energies provide it with a strong, supple musculature, adequate blood storage, an integrated nervous system, and good eyesight for the greatest physiological potential. It is this remarkable strength which, in the masochistic character structure, becomes turned against itself and becomes a prison of contracted muscle mass rather than a springboard for being. The depth of the suffering is only a measure of the potential for ecstasy.

The Wood yang deficient syndrome may take two general forms: one has a primarily physical origin, the other arises out of life struggle. The former may be a constitutional deficiency or a Wood yang deficient condition based on severe Wood disease due to infection (hepatitis, mononucleosis), drugs (marijuana), or other toxins.

The principal focus of this discussion will be the Wood yang deficient condition arising due to unfavorable early interpersonal relationships, which divert the constitutionally healthy Wood energies from normal pathways. The syndrome produced by this life struggle is still by far the more common and important one for our consideration here. However, in a world increasingly contaminated by chemicals, this balance may shift to the physiological rather than the psychological cause of Wood yang deficiency in the foreseeable future.

Individuals with Wood yang deficient conditions of physical origin may retain the visions of the future which they formulated before their physiological disability, and on this level express considerable will and drive. They are unable to make the decisions and the plans to move the visions into action. The Wood does not burn. These persons tend to be phlegmatic, poor achievers, and are unable to mount sufficient energy on their own to finish anything they begin, without a great deal of outside support and push. They account for one part of the population of 'underachievers,' since they may often be quite intelligent. The Wood yang deficient physical syndrome is to be seen with increasing frequency in a toxic world. It deserves a fuller discussion.

WOOD ENERGIES FROM BIRTH TO THREE YEARS

Beginning with movement in the womb, the Wood phase is intrinsically related to the neuro-musculoskeletal manifestations of being. Wood energies administer and engender the entire range of psychomotor development, from the first movements in utero to the final gasp. However, this motor activity reaches its most crucial psycho-social encounter from birth to approximately the age of three. During this period, the response of the parent to the rapid and explosive advances in the psychomotor development of the growing child is crucial to the fate of its Wood energies and to the assertion of its being. It is also the critical period when yang energies can easily be obstructed. During this period the body says "yes" and moves out with enormous energy and curiosity. Verbally it says "no" to any constraint or obstruction. But the parent who cannot tolerate or make room for this natural state of affairs, being bigger and stronger, can succeed to a significant degree in forcing the child to inhibit itself, to stagnate its own Wood qi. The conditions for being will always be compromised so long as our lives are dominated by considerations of power rather than love. The struggle between a parent's ego and a child's unique life force renders 'being' a brutal battleground. The aftermath of the battle can be crippled affect, behavior, and personality.

{ 153 }

Any inhibition of psychomotor functions on a sufficient and consistent scale will produce disharmony. Although this usually occurs in early childhood, it can occur in a repressive relationship at any time in life. By inhibition, we mean the denial, either consciously or unconsciously, of the reality of self. Whenever we are forced to pretend to ourselves, for whatever reason, that we are other than who we are, we are dealing with inhibition. Some years ago I worked with a young woman who had a great dramatic flair, a fine singing voice, and a sense of the theatrical. Her family was threatened by these qualities and labeled her as both sick and bad for being herself. At the beginning of our contact, she could relate only to my dog, because the only living thing which had ever accepted her for herself was the family dog. Slowly we worked toward an acceptance of herself as the 'good me,' and she achieved a state of being which was real and comfortable. The denial in this instance was not so severe as to obviate correction.

The 1945 investigation by American sociologists into early child development in Japan uncovered child rearing practices that led to the inhibition of Wood yang energies. From birth, in the traditional Japanese family, the infant was switched with a heated rod whenever it inadvertently expressed a negative look or sound towards the father, and if it was female, toward any male in the family. By one year of age, the male infant was completely unable to show any form of hostility or defiance toward the father figure, and the female infant toward any male. That part of being had been completely eliminated as a meaningful issue in the life of that person, and it was extended naturally to all authority, especially to the emperor. Up to the end of World War II, the doors of mental hospitals in Japan were made of rice paper. Violence in the mentally ill was unknown. Mental illness was defined almost as any thought or action which questioned authority, especially of the state, and particularly of the emperor, that is, any spontaneous assertion of individual being.

The inhibition of the assertion of being is expressed by the Chinese as an "impedance of the free flow of qi" (for which flow the Wood phase is responsible), leading to stagnant or 'noxious' qi. The inhibition of assertion of being generates the most profound state of impotence which, in most mammals, leads invariably to rage. The vicissitudes of this rage ('noxious' qi) are manifold, depending on many variables of constitution and conditioning. On an energy basis, which is the essence of our orientation, rage and 'noxious' qi are synonymous in cause and effect.

Superficially, the dilemma of the Wood yin excessive and Wood yang deficient persons may seem similar. Whereas both have a problem with assertion, the Wood yang deficient person is being inhibited from assertion, while the Wood yin excessive person has no desire to be aggressive to begin with. The former condition comes from life, the latter from constitution.

WOOD YANG DEFICIENCY

Personality: Passive-Aggressive

The character structure which develops around enduring impotent rage is the passive-aggressive personality. The principal feature of this person's life is passive resistance as an expression of opposition to the blocking of evolving being. Unable as a child, or as a prisoner in any other sense, to oppose openly, he is forced to oppose covertly. Passive resistance is expressed through a variety of maneuvers meant to frustrate and undermine the enemy in such a way that the enemy is unable to act directly against the perpetrator. Accidents which inadvertently destroy the enemy's property (the adolescent 'totals' Dad's car), procrastination, misplacement of valuable property ("Where is my screwdriver?"), and the classic headache every time the husband or wife wants to make love are some examples. Other behaviors include stubbornness, argumentativeness, and even temper tantrums, all of which are meant to evoke in the 'enemy' the same feelings of impotent rage felt by the passive-aggressive 'victim.' Stealing, lying, running away, and truancy are all part of this picture. It can be summed up in one word: spite.

Whereas passive-aggressive responses characterized by irritability, irascibility, and subtle opposition are the most common, the opposite may also occur in people who have varying degrees of impulse control problems from other sources. These other sources, coexisting with the main manifestation of 'noxious' qi, may include subtle minimal brain damage or epileptic equivalent disorders.

Within the framework of the Five Phase system, the phase controlling Wood (Metal) may be weak and fail to maintain impulse control. I believe that another factor in determining whether character structure is more passive or aggressive is the integrity of the Kidneys. A weak 'mother,' the Water phase, may be unable to sustain the Wood yin. If the heat (from deficiency) in the Liver drains the Kidney yin quickly, then one may see more aggression than passivity because both Water yang and Wood yang will increase, leading to a 'flaring up of the fire of the Liver' and a more hypertensive picture, both mentally and physically. The ensuing hyperactivity of Wood yang may be another reason for poor impulse control. The condition of the Fire phase will also affect the outcome in terms of its ability to handle the excessive heat from the Wood yang. Other relationships between the phases may be relevant theoretically but are less obvious clinically. I am, therefore, including some of the childhood conduct disorders, both the aggressive and non-aggressive, in my discussion, as well as the adult disorders of impulse, which may lead to extremes of violence.

Other Attributes of Wood Yang Deficiency

Anxiety takes several forms when the assertion of being is suppressed. Primarily there is a phobia against direct assertion or aggression. Any situation that exposes a Liver yang deficient person's being to the world in an assertive role precipitates terror through the threat of humiliation, the same humiliation experienced when one's essential being is denied by those required by nature to validate it (parents, teachers). This is the fundamental experience of the inhibition of the assertion of being. Direct exposure is most clearly identified with fear. Speaking in public, oral examinations, observation at work, and any social occasion in which direct assertion is involved provokes anxiety. The deep-seated fear is of humiliation. Secondarily, there is guilt. Some forms of guilt are expressions of anxiety about the assertion of being. Whether the disapproval associated with guilt feelings comes from within or without, anxiety is the direct result of a fear of disapproval for having existed. Some of the guilt may also be a consequence of 'being bad,' arising from the spite mentioned above. Spite is an uncomfortable emotional state which feels bad and with which the person eventually identifies. 'Feeling bad' becomes 'being bad,' evoking guilt, shame, and fear of exposure. Both kinds of guilt may be the unconscious rationale for the inevitable masochistic suffering and torture of self and others which must follow 'not being.'

Cognition associated with the Wood phase has traditionally been connected to decisions and planning. The Gallbladder has been the decision maker, and the planner has been the Liver organ system. On the Chinese clock, the Gallbladder (11 P.M. to 1 A.M.) precedes the Liver (1 A.M. to 3 A.M.). Decisions should logically precede planning, and so they do in the Chinese system.

Alteration in cognition reflects alterations in character. The passive-aggressive personality, the tortured, spiteful masochistic character thinks in a tortured and spiteful fashion. We find, therefore, that the spite is expressed in negativity and vengeance and the torture in ambivalence. Ambivalence is the cognitive projection of the 'morass', the stagnation of the impasse between the assertion of being and the suppression of that assertion. Negativity and vengeance is the restorative mechanism with which an entity can maintain the movement necessary to life, without directly threatening that life with the assertion it has come to associate with psychological and even physical death. Ambivalence means indecision, and negativity undermines plans that do possibly unfold. The terror is that of an assertion of being; and the object is to keep moving but go nowhere. Cognition assumes these characteristics, and all thought is contaminated with obsessive vengefulness.

Negativity is a perfect cultural medium for *depression.* With the repression of Wood yang energies comes the entire spectrum of emotions associated with the interference in assertion of being. Low grade irritability, angry withdrawal, and muffled agitation are characteristic of this type of depression, which may be expressed by excessive smoking or overeating. These states also tend to come and go and depend a great deal on how things are going in the outside world. Underneath are feelings of worthlessness, self-depreciation, inadequacy, and low self-esteem, since the Wood yang inhibited person cannot be himself and because he senses that something important is missing. Guilt is also a prominent emotion, as I explained above in the discussion of anxiety. In both men and women there may be rare, explosive outbursts of anger or crying, the latter more especially in women. Suicide is most often fantasized as a violent act (pointed out by Ted Kaptchuk[11]) such as driving into another car or a tree.

With negativity having exhausted all interpersonal relationships, *psychosis* may ensue from prolonged isolation. Under these circumstances, negativity may reach an extreme and become life-threatening. On the other hand, should suppressive forces be weakened and real or imagined humiliations be experienced, the result could be unanticipated violence.

A large part of the suffering experienced by these people is due to their inability to express *love,* which has come to be associated with manipulation and humiliation. The price for it was too high. The message is: "You can make me do what you want, but you cannot make me love you." To quote Lowen: "The aggressive drive is bent inward, as if huge pliers had been applied to the two ends of the organism. As a result, the tender feelings are compressed between the arms of aggression and bound."[12] Assertion, which is suppressed in the Wood yang deficient person, is as necessary for the demonstration of love as for that of any other facet of oneself. The result is frustration in any given area of living. Since love is so central to life, the suffering here is great and the consequences potentially tragic. The restorative maneuver to maintain some kind of feeling contact tends to show itself in the sado-masochistic context of causing hurt either to oneself by provoking others or to others directly.

Because of the difficulty with tenderness, *sexual relations* are usually achieved in the context of pain and suffering, these being sufficient stimuli to evoke feeling. Depending on the degree of suppression of Wood yang energies, we encounter a wide variety of sexual practices, from relatively mild gestures of a pseudo-painful sort to the most extreme sado-masochistic brutality. Sado-masochism is traditionally considered a perversion within the relatively broad framework of what is 'normal' sex. This tends to be assessed according to the values of who is writing the definitions. To the extent that it is a substitute for the ability to feel tenderness, as described above, I assume it can be thought of as a perversion, without compromising the principle "to each his own," as long as the partner is willing and not damaged.

On the other hand, in keeping with the general principle that sex is sometimes an area of behavior where the opposite of the characteristic personality is expressed, we do find some people in this category who are free to show tenderness and love only in the sexual realm. *Bioenergetically* the energic physiology is that described in the general statement on disharmony at the beginning of our discussion of Wood.

A Case of Suppressed Feelings

If there is one category of excess or deficiency that I have encountered most often in my practice, in my life, and in myself, it is passive-aggressive Wood yang deficiency. Yet, from so many examples, the person who springs most immediately to mind is a woman whom I saw during the first four months of beginning my practice of acupuncture. At that time she was middle-aged and presented with severe sciatica. She was a professional person who had functioned most of her life as a housewife.

Her previous medical history included Meniere's Syndrome, hypertension, an ectopic pregnancy, many powerful medications, exploratory cranial surgery, auditory nerve ablation, and a spinal fusion that occurred eight years before our first meeting. From that time she had been largely bedridden and unable to perform household duties such as cooking and cleaning. She had married young, and her children had long since left home — about the time that she took to bed. All that remained was her husband, a successful businessman who spent a great deal of time away from home and especially on the golf course.

She was treated with a combination of Five Phase and local tendeno-muscular acupuncture, a technique I had learned from Dr. Van Buren in England. She responded to the needles and had considerable relief despite the presence of the fusion for a degenerated disc. After the third of weekly treatments, she revealed that she had had a 'nervous breakdown' three years earlier at which time she had been treated with electric shock therapy. She then went on to tell me about her jealousy of her husband, whose good health and enjoyment of life she resented enormously. She was alone in pain, while he cavorted with abandon.

During the next treatment she said nothing more about her personal life, but from the fifth treatment to the seventh and last she revealed and worked through a great deal of suppressed feeling. She said that as a child she was taught, under the threat of severe punishment, never to talk back. Throughout her marriage she would "turn to stone" when her husband yelled at her. She realized that she was angry at herself for "holding back," and that "the reason for always being ill is that it makes me feel better to do something to hurt myself."

After the seventh acupuncture treatment I suggested that we do some bioenergetic work, such as kicking, pounding, and screaming. It took little time to teach her how to do this effectively, and she did it with gusto. Most of her anger was directed at her husband whom she admitted punishing for his domination and neglect by being ill and unable to care for him and his house. We did this together only one time.

By the following week she revealed by telephone that her physical complaints were completely gone. She had confronted her husband with her grievances and demanded money from him for something other than illness for the first time in her life. He readily acceded, and she and a friend went on a three month tour of Europe, the first trip she had ever taken in her life. I saw her three years later. She had been separated from her husband for one year and was working in her profession, where she had strained her back. She was better in three visits.

Perhaps the reason Mrs. P comes so readily to mind is because treating passive-aggressive problems is generally so much more difficult, and because hers were so clear-cut and responsive to the interventions made. Raised in the country, she had fewer of the layers of sophisticated maneuvering that I encounter in city people. The childhood admonitions against assertion were also very clear and direct, which is not the case with ostensibly permissive parenting, where the control is much more subtle and devious. I have found acupuncture to engender an emotional catharsis that is more rapidly available for integration in those whose feelings and thoughts are more suppressed than repressed, as was the case with Mrs. P.

Suppression is a less profound concealment than repression, and I believe this is the explanation for Mrs. P's rapid awareness and subsequent growth.

WOOD YANG EXCESS

Personality: Unremittingly Aggressive

We have all encountered the unremittingly aggressive person whose intrusions on the environment are the lament of all. This is the person who cannot accept "no" for an answer and, in fact, does not even seem to hear it. He hears only the sound of his own voice. Whatever it is that is important to him crowds out any other physical or interpersonal consideration. This is more or less a steady state, and one from which those exposed find little respite. The pressure is unremitting and the escape difficult. This person is totally convinced of the correctness of his behavior and has no insight into the inappropriateness of his actions and expectations. Other people's needs for time and space receive absolutely no consideration in the drive to satisfy his own needs. The reaction to his behavior is usually highly negative, which, however, he rarely notices. People who consistently block this aggression and whom the person is unable to overcome, in one way or another, will cease to exist and become invisible. If they are people of power, the direction of the aggression will shift away from them to a more promising prospect. Combined with high intelligence, the Wood yang excess person may become formidably powerful in a material sense. The tendency is to exceed himself and ultimately fail.

Other Attributes of Wood Yang Excess

There is little evidence of felt *anxiety*, but considerable evidence of agitation, whenever such a person is not getting his way in the fullest. The sense here is that beneath the surface there is, for some, an overwhelming, real anxiety fueling the agitation. To understand this latter group, we need to consider the two possible sources of the Wood yang excess.

As discussed earlier, the etiology of Wood yang excess may be either constitutional or compensatory. The distinction is made primarily by history. The constitutional traits are of uninterrupted and long duration. The compensatory etiology has a history of recurrent episodes whose energy is not continuously sustained. In the case of underlying anxiety mentioned above, I believe we have a person whose aggression is more compensatory than constitutional. The person we have been describing in our earlier discussion of 'personality' who does not have that quality of underlying anxiety falls more into the constitutional than the compensatory category.

The Wood yang excessive person is an outwardly enthusiastic advocate of himself or any current extension of himself. The energy that carries him along is strong and the direction is outward, if not upward. *Depression* is therefore not strongly evident, but there is also no joy. This is not a happy person, just driven. Agitation, with underlying anger, is the dominant mood in the face of opposition. The atmosphere is more noxious than nourishing. More often, these people do not know depression, but they create it in others.

Depression, when and if it comes, is sudden, unexpected, and physiologically cataclysmic. This *psychosis,* however, is rare and represents more a total depletion of the mothering Kidney genetic energies than a collapse in the truly psychological sense. The yin has been depleted by compensating for a Wood yang which has been out of control over the period of a lifetime. The substance of a person has been sacrificed to the ego, and the result is profound emptiness. Once the aggression has exhausted its sources, there is nothing left. The picture is one of total psychomotor retardation, with the loss of all significant drive for even the most elemental life functions, such as food, sleep, clothing, shelter, and sex.

Cognition is constricted in content and breadth by the overriding pressures of aggressive drives and the particular obsession of the moment. Since Wood energies serve judgment and planning, these faculties will be disturbed by the person's irresistible drives of the moment. Judgment will be distorted to serve the irrepressible and imminent compulsion. Such a person does well to align himself with passive but competent people, who are willing to compensate for his endless mistakes and failures in such a way that he never need notice them. In my experience, he frequently does make such an alliance in life. The passive partner seems to thrive on the apparent excitement generated by the Wood yang excess person's aggressiveness. Under these conditions, insight is negligible.

Love, which in part we have defined as the ability to consider experience from another's perspective as well as from one's own, is almost out of the question for someone whose sole outlook is for his own self-aggrandizement. The only possibility for an enduring relationship is with a person who, as I have already mentioned, is willing to subvert his own will to that of his partner. Should the subject be one who has special talents of potential value to the world, the self-sacrificing person would be rendering a service to society by bringing that talent to a world which might otherwise reject it because of its owner's noxious personality. If, on the other hand, the subject has nothing to offer except aggression, our erstwhile benefactor compounds the villainy. The latter, in his own right, could be a person with a very strong Wood yin and a great capacity to retreat; or, on the other hand, he may assume this position as an expression of severe masochistic traits.

[161]

Sex serves the need to relieve tension in order to promote sleep and keep the machine going. The sexual partner services that need and takes what he can for himself in a sexual relationship which falls far short of mutuality. Perversions fall into the sado-masochistic realm, with the subject perhaps finding some relief from his endless aggression by assuming a more passive role, though either role is a possibility for either partner.

Should sex itself be the primary focus of this person's aggressiveness, sexual abuse of any kind would be possible, since the aggression, and not the object, is the issue. However, because fear and hate are not major issues, the likelihood of violent rape is unlikely. Children could become victims when they are the only sexual object available.

Bioenergetically, the subject appears to be the same muscle-bound person whose aggression is turned on himself, whom we have already described in our general introduction to disharmony of the Wood phase. This is contrary to expectations about a person described as driven endlessly forward, whose musculature one would expect to be lithe, flexible and supple. The latter is, however, the picture of a person whose Wood energy is 'normal,' whose ability to store the blood and nourish ligaments and tendons is unimpaired. The Wood yang excessive person must, throughout his life, and especially in the early years, meet constant resistance to his overriding aggressiveness. It is the 'world' that, to save itself, turns this aggressiveness backward toward the subject, creating a similar though perhaps less consistent inhibition of his Wood energies than that which occurs during the etiology of the masochistic character described above. In nature, for every force there is an equal and opposite counterforce. Most of the people I have known with the Wood yang excessive personality eventually self-destruct and fail dramatically.

Another scenario is the eventual exhaustion of the capacity of the Liver to store the blood and nourish Iigaments, tendons, and muscles and for the Liver yang to nourish the nerves. Muscular dystrophies and neurological disabilities may then occur.

A Case of Total Aggression

A typical case of Liver yang excess was a woman artist who came to me because of low energy. She had had a cystic breast and was concerned about cancer. She had also had a thyroidectomy for hyperthyroidism at age 17, a partial hysterectomy, and stiffness in her hands. She responded well to herbs, and her energy returned rather quickly.

What was most remarkable was her personality. Her dominant characteristic was aggressiveness. She never spoke but that she demanded. She required full attention at all times to her needs, and to hers alone. Nothing stood in her way. Though her talent as an artist was considered to be mediocre, her work appeared in galleries to which others far more talented could not gain entrance. It was the only defense that gallery owners had against her onslaughts. She was certain that she was the best, a fact that no one who wished to have the slightest peace was going to deny.

Unfortunately, she was not interested in addressing the problems associated with her mode of relating to others and departed as soon as her physical well being had improved. In the long run, failure to deal with these issues will again deplete her energy.

10

The Fire Phase

The natural function of Fire energies in the evolution of being is the conscious awareness and intelligent formulation of creative visions and concepts and the development of conscious, symbolic, intelligent, interpersonal communication, including verbal, mathematical, musical, visual, and motile forms of expression. There are three dominant developmental eras associated with the Fire phase. The first of these is the creative childhood years (the 'yes' stage), especially when expressive language develops and love feelings draw one to the parent of the opposite sex. The second is during pubescence, when interpersonal relations explode and love blossoms. The third includes the years of creative adult work, especially after mid-life. The Fire energies conduct the entire symphony of the ebullient expression of positive creative being.

What do we mean by 'creative'? Creative explicitly involves bearing newness into being, a newness which distinctively modifies known reality. It implies doing this as part of a continuum, so that something original can 'become' at any time and many times. The net product of this condition is change. Inherent in the creative situation is tolerance of change, whether in an artist's vision or an intimate relationship.

Water yin gives us the substance of the mind. Water yang gives us the drive or force for its evolution and development. Wood gives it direction, and Spleen feeds it. Fire (Heart) yin inspires that substance into awareness, and Fire (Heart) yang gives form to the creative idea.

These energies subserve the basic human need for contact, on the level of the ego. The dominance of consciousness and awareness, of creativity and love, by Fire energies places these energies in the center of all interpersonal considerations. The entire issue of contact in adult life and on an adult level is a function of the ability of these energies to integrate the positive experiences of all the earlier eras into full awareness and expression in relationships.

Also, in terms of consciousness and awareness, the Fire phase contacts the general energy (Heart), distributes it fairly (Triple Burner and Pericardium), and purifies it (Small Intestine). Each of the four aspects of the Fire phase, the Heart, the Pericardium, the Small Intestine, and the Triple Burner, superintend a separate, yet intimately related, segment of the total function, which has given man the power to consciously express a portion of every facet of his being. The Fire phase is responsible for the ability of each of the other phase energies to find a conscious symbolic statement of its special natural functions wherever that is necessary or desirable. The yin energies of the Heart beget the 'insight' and the yang energies the 'expression.' All intelligent and intelligible communication, from the infant's first cry, through the declaration of first love, to the final realization that "I believe," is mediated by the energies of the Fire phase. On the level of feelings, and at their supreme maturation, these energies nourish and govern the awareness and the expression of unconditional love, both for self and for others.

Lawson-Wood states that "joy arises out of the activity of the divinely inspired part of man."[1] Chinese medicine maintains that the 'spirit' *(shen)* is transmitted from one generation to another through the Water phase. During our lifetime, the spirit is said to reside in the Heart by day, where it may be contacted through the quality of brightness emitted by the pupils of the eyes. At night the spirit is said to reside in the Liver and to be revealed in our dreams. A pure spirit does not dream. Some authorities say that 'spirit' is a term reserved for the transcendent person outside of the material body. They prefer the term 'soul' for the incarnate spirit. Confusion abounds in the use of these terms, and I will use 'spirit' exclusively, in the interest of simplicity.

Natural Functions of the Fire Phase System

Heart yin

The inspiration for the creative, original formulations of all forms of art on both an intellectual and spiritual plane of being, including the 'art of loving' as a joyous celebration and fulfillment of organismic well-being, is the energic function of the yin energies of the Heart energy system. Heart yin is involved with the unfolding and visual or auditory conceptual representation of inspired, artistic taste. The Earth phase bears the milk of human 'kindness' and fulfills the basic 'need.' This is the beginning of the sense of self-worth. The Heart yin is the medium which enriches that 'milk' into the 'cream' of human congeniality and fulfills the basic 'want.'

{165}

With these energies, people experience a joy and celebration of the existence of others and of the new life which their love creates. Love in its highest form is the fulfillment of Fire energies: love as unconditional acceptance, as permission granted to another human being to penetrate one's ego as one penetrates and lives in the other's, as setting aside one's ego for the other. For children this is the beginning of self-love. To be special to ourselves we must initially be special to another person. The final realization may be that we are special "to," and perhaps even special "with," God.

The Heart houses the mental energies and controls all higher mental functions. Lawson-Wood says, "The feeling of inspiration and versatility of psychic faculties may be available to man only because of his symbol-forming, interpretive abilities."[2] Heart energies are responsible for the higher, conscious, intellectual-mental 'investigation of life' including: 'awareness,' 'symbol formation,' and the communication of ideas and feelings. In Chinese medicine, the Heart 'opens' to the tongue. It is embryologically close to the throat. There is a Hindu saying that "If one can close off the throat, one closes off the flow of thoughts." The Heart controls the circulation of ideas within and between men.

Heart energies embody the spiritual being, the 'divinely inspired qi,' and the spiritual quality of love transmitted and expressed. Revelation on the spiritual level, in the form of divine inspiration and divine creative love, are the purview of the spiritual component of Heart yin energies. Only through these Heart yin energies do the divine spirit, divine love, and divine will (discussed elsewhere in relation to Kidney qi, yin, and yang) come into conscious human awareness.

Heart yin controls the venous circulation. Its principal function is to cleanse, and its role is diastolic and relatively receptive.

HEART YANG

Heart yang is the active aspect of the circulation (systole), representing the nourishing arterial blood and the force that moves it. Heart yang energies are the active formative principle in the network of expressive Heart functions in which the yin facilitates spontaneous awareness. Yin mediates the externalization of the inspired 'substance,' and yang gives it form. Yin without yang is chaos, and yang without yin is the crushing boredom of uninspired order (bureaucracy).

Heart yang is responsible for the organized, conceptualized, and utilizable communication of the creative 'idea.' Heart yang provides energy to the ego functions, which interpret and formulate inspiration into articulate understanding. Philosophy is the developed statement of this process.

The Heart yang (and Small Intestine) energies systematize the inspired discrimination (taste) of the creative artist into the structure necessary for its implementation in the real world. Architects, interior decorators, poets, painters, sculptors, and musicians owe the awareness of inherent symmetry to Heart yin and the formulation of professional style to the organizing energies of Heart yang.

For example, a sculptor looking at a stone sees a figure in the stone (Heart yin) that he subsequently creates by separating the 'pure' from the 'impure' (Heart yang or the Small Intestine). Thus a balance is achieved in the Fire phase between intuitive inspiration and the organized reasoning necessary to enduring creation.

Whereas 'divine revelation' is the gift of Heart yin energies, Heart yang endows us with the benefaction of 'divine intelligence,' which Western theology calls 'The Word.' The 'Logos' or Word of the Gospel of John and subsequent esoteric writing is held to be the foundation of earthly reality.[3]

HEART YIN DISHARMONY

HEART YIN DEFICIENCY

Personality: Uninspired Bureaucrat

The principal personality problems associated with Heart yin energies center on the vicissitudes of creative inspiration, including the unrestrained awareness of one's unique creative forces; of all spontaneous feelings; and especially of the capacity to joyfully accept one's own loving, caring, tender feelings in an ambiance of mutuality.

The person whose Heart yin energies are either deficient or inhibited will be experienced as a dull, boring, and uninspired person who subscribes to what has already been created by others and who, if Heart yang is in excess, tends to perseverate and proseletyze it in an often dull and pedantic fashion. This is the person who is maddeningly certain. He or she can entertain no sense of the transient nature of the truth as we are capable of knowing it and must believe that the current or past truth is the absolute truth. He has no choice, since he is cut off from the wellspring of the infinite and has no connection with the unfolding process of reality. Change plays a small role in life, and this person often stands very tall, solidly, and stolidly for the status quo. There is often a strong need for the approval of authority. If there is any direction, it is toward the past. Our current institutions, mores, and customs always find their way into this individual's hands. He

carries himself through life with a notable lack of zest or joyful spontaneity, excitement, or adventure. In short, these are our inveterate bureaucrats   [167]
whom we use to defend what we wish to keep and have a devil of a time
dispensing with when we need to move on.

Whereas this is the dominant personality structure, the very nature of a
repressed Fire is to flare up; and so these staid defenders of the faith may often, in the context of their conformity, be irritable, agitated, and even restless. Some may find acceptable outlets for their Fire in the form of hobbies.
Others find it in a double-life, one of repression and the other of expression,
though this is more rare (Dr. Jekyll and Mr. Hyde).

The person whose Earth, Wood, and Water energies are not severely
compromised by defective constitution or poor parenting has the relative
security and intact integrative apparatus to allow the higher faculties of
love — the tender emotions and creative inspiration — a place in his life.
This luxury is a potential that may be realized provided the circumstances
exist in the ensuing course of development for their fulfillment. Parents or
surrogates who can at least partially listen to and hear the inner song of
themselves and others, and who may both experience and express some joy
and pleasure in both, are the prerequisite.

The inhibition of Heart yin energies may occur directly or subtly. On
a direct level, the parent openly identifies the joyful creativity of his child,
or anyone, as in one way or another the "work of the devil." This attitude is
characteristic of those who espouse fundamentalist philosophies and the-
ologies. I saw many patients in New York City during the 1950s and early
'60s who were raised in this atmosphere, usually children of Baptist and
Methodist families who came to New York from rural parts of the country
where these attitudes were ubiquitous. Whereas these people had great difficulty in allowing themselves the sweet joy of spontaneous rhapsodic imagery, they were clear about the source of the problem as rooted in belief, and
about the work that was required to change that belief. The 'not me' was
relatively available in therapy, and the 'bad me' aspects of themselves were
consciously well-defined; otherwise, their self-esteem was often high. They
were also often competent, even happy, in areas of living more involved
with things than people. They tended toward such occupations as engineering, nursing, teaching, and social work, where the relationships are caring
but basically on an authoritarian rather than a mutual level.

More subtle is the situation in which the parent lacks the capacity for
joy in his own existence and is therefore incapable of enjoying his child.
Whereas in the former situation the issue is identified and then forbidden,
here the child's God-given cup of joy is slowly drained by a lack of response

to the experience of wonder before the small and the great of his or her existence, especially to spontaneous 'love' for an otherwise caring parent. The issue never rises to the conscious level and remains as an endlessly mystifying hiatus in the person's development. When the parent pretends to feel a joy and warmth that is lacking, the burden is on the child to offer a comparably disingenuous response or to reject the relationship. With either solution, the young person is not only mystified by the subsequent interpersonal problems that plague his life, but guilty about his inauthenticity and/or anxious when he pretends.

Here, we do not find the ambivalence of the mother who is unable to provide basic mothering. Nor is there the hostility of the mother who crushes the child's self-assertion in the 'no' stage. Both populate the world with people crippled by ill-defined boundaries or boundaries defined by negativity for whom the struggle for existence and sanity precludes the development of a secure ego capable of creative awareness. The parent may be concerned for, attentive to, and even respectful of the child in many significant ways, perhaps all except those that embrace the genuine response to life that smiles 'yes.' And the inconstancy of this response may compound the confusion when, for example, a mother who can feel free to respond to an infant boy is confused at a later age by her more erotic feelings. This is even truer for fathers and daughters.

The loss of the capacity for joy in any one person is therefore rarely total. The earlier in the life of the child that the inhibition begins, the more damaging to the child's development of his or her own capacity for spontaneous joy and love, both experienced and expressed. It is rare, however, to find total extinction of the awareness of these attributes. The growing person 'becomes' with the unfolding of inner, species-specific genetic coaching.[4] This force carries us through timely developmental eras, which life can distort but which only major cataclysmic experience can extinguish. Unmet basic needs are never at rest, even in the most deprived person. The person who appears to be totally devoid of spontaneous joy is engaged in a lifelong unconscious struggle to contain these needs, and suffers at some level, either physically or emotionally.

Other Attributes of Heart Yin Deficiency

Cognition will be marked by constriction and lack of originality. The subject may be quite ambitious and aggressive but will not become a true leader in the world of ideas. He will be a follower. Furthermore, if the Pericardium energies for defense are strong, as we are assuming in this discussion of Heart energies, repression may be a prominent characteristic. On the cognitive level this will be manifested by some amnestic attributes.

The extent of the amnesia will vary from mild to severe and could be total or could be observed in the form of avoidance of specific issues in life, a noticeable selective inattention. Cognition in the Fire phase also depends on Small Intestine energies and will receive appropriate elaboration in the discussion of that aspect of the Fire phase.

Anxiety tends to be of the free-floating type, which I associate with the repression of natural excitement or with the loss of control over this excitement. However, the emergence of this kind of anxiety depends upon the lack of satisfactory completeness of the earlier stages of development. If those energy cycles are adequately fulfilled and their energies in reasonable condition, the subject will have the strength to suppress anxiety in the interest of an efficient, intact ego. Having drunk more fully of the 'milk' of life, they can more easily forego the 'honey'. This will be even more true if Heart yang energies are intact, as we shall see. Somatic symptoms are more likely in that case, including the classical conversion hysteria, which is seen so rarely these days, as well as all of the more serious illnesses subsumed under the aegis of 'psychosomatic'. Any or all systems may be involved. Anxiety will be aroused in relation to any of the myriad aspects of the era known as the Oedipus-Electra Complex involving the creative forces of love. These are discussed more completely under the aegis of Pericardium-Circulation-Sex energies and involve the anxieties referred to as 'castration anxiety' in boys and 'fear of the loss of mother's love and protection' in girls. In all subsequent developmental eras that involve loving relationships, Heart yin energies are at risk in the form of fear of rejection. Anxiety will appear whenever those forces drawing one person to another take shape, either consciously or unconsciously.

There will be *phobias* of any emotional expansiveness of a pleasurable or joyful nature and may take the form of agoraphobia in some situations, especially when the separation aspect of Earth energies is also compromised. During the manic phase, if such occurs, unrestrained expansiveness will prevail, often with a phobia of any restriction, a form of temporary claustrophobia. Any attempt to exercise control over the subject at those times will lead to greater agitation, excitement, and explosiveness.

In recent years, greater attention has been given to the anxieties that appear in mid-life when a person is drawn away from the mundane (though gloriously rewarding in their time) aspects of the family-career cycle. The driving force of Heart yin energies at this point in development is the need to explore the great unknown which we call 'ourselves'. While fear of the unknown is a Water-Kidney issue, making the unknown conscious is a Fire-Heart issue.

Enormous anxieties are generated by the sacrifice of the security of what is known for the intangibles of the unknown. The word 'crisis' is a spectacular understatement for anxieties that approach cataclysmic proportions during this transition. During all of the other transformations up to this era, society has provided a format for the change. Now the individual is on his/her own, since no acceptable 'rites of passage' exist in Western culture to guide one through what is inevitably a shift that is in conflict with society's treasured traditions. Family, work, and the conventional responsibilities all militate against the drive of the organism, through Heart yin energies, to know and realize itself.

Fire Phase Depression

Whenever the Fire does not burn brightly, *depression* is possible. The tendency to depression will depend to some extent on the intactness of Kidney energies. Whereas an excess of the yin of the Kidneys (Water) can dampen the Fire, a deficiency of Kidney yang can do the same by not supplying the 'fire at the gate of vitality' *(ming men)* to the Heart. At this point depression may appear through the cracks in the armor of the person whose Heart Fire energies are deficient.

For several reasons, Fire phase depressions tend to be cyclic. In fact, the entire character structure may be marked by lability and dominated by mood oscillations. Fire itself is a phenomenon that is constantly changing, flickering brightly one moment and subdued the next, depending on the changeable flow of air (the Metal phase) and availability and quality of fuel (the Wood phase). The Fire phase is always associated with restlessness. The very nature of repression, the principal restorative maneuver of this phase, is another factor. Repression of 'being' is a never-ending struggle to keep powerful forces at bay. The effort placed to this end cannot maintain a steady, even control, since the fluctuating states of exhaustion and renewal are constantly taking place. When repression is strong, the character attributes of emotional constriction, humorlessness, sexual repression, dullness, diminished consciousness or awareness deficits, and conversion symptoms may slip into depression in the form DSM-III describes as

> loss of interest or pleasure in usual activities ... , complaints or evidence of diminished ability to think or concentrate, such as slowed thinking, or indecisiveness not associated with marked loosening of associations or inherence, social withdrawal, insomnia or hypersomnia, loss of interest in sex, guilt over past pleasurable experiences, pessimism, decrease in communication, brooding, dysphoria, feelings of inadequacy, decreased effectiveness, psychomotor retardation, sadness, crying, and hypochondriasis.[5]

In periods during which spontaneity, creativity, and its expression break through the repression, we will have the opposite clinical picture, the manic or hypomanic episode. These forces, which have been out of consciousness for the better part of development, will burst through the operating controls governing their repression. They will carry with them and convey all of the chaos of a primitive force that has not had the leavening effect of ego-organization and lifelong acculturation.

According to DSM-III, during hypomanic periods there is an elevated, expansive, or irritable mood and any or all of the following:

1. reduced need for sleep
2. more energy than usual
3. inflated self-esteem
4. increased productivity, often associated with unusual and self-imposed working hours
5. sharpened and unusually creative thinking
6. uninhibited people-seeking (extreme gregariousness)
7. hypersexuality without recognition of possibility of painful consequences
8. excessive involvement in pleasurable activities with lack of concern for the high potential for painful consequences, e.g., buying sprees, foolish business investments, reckless driving
9. physical restlessness
10. more talkative than usual
11. over-optimism or exaggeration of past achievements
12. inappropriate laughing, joking, punning.[6]

The manic-depressive cycle tends to be more severe in intensity and frequency where the preceding stage involving Liver-Gallbladder energies has been traumatic. Wood is the mother of Fire. Suppression of the Wood energies leads to an accumulation of Wood and an episodic over-feeding of the fires of the Fire phase. The Fire will tend, under these circumstances, to get out of hand. Another aspect of this is the exhaustion of the yin (Water) which attempts to control the Fire. If Kidney and Heart yin are exhausted, the yin cannot control the yang, and we say that the 'qi is wild.'

In addition, if the Triple Burner *(san qiao)* system is operating inefficiently, thermostatic controls will break down, and the Fire will rage out of control until the Wood is consumed, followed by a depression characteristic of depleted Liver energies.

Depressions in general tend to be self-limiting because the expanding energies driving toward realization in the 'evolution of being' tend to break through suppressive forces that create depression. Fire energies are more volatile, and the quality and force of expansiveness is more explosive. The lack of awareness and consciousness of the inner self associated with deficient Heart yin energies makes the emergence of the creative forces even more of a shock when they come.

More Attributes of Heart Yin Deficiency

Love relationships lack the overflowing warmth, effusive ardor, and emotional effervescence usually associated with love. The subject will fear 'abandonment' and never be rapturously carried away by inner drives. He or she will appear to be cold and unemotional and will be unable to convey a feeling of warmth. There will be a tendency toward imperturbable stability. During the manic stage there may be all the effusive demonstration and unfocused physical expression of feeling that is ordinarily lacking. However, it is conveyed inappropriately with great pressure, diffusion, lack of control, and is fickle and shallow in quality, lacking the depth of measured affection.

Sexual activities and attitudes and perverse tendencies are dependent upon the functions of the Pericardium and will be more fully explored in that discussion. A defect in Heart yin energies will deprive the person of the heat, light, and passion associated with normal sex. Coldness, unimaginativeness, constriction, and inhibition of the expression of sexual feelings, as well as difficult arousal and delayed or absent orgasm is the rule. Passivity and submission for the female become the pattern, as a way of reinforcing repression and holding onto a partner. In the manic phase, control will markedly diminish, arousal will be too quick, and in men premature ejaculation will be common. There may be a tendency then to sexualize all relationships, and the practice may be 'polymorphously perverse.'

Psychotic episodes will be marked by feelings of guilt about pleasure and real or fancied sexual or other emotional excesses and there will be severe psychomotor restriction. There will be a strong tendency to feel responsible for disasters that occurred to others in the past, in which the subject was only peripherally involved, and to feel that punishment should be forthcoming for these wrongdoings. There may be talk of suicide as one way to expatiate culpability, but the talk and minor gestures in this direction suffice as penitence and are rarely accompanied by a serious threat to life.

The manic phase is marked by delusions of grandeur, pressure of speech, loose associations, and a complete flight of ideas leading to bizarre behavior such as buying with imaginary funds, wildly spending these imaginary funds, and selling what is not owned, all on a highly embellished scale. Attempts to control this behavior may elicit violence.

While it is true that those who successfully reach the age of the first flowering of the imagination are the least in danger of ego deficient psychological states, many creative geniuses become mad at some point in their lives. The problem is not a defective ego. Indeed, I have rarely seen egos that were better developed. The rhythmic flooding of conscious being with the chaotic quintessence of the unconscious is ineluctable to creativity. A powerful ego in which the Heart yang energies are highly developed is necessary, as we shall see, to bring this chaos into the order we call creation. At critical moments in the history of this process, quantum leaps of inner vision necessarily overwhelm these organizing energies, and the yin submerges the yang, just as a river overflows its banks and inundates the land with new soil. This event is heralded by all of the mythologies of the world when the hero separates from his culture, his security, 'leaves his mind' and enters into other worlds not known personally to the 'honest hunters' of this world.[7] Here he conquers himself, his fear (the dragon), and then owns the power inherent in the unknown, which he brings back to mankind. Some do not return. They die or live out their years in madness, isolated and tortured by the blinding insight which they cannot integrate into the universally recognizable architecture of consciousness (like Prometheus, who brought us fire from the gods). Others become mad when their knowledge frightens the honest hunters, who isolate them from the requisite validating radiant warmth of other humans. "No man is an island."[8] A few return to a higher level of awareness and existence as heroes and teachers, often, like Christ, returning from the wilderness to be ultimately sacrificed to the status quo. The uneasy truce between the honest hunter and the shaman was long ago shattered by the emergence of the power of reason as the dominant force in our relationship to the universe.

The inhibition of Fire energies means that there is a 'smoldering' Fire, that the central nervous system does not experience a full discharge of beta activity, so that the other stages of the sleep cycle (alpha, delta, and theta) do not follow in proper sequence. Insomnia has long been associated with Heart energy imbalance. The form of the insomnia will vary with the condition of the Heart. Early in life, when Heart energies are stronger and attempt to assert themselves, there may be a restless pattern, frequent waking and sleeping for short intervals. This is even more true if there has been any kind of early shock to the Heart, either at birth, due to anoxia, or later, from sudden, overwhelming emotional stress. Later the Heart energies weaken, and the pattern is one of delayed onset, about five hours of sleep and early waking with agitation, an inability to return to sleep, and a feeling of incompleteness. The manic phase, on the other hand, is characterized by little need of sleep for days or weeks, ending in total physical collapse. We will return to this subject more fully in our discussion of the 'nervous system.'

In the literature there are reports concerning *dream* content such as rape and being rescued from fire and smoke. I have not personally observed any recurrent dream patterns with regard to content.

Bioenergetics and Heart Yin Deficiency

For the purposes of our discussion, there are two general types of Heart yin deficiency, one constitutional and one from repression. In the former, the *bioenergetic* picture is of an inert, bloodless being who seems to exude little of the electrical excitement associated with life. In the latter we have the loricated, inflexible body described below.

Using Lowen's bioenergetic terminology, people whose other energies are relatively intact but who have problems with the developmental era during which Fire energies prevail are characterized as having 'armored,' 'genital,' or 'rigid' character structures (to which he refers as the hysterical character, especially in women). In order for this to be possible, Pericardium defensive energies must be intact. Muscle tensions are uniform throughout the body in contrast to the 'pre-genital' people, whose muscle tensions are more localized.

Where inhibition of Heart yin is concerned, the issue is control and rigidity. This rigidity is in the service of controlling Heart feelings. "The back is rigid and unbending, the jaw set and neck tight, the head is erect."[9] While the pelvis is contracted, it has more real movement than in the pre-genital personalities (oral and masochistic). The shoulders are tight, straight, and stiff; respiration is reduced; and the entire front of the body, the chest, and abdomen are hard. The result is concomitant with the inflexibility of the personality.

According to Lowen, there are sex determinants in the final character structure of the rigid, armored person. The female is seductive (hysterical character),[10] and the male is aggressive (phallic-narcissistic character).[11] Physically, both are similar. The 'outer tube' from genitals to head (glabella) is complete but rigid, in varying degrees and forms. In the hysteric there is the 'mesh' as well as the 'plated' type. The former's defenses are flexible and elusive and are seen in the type of seductive woman with 'squirming.'[12] In the male there is the phallic aggressive and the compulsive character. In the latter, the rigidity reaches deeper, the character is more conforming than in the former in which rebellion is more characteristic.

The Heart energy disequilibrium produces the 'armored' person with little awareness, stuck at the genital level of development (assuming that all other preceding developmental era energies are intact). This may occur when Pericardium energies are intact. When Pericardium energies are only partially dysfunctional and repression is partial, two other solutions to the Heart energy disequilibrium are possible. For both, the problem is on the level of a closed heart, fear of being rejected in love and sexually by the opposite sex. The expression of such feelings is deeply inhibited and siphoned either toward profound inhibition of aggression in men or toward aggression in ego-related goals in women (for whom it is safer).

In the male we find the passive-feminine physical character structure described by Lowen in the *Physical Dynamics of Character Structure*. The most striking feature is one of physical immobility and diminished emotional expression. The voice is soft, modulated, and feminine; the manner gentle and eager to please; the face smooth, soft, and 'plastic.' Some may appear broad-shouldered with raised shoulders and little movement in the thorax. Other types have a rounded body and narrow shoulders. All show a soft, rounded pelvis; little severe interfacial muscle tension; little skin turgor; a wooden expression in the eyes; and, except for the raised shoulders, little sign of tension and anxiety. Deep muscles are, however, quite tense but not noticeable. There is a sense of lifelessness, often despair and hopelessness, but no collapse. Movements are not self-assertive. Lowen speaks of a displacement from the penis to the breast. Women tend to be more masculine, are rigid above, heavy below, and have hair in a masculine distribution. They may be aggressive for ego purposes but not sexually receptive to men.

A Case of Massive Anxiety

Two months after I first began to treat people with acupuncture, a middle-aged, very successful businesswoman, Ms. R., presented herself. Her reputation as a hard, tough, ruthless competitor had preceded her. Her chief complaints were massive anxiety, multiple phobias, especially of crowds and places she did not know well, a fear of passing out, hypertension, hypoglycemia (she craved sugar), indigestion related to fear of fainting, and a fear of heart disease, which ran in her family. Her fears were accompanied by a hot flush and a rapid heart beat as well as a feeling of congestion in her solar plexus. Sometimes these attacks would be relieved by burping (see Chapter 13 and the discussion of pernicious influences). Her fears were somewhat alleviated by the presence of someone she knew well. She came for acupuncture because she was allergic to medications. She was an alcoholic, belonged to AA, and had not had a drink in ten years. After some years of experimenting with both male and female partners in sexual relationships, she had been living with one woman for eight years. There was a great deal of tension between Ms. R. and her sister. Other members of the family, male and female, were homosexual, one of whom committed suicide, a fact about which she seemed to show little emotion.

Ms. R. came from an upper-class family. The father was a physician and the mother an unworldly 'baby.' Her parents led separate lives after the death of her older sister when Ms. R. was an infant. Her father was very strict, and she was raised largely in a convent school. Her mother was a "street angel and a house devil," who had no joy in life and resented any her daughter had had as a girl and young woman. The milieu was one in which pleasure, spontaneity, creativity, and original-ity were immoral. Though she was a "playgirl" out of rebellion when she was young, this was short-lived, and she developed into a person whose "spirit is empty and who just makes money." She had even returned to the church for solace and had become, like her mother, "a street angel and house devil," a staunch defender of the status quo in society, and "totally ungiving except to my work."

Though acupuncture relieved her tension and "has forced me to look in, which is good," she never ceased to be skeptical about it as an unconventional practice. I viewed her anxiety as arising from sup-pressed excitement and from qi stagnation in the middle burner (the center of the body), with hot qi going to the Heart and temporarily blocking the 'orifices' (circulation of the Heart to the brain).

HEART YIN EXCESS

Personality: Agitation and Restlessness

The person whose Heart yin energies are in excess must deal through-out his or her life with a greatly enhanced awareness of both the inner chaotic world of the unconscious and the constantly impinging sensory and emotional stimuli from the outer world. His extraordinary level of aware-ness calls upon every energy concerned with boundaries (Earth), sorting (Small Intestine), and protection (Pericardium) to assist him in controlling the endless onslaught, and to digest (Stomach) and organize (Wood) the constant flood of material from both directions.

The subject's personality would be marked by agitation and restless-ness, because he is never at rest from heightened awareness. The energy required to maintain stability might leave him extremely fatigued. Often sleep will be interrupted by chaotic dreams which seem very real, as well as by outside stimuli that are automatically screened from the ordinary sleeper. This will add to fatigue; frequently, if asked, this person will report not feeling rested after a night's sleep. In order to minimize his confusion, he will turn either outward to an extraordinary preoccupation with the 'real' world or become obsessively absorbed by the onrush of images, thoughts, and feelings from the inside. If he moves toward his inner world, he will become extremely self-involved and appear withdrawn. As part of the effort to cope with all of this material, the subject will turn to those avenues of self-direction which we call creative, such as music, painting, and writing. In these areas of endeavor, he will find more freedom from the structured demands of a technological society. He may be drawn to forms of psychotherapy which encourage endless introspection and 'processing,' serving the need to cope with this surfeit of idiosyncratic and often frightening internal turbulence by sharing it in a structured arrangement with another, and caring, person. However, apart from this stabilizing relationship, he will always be struggling to maintain a steady focus and will leave behind a hypomanic pattern of jumping from one thing to another in a grasshopper fashion.

[177]

Other Attributes of Heart Yin Excess

Cognition will always be under siege by this flood of ideas, feelings, and images from the inside. The subject will be hard put to avoid confusion, disorganization, and to maintain continuity of thought, concentration, and attention. Under extreme circumstances, consciousness may be flooded by chaotic material from the unconscious, and thinking will become illogical and contaminated. Delusional ideas may emerge from this anarchy, especially if the internal and external stimuli become confused with each other. It is important to appreciate the amount of energy that is required to maintain homeostasis, how this leaves less for overall productivity, and how at times this energy may seem overactive and at other times seem to collapse.

Anxiety appears for several reasons. There is the constant threat of 'losing' one's mind, of being overwhelmed from within. There is also the ever-present fear of appearing irrational or 'crazy' to others. For both reasons, people who have excess Heart yin energies may fear closeness to people, except perhaps to those whom they recognize to be similar to themselves. This may reach *phobic* proportions, because people with excess Heart yin energies are exquisitely sensitive and highly reactive to their environment and to the pain it inevitably inflicts on all of us, and especially on those who do not 'fit in.'

Depression is not an early sign, because, despite his tendency to withdraw, the subject is far too busy trying to maintain stability to become aware of the tragedy of his or her existence. Over a period of time, there is a gradual enervation which, combined with the failure to succeed either socially or vocationally, leads to a loss of hope and a slow decline into a sense of defeat. This too will be cyclic as are all Fire phase depressions.

Love is a problem for the subject, who has considerable difficulty controlling these feelings, which he or she has to an excess, and which may be overwhelming to those for whom they are meant. The latter may have no recourse except rejection of that love, which to the subject is particularly painful, for the reasons mentioned above. Furthermore, the unavoidable preoccupation of dealing with one's vulnerability to what is coming from the inside creates a shield that precludes the full realization of all the interpersonal developmental phases necessary to the maturing of love feelings.

Sexual feelings will also be strong, but, for the reasons mentioned above, they will probably remain confined to masturbatory activity beyond the age when it usually ceases to be the primary outlet. The drive is powerful and, like love feeling, not likely to be matured by experience with others in the variety of ways which makes for subtlety and success. The results may be frightening, and even inadvertently dangerous, to the object of these affections, since loss of control is an ever present possibility.

Psychosis is always a concern for a person whose consciousness is under constant assault by primary process material which may, for one reason or another, slip out of control. The result would be a psychosis marked by a thinking disorder, which may take one or all of its many forms: perceptual, delusional, or formal (logic deficit). During the early stages, or at a younger age, the clinical picture may include a mental overactivity resembling the hypomanic phase of a manic-depressive illness, a part of the effort to regain control. In its later stages, or at an older age, depression could become part of the clinical picture, as the subject loses hope and the energy to restitute.

Bioenergetically the rigid body structure described under Heart yin deficiency holds. The need for control, and the physical rigidity which subserves it, is even greater where Heart yin is in excess, for obvious reasons. The energy required to maintain this control will cause enervation and less overall aggression. However, from time to time, unexpected irrational outbreaks are possible and even dangerous.

A Case of Too Many Ideas

A young man was referred to me for treatment of pain that extended from the right side of his back through to the chest, for excessive urination, and for diminished sexual energy. He was taking a great deal of Western medication. It was clear from the beginning that he was talented in several of the arts but unable to focus his attention on any one area of expression, and seemed overwhelmed by the different ideas which came faster than he could use them. He lived at home with a dominant mother who raised him as if he were a little girl, denigrated his sick father, and convinced K. at the same time that he was too good for an unappreciating world. His mother's very successful store was his prison.

[179]

K. frantically attempted to handle the profusion of inner stimuli primarily by painting, though music and writing competed for his energy. He was controlled by his mother to a remarkable degree, and it was this control that he needed to gain for himself in order to organize and manage his inner world. A great deal of our work had to do with grounding. Though he questioned my commitment to travel with him into his nether world and was terrified that I would abandon him when he was "disintegrating," together we made many "descents into hell,"[13] into his inner turmoil, and out the other end.

The following is my final note after two years of work with K. "In a rather remarkable way, K. has changed physiologically. His chest has expanded, he has moved from being asthenic to having a well-developed upper part of his body with a growing awareness of the lower part and less fear of getting in touch with his sexuality. His appetite has improved and he retains his food. He has a great deal more energy and it is more focused. His fantasy life has become integrated into his art, so that he feels at this point 'mindless,' saying 'that does not feel bad.' K. has formed a meaningful relationship with a young woman who is also an artist, who is devoted and nurtures him in a way that his mother never could, without all of the demands on his 'self.' In addition, K. has become an extremely successful painter." With the backing of two of the most famous painters of our time, K. went on to phenomenal achievements in art, showing in all the best galleries here and abroad.

HEART YANG DISHARMONY

The etiology of Heart yang disharmony is manifold. Of the deficiency states of these energies, the most obvious is that of constitutional weakness, which may occur in all degrees. It is my observation that the constitutional Heart yang energies of certain peoples, such as the Celts, tend to be either tragically weak or excessively strong at all levels of their function. Congenital factors may profoundly affect all Heart energies, since the Heart is especially sensitive to the shocks which accompany all trauma. This is particularly true when the shock occurs at birth, and especially in those deliveries which are delayed or subject to drugs, forceps, surgery, artificial induction, and the immediate post-delivery roughness characteristic of modern hospital deliveries. Many of these practices are now fortunately being reconsidered and reversed as more women are choosing to deliver at home, where both mother and child do considerably better in the postpartum period.

Given a solid constitution and uneventful pregnancy and parturition, the innate drive for self-expression is strong and insistent. There are certain life events which can dampen its intrinsic ebullience. Assuming the normal evolution of Water, Earth, and Wood energies, the most prevalent event is having parents who feel a great deal of love and caring for their child but who can show it only in non-verbal ways. The early stages of development will be well-nourished; but for this child there is no model for the logical verbal expression of the anarchic inner world of what Carl Jung refers to as the "other reality"[14] and little chance of evolving through developmental stages that involve forging a creative imagination from the fires of that other reality, which, for human beings, can come from no other place. For the language of that other reality is the language of God, obscure to man since logic has prevailed. It is, as Jung stated, the substance of creation and the life task of each man to translate his own secret message from God into human language and share it with all men.

A similar fate is in store for those whose drive for verbal self-expression is thwarted by parents who are threatened by creativity and who invalidate it, either through outright rejection or through the double-bind of encouraging and then ignoring or derogating that which they encouraged. And some parents are selective in their inattention, as is often the case when eros emerges in a child who then seeks fulfillment in the parent of the opposite sex.

If Heart yin is weak, the generation of creative awareness will not follow, and its expression will be a redundant issue as far as creativity is concerned. If Heart yin is troubled and there is a relative unawareness of the creative and tender emotions, Heart yang, which is the organized expressive aspect, may attempt to compensate; and the person may talk, sing, paint, and so on, a great deal more than 'normal.' However, because this will be expression in areas which are not subsumed by Heart yin, the expression will lack real creativity and warm tenderness, though it may simulate them. This is the 'as if' situation. If Heart yin is strong but blocked, it will forever seek an outlet through Heart yang energies and will continue to feed the yang on a material level, if not on the level of inspiration. The heart rate will increase and palpitations will be felt. If Heart yin is strong and its way clear, and Heart yang is not adequate for any of the above or other reasons, the following general personality picture will emerge.

HEART YANG DEFICIENCY

Personality: Ideas Without Execution

Assuming that the condition of Heart yin energies is intact, the subject enjoys a plethora of creative ideas without the benefit of effective, organized, realistic expression and execution. There will be many brilliant beginnings and few meaningful or successful endings. He or she will be the bright youngster who never 'lives up' to his or her 'potential.' His spiritual development will likewise lack the benefit of structured, consistent expression. In all areas of living, this person, whose performance skills may be innately good, may be bursting with inspiration and consciously or unconsciously suffering deeply the inability to transform any of it into organized, manifest forms of communication, either to himself or others. This becomes even more true because as yin attempts to compensate for yang, those rich, creative urges represented by yin energies will become even more insistent. Repeated failure will lead to identification with the underdog and underprivileged and will lead to unconventional, bohemian, and anti-establishment activities. As for the suffering, there is as much as one might expect from a condition so fraught with frustration. Attempting to end this suffering, our subject may plunge ahead over and over in the face of failure, never learning from experience or accepting the reality of his situation. A rebound phenomenon may occur, in which the person will seek excitement in the form of daredevil and dangerous activities. These become addictive, requiring more and more to reach a level of meaningful animation.

Other Attributes of Heart Yang Deficiency

Most of the person's many fine ideas will fall by the wayside due to disorganized, scattered, unfocused expression, which characterizes the entire cognitive problem. It is that part of the brain, the temporal lobe, Broca's Areas, and others related to the expression of thoughts and feelings, which is disturbed. The ideas, forms, and images arise intact but cannot be conveyed into meaningful messages. One might think again in terms of left brain and right brain. If Heart yin energies are intact, the right creative side is functioning, and if Heart yang energies are intact, then the left logically expressive ego functions will perform their roles in the total creative production. This part includes form, organization, concept, discrimination, and articulate understanding. All of the higher patterns of intelligence — philosophical, mathematical, scientific, and theological — depend on the integrity of Heart yang energies. Heart yang is identified by all that is implied by 'The Word.'

In contrast to those whose Heart yin is deficient and who do not experience feelings of love, people whose Heart yang is deficient feel love, affection, and warmth but cannot express it. Sometimes, because they cannot formulate their feelings, they may act out and become involved impulsively. People will be drawn to the subject, whose 'vibrations' can transmit these feelings; but this potential will not be concretely fulfilled. This person may, therefore, be a source of great frustration to others, to those who depend on the verbal and physical articulation of these feelings and thoughts, especially children, husbands, wives, friends, and family.

We find a person whose aura seems highly sensual and sincerely full of promise of imaginative *sexual* play, whose actual performance is lacking the organized aspects of excitement that are necessary to sexual fulfillment. The coherent expression of the impulse is lacking. The lack of control may lead to premature ejaculation or an easy loss of erection as a primordial way of controlling excitement. Inasmuch as premature ejaculation is a problem in men and inability to reach complete orgasm a problem for women, due to impaired impulse stability, the tendency will be toward sexual play that does not require either. Both will be filled with passion if Heart yin energies are relatively intact, and yet adult sex will not be easily available with the above handicaps. The tendency may, therefore, be to turn to safer avenues where failure is not an issue, to those whose requirements are less demanding than normal adults, to children, prostitutes, or gigolos, and to oral forms of sex. Violence is always an issue when frustration is high and when the energies of the drive are strong, as we are assuming here.

The inability to successfully express the many creative thoughts and feelings we associate with healthy Heart yin energies leaves the subject with a great deal of unfocused energy, which he or she will come to fear as a potentially disorganizing force in life. This threat is one major source of *anxiety*. Occasions involving 'expression' and all attempts to organize Heart yang energies into an efficient ego structure, either from inside or out, will also be a source of anxiety, because these attempts will become associated with repeated failure. Expression will always be a potential provocation of danger and anxiety. Another wellspring of anxiety is that described by Fritz Perls, emanating from excitement and high energy, which, for one reason or another, cannot be realized in a safe and fulfilling fashion.

Phobias will be of any situation in which the expression of structured ideas or feelings are consistently required or expected. Teaching, public speaking, musical performance will evoke 'stage fright'. In extreme cases, people may become averse to expressing their own name in a public place for fear of losing the ability of saying even that well.

Sooner or later the accumulated pain and frustration of repeated failures to successfully communicate one's self breaks through and may, depending on the relative weakness of Water energies, emerge as *depression.* Although the subject's history may be marked by frequent episodes of lows and highs depending on problems in the Fire phase, if denial has been substantial, this depression will be of the involutional variety, sudden and devastating. The personality is overwhelmed, and strong feelings of worthlessness may prevail. Suicide is a strong possibility, because the underlying forces are strong and the pain, therefore, high.

[183]

Involutional melancholia with delusions of worthlessness and exaggerated guilt may be one form of *psychosis,* as a further development of the involutional depression we have just described. Projection of these feelings may produce a persecutory paranoid psychosis. The difficulties in organizing primary process material may color the psychosis with one or another form of thought disorder. And because the pressure for an outlet is so great, this disorder may, at times, emerge with the force and anarchy of a manic episode.

We have a relatively integrated *bioenergetic* function compared to those stuck in the Water, Wood, and Earth phases; yet, where Heart yang deficiency is the problem, the mind end of the head-genital axis may be functionally weaker. The upper part of the body chest and arms, which are the more physically expressive in terms of gesture and available breath, will be less well developed than the lower parts. This is in contrast to Heart yin deficiency, when the genital end may be functionally weaker.

There will be less armoring, and the process of armoring may take place at a later period, because this person initially is permitted and able to feel a great deal and only unable to organize and express it successfully. Repression is, therefore, not an issue. Whereas he may appear to have a moderate lack of muscle tone compared with the Heart yin deficient person, he is actually less rigid and more flexible.

A Case of Writer's Block

Mr. L. came to see me in my role as a psychiatrist at the time when I was first integrating acupuncture into my practice. His chief complaint was depression complicated by alcoholism, as well as gastro-intestinal complaints. He was a public relations writer who at the time of our first meeting had been out of work for some time. This was one of the more immediate sources of his depression. In his initial biographical note, which was a story of a burgeoning sensitivity to the dangers in the world and a growing distrust of parents, people, and especially himself to cope with life, he stated the following: "I came to believe that nothing I tried could ever work out, every effort was doomed to failure. Adler says that in every failure there is this fictitious personal superiority striving, plus a lack of social interest. I know that well. I have thought at various times I could be a great writer but have a lifetime writer's block. The sin of hubris — fear and self-loathing." He went on to say: "Perhaps the only positive asset I had over the years was the desire to understand and master my fate in some fashion. That had never entirely deserted me. And I have not given up on that transcendental quest. Somewhere, deep inside, the healthy side of me, eros, is still a tiny flame." That "quest" had taken him to five years of psychoanalysis prior to our work and to an enormous search into the literatures of the world in order to "master [his] fate."

During the following three months, using acupuncture, a little *bioenergetics,* and talk, we plunged the depths of his 'dark' side, uncovering black, murderous sadism and a great deal of sadness. Some of the latter he realized was his mother saying, "Poor thing, feelings are hurt, cruel world, don't want to see you suffer, cannot punish you." The acupuncture stimulated many fruitful dreams. In this period, in his words, "I moved from my black, negative, diabolical to the positive side." The acupuncture was a meditative experience, evoking a great deal of feeling and usable insight, and a growing centeredness. He awakened to the need to support his family, and our work ended when he found a good job as a writer in the Midwest.

After 20 treatments he said: "My relationships with my children have improved, I have moved to the positive side and am no longer depressed, I am not avoiding pain, I am facing anger and grief. My alcoholism, smoking, and caffeine addiction I see as a problem rather than a source of self-esteem. I am in touch with my need and my ability to support my family. I have less worry and anxiety, and my body is better coordinated." He added that "I can express myself better, am working (writing) more productively, I am better organized and have fewer false starts."

Heart Yang Excess

Personality: Compulsive Communicator

When Heart yang is in excess, formalized expression becomes the overriding energic and life agenda. And for most people who are so disposed, the expression usually far outruns the creative material available from the primogenial *incunabula.* Prolific creators such as Haydn, Telemann, Vivaldi,

Bach, and Mozart, whose quality matched the quantity of their remarkable harvest of original conception, are the exceptions to whom history has affixed the title of 'genius.'

[185]

Quantity overpowers quality, and we tend to have people whose early material is highly valuable and whose expansive subsequent work diminishes in value, or whose work is always voluble but lacking in development. The tendency is to be repetitive; or, being compulsive communicators and having run out of their own ideas, they become salesmen and sell other people's. They need, therefore, a constant audience, leaning toward acting, salesmanship, and, in the extreme, may become 'con artists.' When the overriding theme is quantity rather than quality, taste may suffer from the discrepancy.

Other Attributes of Heart Yang Excess

Cognition will tend to be clear and sharp, because Heart yang energies are important to the logical synthesis and expression of feelings, thoughts, and imagery. Speech may be somewhat pressured, as, for example, with the 'high-pressure salesman,' with a relative poverty of thought, and with some compensatory embellishment of content. Or, as Shakespeare said, there will be much "sound and fury, signifying nothing."

Anxiety will be experienced in any situation that interferes with the pressure to communicate. Under these circumstances, the degree of anxiety will be commensurate with the suppression of bursting energy, which may at times be overwhelming. The expansiveness of this force may make confining situations or spaces relatively intolerable and be experienced as early agoraphobia. In those situations where the subject had shown early promise and then slackened in quality, there may be an ego issue involving pretense, both to others and to himself. In either case, pretense always carries with it the anxiety of being found out.

Depression with all Fire energy disharmony tends to be cyclothymic, partly because of the changeableness of Fire, and partly because these energies reach out to the world for relationships on which they depend for fulfillment more than any other. This is especially true for those Heart yang excessive people whose drive to express themselves increases this need for a responsive audience. Dependency of this sort is highly unreliable and sets the stage for many mood swings, as the responses vary from positive to negative.

For those whose talent for cohesive expression brings them a natural early advantage in life, but who falter when substance cannot match volume, the awareness, usually in middle age, that at best they have achieved mediocrity and not the illusive masterpiece, and, at worst, little of lasting value, may precipitate a major depressive episode. Because of the expansive nature of Heart yang excess, the depression may be less severe and even show some manic features or, at least, considerable agitation.

Psychotic episodes will probably be an extension of the major depressive episode, should the sense of defeat be in the extreme and the rest of the personality without resources. Whereas mental processes may remain relatively clear, the tendency to embroider content and to be expansive may lead to agitated (manic-like) delusional thinking, especially delusions of grandeur, interspersed with episodes of profound withdrawal.

Love relationships are unfulfilling for the partner as long as the verbal expression of feelings outweighs the substance behind them. Since a person exploits that which he does best in the struggle for survival, the subject will tend to use words as a manipulative tool, exploiting his talent for reasoning to convince the partner that they are indeed getting what they feel is missing. It is not dishonesty or the need just to get his way which drives the subject into the above behavior. More important is the need to keep his audience and to compensate in as seductive a manner as possible for what even he sooner or later realizes is so far out of balance, that there is a superfluence of words, but not necessarily the right ones.

Sex will be simply a matter of relatively more performance than inspiration, more words than action, and more reason than passion.

Bioenergetically, we find a person who appears on the surface to be without any obvious serious defects but shows slight 'qi wild' signs. The excessive drive for expression and communication will place a steady drain on Heart yin energies, which will not have the opportunity for recovery. Frequently, this person seems to be going along physically at full speed and then suddenly collapses. He is usually moving at too fast a pace to notice what is happening inside.

A Case of Unfulfilled Early Promise

The person we are about to consider as an example of Heart yang excess is unfortunately only one of an army of people who sit at their typewriters pouring out material at a prodigious rate while they accumulate an equally astounding mountain of rejection notices from the publishing industry. Ms. A was a 72-year-old woman who came because of a sore back and herpes zoster. She had, in her youth, won scholarships and fellowships in literature and had published a highly successful and well-received novel by the time she was 28.

She broke with her old American family and lived abroad in Paris with a famous jazz musician, joining the exciting literary scene that included Hemingway, Miller, and Stein. She returned to the "states" because of World War II and bought a house in a community that is a center of American art. She lived her life traveling between this rural paradise and the Village scene in New York City where she had a studio-apartment. She was well-fixed financially by inheritance, and although as she grew older the money did not carry her as far, she managed to live quite well by renting a small cottage on her property. She never married.

{187}

Although her literary production was to be envied, it never matched the quality of her early promise, nor was she published again. She nevertheless maintained her dignity by identifying with literary circles in which she continued to circulate by acting hostess to large summer parties of writers and artists in her comfortable home. No one any longer took her seriously, but they did avail themselves of her hospitality. She was not included in the intimate and heavy drinking crowd of currently successful literati.

However, she was not to be ignored. The weekly local paper was filled with her letters to the editor on all subjects, as well as many poems and essays on philosophy and the sheer beauty of her surroundings. There were even some short stories. The editors were excessively generous in the paper and print they allotted to her, which could hardly have been explained either financially or by the mediocre quality of the material. She was a very nice person and, fortunately, recovered quickly from the herpes and her back ache, the latter being associated with sitting so many hours at her typewriter.

THE PERICARDIUM

It is my impression that the Fu (hollow, external) organ of any organ system is the guardian of the Zang (solid, internal) organ of that pair; and, among its other energic physiological functions, it serves the need of security and restoration. If this concept is correct, then it would be sufficient for the Heart to have for its defense only the Small Intestine, which is its Fu counterpart. The need for a special Zang organ to assist in the protection of the Heart rests with the enormous importance of the Heart as the supreme controller, and especially as the controller of the conscious mind and of the spirit. "The Heart stores and harbors the divine spirit."[15] The ancients recognized this, as was implied by the original *Inner Classic (Nei jing)* pulses in which the Pericardium occupies the position above the Heart. The European system has assigned this position to the Small Intestine. (Each may be correct, according to its use.)

Natural Functions of the Pericardium

The Pericardium energies serve as the interface between the communicating ego of a person and the communicating egos of others. These are the energies responsible for the realization of successful interpersonal relations, for the quality and quantity of contact with the outside world that enhances individual development. Winnicott would call this communicating ego the "false self,"[16] which deals with the world, negotiating the best possible arrangement there for the maximum fulfillment of the "true self," which itself never communicates directly. (I think of it as the *shen* or 'spirit,' as the creative potential energy which is the responsibility of each of us to make manifest).

It is said that the spirit *(shen)* resides in the Heart during life.[17] It is the work of Pericardium energies to provide both nourishment and protection for the spirit and the Heart. One must be both receptive and acquisitive in achieving sustenance, as well as clever and sharp, though fair, so that one does not give too much away in the inevitable bargaining that characterizes energy exchanges throughout life, after infancy. (I emphasize fairness because it is a point of wisdom that greediness is a seed of self-destruction.) While one does not cheat, one sees to it that one is not cheated. All of the ego skills contributed by other energic systems are coordinated by Pericardium energies to afford safe human contact while the inner self grows. These include the strategy and planning of the Gallbladder and Liver, the sense of limits to one's powers afforded by Kidney energies, memory from the Bladder, communication from the Heart, the digestion and distribution of thoughts by the Stomach and Spleen, and others that we have already or are yet to discuss.

The most fundamental issue of human existence is safe contact with other human beings. From the beginning, people will take those measures that ensure both their safety and their connection to other people, according to the requirements of the environment. If direct communication is not safe, indirect methods of contact will develop. Their object is not simply to protect, but, more especially, to restore to that environment conditions necessary to obtain what is ineluctable to life.

These stratagems, which I therefore call 'restorations,' were originally observed and described as 'defenses' by people working on a model which emphasized pathology. They were seen only as obstacles to the therapeutic work of unmasking the unconscious and as a nuisance to the therapist who labeled them as 'resistances' to be overcome, as the focal point of an endless, artificial, and needless struggle between therapist and hapless patient.

The positive aspects of these tactics have not been understood or appreciated until recently. All of the primitive displacement maneuvers described by Anna Freud[18] as defense-resistances exist not only as a shield against outrageous fortune, but primarily as a way of making a continuous safe 'contact' with significant others. Introjection, identification, projection, regression, undoing, reversal, turning against the self, denial, as well as the more sophisticated repression, reaction-formation, rationalization, intellectualization, and sublimation, are tactics of the Pericardium energy system to ensure the survival of an organism through 'contact' in an environment unfavorable to its central integrity and existence.

{189}

A case in point is that of a middle-aged professional person who complained that he had been severely addicted to sugar, nicotine, caffeine, and alcohol, with escalating episodes of acute illness during times of stress. He regarded these habits as evil forces that he wished, with someone's help, to eradicate. It did not feel right to proceed with the acupuncture techniques available for these purposes without a clear and mutual understanding about how these cravings fit into his life. As we talked it became clear that he was a brilliant person in his field, who, however, was unable to realize his acknowledged capabilities without being attached to an aggressive person. For the drive and assertion necessary to fulfill his original ideas and organizational ability, he depended on another. His estranged wife, a psychopathic personality, had provided this until she abandoned him, destroying their very successful business. It became more and more apparent that his 'outer self', his ego, was programmed only for war, which he had conducted with his ex-wife and many other authorities over the years, leaving little for the nurturing and enhancing of his 'true self'. This pattern repeated the less-than-adequate care and protection he received from his parents in his early life. Clearly his 'addictions' were a way to feed that inner self which had been left a helpless, dependent spirit, abandoned by his first caretakers and then by his 'self'. His primary function became finding and attaching himself to someone who could 'sell his wares'. To achieve his goal of establishing healthy habits, he had first to see that the 'bad' habits were there to serve the positive purpose of feeding an otherwise starving inner being. In examining all disharmony, we must separate the intention from the result. Only with the understanding that his primary goal through all of the self-destruction had been positive, can we call upon this part of his personality to assist him in proceeding to a more constructive life.

The Pericardium system manages this safe passage through adverse environments so that all other energic systems, especially the Heart, may be spared the drain of restorative operations and devote their full energies to the consummation of their essential natural functions. Restoration is an ongoing and endless task, a constant drain upon the energy required for the Pericardium's other tasks.

The developmental era in which Fire phase energies are ascendant is roughly between the ages of three to five years, though they have already played a significant part in the development of speech. It is a more relaxed time when many of the survival mechanisms are already in place and the growing organism may turn to the 'lighter' side of human existence. It is after the extraordinary exigencies of infant nourishment on all levels, the vicissitudes of the 'no' stage, and the development of a normal gait, coordination, and the ego structures necessary to everyday survival that the growing person is ready for 'affairs of the heart.' Love relations of remarkable intensity and complexity evolve in the playground. Competition, jealousy, and sexual exploration are extended to these new territorial prerogatives as well as at home in the 'Oedipal' situation, until these energies are temporarily diverted to the mastering of written language during the developmental period known as 'latency.'

The relationship with the parent of the opposite sex plays a critical role at this stage of development when affairs of the heart and sexuality make their first inchoate surges. The self-image of the child as a desirable yet respected person in the eyes of the parent of the opposite sex develops or is negated at this time. The family romance, mother and son, father and daughter, must flourish in an atmosphere of joy, acceptance, restraint, and regard. The balance is delicate and rarely perfect.

While Heart energies are leading children toward these new attractions to other people, both at home and abroad, in the nursery school and on the playground, the ego is developing apace, evolving Pericardium energies for more sophisticated psychological strategies in keeping with the increasing complexity of relations.

A related function of Pericardium energies is the unification of spirit love (Heart) and genital love (Liver-Kidneys) through the free and open passage of the middle burner (nurturing and the Spleen) to produce adult sexuality. These energies are deeply involved in the giving and taking and the blending of physical and verbal affective love. Yin, serving defensively, and yang, serving aggressively, participate equally in this work. Related functions are as the messenger from whom joy is derived and as the official ambassador who is the origin of joy and pleasure.

To some observers, the Pericardium is the harmonizer of the various aspects of Fire in the body, including Kidney yang and the Triple Burner. Though I agree that the 'little fire' of the Kidney yang and the 'little fire' of the Pericardium are intimately related, I see the Triple Burner as the harmonizer. To others, the "Pericardium represents consumption of life (Wood) by an internal heating process (transformation). Through this sacrifice (meaning to make sacred), life is drawn up to a higher vibratory level."[19] I see this as a province of Heart energy, and not Pericardium function.

In this regard, Pericardium energies in conjunction with Triple Burner energies are essential to the 'fair' distribution of energy among the three burners. Some sources ascribe to the Pericardium energies the 'official' and formidable task as the "administrator of justice."

NATURAL FUNCTIONS OF PERICARDIUM YIN

The Heart houses the 'spirit-mind,' the spirit carried from generation to generation by Water energies and made manifest in language. During life it is fed through the Wood phase which is the 'spirit-soul,' the part of the spirit which grows during a lifetime. This is the inner core of the self, the 'emperor'; kill the spirit and the organism dies (Queequeg in *Moby Dick*).[20] Protecting the spirit-mind from harm becomes a critical function of the energy systems, second only to, and in conjunction with, providing for its continued nurturance. The latter can be accomplished during life only through contact with other spirit-minds. However offensive that contact may be, we human beings are bound by that reality; we have no choice if we choose life.

The laws which govern that reality require us to give if we are to get. Whereas during the infancy and the early childhood era, dominated by Earth energies, we 'sort by self,' the following eras of development, which are increasingly governed by Fire energies, witness a concomitant shift to 'sorting by other.'[21] The thread that binds mother and child through the invisible energy channel that replaces the umbilicus multiplies as other human beings enter into the child's life and gradually becomes a two-way, rather than a one-way, conduit.

This thread (described so well by the Kahuna, the Hawaiian shamanistic tradition[22]), and the ineluctable need to preserve it, is at once our greatest glory and our greatest danger. While it affords human beings the unique opportunity for spiritual change and growth through an exchange of energies with other souls, it also affords those other souls access to our own soul, both for better and for worse. Once again we tread the tightrope of the universal paradox.

It is the function of Pericardium yin energies to maintain the integrity of this 'thread' and to regulate the flow of energy along it in both directions. While it is the work of the Pericardium yang energies to acquire sustenance, it is the work of the yin to receive it and to prevent the spirit-mind from being drained by others. The Pericardium is called upon to contain the Heart's natural ebullience and desire to reach out to others, to be receptive while not drained. It is called upon to achieve a realistic, healthy balance between what one shares of one's inner self and what one keeps to oneself, exercising the utmost diplomacy and care not to offend the all-important 'others.' In addition to the Heart's openness, there are other internal factors that, in excess, strain the Pericardium's managerial energies; these include Wood's directionality, Metal's propensity to 'let go,' Earth's proclivity for bonding, and Water's chaotic drive and power. The Pericardium must restrain and regulate all of these forces so that there is no outpouring of energy beyond what one receives. Truly, it is said that it is greater to give than to receive, and that the more you give, the more you have. 'Giving' is the Heart's special quality without which it would stagnate and die. In this sense, giving is the stimulus that urges the life force within the spirit-mind to higher levels of creativity in love and in work. This notwithstanding, and whatever may be ascribed to the one-sided energy equations of genius, the Pericardium yin's contribution to safeguarding our essential lines of supply and storehouses of energy from damage by maintaining a balance between input and output is essential to life. Discriminating between those with whom one can safely share one's inner being and those who may not be trusted is always critical to well-being and survival. This is especially true in moments of excess, such as falling in love, when one is off-guard, open, and overwhelmed by the spirit-mind's great affinity for others and its deep terror of isolation. The ancients preferred the Pericardium to keep the Fire "temperate cool, fit, and well," i.e., to keep a balance between passion and reason. The ancient texts caution us against inhibiting Pericardium energies, in which case "the rejoicing person's" soul is laid bare instead of remaining concealed.

Pericardium yin energies sustain all of the restorative stratagems that are sometimes necessary for doing the work we have just described. Even under the best of circumstances, situations arise in which one is called upon to make compromises with one's 'wants.' Sublimation is the process of finding and accepting a substitute activity that gives some measure of satisfaction in lieu of the original 'want,' and it is the most desirable of all the restorative measures. The others more or less drain energy from the Pericardium yin's important function as the energy that joins romance and eroticism, the Word and the Touch, the heart and the genitals, the spirit and the body, rendering adult sexuality sacred.

PERICARDIUM YIN DISHARMONY

Personality in Pericardium Yin Deficiency and Excess

The inhibition or deficiency of Pericardium yin energies renders subjects less than capable of fending for themselves in the interpersonal arena of love, sex, and the creative aspects of life. They are easily exploited because of their eagerness to please in order to be accepted. Even in the best of affiliations they are unable to stand up to others for fear of rejection, and, placing themselves in the position of a 'door mat,' are often walked over and trampled unintentionally. They may feel a great deal and express it well, but they cannot control that expression in the interest of their own well-being. Since they "wear their heart on their sleeves," they are highly vulnerable to being abused by people whose integrity and intentions they are in no position to judge. Unable to substantially control their heart feelings, they are forever impulsively falling in love, forming powerful, clinging involvements that are more like attachments than equal mutual relationships, for which reason they tend to be unrealistic, short-lived, and destined to be quickly and frequently repeated.

Judgment in choosing a mate who could satisfy some of their basic needs is overridden by a denial of reality induced by their inability to delay or sublimate surges of emotion, leading them often to people who are unavailable for a true bond, such as with those already committed elsewhere, or who are otherwise unsuitable for an authentic union. Sooner or later they may stop trusting their judgment and miss the 'real thing' when it does come along.

When a young girl fails to win her father's affection in the Oedipal conflagration, she experiences this as a profound lack in herself. In order to win affection she must appear to be someone else, pretend even to herself—nay, especially so—to be another, playing a role that she associates with success in gaining affection. Depending on the myriad of influences around her, the roles which emerge cannot be easily predicted or classified. Pericardium yin energies play an important part in the resolution of all affairs of the heart. If her father prefers boys, she may become a tomboy. In the past the result was often a seductive, dramatic, and manipulative personality whom we have labeled, with some reproach, the 'hysterical personality.' The cool, aloof, unattainable breaker of hearts and lives as typified by Turandot (Puccini)[23] or the vamp of the silent films, who some of us may remember, are among other better-known possibilities. These restorative tactics seem to change with the times, and where the vamp now lacks an enchanted audience, one may find a martyred, long-suffering soul, clinging because of his or her pitiful plight, arousing guilt and a sense of obligation in others. These are very sticky connections whose ubiquity is a testimony to their effectiveness.

Professional acting may seem like a natural direction for a person who feels he must be someone else in order to survive. The integrity of the Pericardium yin energies is a critical factor in the outcome of this endeavor. Without suitable control of the irrepressibly expressive Heart energies by the Pericardium yin, the 'true self' will suffer from both a lack of inner creative energy for its own development as well as the depth necessary for great drama.

Pretense, both aware and unaware, becomes an important ingredient in a character whose lack of authenticity is referred to in psychoanalytic circles as the 'as if' personality. The over concern for acceptance channels energy excessively toward others and away from grounding in oneself, engendering superficiality, emotional instability, and restlessness. Hypomanic behavior and pressured, rapid, and circumstantial speech patterns are reflections of the desperation to establish and hold contact.

The boy during the Oedipal period wants to impress his mother with his strength, power, and prowess, especially vis a vis his father. An unfavorable parental reception by one or both parents will leave the issue of his potency unresolved, to be settled in other ways, depending on factors such as size and real strength. He could become the local bully, retreat into a fantasy world of imagined, dauntless virility, or turn to less obviously masculine pursuits. If Pericardium yin energies are sufficient, this boy will eventually channel these needs into his areas of strength which he will develop, forging for himself the adequate self-image his parents could not give him. There are always scars from such a struggle, from which, however, a stronger and perhaps more interesting person might develop. If Pericardium yin energies are not sufficient to the task, the bully, the schizoid, and other maladaptive restorative tendencies will persist and grow into major personality problems.

If Pericardium yin energies are in *excess*, the subjects will suffer from the consequences of repressed Heart energies, a condition which Dr. Shen calls 'Heart closed.' They will have difficulty opening their hearts to give or receive, and in the absence of intimacy they will feel empty and isolated. They will have similar difficulty opening their minds to consider new ideas from, or to share their own with, others. They give little of their real selves, make no real sacrifice, and have therefore little that is sacred in their lives. Like the parsimonious Scrooge, they may correctly discern that they receive nothing, for which they will blame others, becoming people who feel cheated, bitter, and vengeful.

Cognition in Pericardium Yin Deficiency and Excess

When the Pericardium yin is *deficient* the energy that is required for the purposes of restoration, which must go on, will be procured from wherever it is available, but first from within the Fire phase. The ego-organizing energies of Heart yang will be among those energy systems called upon to forfeit some of their share, and *cognitive* functions will suffer. Those functions most closely associated with the Fire phase concern the 'process' of thinking, attention, concentration, coherency, clarity, logic, and the orderly flow and appropriate rate of thought and speech. It is these which suffer first when Pericardium yin energies falter and energy is withdrawn from the immediate 'family' within the Fire phase.

When Pericardium yin energies are *excess,* there is an intensively persistent concern for self-protection that diverts energy from the general reservoir available for other ego functions, especially those Fire phase energies used for creative thought and creative relationships. Thinking, while ordered, will not have available the source, the fountainhead of imagery and emotion, which is the hallmark of the 'other reality.' Once again there is a profound sense of emptiness, loneliness, and sadness for one's lost heart-mind.

This reservoir has two sources. The first is from one of the 'singular' organs, called the 'nervous system,' which arises from the *yuan* ancestral energy and is akin to the Kidney essence *(jing)* function of building the 'marrow' of the bone, whence comes the myelin of the central nervous system. The second is called 'mental energy' and is one of the five 'functional energies' which stem from the 'five tastes' that are stored and distributed by the Spleen energies, as well as receiving a direct contribution from each of the organ systems. The distinction between the two is that the former is concerned with Kidney energies and the material foundation of brain activities, while the latter is concerned with the more ephemeral activity of mind and spirit. It is, on the other hand, the Kidney qi energies which convey the potential spirit energies of an individual from their primordial existence to this lifetime and to the protection of the Fire through the Triple Burner system. Very little information is available about these energies in the English language.

Anxiety in Pericardium Yin Deficiency and Excess

In deficient states of the Pericardium, *anxiety* will be experienced in any situation in which a person's restorative behavior fails to bring the desired results of closeness without danger. This becomes more likely as one approaches adulthood and enters into relationships of greater intimacy where the all-important pretense at the core of the restoration may be perceived and uncovered. The overly seductive young woman whose self-esteem is impaired by her father's indifference will become anxious when someone tries to get close enough to appreciate her insecurity. The most important source of anxiety here is that associated with the uncovering of pretense. Nearly as common is the anxiety generated when the ever-surging and ever-yearning Heart energies threaten to break the barriers against intimacy created when Pericardium energies are in excess, or when the Pericardium, in its wisdom, has erected barriers in response to earlier trauma to protect the spirit. When Pericardium yin energies are insufficient to contain these Fire energies, a person might feel more comfortable in contained spaces that reinforce the Pericardium and relieve the fear of losing control. They might be *phobic* of spaces and situations which invite further expansion. Those whose Pericardium energies are in excess are already engirded and will have the opposite propensities: phobias of closed spaces and partiality to the open ones. Their uncommonly successful restorations are barriers against intimacy and lead to isolation and eventually the existential anxiety of significant alienation.

Depression in Pericardium Yin Deficiency and Excess

Depression associated with the dysfunction of Pericardium yin energies would be classified in the DSM-III as cyclothymic. The pattern is similar to the depression associated with a failure in Earth energies where bonding is inadequate, where there is an alternation between euphoria when a love 'object' is found, and dysphoria when it is lost. The difference is one in depth and breadth. The person whose dysphoria is in the Earth phase experiences a much more profound depression which is catastrophically devastating to his entire existence and overall function. The person with a Pericardium yin depression may feel devastated, but he is able, if he chooses, to continue to function efficiently in the rest of his life. Furthermore, the cycles are less frequent because a Pericardium yin person is likely to hold onto a relationship somewhat longer than the Earth phase person, whose bonds are much more tenuous. Nevertheless, the depressions may increase in seriousness with repeated failure to form a successful love relationship, and, at some point, suicidal gestures may be made of both a manipulative and hysterical character, which nonetheless may be successful in the end.

The person with *excessive* Pericardium yin energies suffers great sadness, emptiness, and loneliness for the lack of a creative, mutually nurturing link with another person. The pain of this sadness can be obliterated only as long as the energy is there for that purpose. Eventually it cannot be sustained, and major depressive episodes will occur, especially when another person appears who is loving and caring. At these times the pain is even greater, as the Heart energies press against the stagnating forces of the Pericardium yin; suicide is a serious possibility, as one after another of the surrogate relationships fails to satisfy the ineluctable needs for genuine human contact.

{ 197 }

Love and Sex in Pericardium Yin Deficiency and Excess

The inability to control and manage the compelling need for affection when Pericardium yin energies are *deficient* seriously reduces the chances of exercising good judgment in the suitable choice of a *love* partner. Frequently these individuals will attract people who exploit them, lending a pseudo-masochistic color to the involvement. They do not seek or enjoy the pain but are unable to defend themselves against it.

Furthermore, the overdetermination of these needs reduces the ability of people to 'sort by others.' The reduced awareness of another person's needs renders the relationship rather superficial, unsatisfying to the 'significant other,' and therefore, though sticky, rather short lived. As a reaction to the misery and chaos generated by this way of life, there will be an attempt to keep back Heart feelings by withdrawing all warmth and moving to the opposite extreme. This is rarely successful except for a short time, after which the cycle repeats itself.

Love for the person with excessive Pericardium yin energies is, I repeat, a severely painful experience, to be dreaded and avoided at almost all costs. The attraction is, of course, inevitably there within all whose Hearts are closed, since the outward thrust of these energies towards another never rests.

Sex is frequently used by this person as a device to hold a partner and as a proxy sensation in lieu of Heart feelings. It is rarely successful in holding together a long-term relationship. The Pericardium yin's commission to superintend the union of mind and genitals within the Heart in the service of adult sexuality is forestalled in a person whose Heart is closed to this consummation. The excessive Pericardium yin male has so much control that he is often a desirable sexual companion for short periods or as a gigolo. So also, the excessive Pericardium yin female's emphasis on sexual competence will make her a desirable companion for the male who is in the market for sex without love.

The deficient Pericardium yin person is often inadvertently promiscuous, partly because relationships are not long lasting and partly out of his unmanageable quest for affection, which renders him a quick mark for the transient satisfaction of other people's needs. He also foregoes his own sexual preferences for those of his partner, submitting, often without protest, to sexual practices that he experiences as 'perverse.' Sexual satisfaction is therefore not commonly forthcoming, though it may be feigned to gratify the partner. The relative lack of control over emotion may express itself sexually in men as premature ejaculation, and in women as the inability to focus their excitement to achieve an orgasm.

Psychosis and Dreams in Pericardium Yin Deficiency and Excess

Psychotic episodes are not common when only Pericardium yin energies are deficient or excessive. In assuming, for the purposes of our discussion of the Fire phase, that the previous developmental eras were intact, ego development will have reached a level of stability that obviates psychosis except under the most unusual and stressful circumstances. Everyone, of course, has a breaking point. The course would be difficult to predict. As explained above in the discussion of cognition, Fire energies support the thinking 'process,' which we saw included attention, concentration, logic, coherency and clarity, as well as the flow and tempo of speech. These functions would most likely be impaired. Should delusions enter the picture, they would most likely concern feelings of being very desirable and pursued by the opposite sex, especially by very important people who either wish to or have already married them.

The literature attributes to the Pericardium yin dysfunction romantic *dreams*, including ones about mountains in which there is either a great deal of smoke and heat, or in which there is a great deal of ice and cold. A fear of falling is also associated with Pericardium yin dysfunction.

Bioenergetics in Pericardium Yin Deficiency and Excess

Bioenergetically, the inability of the Pericardium yin *deficient* person to modulate the flow of Heart energy represents a significant drain on the overall energy of the body, leading to fatigue, especially in the morning after a full night's sleep. As a result the person needs an endless infusion of energy from the outside, while seeking at the same time some sort of control from the same source over his emotional life, which tends to go off in all directions.

On a physical level he will appear armored, but the armor is superficial. The difficulty in holding energy in the Heart area will render that part of the body, the upper burner, relatively underdeveloped and somewhat collapsed.

The shoulders and arms will be stiff and tight from the body's attempt to compensate for the Pericardium's unsuccessful defense of the Heart. One will neither find the degree of anxiety nor the total collapse of the masochist, nor the integrated, armored person whose Pericardium energies are intact. *Bioenergetically*, the subject falls somewhere between the two, with collapse occurring in parts of the personality rather than the whole, and anxiety being contained rather than overwhelming.

The Pericardium yin *excessive* person will suffer from exhaustion as his energy is drained to maintain restoration. His armor reaches the deep musculature of the upper part of the body, especially the chest muscles, which become overdeveloped from protecting the Heart.

A Case of Pericardium Yin Deficiency: Need for Attention

The Pericardium yin deficient person is well illustrated by a 25-year-old, extremely attractive woman who came to see me in a depressed and agitated state. She worked professionally as a singer and had one child for whom she was barely able to care because she was in a continuous turmoil over her love life. She was at this time completely hysterical, tearing her clothes, screaming, running from her house into the street, and unable to control her desperate longing for the younger man who had just left her because she had been too possessive and clinging. She confided to me that she could not live without "his penis." No other penis would do. He was forced to leave the area to avoid the scenes that she created where he lived and worked. She was unable to function, to work, or to care for her child who was now living with some friends.

Her history was a frequent repetition of the same story. Her mother had been jealous of her father's affection for her and successfully kept them apart by making both of their lives miserable whenever father and daughter seemed to be close. To keep the peace, her father became aloof and generally ignored her. Consequently, she sought and obtained the attention of boys from an early age and was promiscuous by the age of 14. Her judgment in choosing men was distorted by her need for attention, and she went wherever that wind blew the strongest, whatever the cost. She had a reputation as an 'easy mark,' and she was unable to play any of the boy-girl courtship games that make a girl seem 'hard to get' and much appreciated when 'won.'

While our work together got her through the present crisis, she was unable to focus on her inner self or stay long enough to work through her father-daughter love affair with a therapist. Instead, she gave up her work in nightclubs and turned instead to a religious order which practiced celibacy. The last time that I saw her, she was serving at a wedding to which I had been invited, which her religious order was catering. She wore no make-up and seemed unusually serene and stable.

A Case of Pericardium Yin Excess: 'Heart Closed'

It is difficult to choose one person to represent the Pericardium yin excessive personality, having seen many people with this problem over the years. Let us talk about a young man, aged 30, who came originally because of pain in his right side, both front and back, in his right shoulder, wrist, and left knee. He mentioned at our first meeting that he felt his "life was going down the drain" and that he felt "paralyzed." He had recently undergone a powerful drug therapy and become aware of his sadistic side, at which point he "converted to Christianity." This seemed strange, since both of his parents were Christian and he had never practiced any other religion. This conversion led him to the ministry, about which he was enormously conflicted. His overall pulse had a Cotton quality that suggested an oppressive sadness, and his Heart pulse showed no wave, meaning that his Heart was 'closed.' Since he was staying for only a short time in my area, we agreed to see whether a few sessions could help.

His physical complaints responded well to the needles and they also produced an enormous emotional catharsis. He reported that he was unable to feel, show, or tolerate love. It made him extremely uncomfortable and rejecting of the person who was expressing it to him. Sex was the only way he could be comfortably close to another person. At times, if he were attracted to someone, he could feel the energy going from his heart out through his arms and then withdraw when he was threatened.

All of his physical pain disappeared, and he went on to say that his energy had improved, that he had an opening in his chest area, and that he had become more aware of himself both physically and emotionally. During the last of six sessions he revealed his conviction that in a previous lifetime, during World War II, he was a Nazi soldier who had killed and tormented many people, including many Jews. He felt that in this life he had to atone for these atrocities and had to grow and develop away from the person who did these things. When last heard of many years later, he was a minister in a distant part of the country, married, and with a family.

NATURAL FUNCTIONS OF PERICARDIUM YANG

In the service of the Pericardium's primary responsibility to protect and nourish the spirit, to maintain safe and balanced contact with other humans, the Pericardium yang's contribution is primarily to provide energy for acquisition and for an aggressive shield when necessary. Heart yin provides the basic source material, and Heart yang the ego structure, to express it. Pericardium yang energies provide the thrust, the direction, the precision, the timing, and appropriateness of the expression. The object of these energies is to procure what is required and to fight for it when peaceful methods miscarry.

The Pericardium yang is concerned with strongly and accurately reaching the correct mark with intense, focused communication. The person with healthy Pericardium yang energies will expediently seek and find the appropriate fulfilling response for his expressed love or creativity. He will find the desirable mate, the most suitable publisher for his book, and is able to be persuasive with all. He will generally be at the right place, at the opportune time, with the propitious people, and with the correct material and message.

Throughout the Fire phase, communication is the central theme. The acquisitiveness and assertiveness to which we have referred is largely verbal. The age old question "Are you a lover or a fighter?" is irrelevant to people with good Pericardium yang energies because they are good at both, especially using words. Authentic loving phrases and tender embraces at the appropriate moment establish the circulating network of the essential support and sustenance, the give and take, of human relations. Convincing turns of speech succeed in commanding the best audiences for creativity, whether it is an art gallery, a producer, or a publisher. They win cases in court, sway assemblages in political debate, and obtain the most desirable jobs and promotions from superiors. Physical aggression, though available, is the last recourse chosen by these energies when survival is at issue.

PERICARDIUM YANG DISHARMONY

Personality in Pericardium Yang Deficiency and Excess

Assuming that Heart yin and yang are intact, the subject with deficient Pericardium yang energies has the ideas and the ego organization to express them, but the singular inability to do so when and with whom it counts in a convincing fashion. Unfortunately, he is out of synchronization and fails constantly, despite the value of what he wishes to offer. He is unable to persuade anyone of the value of his love and talent due to the weakness of his presentation. For this reason he is deprived of the recognition and input necessary to nourish the loving, creative, and communicative aspects of existence. Ultimately, he feels empty and frustrated.

The latter may lead to considerable rage, either at himself or others whom he blames for his failure. A compensatory pseudo-aggressiveness may appear which lacks authenticity, purpose, and meaning except to achieve potency for the moment. Domination will displace mutuality as a conveyance of that power, which most often will miscarry, leaving the impression of exploitative and manipulative self-aggrandizement from which the love partner and potential patrons will withdraw, realizing the falseness of the subject's attentions.

The person with *excessive* Pericardium yang energies will falter at the other extreme by relying too much on style and too little on substance, too much on words and too little on real, rather than apparent, action. This was no more eloquently stated than by Liza Doolittle, the transformed flower girl in *My Fair Lady*, who, disgusted with "words, words, words," sang "show me, show me!"[24]

Other Attributes of Pericardium Yang Deficiency and Excess

When there is a plethora or dearth of Pericardium yang energies, all of the appurtenances of Heart *cognitive* 'process' functions such as memory, attention, concentration, logic, clarity, and coherence are compromised in terms of being either excessively or insufficiently precise, concise, and eloquently timed. The consequences are not catastrophic, but sufficient to interfere with the goals of thought and communication. While it may be difficult to imagine how being too precise is a problem, one must only bring to mind feelings aroused by the people who are constantly correcting us for the smallest deviances from exactitude. These could be people who have a surfeit of Pericardium yang energy.

Repeated failure to 'sell' oneself due to the handicaps described above will gradually generate *anxiety* wherein a Pericardium yang *deficiency* is faced with situations in which this kind of assertiveness is inescapable. The problem is not an initial fear of assertion, as one might find in miscarriages in the development of Wood energies. Instead, it is a failure in this later stage of development to generate an assertiveness that is effective in achieving desired results.

The person with an *excess* of Pericardium yang energies will experience anxiety whenever he is moved into a position in life where form becomes less important than substance. This occurs in all large institutions when very efficient people in lower managerial positions are moved into policy areas as a matter of seniority. Some anxiety will also be generated for the person who stumbles into a situation in which he is forced to depend on, or cope with, people who lack the exquisite precision that he has come to expect both of himself and others. The anxiety is even greater when he surmises, for a variety of reasons such as age or illness, that his flawlessness has its limitations and/or is permanently impaired.

When a person is fully equipped, in touch with his or her essence, and capable of organizing as well as defending it but is unable, due to a Percardium yang *deficiency*, to completely implement this potential (to appropriately market himself), the phase of frustration and despair is singularly intense. Since we are still in the Fire phase, the *depressive* episodes tend to be cyclic, falling into the much more severe DSM-III category of Major Depressive Episode. During the involutional period in particular, the anguish of a life retrospective of smoldering dreams which never caught fire engenders agonizing pain, the escape from which is often a genuine suicide attempt.

The *excessive* Pericardium yang person knows a different kind of depression that stems from the dislocation of interpersonal relations as the consequence of irritations generated by his extraordinary exactness, without a compensating essence. These disaffections are baffling and embittering, leading to a depression characterized by emptiness and loneliness.

The person whose only energic 'imbalance' is Pericardium yang *deficiency* is both frustrated and frustrating in love, his persuasive powers failing in time, place, and propriety with a person chosen well, to whom his heart is open in feeling and expression. The bumbling lover is there too late or early, with too little or too much, in a situation that is sweepingly and intolerably aggravating to all.

In contrast is the *excessive* Pericardium yang lover whose extraordinarily methodical thoroughness robs a romantic interlude, or even an extended attraction, of the wild, sensitive, chaotic unpredictability of heart feelings that renders passion so creative and vital to life. He is unable to follow the advice of Fritz Perls, who admonished us to "forget our minds and come to our senses."[25]

The subject is unable to perform *sexually* to anyone's satisfaction for the reasons already enumerated. In *deficiency* it is all a matter of disconcerting disintegration, and, in *excess*, a matter of tedious ultra-technology and little substance. Neither is conducive to the fluid streaming in which two people become one. The strength and focus of the underlying feeling makes the rage which ensues from unabated frustration potentially dangerous. Paid companionship and masturbation may serve to defuse some of this potentially explosive energy, while the monastic life may altogether side-step the issue, except in the realm of fantasy.

When there is a loss of control over consciousness in the Pericardium *deficient* person there will be five ingredients to the *psychosis* which ensues. First will be the delusion of being a great and successful person, especially as a lover, whose verbal supplications and solicitations are irresistible to all, especially to desired sexual partners. The second will be aggressiveness toward those who, usually from among the famous, are selected to play the role of lover. The third will be the need to identify the person or persons responsible for interfering in the consummation of this affair or of any other project for which acclaim is expected. The fourth is the potential danger to all of these people; and the last is some loss (deficiency) or accentuation (excess) of precision in logical thinking similar to the manner described earlier in our discussion of cognition, except to a far greater and disabling degree. Psychosis in a person with *excessive* Pericardium yang will be marked by obsessive-compulsive features and notable emptiness.

The *dreams* of *deficient* Pericardium yang people are ones in which there are endless experiences characterized by profound impotence. Sometimes there are attempts to shoot a gun in which bullets fall far short or wide of their mark. To my knowledge, Percardium yang *excess* dreams do not reveal any consistent pattern.

Bioenergetically the Pericardium yang *deficient* person appears at first glance to be healthy and has a flexible musculoskeletal structure with little armoring. After some observation one will see chaotic breathing patterns and disjointed, unfocused movements of a relatively subtle nature. Under stress these will increase noticeably to the point of disintegration. This is the person who, like the submarine captain in Herman Wouk's war trilogy,[26] functions well with the considerable knowledge he possesses until faced with the test of action. He looks and is great until he must move into a focused activity under pressure. Then he falls apart.

The Pericardium yang *excessive* person will likewise appear well organized and flexible as long as he is stationary. Once mobile, one will observe a subtle lack of fluidity and lack of freedom in which each movement is measured and limited in range. Furthermore, he will depend on an outside authority to direct his movements. Under stress this becomes an inability to move instinctively into performing a task, which translates into "He who hesitates is lost." German troops in World War II functioned brilliantly, if perhaps somewhat rigidly, as long as they followed orders, but they could not operate autonomously, which was a big advantage to the Allies in many situations.

Cases of Pericardium Yang Deficiency and Excess

As an example of Pericardium yang *deficiency*, there was E., a [205] young woman who came to me primarily because of headache, chest pain, menstrual pain and irregularity, insomnia, and diarrhea. Having lived for some time in the Peace Corps in a Moslem country, she had had hepatitis. She recognized the Heart symptoms as due to severe disappointment, because her well-formed plans for using her considerable knowledge of the esoteric Sufi tradition when she returned to this country fell through as the nation passed from its preoccupation with gurus to the age of the yuppies. She was an excellent and prolific writer and speaker, but despite her high degrees and obvious competence in extremely difficult subjects, she could never formulate a program for herself that would give her the recognition she deserved. Somehow she could not package and sell herself, be at the right place at the right time, integrate her considerable talents into a fertile, yielding product.

For Pericardium excess there is Mr. C., who was an elderly man when we met to treat a variety of his physical ills, including arthritis. He was from a distinguished family and in his youth had squandered a fortune. He and his wife had come down financially in the world and retired to an inherited home where they lived in relative modesty. Mr. C. was one of the most distinguished looking people I have ever met. His presence brought to mind a picture gallery of senators from the golden age of oratory. Indeed he was marvelously gifted of speech and could easily persuade even the most perspicacious that he was at least one of the great statesmen of the times.

His main interest was music. His ear was good, as evidenced by his ability for languages, and he had a fine voice. For most of his life he retired to his study to write music, and he was marvelously convincing in any discussion of this pursuit that he was on the verge of writing the definitive music of his time. If I had not met other members of the family, I would believe to this day that I had met the musical genius of the age instead of a pathetic figure who drowned his failure in drink.

Natural Functions of the Small Intestine

The Small Intestine is known as the 'minister of information,' whose ego functions are primarily cognitive. There are three activities that the Small Intestine shares with the Spleen-Stomach energies, whose ego tasks are likewise heavily involved in cognition. These three functions are the 'separation,' 'absorption,' and 'transformation' of ideas. These mental functions parallel the Small Intestine energies' work on a material level.

The Small Intestine energies' principal role in this psychological realm is the separation of ideas, which is an extrapolation of its physiological capacity to separate the 'pure from the impure.' This may include, for example, distinguishing the 'nourishing from the contaminating,' 'creative from destructive,' 'real from meretricious,' and 'love from hate.' Its broadest mandate is the distinction between 'clarity' and 'confusion,' necessary for lucid thinking, analysis, and discrimination.

Small Intestine energies are more subsidiary to Spleen energies during the process of absorption and storage, but tradition states that they are "entrusted with riches which create changes of physical structure" and are therefore important energies for "transformation." Chinese phenomenology teaches and requires us to consider that these "riches" are energies that must have their mental as well as spiritual reality, and that the transformations occur on all levels. We call the internal alchemy of ideas 'metanoia,' from whose creative weave of clear thought, clear reason, intuition, and revelation springs wisdom.

Within the framework of the Five Phase system, the Small Intestine energies, as just described, serve to contribute order and stability within the Fire by purifying and transforming surging Heart yin energies. They join in this regard with the energies of the Triple Burner, Pericardium, and Heart yang, each making a unique contribution to the safe, effective, intelligent statement of a creative, loving being.

Another stabilizing contribution of Small Intestine energies within the Fire phase is their effectiveness in removing excess heat from the Heart which otherwise renders the spirit-mind restless and irritable. This excess heat is, I believe, what the ancients referred to as 'excess joy' and what we know as mania.

The spirit-mind *(shen)*, housed in the Heart, is fed from the spirit-soul of the Liver, which is equipped to exchange spiritual energy with other spirit-souls for the ultimate nourishment and growth of the spirit-mind in the Heart. On a physical level we have the special portal circulation from the Liver to the Heart. When, for a variety of reasons, the Liver energy is stagnant, heat accumulates from the impasse between the expanding forces of Liver qi and the inhibiting forces that stifle it. This heat, and fire, may accompany the aforementioned transfer of new spirit energy from the Liver to the Heart, and if the 'nervous system' is weak, the spirit becomes disquieted and loses contact with the 'self,' leaving the person feeling adrift and lost. The capacity of Small Intestine energies to remove this heat restores the spirit to calm and connectedness.

SMALL INTESTINE DISHARMONY

Sorting, absorbing, and transforming may be considered yang functions because of the good functional heat which is required for this work, and removing heat from a Zang (solid organ) is also a Fu (hollow organ) yang function. The logical approach to considerations of disharmony is to explore the deficiencies and excesses of the predominantly yang character of these energies.

SMALL INTESTINE YANG DEFICIENCY

The person who is *deficient* in Small Intestine energies is one who is having difficulty separating thoughts from feelings, one thought from another, and one feeling from another. Analysis and synthesis are wanting, so that there is a confusion of feelings and thoughts, which contaminate one another. Consequently, there is a tendency to go off in many directions and difficulty in setting priorities. It is of interest to note that dreams classically associated with Small Intestine energies are of "wandering around in a large town as if lost." The subject will be less discerning in taste in all areas of life, including art and people, and in relationships will confuse love and hate.

A subtle rigidity, unexpected in the disorganized, will pervade life, not because this person is unwilling to be flexible and consider change, but because the confusion which defines life leaves him or her unsure and clinging to what is known. Impeded by difficulties with the transformation and transmutation of ideas, he is further limited by a lack of depth and growth. Handicapped in the capacity to move heat from the Heart, mental disarray will be complicated with restlessness, anxiety, and manic behavior. He may talk in his sleep and complain of palpitations, heat, and ringing of the ears, and be subject to epilepsy or schizophrenia should 'phlegm' be present in the Heart at the same time.

The phenomenon of the double-bind may play some part in the disharmony of Small Intestine energies. In this phenomenon, which has been offered as one etiology of schizophrenia, a person is subjected by a significant other to two or more conflicting messages about an important issue at a vulnerable time in his development. The ensuing confusion would place great pressure on Small Intestine energies to perpetually sort what cannot be sorted, enervating and exhausting these energies to the point at which they cannot perform the heat draining and other ego tasks so central to correct mental function and mental health.

A Case of Small Intestine Yang Deficiency

L. was a 64-year-old artist and poet who came to see me because of a severe heart ailment with pulmonary complications. She had this since childhood when she had suffered rheumatic heart disease. While we worked on her physical problems, a myriad of emotional ones flooded to the surface. Though much of it centered on her marital relationship, it became quickly obvious that the main issue was her rampant chaos and disorganization, which reached into every area of her life. L. was a walking disaster, articles of clothing hanging off her like a shedding reptile, pocketbooks spewing forth their contents when she sat down or stood up, books and notebooks dropping like leaves in autumn.

And so went her mind and emotions. She was dismissed from a painting class, despite her obvious talent, because the teacher, who was personally fond of her, found that the upheaval which she created by her mere presence drove him to distraction. For L., every consideration carried equal weight as it entered into the arena of daily life. Her sorting mechanism showed no evidence of having enough vigor to support her even in the most automatic, mundane activities, as, for example, distinguishing one shoe from another. For this reason she suffered from a highly appropriate lack of self-confidence, which made anxiety her trademark. In spite of and perhaps even because of the disorder which was her constant companion, she was very endearing and absolutely unforgettable.

SMALL INTESTINE YANG EXCESS

Those who have an *excess* of Small Intestine energies will suffer from being encumbered by a too 'black and white' attention to differences, from being unable to blend opposites and see the grey areas of life. Compromise will not be easy for these reasons, and creative change will suffer, not because they cannot 'transform,' but because the emphasis is on analysis rather than synthesis. The excessive drain on Heart fire will reduce the capacity for joy and set the stage for a tendency to depression. The Water yin excess left-brained person who extols mankind for its logical mind is not by himself restricted to a choice between analysis or synthesis, and can do both.

A Case of Small Intestine Yang Excess

In contrast to L. (see above), there was another person with whom I worked, for whom the separation of thoughts and feelings was almost a religion. Never were they to occupy the stage during the same performance. Only one prima donna at a time. Feelings were for exact times and places such as lovemaking, weddings, funerals, and patriotic occasions. All other events were to be superintended by pure reason. Nor could one feeling contaminate another, or one thought have associations. Nothing could be considered or executed until it adhered to the rules of pure deductive logic. Mr. M. had a premise for every contingency from which to deduce a response for every contingency. This made living an extremely difficult affair for him as well as for everyone whose lives came close to his, especially those dependent on him. Pure reason proved to be deadly as a formula for life; everybody and everything suffered, including those things one would have anticipated would flourish through its steadfast application. Businesses failed, children made poor marriages, and careers floundered. From knowing this man, who incidentally had a heart of gold, one could only conclude that reason kills, and absolute reason kills absolutely.

{ 209 }

Natural Functions of the Triple Burner

We subsume Pericardium, Triple Burner, and Small Intestine energies under the aegis of the Fire phase, in which the Heart is the emperor, the supreme commander to whom all other energies are subject, to whom they minister and are therefore known as 'ministers.' The Heart energy provides the inspiration and communication of higher thought and emotion. The Pericardium provides the communicative energies for defense and defined, focused assertion of this inspiration as well as the 'reason' necessary for the achievement of enduring creation. While the Heart is the 'emperor', the Triple Burner runs the empire.

The natural function of the Triple Burner on a psychological level is balance, orientation, and socialization. These tasks are principally in the areas of accurate flow, integration, harmony and perception. As such it is responsible for socialization within the nuclear family and with the 'family of man.' Integration of the three levels of the mind — medulla, midbrain, and cortex — through a free and balanced flow of energy is fundamental to mental equilibrium. Integration of the two sides of the brain through the *corpus collosum* is necessary for the effective blending of the creative (right) brain and the logical (left) brain, concomitants of innovation, invention, and original conception.

The term Triple Burner is a misleading translation of the original term *san jiao*. *San* means three, and *jiao* is level, sometimes referred to as 'warming (or burning) spaces.' Hence the *san jiao* refers to the three burners or warming levels of the body, upper, middle, and lower. The relationship of Triple Burner energies to heat or warmth is only one aspect of its principal functions, which more importantly includes distribution, integration, balance, and homeostasis.

During embryonic development, the Triple Burner correctly distributes the source *(yuan)* or original inherited energy from the Kidney organ system to the source points of each channel, and thence to the entire being. Later, the Triple Burner is the 'secretary of the interior,' which is located in the Stomach wall. Controls for the upper level are in the *cardia*, the middle level in the *fundus*, and the lower level in the *pyloric atrium*. The acupuncture points TB-2 *(ya men)* and CV-17 *(shan zhong)* are responsible for the upper burner; TB-10 *(tian jing)*, B-39 *(wei yang)*, and CV-7 *(yin jiao)* are responsible for the lower burner; and TB-7 *(hui zong)* with CV-12 *(zhong wan)* are responsible for the middle burner. CV-5 *(shi min)* is the *mu* or 'alarm' point of the Triple Burner. These three 'energy reactors' draw heat from the Kidney fire at the gate of vitality *(ming men)* to the Spleen for the digestion, absorption, transformation, and processing of physical as well as intellectual food into energy usable on both planes of existence. Through the 'interior duct' of the Triple Burner, 'impure' energy flows to the Kidneys to be further separated into Protective *(wei)* energy and the pure and impure fluids. It is also said to be the "official who plans the construction of ditches, sluices and creates waterways," assisting the Spleen energies to regulate Water distribution. (TB-2 [*ya men*] means "fluid's door" and is the central Water point of the body.)

The Triple Burner has, therefore, a unique relationship to both Kidney yin (Water) and yang (fire at the gate of vitality), and, since we are eighty percent water, which depends on heat for metabolism, the Triple Burner energies permeate the entire chemical environment. The Triple Burner occupies a strategic position to control the correct flow, the balance, and the harmony of all energy between the upper, middle, and lower parts of the body, as well through the source points and Stomach, the outside and the inside. Precise direction and movement, integration, and dynamic stability characterize Triple Burner energies at any level of function.

TB-3 *(zhong zhu)*, also known as 'middle islet,' is simultaneously the controlling acupuncture point of the 'internal duct' and of the sensory organs, especially the eyes and ears. Since the Triple Burner is an integrating force between the three levels of the brain, as well as between the two cranial nerves that control seeing and hearing, the suggestion is strong that it is also involved with the sensory process at cortical levels of perception. Some say that the Triple Burner is the "politician" who can "sense and read the pulse of the outside world." It has also been characterized as a "receiving station and transmitter." All of this implies a strong investment in contact with the outside world, with relationships, and, through its involvement with perception, in the integrity of boundaries which are so vital in human relations. As a mediator of warmth and an orchestrator of harmony, as the integrator of the families within, these energies would seem to be crucial to all close social bonds, especially with friends and family.

INSIGHTS INTO THE TRIPLE BURNER FROM THE PULSE

There is no specific position for the Triple Burner system in the Contemporary Pulse Diagnosis system of pulse diagnosis. According to Dr. Shen, its function is found in all three burners, and there is no single position for it.

I assess the function of the Triple Burner by examining the relationship between the principal positions and the burners. If the qualities are generally more or less uniform, I consider the Triple Burner to be functioning well. If, on the other hand, the qualities vary considerably from position to position or burner to burner, the functioning of the Triple Burner is greatly stressed. I have found this chaos especially in cases of autoimmune disease and severe chronic fatigue syndrome. Students report associations to the right proximal position, which makes this a reasonable area for exploration. For example, one Five Element (Phase) practitioner, treating a patient who she believed to have a Triple Burner causative factor, was unable to make any progress until she found extreme activity in the Gallbladder and right proximal positions. At this point, she resolved the pulse and clinical picture by using the exit-entry points for the Gallbladder and Triple Burner.

Evaluation of Each Burner

Upper Burner. The integrity of the upper burner qi (distal positions on the pulse) tells us how well we can reach out to the world and take the world in, with awareness of our creative being, with the strength to communicate and protect our being and to maintain mental and emotional stability. It tells us how well we can handle shock or recover from grief.

Middle Burner. The integrity of the middle burner qi reflects how centered this person is in life, and of course about the relationship between the moving and recovering qi (Liver) and the nurturing qi (Spleen-Stomach). It tells us how easily this person can handle stress and toxicity, mental and physical, and the organism's capacity for recovery on a day-to-day basis (Liver), and how well it can replenish itself over time (Spleen).

Lower Burner. The lower burner (proximal positions) gives a sense of the root or ground upon which the person stands (the Kidneys). Intact proximal positions tell us that a person has the root or ground to stand on in order to heal. If these positions are reduced in qi at a young age (Deep, Feeble) we may suspect that the constitutional qi is deficient and recovery may be more difficult. If the person is older, I assume that some of this deficiency is more gradual draining due to physical overwork, overexercise, or some other form of abuse (drugs, sex), and that there may be more basic qi with which to work (Reduced Substance pulse quality). In other words, the lower burner pulse positions may indicate both what a person has to stand on constitutionally, as well as what they are making of what they are given.

If the deficiency is primarily of yin, with harder qualities such as Tight, I realize that this person has probably been overworking their mind and central nervous system. At times, one of these deficiencies is so much more characteristic of the person that it appears by itself. This is especially true if yin is being depleted, since the harder qualities (Tight) overshadow the more pliable ones (Yielding or Feeble characteristic of qi-yang deficiency).

More often, in keeping with the realities of life, there are signs of both types of deficiency, which informs me that both processes are occurring simultaneously. Or the proximal position may be Tight (yin deficiency) and Feeble (qi-yang deficiency), or the qualities might constantly change from one to the other during the examination.

TRIPLE BURNER DEFICIENCY

We will confine ourselves to considerations of deficiency since it seems difficult to imagine a person having too much of what Triple Burner energies mediate, except perhaps an overemphasis on form at the expense of content. Once again we will dispense with the division of yin and yang, which has been referred to in terms of the Triple Burner's close association with the distribution of both water and heat, as not relevant to our focus on matters psychological.

Personality: Lack of Integration

The subject will have difficulty integrating the inevitable discordances of his or her being. A classical and continually puzzling example is the German people, whose historically recent excursions into the higher realms of philosophy, music, and art alternate dramatically and exclusively with their ancient passion for war, sadism, and domination. Coldness, hardness, and arrogance fluctuate indiscreetly with softness, humility, and flexibility. Since one part of the personality is out of touch with another, neither can serve to ameliorate the other's more drastic qualities. The tendency is to go rapidly and unqualifiedly to extremes. The attendant disharmony has obvious far-reaching and fathomless consequences on the entire fabric of existence.

This lack of integration will reveal itself in disparities between verbal and performance skills. On psychological examinations, verbal and performance scores will be widely divergent. Some can take apart and put back together an engine without learning to read or write, and others who excel in many verbal faculties can barely unwrap a package. Some, as George Bernard Shaw pointed out, can "teach" but not "do" and others are the opposite and can do brilliantly but never teach. ("He who can, does, he who cannot, teaches." [27]) The subject may have the brilliant vision of Heart yin and the inadequate execution of Heart yang, or just the opposite, leading in either instance to endless frustration. {213}

The subject may also suffer from a lack of smooth and harmonious flow of thoughts and feelings, often becoming 'stuck.' An example would be 'writer's block,' or the mind that 'goes blank'; overall achievement would be uneven. If the flow between the two sides of the brain is impeded, a full articulation of what the creative and logical sides of this person could produce in unison will never be realized.

In relationships there will be, at best, a lack of warmth and withdrawal, and at worst, suspicion, estrangement, and the rupture of kinship and friendship due to misperceptions.

The prototype is therefore a person who seems unbalanced, poorly integrated and coordinated, with wide variations in performance, problems with perception, and seriously disrupted personal relations, especially as pertains to the exchange of warmth and the strength of bonds.

A Case of Split Personality

The person I have seen who most closely resembles this prototype arrived because of fear of himself, having recently brutally beaten his child. Although he felt very guilty, he also felt the child deserved the beating. This dilemma continued in his mind until some time after we stopped seeing each other, at which time the child died mysteriously. It carried over into all aspects of his life. On the one hand, he dealt in a 'trade' that was enormously damaging to people, and, on the other, he expressed enormous compassion for his fellow human beings and wished to become a healer. He was a trained writer who did not write; he was a master mechanic whose car was never repaired; he was an accomplished flyer who never put his plane in the air. Living off his illicit earnings, there was nothing to keep him from his well-intentioned goals. Even with his superior intelligence he could not harmonize and collate the two rigidly divided sides of himself, either in the mechanical aspects of living, or in personal relationships where he was in endless conflict between his ideals and his perceptions of being everlastingly maltreated. Those who knew him lived in fear of his violence, knowing full well that even while engaged in a violent act, he would, in another part of his mind, be thinking of himself only as a reasonable and gentle soul.

11

The Earth Phase

Introduction: Earth Yin and Earth Yang

Earth yin is primarily concerned with bonding and the beginning of the formation of boundaries, while Earth yang is primarily concerned with the maturation of boundaries and separation. Each section is divided into natural functions of these organ energies and the pathologies associated with the distortion by life experience of these functions, first with deficiency and then with an excess of these energies.

[215]

NATURAL FUNCTIONS OF THE EARTH YIN PHASE SYSTEM

The Formation of Bonds

Bonding

Whereas the Water phase is associated with the continuation of the species, with the survival of the individual from one generation to the next, the Earth phase dedicates its energies to the survival of the individual in this generation. From inception through its functions of digestion, absorption, and metabolism of all material substance and energy transformations, it is the life-giving earth mother.

Viewed from one scheme of the Five Phase system, the Earth phase occupies a central position during our lifespan ('later heaven').

The Five Phase concept arose, as far as we know, in a culture that oriented and adapted itself to the natural world, understanding itself as an integral part of the behavior of that world. Hunting and gathering preceded agriculture, and so the original orientation to the larger natural scheme was spatial. The points of the compass—east, west, north, and south—were probably the first abstractions of the universe upon which man projected his own place in the great scheme of things. The earth is, of course, the center, the source of earthly sustenance that feeds and nourishes the other phases during this earthbound lifespan. It is certain that an Earth phase that is unable to perform completely the vital function of providing food energy to its dependent organ systems would leave those organ systems, and the entire organism, in a weak and vulnerable state.

The Earth phase dominates the oral-bonding and first-separating phases of psycho-social development for both parent and child. As the source of all material substances, the Earth phase is the nourishing mother. The capacity of the earth mother for unconditional, minimally egocentric love during the in utero and early oral developmental eras is the endowment which will determine the quality or quantity of the 'bonding' between the earth mother and offspring, as well as the latter's bonding with itself and with the entire human race, as long as it endures here and beyond. The earth's gravity is a centripetal force that, by its fundamental nature, is the bonding energy of our existence.

The trust and self-worth ("I am worthy of such care") that ensues from relatively consistent positive initiative and response by the earth-mother to her offspring in those early encounters leaves an imprint that little less than a lifetime of new experience can alter, for better or worse. Indeed, it is in the context of this exchange that a new person will more or less identify himself as human, or wish to be identified with all humanity. The original potential for this identification rests in utero with Kidney yin and the potential becomes a reality through the bond with the mother (or surrogate). Children born without this potential do not respond to this bonding and are alluded to as 'autistic.'

From its position in the center of the Five Phases, or even from its place between Fire and Metal, the Earth phase feeds all other organ systems; and by its inherent correspondence to the emotion compassion, it also exercises, through the Ko or controlling cycle of the Five Phase system, a direct, mitigating influence over fear (with love) and, indirectly, over anger. This tender ambiance is requisite to the healthy assertion of 'being,' and at once softens, ameliorates, and balances the Wood phase's 'negative' aggressiveness.

Normally, the energies of the Earth phase contribute to the general equation of human affect a sense of quiet, peace, calm, and compassion. These energies balance, with serenity and thoughtful reflection, the more disquieting, aggressive, impulsive, and restricted energies of compromised becoming, such as those associated respectively with Wood (repressed emotion), Fire (excitement and apprehension), and Water (fear and anguish).

The Earth is the phase of evenness and easiness, the oil on troubled waters, the phase of grounding and centeredness.

The ultimate goal of a healthy Earth phase is to reproduce itself through its offspring as a new and joyful provider of nourishment to ensuing strong and centered generations.

Disharmony Of Earth Yin Function

Deficient Earth Energies: Problems in Bonding

Clinically, there are three (and possibly four) distinguishable diagnostic categories of emotional disabilities that are associated with major deficiency in the bonding and boundary capacity of the Earth energies. The first two occur due to intra-uterine and early post-partum lack of support for Earth energies. Most serious in terms of destruction to the life process and cycle of development is a type of 'schizophrenia.' A less severe problem, also originating at the same time of development, is the schizoid personality disorder. Deficiencies at the time of late infancy and early childhood (six months to two years) can result in the formation of an 'oral' character.

INTRA-UTERINE AND EARLY POST-PARTUM LACK OF SUPPORT FOR EARTH ENERGIES (TO SIX MONTHS)

This most debilitating failure of life-organizing energies occurs, I believe, primarily in utero, and, in my opinion, involves the Water phase as a genetic vulnerability. Inasmuch as the Water phase (yin essence) is responsible for sound genetics and the integrity of the development of the central nervous system before and after birth, the healthy evolution of Earth energies must rest, to a great extent, with the Water. It is a fundamental axiom of Chinese medicine that Kidney yang is the progenitor of all the yang of the body, and especially of Spleen yang, which is the heat energy that drives the digestive process. However, the soundness of the digestive-metabolic processes during the post-partum maturation of this system is a function of the Earth phase. Defects in the alimentation-metabolic pathway will impair the work of the Water phase and its central nervous system ('marrow') activities, which is the slowest system to develop to maturity. The two systems (Earth and Water) are thereby functionally reciprocal, so that a developmental affliction of the central nervous system may involve an impairment of one or both as etiologic factors in varying degrees. As a rule, I believe that the higher the function on the evolutionary scale and the closer to abstract thinking we come, the greater the involvement of the Earth energies (though all of the phases play a role in cognition, as we shall see). As the human central nervous system is infinitely complex, involving the integrity of trillions of cells, the failure of Earth and Water phase energies, at this stage, can cause an unlimited variety of congenital defects. Schizophrenia is only one. Which exact failure of Earth and Water energies leads to this and other defects is information that we do not yet have at our disposal. However, it is my clinical impression that rather than separate entities, there is a continuation from the least neurosis to the most disruptive psychosis based on my experience with the different degrees of 'phlegm misting the orifices.'

Once again we have with this disorder (schizophrenia) the familiar reality in medicine that human beings have a limited repertoire of restorative mechanisms, which we observe as symptoms. The same clinical picture may result from a plethora of causes. My impression of the disease is one of multiple origin, having its primary etiology in the intra-uterine environment, which is clearly a developmental era governed by Water energies. Culpability lies in part with the person's constitution and, increasingly, with this culture which has introduced artificial chemicals into food and air, artificial delivery systems, and the greatly increased use of 'recreational' drugs. Ingestion of such commonplace items as coffee and cigarettes has been 'scientifically' implicated as teratogenic to intra-uterine life. The remarkable bombardment of energies all across the electromagnetic spectrum, from high tension wires to computers, plays a role.

Schizophrenia, as distinguished from psychosis (out of touch with reality), was defined by Harry Stack Sullivan as the loss of control of consciousness, and by others as an issue of poorly delineated and highly unstable boundaries. The concepts are equivalent, if not exact. This 'loss' of 'consciousness' or 'boundaries' is highly labile and usually occurs concomitantly with some identifiable stress, which, if chronic, is also cumulative, so that the schizophrenic process is generally a combination of life's exigencies and a pre-delivery insult. There is no question that such an event can also occur without any genetic or intra-uterine predisposition. I have seen such a loss of control under conditions when people had no other way to cope with, or escape from, an impossible life situation. An acute schizophrenic episode generated primarily by a profound, chronic interpersonal failure can be a potential growth experience if handled correctly. More often, it is not correctly approached and degenerates into a way of life which we call 'chronic' schizophrenia. The propensity for such chronicity, I believe, is due to a breakdown of Water energies during the genetic-conception unfolding, and of Earth energies after the birth process. Research into the etiology of this disorder should, I believe, be directed to all pre-parturient stages of development. The medical model and social values, however, play an extraordinary part in creating and perpetuating chronicity.

SCHIZOPHRENIA

Let us examine some of the parameters of this deficiency, which we call schizophrenia, in the pre-delivery functions of the Earth phase. This is, in large part, descriptive material from DSM-III-R with which some of us are not only familiar, but by now largely disillusioned, in regard to its usefulness. It is briefly recounted with an emphasis on energy considerations.

Before embarking on this course, I wish to emphasize that the meaning of the phenomenon I am about to describe seems to be culturally, not scientifically, determined. We have yet to be entirely clear about the syntonicity of the acute schizophrenic experience in 'spirit'-oriented cultures, where it functions as a medium for induction into higher levels of spiritual and healing power rather than a mental hospital.

Personality

Affect is generally blunted, flat, inappropriate, or silly. Eyes are expressionless and "see but do not look." There is a deterioration of work, social relations, and self-care, as well as increasing social isolation engendered by terror of annihilation. Peculiar and bizarre behavior, both private and public, is often founded on delusions. Speech is digressive, vague, overelaborate, circumstantial, and metaphorical. Eye contact is often extremely difficult. The person's attention seems to be remote or fixed. Catatonia, including bizarre posturing, and hebephrenia characterized by inappropriate laughter, are often encountered.

The enduring methods of coping with reality by schizophrenics are:

1. General avoidance of interpersonal stress through withdrawal from both emotional and physical contact with other people, especially from those outside a very small circle of long acquaintance. Often these consist of only one or two people within the family circle.

2. Denial of any reality that constitutes a potential threat.

3. A disorganization of the ego when denial fails, with loss of internal and external boundaries.

Symptomatology such as depersonalization, catatonia, paranoia, and hebephrenia depend, in my opinion, upon several factors in addition to the underlying intra-uterine insult. The degree of the insult and the integrity of the other phase energies, as determined by constitution and post-uterine interpersonal experiences, will play a part in the degree of organization, albeit maladaptive, that the schizophrenic can bring to bear to the massive disorder with which he or she is burdened. The paranoid person is the most highly organized, and the hebephrenic the least able to give order to psychic anarchy. In the more chronic, burned-out stages of schizophrenia, one encounters a severe narrowing of focus as a way of coping with the anarchy.

The principal bioenergetic feature of the schizophrenic is the loss of balance between the inner energies of the body and the external mechanisms that normally control these energies and keep them within the boundaries of the body integument, or at least within a short distance of that integument (the skin). This accounts for the loss of ego boundaries and the tremendous confusion between what is inside and what is outside, the source of much of the terror for people so afflicted. The loss of identity without integument leads to this fluid ego state and to conditions of depersonalization. In Chinese medicine these outer layers are energically referred to as the *wei* and qi levels, or, in another system, as Tai Yang, which Dr. John Shen also calls the 'nervous system.' The integument includes the musculo-tendon system, which on a psycho-biological level is a necessary survival mechanism for offense and defense, for standing to fight or running to hide. The person who has lost clear and secure knowledge of all these resources is indeed in terror and at risk.

A second striking bioenergetic finding is the blocking of energy at all the key transfer points of the body, i.e., the joints of the extremities, the base of the skull, and in the pelvis where the lumbar and sacral vertebrae meet. Chinese medicine teaches that we are part of a gigantic universal energy system. When the energy of the universe moves, our energy also moves. If there are obstacles to this movement, problems develop which may take many forms.

Bioenergetically, the schizophrenic is blocked at all of the above-mentioned segmental joining points of the body, in which case he (or she) becomes energetically disjointed and disconnected within himself. This leaves the schizophrenic with a lack of internal coordination and with confusion that reflects itself in his thought processes, which likewise become uncoordinated and disjointed. (The *shen*, or spirit, is confused.) At the same time, the schizophrenic is unable to allow the energic forces in the world to flow smoothly through his being, and at once he loses synchronicity with those forces and experiences them as adding to the burden of his confusion. Even the energy system of another person, especially a strong one, can be an increased, unmanageable load and considerable source of such confusion. This is one reason why the schizophrenic feels more comfortable in a state of withdrawal. And since the energic forces are quieter at night, many schizophrenics feel more at ease wandering the nights and staying quiescent during the great, dynamic yang hours of the day.

{ 221 }

Cognitive Disturbances

The most serious forms of cognitive disturbance occur with disturbance of the energies of the Fire, Water, and Earth phases. The Water phase energies account for the material parenchymal form and substance of the 'brain.' The other phases are more involved with what we refer to as 'mind.' The Spleen-Pancreas organ system controls the ingestion, digestion, absorption, and metabolism of food. Analogously, it controls the ingestion, digestion, absorption, and metabolism, i.e., the alimentation of thought, and the Fire phase of all of the higher ego functions of the cerebral cortex. Dr. John Shen, in Chapter 14 of this book, adds another dimension to the etiology of psychosis in the qi, food, and phlegm ('misting of the orifices') stages of stagnation in the digestive system.

What are these functions? The Earth and Water phases are responsible for the order inherent in maintaining the boundaries between the conscious and unconscious, the inner and outer world, and for the reliable reality testing that is requisite to successful earthly perpetuity. When the Earth phase fails and internal pathways become fragmented, there is a loss of contact and cohesion between levels of abstraction. The schizophrenic, despite his (or her) brilliance, may consequently be debilitated by this interference with abstract thinking. The result is concrete thinking, which is defined as relating "to a specific or particular item or thing as a whole, a tendency to react to the immediately-given object or situation without considering its relationships or classifications," the opposite of abstract thinking, wherein a person can generalize from a specific.

Internal fragmentation, which is a singular characteristic of schizophrenia, precludes movement from the specific to the general. This fact by itself accounts for the massive confusion that attends all contacts a schizophrenic has with reality. The autism, hallucinations, delusions, illusions, and body distortions follow from this fragmentation and loss of boundaries. The functions of attention, concentration, memory, the accumulation or organization of knowledge and reality are all consequently compromised.

The cognitive clinical picture may include one or more of the following: bizarre delusions and thoughts being controlled by outside forces; persecutory delusions; somatic delusions; grandiose delusions, sometimes religious or nihilistic; auditory hallucinations, usually defamatory in character, though sometimes threatening or suggesting violence; incoherence; marked loosening of associations; illogical thinking; poverty of speech and ideas, or fixed ideation; unusual perceptual experiences of a visual nature; feelings of clairvoyance, telepathy, and 'ideas of reference.'

The organization of ideas into logical, communicable language is the function of the Fire phase. The disorders of language one finds in the schizophrenic process are the result of the Earth phase feeding the Fire phase with energy fragments that were never fully 'digested,' 'assimilated,' or 'transformed' into usable units of 'mental energy.' (Recall that the Earth is the center, storing the 'tastes' and feeding all the other phases.) The Fire phase does not receive qualitatively serviceable energy for performance of its tasks, the consequences of which are the myriad remarkable language disturbances of schizophrenia.

Energy Logistics

According to Simon Mills, the herbalist, the Earth and the Fire have a special relationship in that the 'sweet' flavor associated with the Earth disperses excess tension/activity in the Heart function, possibly working to encourage stability and quiet to an overly-charged situation.

Furthermore, the boundary problems of severely deficient Earth energies complicate even further the quandary of the schizophrenic and the observer in terms of when and whether the person is talking to some part of himself or to others. The hebephrenic phenomenon of sudden, inappropriate laughter may be a confusion of coordination within the Fire phase between its mediation of the emotion joy (the spirit scatters) and its communication function. This would imply weakness of the Water phase (unable to control the Fire), which is compatible with the idea that the Earth phase in schizophrenia has been severely compromised before birth, either in utero or genetically, by a functionally-compromised Water phase. The catatonic process is apparently an attempt by the Fire phase to find safety through silence, and by the Metal controlling Wood to achieve immobility for the same purpose. These energy logistics may all occur as 'phases within a phase,' all characteristics of the other phases as they function within the Earth phase.

Dreams and Anxiety

The dreams of schizophrenics are, most accurately, waking dreams or night terrors. A night terror is defined as "a nightmare from which the dreamer awakes but the terror continues." These night terrors reflect the loss of boundaries between conscious and unconscious—between outside and inside—and the subsequent loss of control which leads from anxiety to terror. One source states that people with problems in the Earth phase, especially Spleen, will not sleep peacefully or be able to sleep on their back.

The anxiety of the schizophrenic is the terror of annihilation. Its source is the loss of boundaries, as previously described, leading to massive confusion of orientation to self and others. The disorganized sub- and unconscious 'other reality,' the organized mental functions, and the body are indistinguishable from each other and from the environment. Terrifying distortions of one's own body image ensue, as well as disorientation in a world that has lost its familiar perceptual navigational guideposts. For this reason, and because of the inability to cope with the energy of other human systems as previously described, the threats of annihilation come from all directions and often they only seem more ominous coming from the outside world. Inasmuch as the schizophrenic has no control over the internal disarray, he tries to focus anxiety outwardly in the direction where, through retreat or attack, he feels a slightly greater chance of mastery and stability. The attempt at restoration is, therefore, to project. In its least organized form, the configuration is called hebephrenia.

The catatonic is the next least well-organized restorative mechanism, which generally carries with it a better prognosis than the hebephrenic. Again, we can say that the Earth energies, necessary to maintain the ego-functions of internal and external boundaries, are greater here than in the hebephrenic.

Paranoia

Paranoia is classically referable to the Water phase. In paranoid schizophrenia, both the Earth phase and the Water phase are involved. The boundaries between internal and external worlds are more highly structured. According to most thoughts on the subject of paranoia, independent of other considerations of degree or content, there seems to be general agreement that the boundaries are maintained but that internal and external are reversed. What is actually inside is experienced as outside, crossing the boundary from that direction. Paranoia could be a confusion within the Earth phase of yin and yang, so that what is inside (yin) is projected outward, and what is outside (yang) is 'introjected.'

The paranoid mechanism of the Water phase provides the boundaries (albeit in retroversion) which the weak Earth energies alone cannot erect. The results are less than perfect. The Water phase cannot truly replace the Earth phase as boundary-maker. Since Water energy is now siphoned to functions which are restorative and unnatural, its own developmental mission is, perforce, diverted and subverted.

Food Allergies

Theron Randolf has demonstrated that schizophrenic symptoms may be caused directly by food allergies, which come from an immune reaction to incompletely digested proteins.[1] The body reacts to these proteins as if they were a foreign substance, for instance, very much as it would react to a virus. Indeed, these incompletely digested proteins are often quite large, the size of virus molecules. Much of the schizophrenic thought disorder, as well as other symptomatology, is postulated to be the result of the effects of these large molecules on receptors and on circulation in the brain. I have treated a schizophrenic with severe food allergies in some depth. As with many patients with pervasive allergies, this person was better for a short period of time when placed on an allergy-free regime. The proliferation of sensitivities outstrips the attempts to adapt to them. In this person, the fundamental defect was in the Water phase, profoundly affecting her entire constitution, and, most especially, her psychological functions from early childhood. The increased demands made on her mother by her extraordinary neediness were not met, and she experienced rejection and incomplete bonding. The failure to be accepted and to bond, so crucial to the 'evolution of being,' predisposed all other systems to inadequacy. The massive food allergies arose from the incompetence of the Earth (Spleen), and the overwhelming inhalant allergies from defects in the Metal (Lung) phases. (Experience shows that the detoxifying functions of the Liver are also a factor in all allergies.) Clinical ecology is a sound and valuable discipline; however, it is dealing with symptoms and mechanisms, not the fundamental energic disharmonies. In this case, therapeutic concentration on the energy, rather than the allergy, produced excellent results.

A Case of Schizophrenia

A 30-year-old mother of one child was referred to me by her own mother, because the younger woman was hallucinating. Since early childhood, R. had had difficulty relating to other children, though she was very intelligent and functioned well academically. She attended but did not complete college, where she met her husband. The marriage lasted only long enough to produce one child. There were many other men along the way and frequent moves and changes of job as she followed these men. There were also periodic hospitalizations for episodes of hallucinations, delusions, and confusion, which began during her late teens when her mother would rescue her from whatever improbable situations she was in at the time of her 'breakdown.' At these times mother would take control, drawing her in to herself while at the same time pushing her out into paths that were totally unrealistic. With this patchwork pattern of living, little of substance was ever accomplished.

Somehow through all this R. had raised her child to the age of 11, when the child began to assert her desire to live with her father. It was during one of her many life transitions that I met her, at which time she was actively hallucinating that an ex-boyfriend was controlling her through voices that were mediated through a computer. These voices accused her of being evil and harmful, curiously, in fact, of being very much the way I experienced her mother to be. R. was searching at this point for some way to help herself without hospitalization and without the use of medications, both of which she found debilitating.

Despite endless interference by her mother, whose prescriptions for her daughter were totally mindless of her defects, we managed, with the use of psychotherapy, acupuncture, nutritional supplements, and some herbs, to eliminate the disabling voices without the need for drugs, except every few months. At these times we would introduce one medication in large amounts for a few days, quickly reducing dosages as the acute disorganization subsided. We then continued with the above regime. R. was able to get a job and begin to put her life into some kind of order. She made plans to escape from her mother and began to learn self-assertion without fragmenting anxiety. When last we spoke, she had begun her life again somewhat more realistically and was searching for someone to continue our work in the area in which she now lived.

Schizoid Personality Disorder

Another less life-disorganizing outcome of a deficiency in Earth and Water energies during the intra-uterine to first six months of life period is the personality disorder called 'schizoid.' Here the primary issue is existence, "to be or not to be," in its most concrete sense. The event leading to this dilemma is one or more life-threatening experiences either before birth or during the first few months of life. Borrowing from the DSM-III, this personality disorder shows the following characteristics: "This person shows an emotional coldness and aloofness, an absence of warm, tender feelings for others. There is an indifference to praise or criticism or the feelings of others. Close friendships are limited to no more than one or two persons, including family members." The need for what has been described as such 'splendid isolation' is the clear sense that destruction is imminent.

A Case of Abandonment

J.'s mother had attempted prenatal abortion of him. His parents had succeeded in aborting a child one year previously, but the knitting needles did not work this time. Clearly unwanted, he was neglected during his early infancy when his mother, to spite his father with whom she had had an argument, would leave him alone in the house. She would call the father's place of business to let him know what she had done, and he would call his mother to go and care for the baby. At the age of six months the child had pneumonia, and his lungs were weak from then on. The ambiance was always physically and verbally violent, and he was beaten by both parents, especially his mother, who was also sexually seductive and sexually exploitive. Later, he became an accomplished street fighter when attacked.

Throughout childhood he stayed to himself and in his own fantasy world, though he was always able to function and distinguish it from reality. He was always treated as the caretaker in the family and acted that role from his earliest years. For this reason he managed after puberty to succeed in school, in the service, and in his work, but he always remained aloof except toward a few friends. When he was 24 he entered therapy with an old woman. Up to that time he could not bear to have anyone touch him. It was literally physically painful, and sometimes, if touched in the street by accident, he would strike out automatically as if attacked. One day this old lady walked over to him as he lay on her couch and placed her large, warm, and worn hand on his chest. J. had a convulsion and then began his long road back to a humanity, including his own, which he long before ceased to experience as anything but deadly. In later years he came to realize that his existence had been tolerated only as long as he was useful.

INFANCY AND EARLY CHILDHOOD LACK OF SUPPORT FOR EARTH ENERGIES (SIX MONTHS TO TWO YEARS)

Deficiencies in the energies of the Earth phase that occur after birth affect the growing child differently than do those which occur genetically or in utero. Life is far too complex to fit neatly into our scheme, and the overlap that accounts for the borderline states is considerable. The necessity to schematize should not be allowed to overshadow the limitations of such schematization. There are many people who have suffered from combinations and permutations of all these insults, schizophrenia, schizoid, oral, symbiotic, and narcissistic. The scheme does help us in sorting out the issues and, one hopes, in improving the prognosis of a management plan.

THE ORAL CHARACTER

The problem of orality stems from significant failures in early mothering. Both child and parent may contribute to this, since some children are born with weak sucking reflexes or buccal musculature, or with allergies to mother's and other kinds of milk. Some children are unable to accept other forms of nurture, such as physical contact, and there is a wide spectrum of autistic states with which children are born that limit contact and communication, from the non-verbal to the verbal.

On the other hand, there are many, perhaps most, children who are born with excellent capabilities to receive nurture in all forms who do not receive it because mothers are, for a variety of reasons, unable to provide it. Some mothers can give it in a form that, for some reason, is unacceptable to the child. There are mothers who can hold but not breast-feed a child. Others are more verbal and can sing to their children but prefer not to have physical contact.

During my years as a child psychiatrist, I occasionally treated children who had been so infantilized by their parents that they never had the opportunity to develop the skills that they needed to survive on their own. Some of these children had initial defects, to which the mother naturally responded with overprotection, and then carried it on inappropriately. Other severely disturbed mothers with profoundly undeveloped ego-boundaries projected their own need for support and protection onto the child and treated the child as if it were themselves. Most of these mothers were psychotic, and the fathers inadequate or absent.

The possibilities for failure at this stage of development are therefore obviously manifold. Naturally, the burden for correctional behavior at such an impasse between mother and child lies with the adult, who alone, in the early phases of the relationship, has the potential resources for adaptation and change. We read about parents who succeed with the most autistic children, but more often about children and adults whose parents were too egocentric or inadequate to effect any accommodation that might lead to some fulfillment of the needs of their children during this 'oral' phase of development. The result is a deficiency in the energies of the Earth phase, which we refer to as the 'oral character.'

There are a number of conditions that fall between and around the schizophrenic process and the oral personality that we need not refer to in detail. These include the personality disorders, 'borderline' and 'narcissistic,' described in DSM-III-R, earlier alluded to by DSM-II as the 'unstable,' 'immature,' and 'inadequate personalities.' Developmental schemata for this period vary from one 'expert' to another. The one that appeals to me states that the 'oral' personality has been separated from nourishment too early; the symbiotic personality fails to distinguish his identity from the personality of others; the narcissistic personality, whom we will discuss, is one trying to cope with problems of too little or too inflated self-esteem; the masochistic personality, whom we have already discussed in Chapter 9, is dealing with issues of control and the humiliation associated with submission, which, though there is some overlap, is in my opinion more a problem of the Wood energies and the assertion of 'being.' With the partial exception of the latter, all of these conditions are rooted in failures of the basic issues of nurturance and separation during the era of infancy and early childhood. These are all 'borderline personalities,' which I consider to extend in a continuum from psychosis to neurosis and not as a separate psychological category. I simply wish to indicate that by describing the 'oral' personality we are also including these other life adaptations that have similar etiologic and characteristic roots.

The Oral Personality

The 'oral' personality is dependent upon others, exceeding the usual parameters for that otherwise natural state of affairs, both in degree and kind. Such persons feel inadequate to care for themselves, and at the same time feel that this care should be provided by others. Interpersonal relations are sticky and clinging, marked by demands for succor of all kinds, including financial support. In contrast to the schizophrenic, they are capable of perceiving reality with some accuracy; however, they cannot face it alone, feeling totally inadequate to the task. Avoidance thereof often leads to a variety of real-life disasters, frequently financial and marital. They have no aim in life except to be cared for, and apart from this, do not know what they want. Work records are generally extremely poor, with frequent changes in employment. The deep feelings of inadequacy tend to make them very egocentric, self-centered, and generally unfeeling toward others, whose needs they cannot imagine to be as great as, or taking precedence over, theirs. They are envious of others who are seemingly more competent and are bitter toward those whom they see as stronger and who do not give them enough. The demands are endless, the satisfaction short-lived, and the resentment quickly evoked. In the past they have been classified as 'inadequate' or 'immature' personalities.[2] More modern classifications are personality disorders of which the 'borderline personality' is characterized by impulsivity, instability, and chaotic relationships swinging from hate to love. Life is experienced in extremes, all good or bad, and as a victim of circumstances rather than due to one's own actions. The central issue, as with the 'oral' character, is above all concern with abandonment, real or imagined. (The 'narcissistic personality' is discussed below.)

The activities of the 'obsessional neurosis' are the restorative measures often found in the borderline personality between the 'oral' character and schizophrenic. This compulsive behavior, which often becomes outwardly quite bizarre, involving, for example, the constant rearranging of objects into a certain inexplicable order, is the preamble to a 'decompensation' of the 'oral' and 'schizoid' character into the schizophrenic condition.

Affect is often flat with little expression, except that of emptiness. Surrounding the 'oral' character is a sense of loneliness, which will often lead them into relationships with people who need to be helping, caring, mothering figures. There are mood swings of euphoria (inflation), when someone appears in their life who seems willing to assume that role; and dysphoria (deflation), when that helping person also has needs and is not the perfect mother. (Cyclothymic in DSM-III-R; also see Fire phase).

The oral character may go into deeper depressions when the mothering figure actually abandons them. This depression resembles the anaclitic depression (despair), so well described by Winnicott in infants who lose their mother somewhere between six months and one-and-one-half years.[3] (Anaclisis is defined as "dependence on another or others for support, especially for emotional support.") In contrast to the endogenous depression (Recurrent Major Depressive Episodes in DSM-III-R) related to the Water phase, or the Dysthymic Disorder related to the Wood phase, this depression will lift eventually, when a new, promising mother figure appears on the scene, though I have found the event to be registered energically on the pulse. Recently, while teaching about the pulse, I took that of a young man whose Lung pulse was Flat, indicating that he had suffered a deep disappointment early in life. Examination of his ear placed the date in the first two years of life. He told us then that at that time he had been separated from his mother, when he was put in a hospital for an operation. The apparent depression lifts, but the residue is physiologically and psychologically significant. As long as that Lung wave is Flat, difficulties with receiving and moving the qi and consequent tendency to sadness and respiratory problems will persist. He reported that for as long as he could recall he had been unable to take a deep breath.

Falling Dreams

The recurrent dreams of the 'oral' personality are those of falling. They vary widely in the exact content, and generally there is fear, qualifying the dream as nightmare. They seem, of course, quite real; but they are not the living dreams of the schizophrenic, the night terrors. The 'oral' personality usually awakens before hitting the ground, though I have worked with some people who have dreamt that they actually had been killed. Upon waking, there is a sense of relief and a recovery from the fear. In those who did reach the ground and died, I have known a few who were actually suicidal. These were the 'oral' characters who had been through the inflation-deflation cycle too many times, or those who were deeply into anaclitic depression and had given up hope. The gestures lack conviction but do sometimes inadvertently succeed.

The 'oral,' Earth energy deficient person may also have recurrent dreams of hunger or thirst. This may depend upon which aspect of the Earth phase is deficient, since the Spleen-Pancreas prefers dry (food), and the Stomach prefers wet (beverages). The craving may, of course, be for both. Classical Chinese medicine also reports recurrent dreams of storms and the construction of houses and walls in Earth energy deficient people. I have had occasion to record a few patients reporting this.

Bioenergetic Assessment

The 'oral' character is distinguished bioenergetically by a lack of energy, easy fatigue, and a general lack of aggressiveness. Physically, the chest is deflated and often the sternum is depressed. Spleen energies, which normally rise, are too weak. The arms and legs feel weak, and the person will tell the doctor how weak, impotent, and ineffective they are. The legs are thin, and they stand with knees in a locked position. This makes it necessary for the spine to carry all of the body weight, ultimately weakening the back. The neck and head are forward, the belly protruding, and the pelvis back. The forward extension of head and neck will lead to extreme neck tension and headaches. The neck may be quite long.

Problems with Cognition

The person whose Earth energies have failed at this stage of development has difficulty with the digestion of thought. Information is overwhelming because the 'oral' character is unable to break it down into its component parts so that it may be more easily and usefully absorbed. The thinking of the 'oral' character may seem unfocused and scattered, confused and unorganized because he cannot digest information into usable, recognizable (by the brain) thought building blocks. These people often develop food allergies, because they absorb incompletely digested proteins and are the ones who most often have a craving, dependent, addictive relationship to food. They are also those who most often are subject to what is described by the clinical ecologists as 'brain allergies,'[4] especially those marked by confusion and overwhelming anxiety. They are often 'hypoglycemic,' which has more recently been seen as a function of the food sensitive person and has similar symptoms. The patient described as Kidney yang deficient whose Kidney yang could not support the Earth energies (Spleen yang) exhibited all of the above symptoms.

Another characteristic of the thought processes of the 'oral' personality is the presence of obsessive worry as a maladaptive maneuver to manage anxiety. In contrast to the Metal personality, who is an obsessive, compulsive perfectionist with marked rigidity, the 'oral' character is relatively unstructured; the obsession stays within the mind in the form of constant, free-floating worry. During psychotic regressions under stress, bizarre compulsions will appear as a restorative measure in those decompensating toward schizophrenia, along with many of the other symptoms of that condition described above. A characteristic that distinguishes between the decompensated 'oral' and the person suffering from earlier, more pervasive damage is the former's relatively rapid recovery in a protected environment.

Another quality of thought processes in the 'oral' character is concreteness. While they are more capable of abstract thinking than the schizophrenic because boundaries are more firmly established between conscious and unconscious processes, the immediacy of their need for emotional and financial support (food, clothing, and shelter) directly influences their thought processes toward concrete concerns. The capacity for abstract thinking is present, but preoccupation with the concrete precludes its maturation.

The person who tends, on the other hand, to do much of his thinking while he or she is eating will often develop serious digestive problems, depending on the extensiveness of this habit and, of course, the constitutional status of the gastro-intestinal tract. Again, the kind of disorder that will result depends upon the nature of the thinking and of vulnerability of the organ or area.[5] The worrier will have incomplete digestion (the Earth phase); the person with angry thoughts will develop Liver difficulties with sour regurgitation; and people with decisions on their mind while they eat may have Gallbladder problems. In Chinese medicine, the Lungs, which digest (dispersing function) 'mucus,' are part of the digestive system.[6] Should mealtime be chronically marked by rigid repressive practices (no talking, strict discipline, and little gaiety) or by thoughts of grief, excess mucus may appear, as well as problems with elimination. Excessive joy is not often a chronic habit. In states of excessive joy, which we would call mania, people are often too hyperactive to eat. Emotional shock while eating will affect both the Heart nerves and general circulation, and also the nervous innervation and circulation of the gastro-intestinal system. Problems with digestion on many levels will ensue.

Anxiety

The anxiety of the 'oral' character is most specifically related to deprivation. The issue is survival, and terror is aroused by the ever-present, ubiquitous expectation of the loss of sustenance. Although it is largely a matter of being deprived of love, the oral character experiences this in very concrete terms, since he often has great difficulty establishing himself in the real world of work and financial stability. Survival is a question of having someone who is committed to his physical survival first, and spiritual survival secondarily. The possible loss of this commitment is a constant source of anxiety. It is aggravated by his egocentricity and lack of concern for the needs and wants of the other person, whose inevitable ambivalence will sustain the expectation of abandonment and concomitant anxiety.

Another source of anxiety is the compensatory state of the Spleen-Pancreas, which is referred to as 'hypoglycemia'. In this condition there are wide fluctuations of blood sugar which, when elevated, leads to lethargy, a decrease in concentration, and exhaustion; and when low, to anxiety, dizziness, and extreme weakness. Other organ systems are involved, including the Liver and Kidney (adrenal), but the principal defect lies with a Spleen-Pancreas overburdened by the heavy sugar intake of those whose oral needs were sufficiently deprived to sustain a lifelong craving for the sweetness they missed. In varying degrees we are most of us thus afflicted.

A Case of Dependency

E. was 29-years old, a rather disheveled but attractive woman at the time she was referred by her sister. At the time, she was unable to cope with the care of her husband and one child and appeared in a state of tortured confusion and severe agitation. She was the eldest of five children. Her parents operated a bar and she was raised in this atmosphere, as one child after another arrived, the second only one year after she was born. E. was pushed out of the nest almost immediately and was used to raise the other children.

She left home at the age of 17 and married a bi-sexual man who was a pimp, and for whom she was a high-class prostitute, until he absconded with their child. In 16 years she has not been able to trace either of them. She continued to lead a marginal, impulsive, and highly unstable life until she married a carpenter with whom she has wandered from place to place, finally moving into her sister's house, and forcing the latter out.

E. was extremely dependent on her husband for almost everything. [233] She was afraid to learn to drive; she could come to therapy only at the whim of her husband who opposed her treatment. Her dependencies included drugs, both prescribed and recreational, which she used when she could not get what she needed from people. She had many obsessions. In order to allay her anxiety, everything had to be in a particular place and be done at a particular time and in a particular way. If it was not, she would withdraw, go to sleep, stay in bed, and not function. She personalized most of what occurred around or was communicated to her, leading to considerable distortion and conflict.

There were frequent changes of mood directly varying with whether she felt cared for or not. She said "All I want is to be loved unconditionally" and was in a rage if she was not. Though she said that she was afraid of being made a fool, of giving without getting, she had no resistance to anyone who appeared to be willing to take care of her, and no judgment about the people who made these promises. The venom that followed their defections was monumental, though short-lived. Her everlasting hope was that "something will happen that will make everything nice." She responded well to the needles and some talk, and presently, eight years later, she is doing well. She is independent, with a career, and has raised her son to be a fairly well-adjusted adolescent.

Permissive Parents

Changes in parental attitudes since World War I, and especially since World War II, toward a more permissive environment for children have been misconstrued by some people to mean the setting of absolutely no limits and have led to a new form of the oral dependent person. All of the pathogenic outcomes of child development have become, consequently, marked by greater confusion and disorganization. This unstructured and untrained, inadequate person has been with us throughout history and is now here in new and more virulent forms since the loosening of parental disciplines.

When little is expected, there is little chance of developing a feeling of adequacy or self-esteem. Whereas in the past the parent paid a great deal of attention to the child's development, often excessively, recently the child goes his own way relatively unguided. These people do not have the organizational ability to enslave others to their needs in a series of intense relationships, because they never experienced such intensity in their original relationships. Instead, they themselves become enslaved to their lack of preparation for the pain and frustration of daily life. So painful and intolerable is reality to them that escape, especially through readily available drugs, is irresistible. As one recovering drug addict told me in the 1960s, "Man, I need a human tranquilizer." He lived his life in a wealthy ambiance of total emotional neglect. Another told me that he had the "Long Island syndrome," meaning that "no one ever expected anything from me." Most of these young people report having been told by their progressive parents, while longing and begging for guidance, that indeed these parents had every confidence in them that they could and should be able to guide themselves, that their counsel was not necessary, or even desirable. The absence of models from which to learn and authority against which they could test and build their own strength has left a scarred generation. Many other factors have contributed to the pain-phobic drug culture. Not the least, I believe, is this new wrinkle in the distortion of Earth-bonding energies.

A Case of Formlessness

C. was a 20-year-old college junior who was extremely agitated. He stated that he felt nothing, was completely apathetic, withdrawn from any interest in or caring about anybody or anything in life. He likened himself to his older brother who was in even worse shape, and to his father who was a salesman and was totally passive, with no interests. His mother, who came from a wealthy family, stated that "happiness equals money and that is all I know." He felt that his problem centered in the fact that he was never expected to do anything or assume any responsibility even for himself. No one paid the slightest attention to his obligations in school or had the slightest curiosity about how he was doing. On matters of utmost urgency with regard to his development in the real world it was assumed that he could figure it out by himself. At home his care was total, and in fact, even until the age of 16 his mother would wipe his behind for him after defecating, so that he would not have to do it himself.

His feeling was one of amorphousness, and formlessness, having no 'definition' to himself and his life, and no limits. He simply did not know where he was or where the rest of life was and he had an almost total disorientation to the essential issues of existence. He deplored his lack of education, having done nothing in school up to this point. It left him feeling that he was inferior because "I don't have the tools to expand on thoughts." However, seeing his brother in the same place, but five years older, he was gripped by the fear of that deadness, which he sensed in himself. This fear was a spark of his life that could be fanned into a flame of being.

THE MATURATION AND TRANSFORMATION OF BONDS

Trust in mother is, paradoxically, the condition that allows human beings to believe that it is safe to expand this bond to others and thus fulfill their developmental destiny as adults. This earth-trust is the fertile soil for all natural separations in the 'evolution of being', the first of which is the gradual emergence into the newborn consciousness of awareness of another being, necessary and helpful, and yet with their own needs.

Bonding, and especially the process by which bonds mature, is the enduring symbol of the energies of the Earth phase. In the early era, it establishes the human bond (yin function), and in the later era of early childhood, it creates the conditions for the expansion (yang function) of that bond to other phenomena, both human and otherwise, which occupy this space with us. Though not entirely individuated from the primary bond, the child begins, with the help of the trust these energies engender (and with Metal phase energies which serve transformation and expansion), to identify, not only with the immediate, but with the larger world of people and things. The existential family begins to become included as part of one's self ('being'). The Earth is the glue that bonds, and trust, its child, the solvent that separates, always at once in the same process.

Even failure to bond well with the original caretakers can be remedied to a reasonable extent by the formation and expansion of bonds with surrogate caretakers. This is especially important to health care practitioners such as Chinese medical practitioners who are surrogates in the same continuum of bonding.

A Case of the Extended Family and Surrogate Caretakers

A young woman was born into a family with a very immature, impulsive, and violent mother and a largely absent father working very long hours. Their marriage was forced against the father's will due to her pregnancy at the age of sixteen. The child was not welcome and the mother beat the child whenever she was emotionally stressed.

Shortly after her birth the mother began to drink and the infant and child were largely neglected except for the nearby presence of her paternal grandparents and paternal aunt and uncle, who also became involved in her care.

The child was fearful and exceedingly cautious in her early years but gradually came more and more in contact with friends of the family as well as other relatives that seemed to increase her courage. Counselors in summer camp, teachers, special attention by significant family friends, and finally friends her own age and older played a greater and greater part in her maturation into an independent person who left home early. Later, psychotherapy and other healing modalities that she pursued built upon the strength she gained from her surrogate caretakers and friends, allowing her to create a successful personal and professional life.

DISHARMONY OF THE TRANSORMATION AND MATURATION OF BONDS

Wherever the original bond is dysfunctional, the maturation and transformation of bonds is determined by the extent to which the infant is genetically unable to participate in the original bonding process (autistic), the degree to which the caretaker is unable or unwilling to allow this maturation, the unavailability of surrogates, and a deficit in Metal transformational function, or some combination of the above.

The result, as illustrated below, is a person damaged socially and interpersonally as well as often neurologically. While a wastebox diagnosis, the description of Asperger's Syndrome is illustrative of many of the permutations and combinations of the insults mentioned above. Some of the symptoms are: lack of social skills; dislikes changes in routine; appears to lack empathy; unable to discern subtle cues in others' behavior, facial expressions, and tone of voice; avoids eye contact and has unusual facial expressions; restricted and unusual interests; awkward motor development; easily over-stimulated.

Any of the categories of disharmony given under Earth yin deficiency and excess can also be examples of a deficit in the transformation and maturation of bonds.

A Case of the Failure of Spleen Yin

A young 32-year-old man was interviewed who had become massively depressed when the only girlfriend he had ever had ended their relationship. He was hospitalized, given drugs and shock therapy, but his depression became greater, including a steady withdrawal from society, and even from his own family. Sensory deprivation therapy was followed by an ongoing delusion and even hallucination about distant family members who were going to disenfranchise him when his parents died. At times this involved smashing walls and furniture when he felt threatened, though never against another person.

His history included his mother's previous miscarriage, toxemia of pregnancy, her abandonment of him as an infant for eight months, and two inguinal hernias at the age of three. Parents are self-described as perfectionistic and demanding; he could never defend himself against them.

He was extremely sensitive as a child, with considerable difficulty with peers, and withdrew into a world of fantasy involving Camelot and all of the adventures associated with the Knights of the Round Table. He has stayed in that world ever since, and despite an IQ of 158, he did not do well in school.

In college he discovered that if he took enormous amounts of coffee, caffeine tablets, and Dexedrine he could think clearly and perform outstandingly such that he earned a Masters Degree and acceptance into a prestigious doctoral program. Here at last, with the rejection by his girlfriend, he fell into the massive depression mentioned above.

A central and ongoing feature of his problem is his experience of himself as totally unable to think and a complete sense of unworthiness. Any compliment is experienced as mockery. He feels that his brain has been damaged and that he is autistic. A neurologist recently made a diagnosis of Asperger's Syndrome, a form of adult autism. He avoids people, closes his eyes when he talks to them and continues to use caffeine stimulants in order to participate even in a limited way in society. My experience with chronic users of amphetamines and high caffeine stimulants is brain damage, often irreversible.

Here we have a combination of almost all of the insults listed above to make the maturing and transferring of bonds unlikely. Evidence of in utero damage and Kidney essence deficiency are the `toxemia of pregnancy', placenta previa, the double inguinal hernia at age three, extreme sensitivity, and the prolonged flight into fantasy life as a young child. Abandonment by his mother during the first year of his life did not provide him with the Earth nurture that could have created the bond that would have permitted a maturation of that bond and transfer to others. The pressure to succeed forced him into an addiction that I believe created a realistic brain deficit with the consequent downward spiral that included damaging medical intervention.

EXCESSIVE EARTH YIN ENERGIES: PROBLEMS IN TRANSFORMING BONDS

Increasingly in recent years, the problems have moved toward difficulties in breaking bonds rather than in forming them. I would argue from clinical experience that the therapeutic task is easier for both the patient and the therapist when the bonding is deficient and the patient is an 'oral' character or a schizophrenic, rather than the situation where the bonding has been too strong. Where, in Chinese terms, the Earth energies have been excessive in bonding, the person thus afflicted has been equipped with a sophisticated apparatus to manipulate the world to their way, in contrast to those whose Earth energies have been deficient in bonding. Again, for the sake of discussion, we are oversimplifying a truly complex situation that, in reality, is usually a mixture of excesses in some areas and deficiencies in others, in any one person's life. The ideal is balance, in which a good parent gives and withholds when it is most in the interest of the healthy development of the child. Inborn patterns or tendencies toward patterns of behavior have been extensively studied by Chess and Thomas,[7] showing that the child is not a 'tabula rasa'[8] and has a significant input to the odyssey of his or her own development. The challenge to mature parents is to cope with their own egocentricity and to adapt their energies for bonding and separation to the individual child.

I refer here primarily to the character structure of the person in whose development the Earth energies involved with bonding have been excessive, such as the narcissistic personality.

NARCISSISM

When a child has been made to feel that he or she is the center of the parents' universe, beyond the developmental period in which this is reasonable and in the child's best interests, the general features of narcissism are likely to emerge. This more often occurs in only children, though it is not confined to them. There are, for example, situations in which a child has been the only one, and excessively the center of the parental-family universe for a considerable period of time, until another child comes along, supplanting the former. Other life situations may also interrupt this exclusive relationship, such as death of a parent, and may alter the classical narcissistic personality. We are speaking, therefore, of a theoretical average.

From the child's point of view, he is living in a paradise in which he is the central concern in all relevant matters and is all-powerful in the decision-making process. He does not realize that, in fact, he is actually quite powerless and that the someone else who is in power has, for their own reasons, been willing to allow the child to feel omnipotent. The problems begin to arise when the child, in the normal course of events, must deal with people who do not wish to concede such extraordinary power to him. This is, of course, inevitable and, depending on the degree to which these bonding energies have been in excess, one has relative disaster.

The clinical picture depends upon the exact point in this history that one looks in upon the person. This is the spoiled child, whose behavior is endlessly demanding, whose frustrations are marked by uniquely intemperate tantrums, who may go through life, until and unless correctional action is taken, expecting everyone with whom they come in contact to subsume their own needs and defer to them, immediately and at all times. They are experienced by others as self-centered and egocentric, which characterizes their thinking processes in childhood, adolescence, and adulthood. Cognition is based on the premise that they are the focus of all concern, and they often develop 'ideas of reference' at some point in life, even by the age of four or five.

The characterlogical consequence of such false omnipotence is a life of endless frustration and confusion. These people feel that they know everything; and yet, since they have been expected to do little for themselves or others, they are actually inadequate. Though they cannot function, they feel that their opinions are superior and should hold sway. The ever-growing awareness of the disparity between the fantasy and the reality of their abilities and their ever-increasing failure to dominate the world creates enormous anxiety, endless feelings of inadequacy, and brings into action every imaginable maneuver to manipulate other people, so they may again feel powerful. Any responsibility will evoke this anxiety and, concomitantly, all the tedious and difficult interpersonal machinations that are available to escape it. These are among the most difficult people in the world with whom to live. As the years progress into adulthood, they will seem, to those who get caught in their net, as not only inadequate and impossible, but also extremely immature. They rarely cease to attempt to invoke extreme guilt in anyone who does not accede to putting their needs before all others. They develop a clinging quality, which is best described as sticky; and sooner or later, they become extremely vengeful to all who fail to show absolute obeisance. Throughout their reign of terror, they are, out of their own inadequacy, extraordinary worriers, who burden everyone with their projected concerns, most of which usually are highly exaggerated. Everyone so unfortunate as to be susceptible to their 'guilt trap' will be obligated to either dedicate themselves to these worries, to the exclusion of their own problems, or suffer the consequences of retribution. Indeed, when these people look at life they see only themselves.

A Case of Helplessness

T. was born to a middle class family which had known very hard times in the country from which they had come. Mother was one of many children, relatively neglected, with no opportunity for an education or advancement until she met her husband. He was very bright and won scholarships and other academic honors until, with her aggressive support, they achieved financial security. When she had a child, she wanted it to have everything she never had. The little girl became the center of her life and that world did revolve around her. Every wish was gratified, everything she did was greeted with unrealistic praise, and any dissent was ignored and discarded. T.'s father was pressed into this mold, and since he was a thinker and a dreamer, he accommodated his wife and was glad to be left to himself.

When she was five years old, a brother was born. Mother dropped T. in favor of the son, a much greater prize in that culture, and T., at the same time, had to begin school and thus to face a world for which she was unprepared. She formed no friends there and was lonely both at home and away. As she grew, the relationship with her mother increased in ugliness and deteriorated at the same time into a symbiotic mess. T. could barely function in school, but she was physically attractive, a good dancer, and married quite young. Her husband, who was expected to restore her to her previous exalted state, found himself performing not only his own duties in life, but all of hers as well. Despite her helplessness, she insisted that she alone was capable of decisions and expected total and immediate compliance with her determinations.

The world, including her husband, did not give her the homage she demanded. She seemed to have no residual shred of hope that she could leave her narcissistic world and become an adequate person and turned instead to using her considerable basic intelligence to manipulate and connive what she could not command. Gradually the marriage failed, and while not abandoned financially, she was left to fend for herself interpersonally. Over and over she alienated people, especially men, by insisting they abide by her superior judgment and allow themselves to be swallowed up into serving her narcissism. Therapy was another demand on her part for an appreciative and yielding audience and was not a resounding success. Sadly, she died suddenly and young.

NATURAL FUNCTIONS OF THE EARTH YANG PHASE SYSTEM

Ego Development and Boundaries

The rational, orderly, and compassionate use of the mother's Earth energies during the pre- and post-partum eras is the foundation for sound ego development. Cognition is a major contribution of Earth energies to 'being.' The Earth phase energies are responsible as much for the ingestion, digestion, absorption, metabolism, and, to some extent, excretion of thought as they are of food. Metabolism of thought involves the organization of information necessary to meet the demands of survival and is necessary to the enhancement of what we call 'ego.'

[241]

The capacity to engage successfully in these activities is determined in utero, increasing exponentially with the formation and growth of the placenta (Water phase). The opportunity to do so occurs after birth. At either point the process may be compromised. Generally, the earlier the insult, the more profound the unfortunate consequences. For those whose intrauterine development is incomplete, the dependency on a symbolic 'placenta' and 'umbilical cord,' expressed as an inappropriate need for ego-organization from the outside, will be a determining influence on their life. A quantitatively sufficient insult to cognitive development after birth can mimic the dire consequences to ego development of damage occurring in utero. We have indicated that though the two consequences may seem identical, the latter individual will be at a higher level of maturation when the insult occurs and has, therefore, the greater organizational capacity for recovery.

In adversity, should the Earth energies partially fail in their critical function of digesting, absorbing, metabolizing, and excreting, the normal serenity is distorted into listlessness, thoughtful reflection into obsessive worry, compassion into an excessively sweet and clinging over-concern, and quiet calmness into catatonia. These are the restorative functions of the human organism when its timely needs in the Earth phase are significantly unfulfilled.

While obsessive worry has been classically associated with the activity of the Earth phase, I find it to be more of a function of the Fire phase, and especially of the Pericardium yin maladaptations to stay in `contact,' to stay `intact'. My own findings suggest that obsessive worrying is a function of a lack of trust, a deficiency in parenting at a basic level in dealing with the unknown and its associated fear. However, while over-concern and inordinate compassion for others is linked to a deficiency in Earth energies, I find that excessive compassion is the result of a defect in boundary formation.

Capacity for boundary formation begins in utero (Water phase) as a consequence of many factors. The integrity of the placenta plays a particularly significant role in clearly delineating parent from child. A defective placenta that allows an abnormal exchange between mother and fetus may be responsible for a variety of physical problems, including those with Rh factor. We know that brain damage to the fetus, to varying extents, is a consequence of such a breakdown in boundaries. The danger to the mother is equally well documented.

These mental-physical disorders are intermixed pathologically. The physical breakdown of these boundaries has a profound effect on mental function. Any damage to mental function of the newborn, or to the physical well-being of the mother, will compromise the normal evolution of that relationship from bonding to separation. The bonding will become stickier for obvious reasons if the child is defective, and more tenuous if the mother's health is compromised.

The normal development of boundaries is the foundation on which that bond can safely expand to include others in the process of separation from mother and is a function of Earth yang. Should the boundaries be less than optimal, that expansion and separation will be fraught with difficulty.

At the other end of the scale from the development of bonding, the earth-mother's energy role in child development is to encourage, with the strength and guidance of Metal energies, the transformation of that bond and the expansion of being to an identification with peers and new surrogate parents. The bond to mother should not at this point be broken. Rather, it should be encouraged and allowed to expand and stretch to new interpersonal horizons, while the old bonds are quietly but continually nourished in the background. If the Earth energies for separation are excessively strong, the resulting separation process is carried out too rapidly, too abruptly, or even brutally. On the other hand is the situation in which the process is prolonged inappropriately or, in fact, never truly begun. Like fruit on the vine there is a point of maturity when it is time for the fruit to fall, before which it is too green, and after which it is overripe. We shall consider each possibility in its turn.

DISHARMONY OF EARTH YANG FUNCTION

Deficient Earth Yang Energies: Problems in Separation

There are significant similarities between the personality outcomes for those whose bonding has been excessive and those in which energy for separation has been deficient. In the latter instance, we are considering a situation in which a child may have been sheltered from socialization with peers and adults until the time society demands this socialization at the age of mandatory school attendance. These children are not, as with the narcissistic children, necessarily overindulged. Their sense of inadequacy arises from lack of experience rather than from either the psychological vote of no confidence that comes from a lack of expectation or the sense of inadequacy that comes when one's false omniscience is exposed. These children, in whom the expansion of the mothering bond is under-energized, cling from fear of the unknown. Affect may be flat, from lack of contact, broken by spells of tearfulness in situations in which they feel out of place. The most obvious behavior problem is school phobia, and the anxiety in this symbiotic situation is that of separation. Frequently these people will, if strong enough, develop obsessions and phobias as a way of controlling the anxiety, school phobia being the earliest and most noticeable. If the bonding energies of Earth are poor and the energies of the other phases, especially Water, are severely compromised, a schizophrenic outcome could occur. Often, these people do become 'schizoid,' remaining detached and avoiding others.

A Case of Missed Opportunities

I am reminded of a young man, G., whom I met when he was about 17, prior to the Vietnam war. Both of his parents were deaf, and he had emerged in early childhood as their caretaker, a role in which he performed splendidly. His life revolved around them almost exclusively, and as he entered each of the developmental stages, he missed the growth opportunities that existed for others. He was completely lost in the larger world, a ship without a rudder. Therapy, we both agreed, was not sufficient to replace what he had missed, and we finally hit upon the army as one place where he could find an organized authoritative regime that would provide him with the structure he lacked, and out of which he might develop a social self. In the beginning of his military career he was actively suicidal. His commanding officer stayed in close touch with me, and his sergeant took him under his wing. Within three months his life began to turn around. He found a template on which to build a self, models and facilitators to provide roles and direction. Within a year and a half he had a German girl friend and traveled with her through Europe and the United States on his leaves. We stayed in touch for several years during which he found himself and built a real life. All he lacked and all he needed was the experience and the right environment in which to use it. The adequacy was always there, in contrast to the lack of it in the narcissistic child from whom nothing had been expected.

Symbiosis

The symbiotic relationship is another separation aspect of bonding with apparent deficient Earth yang. Here there a pact between parent (usually, but not always, the mother) in which separation is not an object since each is serving a vital function for the other. These relationships often occur with only children, though sometimes one child and one parent make the decision to make a life together forever that is special even in a large family. While in those special ways others are excluded, in other ways they may relate functionally, parents to other children and child to other siblings, as in the case history given below.

I observed a few of these arrangements during my years working with children, adolescents, and families. The symbiotic relationship is apart from the commonly acknowledged patterns observed in family therapy: that each member of the family, especially the children, is given a role. One is the caretaker, another the troublemaker, another the victim, and still another the helpless one. In this context, Mommy and Daddy each usually has at least one ally. These kinds of relationships are unstable and eventually succumb conflictually to the inherent need of a child to become an individuated adult with a new life and family.

In my parents' day, among immigrant families, one child would be mysteriously chosen as the one who would never marry and would stay to care for the parents in their old age. This arrangement has been the source of plays and books and is found in many cultures. In many families I observed, the overprotected child is often instinctively identified by the mother as defective, even at birth, and in need of special care and protection.

The symbiotic partnership is different. It seems mutually chosen by often substantially competent participants and is satisfying to all concerned. The bond is special, enduring, benefiting both, and transcending all other relationships.

Father and Daughter

A young woman, the second of three children, was born into an immigrant family in which the marriage between the 16-year-old mother and 26-year-old father was arranged against the mother's will while still in Europe. The father came first to this country, followed three years later by the mother, who for her entire life despised her husband. After she arrived in this country, she apparently conceived her first child and then traveled back across the Atlantic Ocean to Eastern Europe to give birth. She then returned to the U.S. with her entire family of origin, including parents and ten siblings. She then had two more children. The paternity of the first was in doubt.

The father was dedicated to his wife and children but essentially had no true wife or partner, since the mother, upon arriving in this country the second time, asserted her independence and lived a separate life except for basic duties. The second child, a daughter, took her role when she was very young as 'wife' and companion to her very hard-working father. She became his secretary and bookkeeper even at an early age, and though she married, she lived with or close to her father until he died, caring for him through 70 strokes in the course of six years, even while working. Her admiration of and devotion to him was quietly observed and acknowledged by the family, but never mentioned. The father even took her husband, who failed at his own profession, into his own and trained him.

Excessive Earth Yang Energies: Problems in Separation

HARDEN OR PERISH

People who are evicted from the nest before their time either perish quickly or become hardened. The outcome depends so much, of course, on what took place before the eviction. Those whose first two-and-a-half years were relatively good, whose Water, Earth, and Wood phases of energetic development were complete, and who were rejected between the ages of two-and-a-half and five years, are strong enough to harden their hearts against the loss of love and survive. While the early Fire energies cannot have their first flowering in the 'Oedipal' drama, while rapture and joy will not sing in their hearts, they do become the bioenergetically armored people whose primary restoration against further rejection and hurt is the acquisition of enormous power. This quest for power may take legitimate or illegitimate forms. One is a socially acceptable exploiter of his fellow man, the business tycoon; and the other is called criminal and is considered socially unacceptable. The unfolding, in one direction or the other, is not always, but often a function of environment and opportunity. Those who come from the middle or upper class are more likely to operate within the law (not always); and those from the poorer classes who are evicted too early are more likely to operate outside the law (again, not always).

Anxiety is evoked by closeness, tenderness, and warmth, and depression is a rare response to a setback in thrust for might. Thought processes are obsessional, with power being a common preoccupation. Love is fundamentally an exploitative means to the same end and sex is without tenderness. Affect is hard, and behavior in all relationships is marked by ruthlessness. Other people can make an impression on them primarily by strength, which they enjoy as a challenge, though for those who are helpless and are no threat, they may show the compassion which intact Earth energies allow them to keep in reserve. They may, once their power is established, become the philanthropic godfathers in whatever sector of society they dominate. They do not, as with the power-driven people with Water energy disharmony, necessarily need to lead and bend the will of masses of people. Whether businessman or criminal, these are professionals. Often they are brilliant. Few can withstand the intense heat of their burning drive for personal power. They are tough.

I speak of these matters from personal experience, having been raised from age six to 16 in an area of New York City dominated by lower middle class Irish and Italian first and second generation families. Both groups had many children. It was the Irish mothers who seemed to relate only to infants and very small children. After the age of approximately two-and-a-half, their children were in the streets, and their primary allegiance was to the gang that raised them. In this culture, as I understood it, with a difficult birth where there was a choice between saving the life of either the mother or child. The decision, according to the priests, was that the mothers tended to die, so some children never knew their real mothers and were raised by older siblings until the gang could take them.

The Italians, on the other hand, remained within the family of origin and fought other families for dominance in the streets. By the time I left home at the age of 16-and-a-half, one half of the Irish, and a few of the Italian, children I knew were in some kind of juvenile detention, having become the prime front line troops of the Greenpoint Gang, a subsidiary of Murder, Inc. These were the socially unacceptable, some of whom later became powerful in crime circles.

The socially acceptable 'criminals' I came to know only later in my life, after the age of 40, when I became acquainted with the modem day robber barons. As Mack-the-Knife reflected at the end of the German movie version of the *Threepenny Opera*, "It is certainly more profitable to start a bank than rob one."[9] Let me give you a concrete example of this thesis, not from my professional files, for these people do not seek therapy, but from personal experience.

A Modern Robin Hood

P. was raised in two of the most significant ghettos of his home city, in extreme poverty. His mother had a proclivity for petty crime, and though he was well cared for during his first three years, he was pushed out into the streets to fend for himself at this time. Several years later he was joined by his younger brother who survived childhood with only one eye. P. went to work as a shoe-shine boy when he was about nine years old. He also ran numbers for the older racketeers. Though he never attended school, he had a photographic memory and a natural talent in mathematics. By the time he was in his early 20s he controlled all of the shoe-shine parlors of the largest ghetto and, along with them, all of the numbers racket. His brother was the finger man, the one with the gun. By the time he was in his mid-30s, P. was the head of all the rackets in the state in which he lived. Most of his day was spent in bed taking phone calls from all parts of the state, recording in his mind thousands of bets and all of the odds.

P. entered legitimate business and made a fortune when he sold this business to the government at the beginning of World War II. It was at this point that a famous prosecutor, later governor of the state, made his reputation by pursuing and eventually forcing P. out of the state. By this time he had many other businesses and rackets in other states, and lived in opulence.

P. was always generous to people less fortunate than himself who did not stand in his way. He supported his in-laws and always gave when asked. He was a modern, rough-and-ready Robin Hood, with a good sense of humor, not personally violent, yet not capable of showing overt affection. The end of his odyssey came at the hands of the two people against whom he never took proper precautions, his own mother and brother, who robbed him of all his empire. There may be honor among thieves, but not in the same family.

No Sense of Self

For those whose first few years are not adequate, premature separation will of course result in disaster. Depending on the endless variables, it will produce results all along the line, from death through the extreme psychotic states to which we have referred above, to at best the 'oral' personality that we have already described under insufficient bonding. Most of those whom I have known who were separated at a very early age from their families were raised in institutions. When I worked on the adolescent girls' ward of Bellevue Hospital in New York, I admitted and worked with many girls from the Catholic orphanages, which abound up and down the Hudson Valley and in Staten Island. We saw the ones who 'acted out,' who broke windows and otherwise refused to become the automatons for which they were being programmed. The problem was so great that a social worker nun was assigned as a liaison with the hospital and all these institutions. She realized what was happening and was endlessly frustrated by her own people, whose repertoire of contact with these girls was a rigid, detached, punishing coldness. A study made during the mid-1950s to which I can no longer directly refer showed that a large majority of the women coming from these homes became prostitutes. They expressed almost no sense of self and were grateful to have some place and purpose in life, whatever the cost. Existence was the only issue.

A Case of Detachment

N. was adopted at the age of 19 months, at which time he was in poor physical condition, suffering somewhat from malnutrition and lagging in all areas of development, including speech and contact with people. He also had a heart murmur. He did not, after being adopted, become close to his mother, but seemed more at ease with his father. He was unable to accept tenderness or affection of a physical nature and apparently was unable to tolerate any strong emotion, which his mother tended to show more than his father. N. was seven years old when his father, the one person to whom he could allow some closeness, died. At that time it was noted that he showed little or no emotion at the news of his father's death. Within a few years his mother married a widower who had been a friend of the family, and who had known N. since his adoption. N. again felt closer to him than to his mother, although he feared him a great deal.

N. had difficulty in school with both reading and speech and had remedial training in both. He had always been very popular but not particularly close to anyone, and his parents felt that N. did not get involved and committed because he was afraid to fail. He set very high standards for himself and was unable to tolerate the smallest deviation from them. He solved the problem of commitment by running away from it. Connected to this issue was his need to feel 'independent,' which meant that he could not ever acknowledge to himself that he depended on his fellow man for anything.

N.'s school experience, especially in high school, was filled with delinquent behavior and a negative attitude toward learning. After leaving school he changed jobs frequently. He was, however, reported to be a good worker, his restlessness notwithstanding. N. joined the army, spent three years in the service, part of which time he served in Vietnam where he saw a great deal of action and was wounded. His negative attitude toward learning prevailed in the army where he lost several chances to get training in the specialty schools.

N. expressed his fear of intimate relationships in terms of being tied down, being hurt, and not being good enough to be loved. With regard to the latter he felt like a colossal failure. His original failure was as an infant in an institution where he was unable to get the warm empathetic response of a caring person that an infant usually finds in a mother. As with all infants who fail to get this response and must protect themselves in order to survive, he ceased crying for the things he needed. By the time a meaningful, consistent, sufficient human reaction was available, at the age of 19 months, it was too late. The barriers had already been erected. N.'s inability to respond at that time led to his being labeled as a 'cold' child, which turned off the people around him, perpetuating the emptiness that had existed from the beginning.

His father's death at the age of seven was another failure, for at that age he could only have interpreted it to mean "If I had been better, he wouldn't have gone away." He responded by becoming more detached and unresponsive, and in order to altogether avoid the pain associated with love and attachment, he chose a line of behavior that aroused disapproval, this being more tolerable to him than affection. The first real break in this barrier occurred during the war, when N. saw men whom he knew die, and when he read their letters to their dear ones, in preparing to send their belongings home.

The second break was the stimulus for his referral by a local priest. At that time N. had returned from the service to enter college. He described himself as a "loner," a "smooth operator," and a "manipulator," especially with women. For a short time prior to the first interview he had lost all ambition, was depressed, extremely nervous, and shaky to the point of trembling. N. recognized that these feelings centered around a struggle within himself concerning a young woman whom he had met in college and with whom he had fallen in love. N. did not welcome that feeling. with which he was unfamiliar, and from the beginning tried to resolve the conflict by cutting off his feelings and erecting an emotional wall. In the course of time, his constantly fluctuating position began to drive him and the girl to distraction. Despite the internal struggle, these feelings of love inspired him to do well in school for the first time. The conflict became overwhelming; he withdrew from school and sought help from the priest, when he found that his anxiety was not assuaged by the distance from this girl whom he still loved.

N. had placed the battle outside himself and tried to resolve it by getting the girl to reject him. He found that the conflict was his own and that he would have to settle it himself. The barrier had been

[249]

[250]

breached, and in the course of therapy, N. decided, for better or worse, to join the human race and to commit himself to the things he cared about, despite the possibilities of rejection, failure, and pain.

12

The Metal phase

Natural Functions of the Metal Phase System

Transformation of Bonds

Whereas the Earth phase energies are responsible for the maturing of bonds into mutually growth-producing relationships, the Metal phase serves the process of individuation by lending its energies to the transformation and expansion of existing bonds. It accomplishes this by letting go and re-attaching, thereby engaging an ever wider spectrum of variegated mortals. These transactions begin to operate by parturition at the latest, during the transformation from the placental bond to the maternal bond (the breast), but probably serve this function from inception to death, and beyond. It is said that the first breath brings with it the heavenly spirit, which makes a newborn human, for without it one does not begin to exist on earth as a living being. From birth onward, Metal energies regulate the release and renewal of the lighter, finer energies that we associate with the air we breathe and with 'spirit', in contrast to the coarser, more material energies of the foods we ingest, which are processed by Earth energies.

The trust engendered by the successful evolution of Earth energies enhances the loosening of the family bond to include surrogate parents in the form of teachers in school, counselors in camp, the policeman on the block, and surrogate siblings or playmates in the neighborhood or school. This metamorphosis, which increasingly engages Metal energies, accelerates during the pre-adolescent, adolescent, and young adulthood stages of development.

During these years there is a rapid loosening of the primary bonds to include the bigger world. This occurs in a rhythmic fashion of expansion and contraction, analogous to the expansion and contraction of the lungs, or the elimination and holding of the large intestine. The contraction aspect is important since the new bonds that are formed during these eras seem as if they will last forever. The first shift in pre-adolescence is to the peer alliance, and there ensues the rebellion in which the need for approval is transferred from parents and surrogates to relative equals. This is a most precarious and anti-social time and one from which many people never evolve; they end up leading lives outside of, or on the fringes of, society. Most of the anti-social activities of adolescence have little to do with the actual work of that period of development, and they signal a lack of development from the pre-adolescent, peer-gang bonding and loyalties.

In the normal course of events there is a shift away from the group toward a relationship with one other person of the same sex, which Harry Stack Sullivan described so eloquently as "chumship."[1] Sullivan suggests that chumship occurs between the ages of eight-and-a-half and ten. While it is true that a selectivity does occur at this age between people of the same sex, the potential for fellowship is greatly circumscribed by the limited maturity of a nine-year-old child. The true flowering of this comradeship occurs, in my experience, closer to the age of 14 or 15. By then, a significant blossoming of inner-awareness creates the pressure to share the new pains and glories of this extraordinary unfolding. Sullivan had little contact with children as an adult and was raised in a rural area, relatively isolated from other children. Despite his remarkable insight, I believe this interfered with his accuracy in estimating the age of "chumship." On the other hand, I also believe that the exact age of this remarkable occurrence, when and if indeed it occurs at all, varies widely with education, opportunity, and social milieu. I agree with Sullivan that it is an innate capacity of the evolving person: indeed, its fulfillment is essential if we are to reach our greatest potential as human beings.

Intimacy under the guidance of Fire energies has its initiation as one discovers through another person that, as Sullivan put it, "we are more simply human than otherwise."[2] Our existential isolation is alleviated through intimacy with the discovery that we are not alone or unique in our sufferings, concerns, and joys; rather, we share them with at least one other person and probably many. We come to perceive ourselves as social beings with an evolving capacity for compassion and empathy. The exultation of two becoming as one for the first time can never be replicated even a short time later when sexual energies infuse personal ties with the most extraordinarily passionate and volatile emotions. There is some evidence from my work with young people who have grown up since World War II that chumship with another person of the same sex may be a disappearing phenomenon, displaced by an earlier and earlier maturity that interjects sex as a principal ingredient between people and precludes the opportunity of finding a pure 'soul-mate' of the same gender.

{253}

YIN METAL FUNCTIONS

Yin Metal energies are available for the interactions needed in that phase of bonding at which point peoples' auras have mutually engaged each other through the threads of energy so well described by Long.[3] These threads, which emerge from the umbilicus (the *hara* or *dan tian*) to join those of other people, were well understood and manipulated by Polynesian Kahuna shamans (for both good and evil).

The attraction of highly disparate energy channels for each other mystifies the rational mind, which is frequently puzzled by the unexpected affinities that develop between people. The often heard, "Now what did she see in him?" expresses this mystification. This attraction, which may be an expression of multiple existential factors, including karmic adjustments, is, in my opinion, expressed almost purely as a 'physical' energy phenomenon *'chemistry',* which is why I believe the Metal phase in Chinese classics is associated on a spiritual level with the 'animal soul.' The further development of the bond depends on the integrity of the Earth energies that foster the binding qualities of loyalty, dependability, and faithfulness. Literally and figuratively the relationship at this level is 'nurtured' and 'mothered' by both members of the bond, and is partly conscious and partly not. Love is a step beyond, in which the two people literally wish for and require communication and union, and is mediated by Fire energies.

Yin energies are closest to the state that is most solid, called 'mass' in physics and parenchyma in physiology. Consequently, the interlocking 'threads' of yin Metal energies have a holding, centripital quality that lends a firmness to the bond. These energy threads are the conduits for the energic ingredients necessary for the continuous renewal of the bond. This replenishment includes ideas as well as feeling, and concepts as well as emotion.

The pain we call grieving, which ensues when these threads are severed and bonds broken, is mediated by those yin Metal energies whose principal conservative propensity is to join and fasten, to hold and bind. Let those who treat these threads lightly, who break them with apparent impunity and ignore the grieving that must follow separation, beware of the inevitable embodiment of these loose, broken, unresolved fibers in the form of physical pain, deterioration, and serious illness.

Yang Metal Functions

Yang Metal energies are centrifugal in nature, serving expansion, release, and letting go of attachments to ideas and beliefs, as well as emotion and people. In contrast to the grief associated with yin Metal energies, the yang energies are filled with the excitement of moving on to new and changing interpersonal and intellectual vistas. Grief for what one gives up is replaced by joy for the new life one embraces. Release includes forgiveness and surrender, the ineluctable ingredients of personal and spiritual growth. Once the 'fear of the unknown' is reasonably assuaged, these energies tend to be associated with the almost uncontrollable celebration of new found 'freedom' during the pre-adolescent and adolescent era, which can lead to enormous conflicts with established conventions. During this era there is an explosive quality to these energies that can be dangerous if the yin-holding energies are insufficient to maintain the stability afforded by strong, healthy past and current bonds.

The Self

Self: Yin Metal Functions

As another major developmental function, Metal yin energies guide us to a more profound sense of our own identity, to a more sure knowledge that 'I am.' This represents a further enhancement of the constitutional 'identity' transmitted by Water energies, of the Earth's establishment of 'boundaries,' of the Wood's 'negative' assertion of 'being,' and of the Fire's positive assertion of that 'being' (as well as the sorting of Small Intestine energies of what is, and is not, 'me'). As our horizons expand and grow during this era, our roots must sink deeper at the same time in order to retain stability.

A principal ingredient of the growing sense of self during this era is the gradually increasing assumption of ownership of one's own inner authority and a relinquishing of dependence on the external authority of parents and peers. In this developmental period, the self becomes a laboratory in which the incorporation of sovereignty into oneself is tested over and over in an unavoidable struggle against the authority of others, until it knows itself and its safe, valid, and appropriate place in the social milieu. This increasing sense of self in a developmental period when the controls engendered by an equivalent sense of responsibility are still unformed makes going beyond limits irresistible as the energies surge ahead toward fulfillment. There are both healthy excesses in the service of experimentation, and unhealthy ones that can result in the development of enduring, maladaptive rebellious patterns. An ameliorating factor is the renewal of ideas, ideals, and values through Metal yin's energy links with the outside world, balancing to some extent the simultaneous and often reckless requisition of authority.

In this struggle the Metal phase assumes the task of the continued development of ego boundaries and realistic limits begun by the Earth phase. The conclusive establishment of these boundaries, and the further deepening of a sense of self, is a function of the assumption of full responsibility. This usually (and hopefully) occurs in another, later, era, often upon the assumption of 'parenthood' of either a child, work, or dedicated service.

The flowering sense of self in these eras grows in many other media, including the endless testing of oneself in a world of increasingly complex challenges on both an intellectual and personal level. From the successful engagement of these tasks, or the ability to learn from failure, emerges an accurate, realistic self-confidence and self-esteem. This growing self-worth is fed by the independent stand one takes against peers and parents, especially as it includes increasing responsibility; and it is simultaneously a source of ever-escalating strength for this stand.

This time may mark a turning point for the better in a person's life, a time when many earlier gaps in development may be at least partially and satisfactorily filled. However, because it is a period of such rapid growth, there is great vulnerability as well as sensitivity, and great harm as well as good may come.

All of the phase energies are operative in this progression: the Water for courage to face the unknown, the Wood for direction, the Fire for expression, and the Earth for compassion. The yang Metal energies provide the impetus for moving on to new conquests, but the yin Metal energies, if they are viable, see to it that one stays with the task to its reasonable conclusion.

Self: Yang Metal Functions

Yang Metal energies serve, in the areas related to the development of the self, to help that self find and wisely use the best that the society and culture in which it develops have to offer for survival and satisfaction. The process of socialization and acculturation begins at birth with the first separation. It may begin even before, if the mother is a drug addict, or otherwise abused, subjecting the fetus to alien chemical, emotional, or physical stresses. Socialization is essentially a bonding and boundary issue, which, as we have seen, is a function of all the energies to different degrees at the various stages of development.

It is perhaps no accident that the earliest social lessons occur at both ends of the gastrointestinal tube. Waiting for the breast and waiting to be 'changed,' biting the breast and toilet training, eating and toilet habits, all relate to Stomach (mouth and stomach are one in Chinese medicine) and Large Intestine energies. Here begins a process in which the individual's natural instincts are suppressed or redirected to satisfy the requirements of society. It is these energies, the Earth, or 'mother' at home, and the Metal, or 'father' out in the world, which continue throughout life to dominate the process of socialization. At each step along the way, the other energies provide the setting and story line for the endless emerging drama. The 'no' stage of Wood energies, the Oedipal theater of early Fire, are eloquent script material in which the Earth and Metal forces take the opportunity to support the personal ethical and moral code of the nuclear family. As Metal energies push for the expansion of bonding to the larger framework of school, church, work, and through friends to other nuclear lineages, the code of the clan comes under some revision and considerable elaboration.

In every society there comes a crucial point when the growing person is initiated through 'rites of passage' or 'threshold passages'[4] into full adulthood. In non-industrial societies this passage from childhood into adulthood is sudden, quick, and complete. In some cultures the journey is filled with personal danger and may end in death. It is a time of testing for fitness to enter and play a useful, responsible part in an exacting existence, an opportunity to teach the totems, taboos, magic, and ritual, and an opening to permanently fix that person's role in society.

As societies become more complex and the world shrinks, the goals of the nuclear family may be at variance with the principles of society. The 'passage' has become long, convoluted, and tortuous, involving less physical risk (auto casualties) and, as evidenced by the growing number of adolescent suicides, more emotional and spiritual danger. Indeed, the 'rites of passage,' which in our time begin in the cradle and end with death, are an extended training for competition sponsored by established authority to develop a cadre of the most fit to take their appropriate place in the production line. The guiding ethic is above all to win at any cost, while publicly espousing love and brotherhood in church on Sunday. This 'survival' mentality furthers the development of boundaries, balancing freedom with responsibility within the framework of this 'double bind.' It has also become a difficult, hazardous, and lamentable task for both the individual and for the society in which this individual seems to be lost and running wild, without constraint or ethical navigational aids. The result is the ineluctable confusion that attends all transitions, great and small, and which conservatives lament, never understanding that it is only from confusion that something transcendent may emerge. We have always lost a few to transcendence, in static cultures as well as in our own. We must work to minimize that peril, without sacrificing the discomposure, which, however uncomfortable to all, is so necessary to our spiritual growth and salvation. That salvation is becoming a universal, yet personal, mission in our time.

METAL FUNCTIONS AND SPIRIT

Within the Metal phase there are two apparently exclusive trends that, in order for a person to be whole, are nevertheless ineluctably, mutually interdependent. Metal yin energies work toward an increasingly refined individuation, achieved by strengthening energy threads from the *dan tian* to the soul (God) through meditation. Simultaneously, its threads to the outside attempt, with the help of ever-expanding Metal yang energies, to integrate this highly individuated soul into mutually nourishing relationships with other individuals in the society, involving shared freedom and shared responsibility. Within the human condition, a tension is thereby generated, from the moment the gametes join, between the forces for individuation and those for integration. As this society has become more intricately multifaceted, sophisticated, and global, our spiritual institutions — traditional forces for union inherently organized for power rather than spiritual creativity — are swiftly disintegrating. As a result people are, on the one hand, attempting to regroup as extreme fundamentalists and, on the other hand, to seek spiritual guidance from other cultures and traditions.

The burden for deliverance and redemption, so clear to me and so eloquently elucidated by Krishna Murti,[5] has shifted away from outer authority to the jurisdiction of our autonomous inner selves, to the gods and guides of "the kingdom of heaven within."[6] The forces for individuation and those for homogeny are becoming one and the same by joining to unify the individual with the universal god within, thus unifying humanity in a much more profound way than ever before. By embracing and embodying authority as our personal responsibility, we will be free to invest the powerful energic threads of our connections with others with the same love we have discovered for ourselves in our oneness with God.

Becoming one with God is a passage into the unknown that is fraught with danger for the neophyte as well as for the experienced traveler. It was Jesus who said, "He who loves father and mother more than me is not worthy of me; and he who loves son or daughter more than me is not worthy of me; and he who does not take his cross and follow me is not worthy of me."[7] This was his invitation to journey with him as guide into that perilous space.

Incorporating authority in the 'self' (responsible individuation) is a recent and highly insecure development in human history. It is one on which all of our democratic institutions depend for their ultimate success. These institutions are intended to support that process by protecting the individual from organized power. Unfortunately, the system barely functions, since only the rich can afford to defend themselves, and it seems to exist only to protect the rich from each other. The seductive part of the operation is that 'anyone can become rich' and buy the protection. Nevertheless, because it is a first step toward individual autonomy, Western democracy unwittingly enhances spiritual unity; it is the 'best act in town.' Despite its materialistic, profit-oriented motif, it is unknowingly a part of a gigantic spiritual revolution. Every other system requisitions the Metal yin energies from the process of individuation to itself, enhancing its own power and decentralizing individuals who can never become complete. Totalitarian systems of the more organized and enduring kind such as exist in the communist countries, commandeer these energies from infancy. They offer the security of what is known and take the responsibility that the human race is perhaps ready to take for itself. The reclamation of these energies by the individual for personal autonomy is the only avenue that will lead to a society of genuinely self-responsible people where power is within and between rather than above and over. A recent emigre from The People's Republic of China whom I came to know while I was there summed it up in a letter: "Now I am used to the American lifestyle, which is fast and sometimes hard. But I enjoy it. I feel I am 'I' in this country, whereas there, I was nothing but a reflection of a government and some leaders or some political policy."

The Metal phase is said to be the 'Minister for Ecclesiastical Affairs' in the pantheon of officials of the Five Phase system. It is the interface of an organism with the finer energies of the universe, refining and renewing our spirit with each breath. Though we may become symbolically united with Christ by eating his body and his blood, we share with every living entity each breath we take from the earth's atmosphere as a practical act of union. And since we have some control over this precious breath, we have learned over the millennia, using respiration and sound, to refine this union with self-realizing and self-fulfilling meditative practice.

DISHARMONY OF THE METAL PHASE

METAL YIN DEFICIENCY

Personality: Inability to Form Relationships

This person will have great difficulty in either producing the energic threads necessary to form new attachments (Water in Metal), difficulty in producing threads that have the strength to hold (Earth in Metal), or difficulty in directing energic threads to their correct destination (Wood and Pericardium yang in Metal). Whereas each particular deficiency will have its own unique personality outcome, the result that they have in common is an inability to form new or lasting relationships. Those who cannot produce energic threads have most likely had severe deficiencies in the constitutional *dan tian* energies and are most likely to be overwhelmingly handicapped people. Those whose energic threads do not have the strength to hold will constantly lose relationships and will feel entirely inadequate, or, if they have the strength to 'project' this inadequacy, will feel terribly misused and abandoned by the human race. The imperativeness of 'contact' to human survival may lead to violence, for some, as the only alternative to an otherwise total failure to establish this contact. The third group, which loses direction, will miss the karmically significant attachments and encounter a lifetime of meaningless relationships, ones which, even if they are incidentally non-conflictual, will lack the promise of growth that characterizes all good matches.

{259}

If the ground energy in the *dan tian* is sufficient to hold threads from other people, the contact will be one-way, caring, dependent relationships in which the other person will be the giver and never the receiver. The lack of firmness and solidity in the substance of the subject's threads compared to those of the other person will render him or her wavering, irresolute, indecisive, and weak in all interactions. Mutuality will be impossible under the circumstances.

Autonomy is a luxury these people cannot enjoy without the long period of the expansion and transformation of bonds, which they have not made substantially in the first place. 'Self'-development and 'self'-awareness will not occur without a period of testing and contesting authorities and peers during adolescence. The lack of solid relationships makes this testing impossible.

What meager sense of 'self' does develop will not be enriched by an easy relationship with the "kingdom of heaven within," nor will the experience of this lifetime add significantly to the growth of the soul. The internal mission of mutual spiritual enhancement will suffer without strong energy threads, as will the external object of oneness with man and God.

Without substantial and functioning energy threads, the sources for renewal of soul, spirit, ideas, and feeling which come from human contact (as well as from communion with God, within and without) will be insufficient to support growth or creativity. Life will be insipid and wan, cognition stale and repetitive, and spiritual development uninspiring. Early promise brings pale bloom and sparse fruit.

The stages of development that depend on an evolving series of relationships, ever more distant from the family and clan, in which there is an increasing incorporation of authority into oneself, are incomplete without viable energy attachments. The individual will obey the authority of others in lieu of his or her own. He will escape from the responsibility that is implied by inner authority to a dependency on others who will be worshipped in success and damned in failure. Eric Fromm captured the character of this person in his first book, *Escape from Freedom.*[8] For the subjects of his study it was less frightening to subscribe to the prevailing 'ethical' code than to transform that code to the more precarious personalized code of individual conscience and moral responsibility.

When the energy threads are broken suddenly for any reason, grieving is the natural reaction as a way of relinquishing the bond in a more gradual and less traumatic fashion. Metal yin is the medium for grieving, and, if it is deficient, there will be either sudden collapse or flatness of affect, buried hurt, pain, resentment, and either an ultimate and inappropriate explosion or physical illness.

Other Attributes of Metal Yin Deficiency

As a result of the initial failure to establish age appropriate liaisons, *anxiety* will be aroused either when desiring a new relationship or in the incipient stages of a new one. Situations that dictate the assumption of a position of strength and authority, or behavior that is counter to, or challenges, existing sanctioned jurisdictional prerogatives will create conflict and induce anxiety. However, the relative incapacity to sustain strong feelings will obviate any intensely felt apprehension, which will most likely express itself in physical symptoms, avoidance, or unrelated irritations.

Depression, the genesis of which is unremitting vital unfulfillment and cumulative incomplete grieving, especially for one's lost or incomplete 'self', will likewise not be a strongly felt experience. Rather it will assume the form of psychomotor retardation, the source of which our subject is largely unaware. These are the kinds of depressions that do not lend themselves well to insight therapies. *Psychotic* episodes may formulate as a progression of this psychomotor retardation, with feelings of low self-esteem. The person experiences himself as the object of widespread rejection, the reason for which may not be understood except in delusional terms. The danger of violence against others, and at this stage even against himself, is real for the reasons just mentioned and as a last desperate and paradoxical attempt to make contact.

Love beyond infatuation is not likely to have an opportunity to take root, grow, withstand the vicissitudes of daily life, and flourish. As mentioned above, all relationships will at best be one-sided. The subject will be the recipient and not the giver, if indeed he or she has the ground in the *dan tian* to receive. One-way affiliations of this kind are not uncommon in this world and serve both partners well in that they are non-threatening to a giver, who has a real fear of intimacy or a high level of insecurity about his ability to hold an adequate partner. They also provide simultaneously an absolutely unassailable reason to complain. The advantages to the receiver are obvious, provided (s)he is able to coexist with endless grumbling and groaning. Sex would offer little solace to either partner, since, without energic oneness, the connections would be primarily genital and ultimately experienced as mechanical and unrewarding, except as a release of tension.

[261]

Bioenergetically the *hara* or *dan tian* is deficient and soft to palpation. The overall conformation varies with the type of problem; those who cannot create the threads are weakest and those whose threads lack direction are somewhat stronger. Generally they will be weaker below than above and tend to compensate by tightening the upper musculature, especially in the epigastrium.

A Case of Isolation

W. was seen initially during her freshman year of college. She came at that time in a panic, with deep feelings concerning her alleged part in the breakdown of a male student who had left the college. She was in a great state of fear that I would kill her for her crime, even though her real part in the breakdown, with which I was intimately familiar, was negligible and tremendously blown out of proportion. However unrealistic, the terror of the retribution she expected at my hands was profound. W. felt isolated and alone, suspicious of everyone's motives, misused, abused, and terrified in her isolation.

Both parents were alcoholic, though her father had stopped drinking shortly before his death, which occurred through a tragic accident. W.'s mother continued to drink herself into violent rages, at which time she would strike out at W. unexpectedly. W. was always terrified that her mother was going to kill her. She fixed this fear on one sexual episode with her younger brother, about which she was sure the mother would find out and then murder her. The mother died as a suicide while we were working together.

Upon her father's death, W. and her four brothers inherited one million dollars each. Sixteen years old and grasping onto some casual remarks made by friends of the family, W. took it upon herself to replace her father as the authority in the family. She executed this role literally and to extraordinary extremes, much to the resentment of other siblings, three of whom were actually older and more mature. As time passed and her siblings formed new relationships, her inability to trust men and form relationships of her own made her turn more and more to the past; she returned often to her home town where she had been a homecoming queen and where she had once had a date with a boy whom she had idealized.

For some years she struggled with the idea that she was homosexual, though she had never had such a relationship. After leaving college, she experimented with a number of alternative lifestyles, finally joining a violent, confrontational therapeutic community for drug addicts, even though she had no drug problem. It was at this time that she became a follower of the community guru who exploited her financially and robbed her of several hundred thousand dollars. She tried to buy her way into a connection with others and was unavailable for counsel on this matter during that time.

W. suffered from extremely low self-esteem and an absolute certainty that everyone looked down on, and made fun of, her. She carried this feeling into every social situation, encumbering herself with the conviction that she was obligated to prove herself continuously, and feeling that she continuously failed. This left her extraordinarily tense, with men in particular. For years she could not share her fears with any of the boys she infrequently dated. She was not able to see men as simply human, having the same weaknesses and failings and the same longings for closeness and acceptance as herself. She was locked into the conviction that men expected women to fit the mold of the all-American Hollywood female.

From her early history we must acknowledge that W. came by all of her problems quite honestly. At the end of our work she was somewhat more at ease with life and able to finish college, but unable to feel safe enough to extend to, or accept from, another person one thread of Metal yin energies. After eight years of discontinuous therapy, but continuous support, W. was convinced that I was arranging her life, that I brought people in at the time of her appointment to say things to her while she was in the waiting room, and that all these things were being engineered not only by myself, but also by some of her teachers. There was no way to convince her of my respect or to shake her of these convictions, which she needed to maintain so that we would never truly touch each other's essence, so that no one would be able to get to her core and annihilate her. The best she could do was to acknowledge that all this manipulation was meant to benefit her. She left at the end of college to live near her home, and fortunately, to resume therapy.

{ 263 }

METAL YIN EXCESS

Personality: Domineering and Possessive

This is a person whose energy threads are so powerfully affixed to and focused upon a specific other that the 'other' will perish as an individual unless he has a colossal sense of self and is endlessly vigilant. (Perhaps that is the latter's Herculean karmic assignment.) All-consuming and engulfing in a monolithic relationship, the subject will drain the partner of energy, ideas, spirit, and emotion and, after suitable feeding time on these ingredients, will replace them, if allowed, with his own version, for which he will assume total credit. This is not a creative melding of ideas since the acquisition is taken for the purposes of possession and not for growth. There is none of the respectful give and take that is implied by the healthy renewal of all these qualities of being (abetted by Earth energies) that occurs after the formation of strong energy threads during the bonding covenant. The connection itself is more important than the person to whom he is connected. This is partially due to the tendency also to incorporate and monopolize authority inordinately and become a domineering and possessive 'law unto himself,' including the 'law' of God, without a counterbalancing well-developed sense of responsibility. His bonds to his own eternal spirit-incarnate, his soul, are similarly all-devouring, leaving this earth at the end of life with less to pass on than when he came.

Other Attributes of Metal Yin Excess

The latter quality combined with the former, the tendency to appropriate the ideas and creations of others, leads to almost inadvertent plagiarism. *Cognition* is governed by this rigidly focused, almost monomaniacal fixation on one person or one theme, the latter often involving a preoccupation with ecclesiastical and spiritual considerations. The ingredients for autocratic despotic leadership are abundant in this person who has little need to answer to external jurisdiction, is self-absorbed, and makes heavy demands on the attention and vitality of others. The dangers are heightened, on the one hand, by rigidity and the concentration on religious issues but lessened, on the other, by a concomitant brittleness and a lack of originality. Plagiarism, engendering no life of its own, is the seed of its own destruction. Even with this mitigating factor, the disruption in society and in individual lives can still be considerable.

Anxiety will be experienced in the presence of people who are able to maintain their boundaries in the face of the subject's intrusiveness. Dealing as we are with an 'excess' of heavier yin energy, loss of control over others will more likely be experienced as *depression* rather than the more effervescent emotion, anxiety. The normal process of bereavement becomes prolonged and highly exaggerated in depth and is further magnified by the subject's rigid over-involvement with religious dogma. This kind of depression can generate a good deal of guilt in those who try to create some distance from the subject.

Psychosis will follow a similar pattern, with some phases of delusions of lost grandeur (authority) and feelings of persecution since, for this person, you are either with him (succumb) or against him (resist).

Love is conditional on the willingness of another to be possessed, dominated, and used. The needs of the significant other to assert himself as an independent person in a mutually sharing relationship, in *sex*, or in any other way will be rejected as a threat to the subject's integrity, since his energic nature demands total mastery. Those who submit will be 'loved' and 'made love to' ponderously and with vigorous insensitivity. This is not sadism or masochism, since there is no need to cause or experience pain, only to 'hold' and be 'held', to dominate.

The *bioenergetic* configuration is tension and spasm below the umbilicus, with pain and tenderness either throughout or on the right or left, especially in women during ovulation. This represents some degree of blood and fluid stagnation due to the excess yin. The area above the umbilicus would be concomitantly underenergized, and there might be 'flushing-up', a condition in which the yin in the lower part of the body loses contact with the yang qi, which rises, giving the sensation of heat.

A Case of Invasiveness

S. was a very attractive 46-year-old mother of three children who presented herself after surgery with inoperable cancer of the ovary. Throughout the years before coming to see me as a patient she was known to me and to others as the most invasive, acquisitive person in the community. Once she had met you, she owned you. She used and consumed us as the need suited her, often for good causes, but with little heed to our individuality or privacy. She scheduled talks, used our materials, misrepresented herself to authorities as having our permission to speak on our behalf, without prior consultation. She assumed the leadership of a movement without the knowledge or consent of those she intended to direct.

S. was a nationally known person in her profession. She had won the highest national awards and traveled to foreign countries as a consultant in her field. She founded a postgraduate school, which she directed until her illness; and throughout her life she was actively on the move, apparently invading many spaces other than the one mentioned above. Including travel, she worked about 15 hours a day. A note I received from another physician who saw her with her husband reveals the kind of relationship she had established. "My personal opinion is that C. resents his wife's patronizing attitude, which makes him contract. She pats him like a dog, lie down, roll over, beg, etc. He says nothing, but his facial muscles start working. This is just one instance. I can give you more."

S.'s symptoms, diagnosis, and death occurred within about two months. She had not the time nor the sensitivity to notice the messages from her own body telling her that she was getting ill. One might say that her energic threads were so deeply embedded in the *hara* of others that she lost touch with her own. During that time I treated her with acupuncture and herbs, and we talked. Her pain was under control without medication up to the moment she 'passed over,' which occurred within a few hours of entering the hospital.

I participated during this short period of time in the most unexpected and amazing transformation I have ever experienced. An incredible spiritual awareness and sensitivity appeared, which swept me along with it to a beautiful, dynamic, but peaceful place in which we could share the most positive, loving acceptance of life and oneness with all of existence. No bitterness or anger prevailed. She surrendered to the forces that had overtaken her and understood the message. She realized that her life-long quest for information had led her down the wrong paths and that she finally had the knowledge she needed and wanted. Death was her teacher, and she, unlike so many I have known, was able to learn. The Tibetan Buddhists say, in their *Book of the Dead*,[9] that it is the last moment, as one leaves this realm to journey to the next, that is the most important to one's spiritual development and place in the next world. Life is an endless paradox, and none of us can know who we will be when that moment comes. S. rose to the occasion, against all the expectations by which we would have so wrongly judged her. Her soul, I am sure, does rest in peace.

METAL YANG DEFICIENCY

Personality: Lack of Energy

In contrast to the yin excess character, who holds with focused intensity, our yang deficient subject holds out of the inability to let go. One way of viewing this would be that Metal yang is not strong enough to feed Kidney yang, which is responsible for dealing with the existential 'fear of the unknown.' However, it is important to be clear that it is the energic inability to let go rather than fear of the next step that is primarily responsible for the personality qualities that follow. Such persons are unable to let go of people, ideas, beliefs, and cling to the known rather than expand their horizons to worlds beyond. At each stage of development they are slow to leave the one to which they have grown accustomed and move to the next. They will appear to be reluctant to leave the womb, for example, and may be among those who are either several weeks late or who show little inclination to push their way out when the time does arrive. They will be slow to give up the nipple and not out of the need for nurture; toilet training will be prolonged and there will be a tendency to encopresis, not because they are passive-aggressive, but because change requires an energy that they do not have in sufficient quantity.

This energy is lacking also in the simple act of breathing air and for their connection with the larger world and universe, both on a physical and spiritual level. A deep sense of loneliness will be experienced at some level of awareness beyond our inescapable 'existential' allotment.

Other Attributes of Metal Yang Deficiency

All stages of development are prolonged, and the next stage resisted. Throughout, they will appear to be extremely cautious and unable to surrender to the flow of life. *Anxiety* may arise when they are confronted with leaving old, familiar situations and people. However, resistance, and not anxiety, is the primary response to newness, and the latter is more a secondary by-product of the struggle and conflict with the ever-pressing world.

Avoidance behavior such as apparent school phobias and later the equivalent of agoraphobia and social phobias will occur. These may be crippling, both cognitively and socially.

Cognition, which may be inherently sound, will be hindered by the lessened exposure to learning and outside influences and remain immature and characterized by perseveration. Acculturation and the 'rites of passage' will be retarded because of their difficulty with letting go of the familiar, which will hold them back from the absorption of new ideas, values, and behavior from teachers and during the stages of peer identification. Especially missing the latter, they will lack the experiences that are necessary for moving from the authority of the clan and family to their own in later adolescence. The potentially massive developmental lags can lead only to a very low self-esteem, except in the most isolated parts of the world where the clan dominates and nothing changes.

Throughout life they will be dependent on outside authority. Because of their inadequate socialization, they will tend to be in difficulties with the law. In addition, they will unwittingly be searching in this way for the limits they have never incorporated and that are most available in the form of law enforcement officers. Though there are other developmental abnormalities that likewise lead to the tendency to be in frequent, though not serious, trouble with the law, this is a common one. Their transgressions are of a nature that lead them to being easily caught, and frequently those people who do not have a secure nitch in a strong clan tradition feel most comfortable in jail, a place that never changes its routine, is entirely predictable, and makes few demands for innovation.

Due to the limited personality development, the depth of being that is a prerequisite to the sense of loss inherent in most *depression* is lacking in these people. Loss of the familiar will create more anxiety and possibly something like an anaclitic reaction, especially at an early age, but the most common form of depression is flatness of affect and an agitated boredom. Outside the clan there can be considerable hurt from critical surrogate parental figures and rejecting indignities by peers; these are not easily forgiven because, along with the general problem of letting go, letting go of grievances is also difficult. *Psychotic* episodes may occur when the clan support system is no longer viable; they will be colored by exaggerated or imagined offenses as well as by poverty of thought.

Love is limited to clinging relationships within the clan, which lack the mutuality and growth aspects that we ordinarily associate with the meaning and significance of the phenomenon. A useful place may be found for these people within the clan, often in a servile capacity, and he or she may be sincerely loved by parents and siblings. Within the clan system where the concept of loyalty and duty are more important than love and devotion, as in the Oriental tradition, these subjects will be completely syntonic with their culture and find an easy place, with no conflict regarding love, which is never an issue. In modern Western societies where adult love is at least a concept and an ideal modality for personal growth, they will be dystonic, except in those isolated instances such as the Sicilian mafia where the clan mentality endures from feudal times.

Sex will most likely be incestuous and remain within the family, either overtly approved, as occurs in some of our own isolated American mountain communities, or overlooked through self-deception and denial, which we are beginning to realize from recent studies is extraordinarily common in many families. The men (in these studies) who have exploited their daughters are frequently isolated loners who have managed to simulate some measure of individuation while in fact never truly developing beyond the rudimentary bonds to their family of origin. In the Springs area of East Hampton, New York, where I lived for over 20 years, it was once common, and the practice persisted in my time, to see mother-son 'marriages' with progeny. The retardation rate in the Springs was then (in the 1970s) one of the highest in New York State.

The *bioenergetic* configuration is a pronounced appearance of immaturity. There is none of the 'presence' of a mature personality that conveys strength balanced with flexibility on a continuum from head to ground. These subjects will always carry something of the little boy or girl, which may reveal itself by the absence of facial lines and contrasts, or a little baby fat, especially in the face.

A Case of Clinging

V. came originally to consult me about his younger sister who had been diagnosed as schizophrenic. The original breakdown occurred when she was 18 at which time their father was dying of heart disease. Since then she had withdrawn, refused to work, slept excessively, refused to discuss anything or, when she did, was incomprehensible. V. wanted advice as to how to handle her.

During this session many personal and family secrets were reluctantly revealed, accompanied by considerable guilt. One was that, since his father's death, he had taken over the care of the mother until his older sister returned home without a husband and displaced him as the caretaker in the home. He was very angry about this because he had always been considered the 'stubborn,' unaccepted sibling until he assumed the role of his mother's caretaker. He had never taken any steps to be on his own, to have a relationship with a woman, though he desired to make love, and could never find a job outside of the family business, where he was exploited. Though he denied any need for help, it was clear that at the deepest level he was afraid that I also would find him to be 'crazy.'

Leaving the details aside, over a period of many years of discontinuous contact, V. has never ceased to make plans, with me or alone, to move away from his family to some kind of independent life. He was handsome, had a good education, extraordinary talents, and many skills with which he could easily have made a life almost anywhere. Instead he clung to the same concerns about his family and is unable to gather the strength, the Metal yin energy, to expand these ties to others.

[269]

METAL YANG EXCESS

Personality: Drifter

The chief personality trait of a person with Metal yang excess is lability. This is a person who can make sufficient contact with people and with ideas, with adequate energic strength to hold these connections, yet is curiously carried away to novel encounters by the sheer excitement of newness. This is done without the pressure that one sees or senses behind the manic illness. Instead, the subject seems to be floating effortlessly through relationship after relationship, work interest after work interest, idea after idea, belief after belief. This is what Neuro-Linguistic Programming describes as the "in time" person for whom the moment is forever.[10] While he is in that moment, his declarations of fealty to the immediate are total and sincere. He himself never suspects that the next wind shift will have him off and running along new shores and into strange waters, almost as if the last did not exist except as a lesson or a memory. His surrender to fate is marvelous to behold except to those who are left behind, hurt and unintentionally rejected. He does not live by the old homily that says "God helps those who help themselves," a condition of life in which fate is supposed to run a poor second to intention.

This is the 'drifter' whose loyalties are as tenuous and vague as the world is round. Family and clan, country, religion, and ethnic identity are subordinate to his own impulses, which expand to the edges of the universe. He is mentally and spiritually as scattered and ill-defined as the rarefied air of the upper atmosphere.

Other Attributes of Metal Yang Excess

Cognitively, his mind is like the proverbial grasshopper and his *love* life a rapid series of powerful affairs, with passion and *sex* playing an important role in each, as is usual in relationships that never progress beyond newness. This playboy semblance is due to an excess of that energy which enables us to perform the important and necessary task of 'letting go' and is not the manifestation of a deep-seated Don Juan or Tristan complex involving the search for the elusive anima. The latter exists but does not account for all of the behavior which we have described above in the context of love.

Anxiety arises in intimate situations wherein the subject is blocked from being the immoderate, aimless wanderer he is energically programmed to be, and *depression* would follow any prolonged inhibition of this rapid flight of passage. Depression may also come during the involutional period of life when the lack of substantial personal development, which must follow from a lifetime of shifting instability, has left a large measure of emptiness for which the self (however elusive) must eventually grieve.

Phobias of closed places are predictable, and *psychotic* episodes are possible within the context of the propensity to let go, in this case of reality. I have no memory of this occurring within my clinical experience.

Bioenergetically, the subject will appear substantially mature, having absorbed a sufficient smattering of each developmental era to permit the appearance of a generalist in the best sense, but on more careful examination he lacks grounding and will appear rootless and almost floating a little off the ground. For this reason he is really a 'pushover' when 'push comes to shove.' In his presence one may even have a pleasant sensation of lightness, which should arouse caution. He can easily sweep you off of your feet, and one may float delightfully until suddenly dropped when something new comes along. He is a little like the leprechaun in *Finnian's Rainbow* who sang, "When I am not near the girl I love, I love the girl that's near."[11] He may also be easily lofted into nether spiritual spaces and be drawn to spiritual leaders and practices, again one after another, for short periods of time, with little spiritual advancement.

A Case of a Dilettante

A. was referred to me for a chest disturbance and recurrent upper respiratory infections, which did not respond to conventional medical care. In addition, she had several kinds of chronic venereal problems, including venereal warts and herpes. She was 30 years old and had inherited a business from her father, which subsequently failed. She drifted from school to school when she was younger, always backed by her indulgent father and generally ignored by her mother, from whom she had been physically separated by divorce since she was quite young.

She never acquired a valid skill or profession. She was a dilettante in vocations and avocations, but most especially with men. Always searching for the right one, she went from one to another, accumulating, for a woman, a most remarkable record, normally the kind attributed to the 'Don Juan' man. Each man in turn was carefully dissected with regard to his qualifications as a husband and rejected, for one reason or another, with the thought that a better find was just around

the corner, and because she was unsure that she could ever be satisfied
with the same one for any length of time.

When last seen, her physical symptoms had abated. Although she
had remained with one person for almost seven months, she was still
floating freely on the surface of our culture, moving with the currents
and the seasons, staying in one place in one employment and with one
person only until the inevitable expectation for some form of commitment appeared to be taking shape. At that point an entirely new cast
of people, places, and work moved on stage. The only consistency was
her endless concern for her health and eternal youth, and her endless
search for the 'right man.'

13

ANXIETY AND DEPRESSION

ANXIETY

Anxiety has a wide variety of definitions, but the one most commonly agreed upon describes it as "a feeling of threat, especially of a fearsome threat, without the person's being able to say what he thinks threatens." I shall add to the confusion with my own concept of the nature of that threat, but in general we shall be operating within the framework of the above definition.

Anxiety is defined by *The Psychiatric Dictionary* as "an affect which differs from other affects in its specific unpleasurable character. It consists of a somatic, physiological side (disturbed breathing, increased heart activity, vasomotor changes, musculoskeletal disturbances such as trembling or paralysis, increased sweating) and of a psychological side (perception of specific unpleasurable feelings and sensations, apprehension). Anxiety is differentiated from fear; the former is a reaction to an unreal or imagined danger."[1] Fear, the Chinese say, is an emotion that descends to the Kidneys, and anxiety is an emotion that ascends to the Heart.

Whereas the perceived danger (conscious or unconscious) may be logically unreal by conventional standards, it is quite 'real' to the person thus afflicted. At some vulnerable point earlier in the person's life, a series of relatively catastrophic events occurred, which placed an extraordinary strain on the capacity to respond and adapt in a fashion that would be productive in an adult ambiance. At the time they occurred, the reaction may have been the best available under the circumstances. However, the traumatic aspects of those events, and all of their maladaptive restorative maneuvers, one of which we call anxiety, continue to be evoked by any incident that is consciously or unconsciously perceived to be the same or similar to the original.

Anxiety is a multi-faceted phenomenon, which may also be classified as acute or chronic. Combinations of acute and chronic anxiety may be observed in, and experienced by, the same person. The two-fold response to acute anxiety has been described as 'fight or flight,'[2] each being an enduring trait in any one person. Each has been characterized in physiological terms, the former, fight, as a sympathetic autonomic response, and the latter as a parasympathetic reaction. Lawson-Wood describes the two respectively as "stiff" and "limp."[3] Anxiety, as we shall discuss it, will include all of its known expressions, emotional and physical, felt or repressed (such as conversion hysteria), acute and chronic.

Anxiety is, however, not only a signal that all is not well, but also a declaration that the organism is still capable of responding. It is, after all, a sign of life and an indication that the person still has the strength to struggle with his malady (*shi* in Chinese medicine, a 'strong confirmation,' and a strong or excessive disease). Depression is a signal that the struggle is over, that the organism is no longer capable of the conflict necessary to move on to new horizons.

We shall deal with two models in our discussion of anxiety, one the Chinese model, as expressed by the Academy of Chinese Medicine in Beijing, and the other my own, based on concepts discussed in the first part of this book. The two constructs are completely compatible.

THE CLASSICAL CHINESE MODEL OF ANXIETY

The classical model lists five causes of anxiety. The first is due to a combination of a weak constitution and a sudden fright. The symptoms are palpitation, restlessness, dream-disturbed sleep, and anorexia. The principal effect is on the Heart. The pulse is Thready and Weak and the tongue is normal. The object of the therapy is to calm the Heart and thereby soothe the mind, which in Chinese medicine is said to be controlled by the Heart. This is done by promoting the circulation of Heart qi, using such points as B-15 *(xin shu)*, CV-14 *(ju que)*, H-7 *(shen men)*, P-6 *(nei guan)*, and P-7 *(da ling)*.

The second cause is deficiency of the blood of the Heart due to blood loss and chronic disease. The predominant symptoms are impairment of memory and concentration, palpitation, pallor, dizziness, vertigo, and blurred vision. The principal effect is, once again, on the Heart, but this time it involves blood more than qi. The objects of treatment are three-fold. The first is to build the blood by strengthening the Spleen, which governs digestion—the principal source of nourishment for making blood. The second is to move the blood, and the third is to reinforce the Heart. Points such as B-20 *(pi shu)*, B-21 *(wei shu)*, S-36 *(zu san li)*, B-17 *(ge shu)*, points on the Heart channel, and Heart *shu* points are used. The third cause of anxiety according to the traditional model is excess fire due to yin (water) deficiency. The principal symptoms are palpitation, irritability, insomnia, dizziness, and tinnitus. This is a water deficient condition of the Kidneys and Heart, which often occurs simultaneously with a condition of blood deficiency. The object is to tonify the Kidneys, remove heat from the Heart, and soothe the mind with such points as B-14 *(jue yin shu)*, B-23 *(shen shu)*, and K-13 *(tai xi)*, plus the Heart points already mentioned.

The fourth cause is internal retention of harmful fluid due to a deficiency of the Spleen and Kidneys. The symptoms are palpitation, fullness in the chest and epigastrium, lassitude, and cough with sputum. There is thirst with no desire to drink. The pulse is Strong and Slippery, and the tongue is covered with a white sticky coating. The object of the treatment is to tonify the Spleen and Kidney yang using such points as B-20 *(pi shu)*, S-36 *(zu san li)*, CV-6 *(qi hai)*, CV-17 *(shan zhong)* — to warm the qi of the yang, and B-22 *(san jiao shu)* — to regulate the water of the Triple Burner. This also warms the yang and removes water retention.

The fifth cause is internal phlegm-fire. Phlegm comes from a long accumulation of dampness and is the approximate equivalent of what we call mucus. Phlegm comes from Spleen deficiency and fire from excessive heat due to severe stagnation in the Liver-Gallbladder energy configuration. The heat dries out the water from the dampness, leaving the heavier residue, which we call phlegm. The cause of the heat in the Liver-Gallbladder is due either to suppressed emotions or to chemicals, including alcohol, caffeine, and recreational drugs. Prolonged illness may be another contributing factor. The symptoms are palpitation, irritability, quick temper, obsessions, and excessive dreaming. Schizophrenia and epilepsy are associated with this condition. The treatment includes points to remove phlegm, such as S-40 *(feng long)*, CV-22 *(tian tu)*; points to remove heat, such as GB-34 *(yang ling quan)* and Liv-2 *(xing jian)*; points to remove both from the Lungs, such as B-13 *(fei shu)* and L-5 *(chi ze)*; points to remove fire and/or phlegm from the Heart, such as B-14 *(jue yin shu)*, H-8 *(shao fu)*, P-8 *(lao gong)*, P-4 *(xi men)*, and SI-13 *(hou xi)*, may also be used. Ear points such as Heart, Small Intestine, Shenmen, Sympathetic, Subcortex, Spleen, Stomach, Kidney, Triple Burner, and Lung are also recommended.

ANXIETY AND ENERGETICS: AN ONTOGENETIC MODEL

Turning to my own ontogenetic model, I define chronic anxiety as a distinctly unpleasant felt experience that occurs when a person unconsciously perceives a threat to his or her "becoming" in the process of the evolution of his or her being. I have found these threats to fall into seven general categories, each of which is associated with one of the stages of this evolution and equally associated with the phase whose energies play the major role in that developmental stage. I am certain that with time this classification could be expanded to include other categories.

Fear of the Unknown

The first and perhaps most ubiquitous form of anxiety is the 'fear of the unknown.' It is the natural 'rite of passage' through each transition from one stage to the next in the 'evolution of being'; an inherent, unavoidable condition of life that we must all find the courage to face and pass through, either alone or with others. The alternative is to remain behind and live what Thoreau referred to as a life of "quiet desperation."

This anxiety will also be experienced whenever a person is faced with a situation that is dystonic to his personality organization. For example, the Kidney yin deficient personality centers on the premise that the world is a hostile environment and is thus prepared for the 'worst' but unprepared for expressions of friendship, which, when pressed upon him, may precipitate an acute state of anxiety.

The Water phase energies normally manage the primordial archaic fear of the unknown and its most profound manifestations in terms of our cosmic identity and ultimate fate beyond death. These energies are most closely associated with the exigencies at the thin barrier between life and death, both in the beginning of life and at the end. We denote the anxieties associated with these issues as cataclysmic in scope and terrifying by name. People who go through life with chronic terror as a constant companion, both night and day, but especially by night, are those who suffered damage to the Water phase through some basic insult in the intra-uterine era. Many have been documented as having survived attempted abortions.

It is my impression that damage to the Water phase predisposes people to anxiety and fear in any and all of its manifest forms. It is the substrate, the prerequisite for the chronicity of anxiety, however it arises, and whatever its etiology in the distortions of the natural functions of the other energy systems.

Kidney yin, Kidney yang, and Kidney qi energies guide us respectively through the death of the body, the death of the ego, through divine love, divine power, and divine spirit, to resurrection. Thus the 'red bird' self-immolates and 'flies' again and again until Water energies lead us, with faith, beyond the fear of the unknown, to salvation (nirvana).

Separation Anxiety

The second form of anxiety I wish to discuss is separation anxiety, a special form of 'the fear of the unknown' marking the several transitions from one stage of life to another. Each of these stages is described in detail in that part of the text which deals with the phase most involved. However, just as the Kidney energies (Water phase) are involved with all chronic fear and anxiety, so in my opinion is the Metal phase involved with all separations, less obviously at the beginning of life and more so later. The Metal phase energies, for their own reasons, always lend themselves to accepting and letting go, whenever the other phases are engaged in this process.

Thus, while the impetus for letting go of the old and taking in the new is the unfolding of the 'life force,' the capacity comes from Metal phase energies. The substance for the new bond is from the Earth, the passion from Fire, the direction from Wood, and the power, as ever, from Water. This is the basic format for, and integral part of, all of the transitions that I have and will discuss, though not necessarily reiterated as such with each discussion. Within the sea of endless bonding and disengagement are roughly ten major separations during life.

The First Separation: Mitosis

The first separation occurs shortly after conception, which is the first union or bonding in the evolutionary cycle. When one cell becomes two, a process of mitotic disengagements begins, which ceases only at death when the soul leaves the body. At this auspicious beginning, Water energies are directing operations, with, I believe, some help from Metal energies. A significant breakdown at this point is cataclysmic.

Even the most obscure adversity with the complex process of mitosis and shifting of genetic material, at this very early stage, can set in place an enduring template of defective perception and reaction. A lifetime of grief with bonding, separation anxiety, and other debilitating, unpredictable developmental disorders may follow. It is my impression, based on 30 years of observing children and adults, that most subtle personality problems are the result of infinitely minute and fortuitous insults to a small, random number of brain cells in utero, or during delivery. Given the trillions of cells and connections to choose from, no single pathological event could be repeated twice. Each minor or major catastrophe is unique. We are a society of minimally brain damaged people, plagued by 'soft' neurological signs, which, together with the "slings and arrows of outrageous fortune," leave us psychological cripples.

The Second Separation: Birth

The second separation is birth, the separation of the fetus from mother. At this critical point the child has developed two major functions independent of the mother. First is the ability to oxygenate its own blood, and the second is a digestive system mature enough to break down food into its basic constituents, to separate what is nourishing ('pure') from what may be detrimental ('impure'), to absorb the former and to eliminate the latter.

Other physiological parameters, such as temperature stability, and all the activity on an atomic and subatomic level, may also reach their penultimate maturity at birth, sufficient to permit this second great separation. The process is described in energy terms in the chapter on the Water phase. In consideration of the monumental misfortunes that too often attend parturition, it is incumbent upon society to gain the best possible understanding of all the variables of this event. In my capacity as director of a child guidance clinic I studied the school system of an upper middle class community and found that, in the opinion of the school psychologists, over 50 percent of the children in the classroom had some organically generated learning deficit. In the clinic, most of these problems could be traced to pregnancy or birth trauma.

The energies attending this sublime and terrible occasion are both Water and Earth. The former we have already discussed as attending the transfer of life from one generation to another, the passage of the essence *(jing)* (the 'water of life') and the fire at the gate of vitality (*ming men,* or basal metabolic energy), first on the genetic, and now on the aggregate plane. Even more important at this great step forward is the fundamental part that Kidney qi plays as the general supervisor of all growth and development. It provides the force *(ming men)* and primitive intelligent will that drives life ahead to maturity against the forces of entropy which exist and operate at all times, in both mother and child, to maintain the status quo. Both the 'life force' and the opposing entropic energies are ineluctable to the thermodynamic balance that is so indispensable to energy conservation and survival, momentarily and over the long haul of our existence on earth.

All energies serve the ultimate purpose of creating fruitful and productive life on earth even when these energies are in apparent conflict. The entropic aspect of bonding, for example, that impedes development I view as ordained and necessary to insure the augmentation and fullest amplification of an evolutionary stage before moving on to the next. Thus a force which may appear to be negative is as necessary to the final goal as one which is obviously pushing us ahead.

Bonds have a life of their own. The Earth energies are involved at this level of separation because the bond that exists between the host and the guest outlives its benefit for both. There is no more comfortable room in mother for either of them. So the bond must change, and, with the help of Metal and Water energies as well as its own, the Earth engineers the separation that we call birth.

{ 279 }

Inasmuch as the Earth phase provides the energies for the richest and most fully engaged bonding, for the establishment of boundaries, and for the consequent trust that permits the expansion of bonding from parents to peers, the anxiety associated with the Earth phase is related to a significant failure in one or more of these developmental functions.

The security of the bond with the mothering person determines the extent to which the biological alarm systems of imminent danger to the integrity of being are mobilized. If these systems are mobilized with sufficient frequency and with consistent lack of reasonably rapid relief, a profound insecurity which we will call the 'terror of annihilation' will become an enduring imprint on the child's panorama of commonly felt experience. The strength and depth of this early bonding experience is also the template on which the growing child builds the distinction between himself and the outside world, the boundaries between what is inside (me) and outside (them). The outcome is a function of both the potential of the child and the permission of the parent.

If the bonding process proceeds without excessive strain, the child feels secure enough to allow that distinction to develop because he knows that at any time of need he can rely on the 'outside' to close the gap between him and them so that he may feel secure. If that recall to the closeness of the bond is not reliable, the child will not feel safe to allow the distance necessary to develop a sense of 'self.' Without a clear distinction between the two worlds of 'me' and 'them,' the ensuing confusion and disorganization will evoke a profound anxiety and vulnerability, which is the equivalent in intensity to the 'terror of annihilation' mentioned above. The energy of other human energy systems is experienced as especially ominous and the danger will seem to cone from all directions. In the extreme, we identify this personality configuration as schizophrenia. Whereas the schizophrenic has no control over the internal disarray, he will focus his anxiety outwardly in the direction where, through retreat or attack, he feels a potentially greater sense of mastery.

I am saying that healthy bonding is an ongoing resonance between a response that creates security and the forces which the security releases that drive for separation and individuation. The two processes are inseparable.

For human beings all separations in the 'evolution of being' are necessarily expansions of bonds already formed as well as a growing capacity to make new and more individually creative bonds. Problems in the balance between the two, especially in the early stages of life to which we are referring, are synonymous with catastrophic anxiety.

The Third Separation: Assertion (The 'No' Stage)

From birth, mother and child are now physically separate individuals with their own, often conflicting needs. The fate of Wood phase energies, those energies that assert 'being' for the growing child and succeeding adult, depends to a large extent on the vicissitudes of the inter-personal encounter between the child's assertion of 'being' and the parental response. If that assertion does not get a favorable reception in a stable balance between these conflicting needs, and consequently becomes the nodus of a power struggle, the 'assertion of being' will become a ceaseless well-spring of anxiety throughout life. The opportunities for this struggle begin with the first cry, escalate with the first stand, and explode with the first 'no.' It is during this 'No' stage, the 'terrible twos,' that the conflict takes its enduring shape.

Anxiety takes several forms when 'being' is suppressed at this juncture. Primarily, there is a phobia against personal assertion or aggression. Any situation that might expose 'being' to the world precipitates terror through the threat of humiliation. Direct exposure is most clearly identified with fear. Speaking in public, oral examinations, observation at work, and any social occasion in which direct scrutiny is involved provokes anxiety. The deep-seated fear is of humiliation.

Guilt is another form of anxiety that is the direct result of a fear of disapproval for having 'been,' coming from within or without. Guilt is also associated with deep-seated, negative, spiteful feelings which accompany the entire spectrum of passive-aggressive behavior ensuing from this struggle for power between parents who need to control and the child who needs to assert his 'being.' While spite may reward us with the satisfaction of revenge, it punishes us with the disagreeable sensate consciousness and sensory experience from which hate and malice are inseparable. This transposes into guilt through the psychological mechanism which says to the child, "If I feel bad, I must be bad." The spiteful child's fear of being exposed as a 'bad person' becomes a lifetime source of anxiety and self-torture.

The Fourth Separation: Oedipus/Electra Complex

The fourth major separation that has the possibility of provoking major anxieties is summed up by Freud and his elaborators as the Oedipus/Electra complex.[4] Whereas competition between siblings for both parents' love may last a lifetime and begin with the birth of the second child, we now encounter a competition between the parent and child of the same sex for the love and attention of the parent of the opposite sex. The anxieties associated with this complex have been discussed *ad nauseam* and the reader is referred to these writings. Suffice to say here that the boy fears castration and the girl the loss of her mother's love.

Whereas all of the elemental energies are operational at all times either on their own or as 'a phase within a phase,' one or more play a more crucial role in a particular era in the 'evolution of being.' At the Oedipal stage we encounter the Fire energies in their first major role.

The Heart and Pericardium are involved with the expression of love, both carnal and spiritual, as part of their function and therefore play a large role in the unfolding of the Oedipal drama. A father's capacity for handling two women at one time, making them both feel loved and special in their own way, goes a long way to mitigating the neurotic outcomes so often associated with the Oedipal period. In order for a young girl to feel beautiful she must experience that beauty through her father's felt and expressed appreciation of that beauty. That expression must be both physical and verbal with all of the restraint appropriate to a relationship between a grown man and a small child.

Hesitation and embarrassment by the father at this point will engender low self-esteem in the girl and all the attendant fears of rejection now associated by her with the expression of femininity and sexuality. Different patterns of seduction or withdrawal will emerge depending on the condition of other energies such as the Wood in terms of assertion, the Kidney in terms of power, and the Earth in terms of security in relation to mother. The mother's understanding and ability to identify will, of course, play a large part in whether the child will even have the opportunity, to say nothing of the approbation, to get close to father. The drama is essentially the same for the little boy except for reversal of roles. The father must be secure enough to allow his son to displace him to some extent and win his mother as a 'hero-boy' instead of as a baby, again within the limits of an adult-child relationship.

The vicissitudes of this 'drama' depend on the capacity for relatively selfless love on the part of the parents, for each other as well as the children, which is largely a function of the Heart and Pericardium energies. Apart from affirming those energies in the growing child, the parents are here serving as role models in terms of what to do with that love and those energies in all ensuing relationships. The energies of the Heart feel and express, and the energies of the Pericardium protect, giving energy to all of the restorative maneuvers people develop to avoid anxiety.

The Fifth Separation: Transition to Surrogate Parent

The fifth significant step in the process of separation is the one most commonly associated with separation anxiety: the move from the original parents of the first few years to surrogate parents in the form of teachers and other adults. At all points of separation we depend on Metal energies to allow the letting go. Up to this point in our discussion it has been Metal as a phase within a phase, Metal assisting Wood to say 'no,' and Earth to deliver a child, for example. At the point of separation from parent to surrogates, the Metal phase is, by itself, playing a larger role, though still in conjunction with the Earth energies, since the new attachment is, after all, very much in the mode of the original. For argument's sake we may say that we are dealing with the Metal within the Earth.

The anxieties associated with this adventure depend on the course of the evolution of being up to this time. If the child is secure that the love of its parent does not cost too much in the way of sacrificing its own 'being,' and that its being has been sufficiently affirmed, this 'rite of passage' should go smoothly with the appropriate anxiety associated with facing the 'unknown.' If the evolution of being has not gone smoothly, enormous anxieties may be generated, which, if not properly handled, can last a lifetime. The most obvious one at this point is school anxiety. Metal energies which are available to help the child let go and take in 'the new' are not strong enough either because they are inherently deficient or because they and other energies have been blocked. If the Earth energies could not be absorbed from the mother (autism and schizophrenia), or the assertive energies of the Wood have been blocked in a struggle for power, the child will lack the strength or the capacity to assert himself in new relationships. Being placed in a position in which one is not prepared to function socially is attended by enormous anxiety.

Together with the danger attendant upon this transition is, for the first time, the possibility of changing and altering already established patterns through new and more favorable relationships. In a former time this possibility was sometimes available with members of the extended family, but the increasing isolation of the nuclear family obviates substantial new experience until school begins. A small mitigating grace attending the current social environment is the existence of day care and Head Start schools, which intervene in the child's life at an earlier age.

The Sixth Separation: Forming Peer Relationships

The sixth important separation and opportunity for separation anxiety is the transference of significant loyalties from adults to peers, which probably occurs gradually but seems to blossom suddenly in the pre-adolescent period. This is a colossal move on both psychological and energic levels. Authority and the need for approval has shifted from the adult world to the peer group. It is here that the growing child looks for direction and a new form of love, group approbation. While his expanding individuality has always been submerged in adult authority, it is still submerged, but in an entirely new authority, whose sole purpose seems to be challenging and overthrowing the old one. Energically the roles previously assigned to each of the phases hold true, except that the Wood assertive energies loom larger.

This is the beginning of one of the most vexing and dangerous periods of growth. Since the pre-adolescent stage is predominantly anti-social, children who become stuck in this developmental place may continue this anti-social behavior for the rest of their lives. This is the age-entry point into the 'gang' when a new authority enters the picture, the gang or 'pack' leader.

Another step between the bond to the peer group and the next great leap forward in individuation, the vesting of authority in oneself, is what Harry Stack Sullivan called "chumship."[5] A person chooses another of the same sex from within the peer group. All the passion that had gone into the 'gang,' from which one now begins to separate, is invested in that 'chum.' A special attachment forms that has no equal in the rest of a person's life. A great and marvelous discovery is made. One is not alone in the world of deep secrets, in the realms of wonder, awe and pain about existence, and in experiencing all of the passionate feelings that living this long has aroused. There commences a colossal outpouring of one's own soul and deep penetration into the reality of another's. A 'soul-mate' exists and one will never be quite as alone again, for one has a new identity as one human being among many, not only on the level of mutual rebellion against authority, but now on the plane of positive consciousness.

The principal anxiety in this context is engendered by fear of separation from one's soul-mate, brought about by family expectations, which are now seen as an even greater interference with one's happiness than ever before. Two have become as one as will truly never happen again, even in subsequent 'love' relationships with the opposite (or same) sex, except rarely in the most mature and developed people. The 'chumship' relationship may have passed into historical oblivion now that young people commence relationships of a highly intimate nature with members of the opposite sex about the same age (13 to 15) that 'chumship' usually occurs. If this is true, human development is being deprived not only of a singular joy but of a key step in the formation of an identity, especially one that has 'humanistic' qualities. I believe that compassion begins with the 'chumship' relationship.

It is the laboratory whose research provides us with enormous knowledge of others and of the race and is the foundation of sympathy, empathy, and forgiveness. If it is gone, what will replace it? The sexual overtones of the new pre-adolescence saturate it with powerful emotions that deprive it of the pure focused energy it requires to accomplish this rich human growth. I hope that I am wrong and that the 'chumship' experience is still available to young people.

The Seventh Separation: Investing Authority in Oneself

The seventh major separation is an expansion of the bond from peers to self, an expansion away from the authority vested in others to authority vested in oneself. (This new separation changes the peer relationship which continues in a new form). With this investment comes a deeper sense of oneself as an independent entity who thinks, feels, and acts from himself more than from others. This new self wants to soar in the sky, it wants total liberty without reservations. While the self-determining aspect of authority has been absorbed, the responsibility part lags behind. This creates new struggles with old authorities, including parents, parent surrogates, the 'pack,' and one's 'chum,' and becomes one of the most conflicted periods in a person's life.

All of the elemental energies are at work here, but most obviously the letting go and taking in of the Metal and the assertion of the Wood. The new bonds, this time to oneself, are always nourished by the Earth. Anxiety is, of course, attendant upon any steps into the unknown, especially defiant ones characterized by the disapproval of those on whom one still depends. A new and very special kind of anxiety appears at this point, aroused as a concomitant of autonomy. It is the need, now that one has asserted one's independence, to think for oneself, to make one's own decisions, accept responsibility for one's thoughts and actions, and to relate on an equal level with other people.

While, at least in the Western world, the individual is struggling through these passages with the greatest difficulty, the entire human race likewise is in the process of a similar evolution. To a very great extent, not only individuals, but the race as whole is blocked at this level in the 'evolution of being.' As a result, masses of people are profoundly anxious about assuming individual authority and responsibility. They are only too eager and happy to regress to the pre-adolescent 'pack' and invest their autonomy in charismatic leaders, representing various shades of megalomania, such as Hitler or Napoleon, whose sagas permeate the chronicles of history since the Bronze Age. All of this has been so brilliantly stated by Eric Fromm in *Escape From Freedom*.

The Eighth Separation: Love of Others

The eighth great separation and expansion of bonds is from self-love to the love of another. It may be well to mention the obvious at this point in our discussion, which is that the accomplishments of each era are cumulative and remain throughout life, and in the opinion of some, even into the next life. The ability to relate to surrogate authority, to the 'pack,' to another of one's own sex in friendship ('chumship'), and to oneself are each now a part of the person, as well as essential to the next step in individuation.

Love is the unconditional acceptance of another human being in a relationship that is universally intimate, sharing, and forgiving. Few of us ever achieve these attributes even toward ourselves, to say nothing about another, though the degree of one's capacity to love another is a reflection of one's capacity to love oneself. It is said that self-love must come first, but experience shows that life is not linear, and that the process is an ever shifting amalgam of contradictions and paradoxes that fit into no neat package.

The working through of love, whether for oneself or another, is the task of at least one lifetime. It involves marriage, children, work, and is heavily laden with tradition. It is a time when all of the energies are sorely put to the test to complete the task which 'tribal' social tradition dictates, most of all the Earth nourishing energies. In the Hindu tradition it is the time of the 'householder.'

This is a conservative period in which creativity is primarily interpersonal, though a small number of people may have the good fortune to express these Fire energies in their work. It is very clear from examining a great many adults that the foundation and storage 'power pack' energies of Water, which are the most difficult to replace, are rapidly and sorely depleted by overwork, pregnancies, and births in the normal course, and by excessive living on all levels by some (alcohol, sex, drugs, and food).

Among the myriad of obvious anxieties during this period in which one must insure the survival of one's family, as well as oneself, is the growing fear that one has lost one's 'self' forever in the service of convention and the survival of the race. For most, this phase of life consumes them, leaving little energy for further expansion into new epochs of growth. A few may be spurred by this anxiety to break loose, the majority of those who are aware succumb eventually to deep depression.

The Ninth Separation: Exploring One's Self

The ninth separation is perhaps the most difficult of all to confront an evolving person. It involves leaving behind tradition and all the security it guarantees to enter the most 'unknown' world of all, one's 'self,' and especially the uncharted seas of one's unconscious whence cometh the creative being who once was and might yet again be God. The terror of this unknown is immeasurable, and only a very few souls venture therein. As the Bible says, "Many are called, few are chosen." This is the season of life when the Fire energies are fully realized, translating this inner world of 'self' into symbols that others can eventually acknowledge. Without this recognition, our adventurer into the nether world of the creative unconscious will be in the greatest danger of isolation, alienation, and insanity. So many of the celebrated creative minds of their own, and of all times, have burned out in the asylum of dying creativity.

The creative process is perilous but the alternative to it is depression and death. Life is movement, and when it stops, the great experiment is over. If it is over too soon, the great lessons are not learned. As George Sanders, the great English actor, said just before he shot and killed himself at the age of 65, "Enough is enough." The transition from our routine consciousness to our creative being leads us into a world in which enough is never enough. Sanders, like most of the human race, did not make that transition. And like him, we die before our time.

The Tenth Separation: The Great Departure

The creative, mid-life crisis requires the letting go and taking in of the Metal energies, the inspiration of the Fire, and the thrust of the Wood. When the Wood is fully burned by the Fire we are ready to surrender in our later years to the pure, contemplative energies of Metal. The quiet taking in and letting go of the breath succeeds the tempestuous raging of the creative Fire. We have reached the penultimate point of our existence in which the only anxiety left is that posed by the truly great 'unknown.' In some societies these steps into contemplation, away from the material world and into the spiritual realm, are accepted and desirable. The final years and, especially, the final moments of life are considered to be a time to settle the outstanding issues of one's karma and to prepare for transmutation. Metal energies lead us toward the final separation and expansion of bonding. Profound ceremonies guided by ancient texts, such as the *Tibetan Book of the Dead*,[6] are available for direction. Water energies, which superintended the first union of gametes, the initial bond, and the first separation, are available to us for the great departure and for reunion with God and the cosmos.

There is no provision in Western societies for this transition. With the unresolved terror of annihilation driving us, death is denied with every painful invasive device or narcotizing drug that technology has available. There is no peace, comfort, or preparation, within or without. Those energies that nature has provided for settling our spiritual incongruities and for passing peacefully to the next plane of existence are left unrealized. With these energies untapped or exhausted by tragic irrelevancies, our spirits leave this world restless and agitated, never ceasing to search for resolution in this world or in some other.

[287]

PRETENSE

Next to the 'terror of the unknown' and to 'separation anxiety,' the most prevalent anxiety is, I believe, associated with pretense. Whenever and for as long as one pretends to be something or someone other than one's real self, one experiences anxiety. The only possible exception to this rule are those people whom we describe as psychopathic personalities, who report none of the symptoms of anxiety that normally accompany dissimulation. No one has, to my knowledge, followed these people over a long period in order to assess the occurrence of chronic physical symptoms associated with prolonged repressed anxiety.

This pretense is largely unconscious and the cause for anxiety is outside of awareness. Pretense begins early in life, before the age of awareness, as an attempt to adapt to the pressure of circumstances unfavorable for the person to be his 'true self.' The hidden, real 'self' has not had the opportunity to pass through the evolution of being' and remains for the person largely undeveloped and vulnerable in relation to the outer world, which now becomes a forbidding place. The 'self' suffers its repression poorly and drives always for expression. This is an endless source of anxiety, along with the fear generated by the deep subconscious knowledge that one is not oneself, and that one "cannot fool all the people all of the time."

Low self-esteem has one of its sources here in this rejection of the 'true self.' The self that is esteemed poorly is endlessly anxious and concerned about discovery and rejection. One other source of low self-esteem is also worth mentioning in passing, because of its relationship to pretense. The narcissistic personality, for whom bonding has been an exaggerated experience and who expects to remain the center of the universe, will suffer profound wounds when they are violently rejected as the 'messiah' and must for the first time sustain themselves on their own self-esteem. In this instance they experience first the 'unknown,' as they innocently plunge from the unreal world of home into the real one, a world without idolaters, and then know the 'terror' of profound disorientation in the profane realm of affairs and people. This is the reverse of the usual unfolding in which the 'terror' precedes the leap.

Pretense is one of the defensive maneuvers that I have referred to in an earlier part of this book as 'restorative' more than 'defensive.' These strategies require all of the phase energies to be operative. One, the Pericardium, is foremost, and coordinates the others into whatever pattern emerges. As the defender and orchestrator of the Heart energies, the creative expressed intelligence, the Pericardium becomes pre-eminent in the restorative process.

SUPPRESSED EXCITEMENT

Another extremely common anxiety is suppressed excitement. Fritz Perls[7] was the first in my experience to recognize and describe it. For many who learned early in life that the direct expression of positive excitement was dangerous, its arousal was siphoned into another more acceptable or more easily hidden experience. In many families, joy is a sin. The reasons may be religious, superstitious, or sheerly spiteful. Misery likes company. One may be certain that the reasons (rationalizations) for suppressing another person's joy are always 'good.' Individuals who begin to recognize their anxiety as repressed happiness, in the course of therapy or some other liberating experience, generally come to realize that anxiety is a sign that the life in them has not been completely eradicated and that its suppression was, in fact, a creative, restorative maneuver that saved their life. They often experience this new awareness as a revelation, a rebirth, and new beginning.

Obviously, we are dealing with Heart energies when we are dealing with 'joy,' and we are dealing with Pericardium energies as the protector and facilitator of the Heart. Anxiety is the consequence of the defense whose purpose is to hide something precious that is in danger of annihilation. Whereas with pretense the Pericardium has borrowed creative energies from the Heart to build a substitute personality, in this situation it has only been doing the work of suppression and repression. The cost to the Fire phase is, of course, more profound with pretense than with repression, and even less with suppression which is a more superficial process, closer to consciousness.

A COMFORTING EMOTION

A related form of anxiety is felt emotion associated with simply being alive. This is observable in children and adults who have experienced their mothers in an ambience of anxiety from a very early age or even in utero. Mother and anxiety become synonymous. Since mother is by nature associated with life, protection, security, and survival, anxiety is then, paradoxically, the comforting emotion coincident with bonding and safety. While the tempo-

rary absence of anxiety may be experienced as pleasant, the profound terror evoked by its prolonged absence obviates its sustained dissipation. The
Earth's 'bonding' energies and, to a lesser extent, the Heart's 'love' energies,
are involved with this subcategory of anxiety.

MAGICAL DEVICES

Closely associated with both of the last two types of anxiety is another, in
which some unpleasant experience or emotion has become a magical talisman by which to ward off harmful events. Worry is closely affiliated with
this type of anxiety. Freud described worry as a rehearsal. Within reasonable
limits which do not interfere with other life activities and with physiology,
rehearsing is a valid, useful tool. Both have replaced the time-worn rituals
associated with dispelling the 'evil eye' so well known to our grandmothers
and so anathema to us in our age of sophisticated reason. We have paid an
enormous emotional price for 'progress.' Obsessional thinking is still another magical restorative device mediated through Pericardium energies,
but which must eventually affect digestion and feed back through disturbed
Earth energies to even greater obsessive rumination.

GUILT AS A TALISMAN

A related form of anxiety that we have already touched upon is one that appears in the form of guilt. It is only another accommodation to the atavistic
insecurity which has been our steady companion since the dawn of time,
and which we have assuaged through a long and varied series of rituals
either to enhance our own power or diminish that of our unseen enemies.
Since the Old Testament, guilt has superseded many of these in the service
of mitigating the disapproval of our 'gods,' both earthly (parents, priests,
conscience, leaders) and cosmic. As long as we feel guilt as an equivalent of
anxiety, we feel safe and less uncomfortable than with the latter. Guilt represents the failure to incorporate one's own authority in the sense of being
one with God.

EXISTENTIAL ANXIETY

In contra-distinction to the accepted definition of anxiety as fear of the
unreal, there is another definition that has recently been advanced by existential philosophy. Anxiety in this context is a healthy emotion that may be
used as a guide to otherwise unattended events, both inside ourselves and
in the external environment. Awareness of these unattended events may be
essential to our existence, or even survival, but is for some 'good' reason
preferably avoided. The uncomfortable feeling associated with such a situation may alert the recipient (whether awake or in a dream) to a readiness

and vigilance that may, either in the long or short run, be life-preserving. Once again, the Fire energies of creative intelligence and the Pericardium defensive energies are involved in this interplay between knowledge and awareness.

ANXIETY AS MOTIVATING FORCE

Anxiety is known to some as a 'motivating' force. Those who never completed the incorporation of their own authority during appropriate developmental eras require some other force to propel them throughout life. Anxiety, experienced with significant dominating authorities in childhood, serves, by association, as a continuing internal imperative in the performance of unpleasurable but necessary adult activities. These people never take the full responsibility and therefore never experience the fulfilling pleasure. They may accomplish much, depending upon their abilities. However, this accomplishment gives them little happiness, since it is never free from the unpleasant accompaniment of anxiety.

ANXIETY AS WAY OF LIFE

The widespread acceptance of the positive aspects of emotional catharsis and abreaction to mental health has witnessed excesses never imagined by Breuer and Freud,[8] who challenged, on medical grounds, the stoicism of our forefathers. From the beginning, and reaching its zenith during the late 1960s in the Encounter Movement and Bioenergetics, it became fashionable to share, indeed shed, one's anxiety on anyone who was willing to participate. Anxiety became, for some, a way of life in which the balance was never encouraged between healthy sharing and the development of a capacity for living with, and containing, anxiety. Thus a generation was kept alive by the medium of anxiety, in the guise of openness, as a primary form of contact. Woody Allen's movies may be seen as a contemporary expression of this theme.

Indeed, it is extremely important to acknowledge one's anxiety. To rely upon it as a primary way of making contact, rather than as an experience to 'work through,' is actually an avoidance of the many leaps in the dark that we must take to grow. It makes only for another pseudo-mutual pattern of relating, both with oneself and with other people, avoiding the honest confrontations of love and its demands on the self to shift one's focus from 'me-me-me' to others. The energies most involved in using anxiety as a bond with others are the Earth, which is the primary source for this work, and the Metal, which is the energy most involved with the expansion of bonds or separation. Anxiety as a form of expression also involves Fire energies.

DEPRESSION

From conception to the grave, and perhaps beyond, there exists an evolutive series of potentials for growth, development, and expression. Any experience that inhibits these potentials will evoke an atavistic, organismic protest. If that protest fails during periods of development when the evolving person is still substantially dependent on others for sustenance, the same survival mechanisms will sound an alarm, which we call anxiety, signaling the person to find a more immediately safe solution. What is called for is a creative alternative, which I call a restorative maneuver. This will restore a relative state of harmony in which basic needs may be met and the cataclysmic effects of the protest attacking the 'self' may be avoided.

Productive resolutions of this dilemma may not always be forthcoming. The best possible solution ensuring current sanctuary may unavoidably include turning the protest away from the inhibiting force, inwardly, where it will vent its unspent energy by attacking the weakest link in its own organismic chain. Should these maneuvers, which others erroneously refer to as "defenses," also fail to maintain a reasonable homeostasis, the protest may assume the posture of withdrawal, which we call depression. Within this framework of silent protest the person is saying that, "If I cannot be myself (within reason), I will be nothing." Under some circumstances, for example, if assertion might bring destruction from more powerful forces, the retreat may he the safest and most expedient tactic.

Life, on the other hand, has another agenda. It is perforce a growth process which, despite periodic strategic retreats, is basically expansive. Depressions therefore tend to be short-lived. Prolonged retreats such as depression cannot resist the forward thrust of these drives, and it is the pain that ensues from this struggle that becomes unbearable and leads to suicide, the final retreat on, and from, earth. It is a monumental paradox that in depression the stronger the life-drive, the greater the chance of a person taking his own life.

Maladaptive living patterns eventually dissipate these positive energies, and, unless a therapeutic process intervenes to alter these patterns into a more nourishing lifestyle, they slowly lose their power to overcome the retreat. One may see a lifetime of surges and collapses, advances and retreats, in what is now referred to as a Cyclothymic Affective Disorder. With age our energy decreases naturally. In middle and older age, especially with the additional discouragement of unfulfilled aspirations and lost identities, we are less equipped energically to countermand the forces for unproductive retreat.

Apart from developmental considerations, depression may result at any time there is a profound loss of energy. This may occur after a long illness or a serious operation, but I think it is best illustrated by the postpartum dysphoria which many women experience in varying degrees. Along with a significant loss of blood and fluid there is a loss of energy. Without the requisite rest, and the herbs which are available to women in China during and after pregnancy, a woman may never recover her blood, fluid, and energy. The result may be post-partum depression, the degree depending in part on the viability of the organ system energies, in particular the Heart, Liver, and Kidneys. The Heart controls the circulation, the Kidneys store the essence necessary to the formation of blood, and the Liver stores the blood and thereby restores the energy for all the systems. The loss of circulating blood affects the Heart, which in Chinese medicine is said to control the mind and is associated with joy. Impaired Heart energies will adversely affect mental functions and the absence of a capacity for joy may lead to prolonged and recurrent depression.

In this connection, a 60-year-old female patient comes to mind. Despite many debilitating physical symptoms, after six full term pregnancies, seven miscarriages, raising her family alone, working as a nurse in a hospital during the midnight shift, and undergoing four major operations, she was referred to a psychiatrist for depression. Attention to her energic needs reversed this state and the myriad of disharmonies which affected every system of her body.

PHASES OF INDIVIDUATION AND THEIR CHARACTERISTIC DEPRESSIONS

The nature of a depressive episode will depend to some extent on the era of development during which the 'self' experienced its original or greatest defeat. Depression, as mentioned above, is largely a restorative self-help maneuver, an expression of 'being' alternative to the one that failed in the normal course of growth. At the same time, it is a form of mourning throughout the life cycle for part of the self which is spiritually and physically dying from repression. Chronic depression is one response to the persistent failure of any personality organization to fulfill its own expectations.

Each developmental phase has associated with it a characteristic depression and is dominated by the energies of one of the Zang (solid organs) spheres of influence. Within our discussion of the natural functions and the disharmonies of these spheres pertaining to personality, depression has already been examined more closely as a function of the excesses and deficiencies of the yin and yang polarities of these energies. Here, at this point, we will search the 'evolution of being,' and each era of that journey, in a more general fashion for the variety of faces by which depression shows itself to the world and to itself.

{ 293 }

ENDOGENOUS DEPRESSION

A lifelong tendency to respond to stress with depression has its roots in severe Kidney energy deficiency. The origin of the depressive personality lies in the failure of genetics or very early intra-uterine life to provide these energies adequately. This adversity is the root of all habitual depressions and the source of the spiritual poverty (Kidney qi), which we call 'endogenous' depression.

More specifically, the loss of 'will' and 'drive' associated with Kidney yang (the fire at the gate of vitality, or *ming men*) deficiency is an intrinsic deficit associated with all sustained, profound, or recurrent depressions. Kidney 'Fire' is the functional heat energy that 'drives' the entire physical plant to provide the force behind the 'will to live.' Without this will, the inclination is to collapse well before retreat is expedient.

Kidney yin provides the substance, the basic grounding material, upon which we must all fall when we go down, and the fundamental stored essence *(jing)* that is the principal reserve with which to bounce back after defeat. It provides us with the capacity for rational evaluations of our limits so that we can make strategic retreats (in conjunction with Liver yin) in situations where advance would lead to major defeat and subsequent grounds for depression. Kidney yin endows the spiritually evolved person with the capacity for the divine love needed to "forgive us our trespasses" when we falter. Kidney qi endows us with the ability to live in the present, to confront issues now, to live with our feet on the ground even when we are dreaming, all qualities which stand us well in the face of defeat and the inclination to withdraw into depression.

ANACLITIC AND CYCLOTHYMIC DEPRESSIONS

Within the purview of the Earth phase energies are both the anaclitic depressions, associated with precipitous failure to retain the maternal bond, and the cyclothymic depressions of those whose bond with mother was continuous but tenuous, sufficient to evoke hope but always falling short of satisfaction. The former is documented by Winnicott in a remarkable movie made at the Tavistock clinic sometime in the 1960s.[9] In this movie we witness the physical and mental decline of an inconsolable infant separated from its mother by her illness. The total loss of cheerful, contented affect, and the obvious state of mourning, is even more heart-rending than the gradual state of marasmus which follows. We know that many of these children do not survive infancy (note Eva Peron's sterile orphanage). Those who do survive live their lives without a tolerance for, or awareness of, joy. We meet people occasionally who never smile and never laugh, presenting to the world, and probably to themselves, a dispirited, flat, and colorless affect. More rarely we encounter this syndrome in adults who have experienced substantial loss, and occasionally they do not recover.

For those who have had a continuous but tenuous relationship with a mothering person, the picture is one of a constant search for a dependable mothering figure, who could in fact be a man. When this person is found, there is euphoria, and when he or she is inevitably lost, there is dysphoria. They are always either in a state of hope or despair and there is little affect between the two. These people are the extreme of the 'cyclothymic' depressive syndrome, and I suspect that wherever the condition is truly serious, this kind of history is involved. They fall into the category of dependent personalities. (I wish to reiterate that even here, without underlying deficient Kidney energies, the depressive solution is likely to be less severe).

AGITATED DEPRESSION

Failure to reach a reasonable autonomy in the process of 'becoming' in the 'no' and psychomotor stages (ages one to four) is a defeat for the Wood phase. Interpersonal encounters with meaningful authority figures in which the drive toward assertion is stifled in this era will inspire the paradoxical response, "If I cannot feel alive by 'being,' then I will feel alive by actively 'not being.'" The result is spite, and the entire negative behavioral range that is included in the spectrum of the passive-aggressive personality. The emptiness of an existential stance that is sustained by negativism and 'not being,' both for oneself and others, must inevitably lead to the affective equivalent of this restless spiritual poverty, 'agitated' depression.

Even within the framework of this antithetic posture, the 'self' attempts to survive, and even flourish, through devious maneuvers. Some people circumscribe the spite with which their archaic defeated ego secretly identifies so that they lead parallel lives of 'negative' and 'positive.' This solution may have a significantly salutary effect upon interpersonal relations and please others. For themselves, the need to selectively inattend one aspect of their personality in order to maintain internal consistency and external approbation is both draining and unfulfilling. The combinations and permutations of these opposing forces in terms of character formation are, of course, endless. A persistent theme of all is recurrent depression, marked by irritation, anger, and agitation.

HYSTERICAL AND REACTIVE DEPRESSIONS

The 'hysterical' depression is partially a manipulative threat to create guilt and make us all unhappy "if I do not get my own way." It is characterized by strongly seductive overtones and is most obvious in women who have not succeeded in winning a fulfilling love relationship with the parent of the opposite sex. These are people who often wear their 'hearts on their sleeves,' and who succeed in repeatedly 'losing in love.'

These failures are related to the Fire phase and in particular to deficiencies in the Pericardium. These are 'reactive depressions,' often 'cyclothymic,' the person's immediate affective state depending on the vicissitudes of "he/she loves me, loves me not." However, in contrast to the cyclothymic picture associated with the Earth phase, the depths and elevations of despair are relatively shallow, and though rhetorically more embellished and florid, far less substantive and less devastating to the entire ego structure. Unlike the characteristic withdrawal of most depressive states, these people tend to pout and, even at their worst moment, love to talk. Excesses in Pericardium energies lead, on the other hand, to a 'closing of the Heart,' a masking of affect, a diminishment of normal mood cycles, and a tendency to vengefulness.

DYSPHORIC DEPRESSION

Disturbances in the Triple Burner energy function of creating harmony in the Fire phase will alter the reactive depression, described in connection with Pericardium energies, into more serious ruptures in relationships. In chronic conditions, the outcome may be a form of depression resembling the more serious schizoid personality of defective Water and Earth energies. Like the schizoid, it is marked by withdrawal from social contacts into a 'splendid isolation,' by suspiciousness, hostility, despair, and restlessness if the isolation is too complete or prolonged. Defects in the Small Intestine energies will color these depressions with increased and sometimes agitated confusion, due to the inability to discriminate on a cognitive level. This is more pronounced in the elderly and in children, or wherever cognitive processes are already either undeveloped or compromised. Constitutional deficiencies in Heart energies are associated with 'dysphoric' depressions, marked by sadness, loss of interest in and guilt about pleasure, some withdrawal, and minimal psychomotor retardation.

BIPOLAR DISORDERS

Interference with the development of creative expression on the verbal cognitive level will also adversely affect the Fire phase, primarily the Heart organ system. The agitated depression associated with inhibition in the 'no' and psychomotor (Wood) era develops, with similar inhibition in the 'positive' (Fire) stage of self-expression, into the bipolar disease that we formerly designated as manic-depressive. It is the repression of both assertion and creativity, stagnation of the qi of both the Liver and Heart, that brings Heat and burns the Wood and builds the Fire, that Water is eventually unable to control. Bipolar episodes may be precipitated by stress in another vulnerable energy sphere, such as the effect of abandonment on the Spleen energies, or separation on the Metal energies.

The depressed intervals, when the Fire is still being quenched by the Water, are observable periods of quiet reasonableness, restriction, and exaggerated quiescence in the areas of verbal, intellectual, and artistic creative assertion. In people with strong Wood the manic phase may be longer and more pronounced than the depressive phase. The person may report anxiety during the non-manic phase rather than depression. The crash into the depths of depression occurs when the Wood is burned past the point where it can continue to feed the Fire.

These energies are irrepressible. The manic phases are episodic breakdowns in this inhibition when the Water is sufficiently depleted to allow the Fire to burn out of control. Bipolar episodes may be precipitated by stress in another vulnerable energy sphere, such as the effect of abandonment on the Spleen energies, or separation on the Metal energies. The Triple Burner, one of whose functions is to regulate temperature, is pushed beyond its capacities. The Heart qi is 'wild,' and the Heart yin cannot control the yang. The 'mind,' which the Heart superintends, is now in a state of havoc and highly vulnerable to other adverse pathogenic factors such as phlegm or dampness from the Spleen. In people with strong Wood the manic phase may be longer and more pronounced than the depressive phase. The person may report anxiety during the non-manic phase rather than depression. The crash into the depths of depression occurs when the Wood is burned past the point where it can continue to feed the Fire.

I believe the bipolar disease is often a constitutional defect in the thermostatic control of the Wood-Fire-Water cycle by the Triple Burner system. Supporting the Triple Burner system's ability to regulate the consumption of Wood by Fire may avoid this pyschological and physiological catastrophe. When sufficient *Kidney yin* is depleted, one finds oneself in the manic phase. Eventually, Kidney yin deficiency transforms into a *Kidney yang* deficiency, is exhausted, and a profound, almost treatment-resistant depression can result.

NARCISSISTIC DEPRESSION

Another melancholia that has its roots during the first five years of life is what I call the 'narcissistic' depression. The subject of this often lifelong misery is someone, often an only child, who during the first years of life was made to feel irrationally important by the parents, usually by the mother. The let down occurs soon after the subject is thrown into a situation with other children and surrogate authorities such as at school or camp. Here, the discovery that he or she is not special is extremely disorienting, and their behavior, both before and after the 'fall,' is unintentionally very alienating to everyone. The child is an innocent victim of inaccurate acculturation by inadequate parents, a child who wants to belong but does not know how. The result is isolation and painful loneliness. These children try and fail, over and over, to be accepted, and, unless they get help, these repeated defeats lead to severe depression and even suicide. The issues of bonding, separating, and communicating involve the energies of the Earth, Metal, and Fire phases, respectively, all of which have been damaged through the parental relationship. One might think of it as the Fire being caught within the Earth or, in neuro-linguistic terms, as being able only to 'sort by self' (Earth) and unable to 'sort by other' (Fire).[10]

SECONDARY ANACLITIC DEPRESSION

The next class of affective disorder I call the secondary anaclitic depression. Whereas the narcissistic child is perfectly willing to expand the parental bond to others but does not have the tools to succeed, the secondary anaclitic person does not wish to make new bonds except in a setting where mother is within easy reach. This person is always longing to be with a parent (usually mother) and becomes both anxious and then very depressed when separated from her. The school phobias include some of these people. Choosing to live outside of their peer group, they are alone, but not lonely. They do not wish to belong and prefer to build an isolated existence as a pseudo-schizoid personality. In energic terms one might say that the Earth does not feed the Metal, the energy principally involved in the expansion of bonds, or perhaps that the Metal (separation) is trapped in the Earth (bonding).

GRIEVING-FOR-SELF DEPRESSION

The next stage in the evolution of the expansion of bonds, as mediated by Metal energies in the service of the Fire (communication relationship), is a move from principal bonding with parents and other authorities to the peer group. It is the period when the pre-adolescent joins the peer group rebellion against all adult institutions, including the one that continues to support and protect him. It is a time of flux between the expansion away from the nuclear family and the ties to the original bonds, which are still needed but resented. The 'good' child who does not join the 'happy hunters' is more adult oriented and not 'one of the boys,' experiences none of the joy of running with the crowd, the ecstasy of breaking loose from the childhood prison of adult supremacy. The joy in oneself that comes from having dared is joy that continues to be missing in this person's life. This engenders a lifelong form of a diffuse, unformulated lament, an unarticulated grieving depression for a lost part of themselves.

INVOLUTIONAL DEPRESSION

The next step, again mediated by Metal energies (expansion of bond) in the service of the Fire phase (communication, love, relationship, and creativity), is the transition of 'being' from all surrogates, including peers, to identity with the personal value of 'self.' We are talking about that part of the process of individuation during which we incorporate authority within ourselves with an emerging, yet inchoate, awareness of the responsibility that accompanies authority. Those of us who do less than meet this developmental prerogative suffer from, or spend a lifetime running from, a sense of profound incompleteness.

Life provides a wide variety of obsessions by which to avoid this knowledge, including family, work, and play, all of which are tinged with a driven quality. The mid-life crisis presents itself when a variety of circumstances, such as children leaving home, retirement, job displacement, widowhood, or divorce, obviate avoidance and precipitate the void. The mid-life crisis is, in fact, an ongoing but unnoticed one from adolescence forward through subsequent decades. If the crisis occurs in a person with sufficient resources to reattempt the individuation that he failed to make at the appropriate time, in late adolescence (especially if Heart and Kidney energies are strong), then the result may be enhancement and satisfaction. If, on the other hand, such resources are not available, the result will usually be some form of 'involutional' depression marked by a deep sense of barrenness and unworthiness.

LONELINESS

The continuation of the incorporation of responsibility into the individuation process leads from the primary 'sorting by self' to the ever-increasing ability to 'sort by other' without losing oneself. The confidence to do that makes creative intimacy possible. Here the integrity of the Fire phase energies, including the Heart which mediates excitement and expression, the

Triple Burner whose energies stabilize and harmonize family and social ties, the Small Intestine whose energies enhance clarity in relationships, and the Pericardium whose energies enable us to find a realistic balance of openness and caution in our worldly affairs, are all indispensable to successful and gratifying love relationships. For those whose energies are not intact, there is a lifelong yearning for the fulfillment of intimacy and a deep well of loneliness.

DEPRESSION OF THE SOUL

The next step involving Fire phase energies is the drive to know and to communicate in a coherent fashion the entirety of oneself, to explore the known and the unknown regions of one's 'being.' One moves at this stage from giving one's self to loved ones, to giving one's self to the Word or the Logos, as expressed in the Gospel according to Saint John, which says, "In the beginning was the Word and the Word was with God and the Word was God."[11] In this process of giving one's self to 'creation' there is a certain abstraction of self that requires one to "march to the beat of a different drummer." So it is a time when we begin to stop bending to the will of our own 'ego' and to the 'egos' of all those upon whom our lives impinge. Few human beings reach or live through this transition, for it is a difficult journey during which "many are called and few are chosen." And yet the price for holding back is lifelong frustration and lack of fulfillment, indeed, the 'depression of the soul.'

DEPRESSION OF THE SPIRIT

The final scene in our drama returns us to the Water and Metal phase energies, during which we move from the creative self to the divine self. From a realization of our uniqueness, in the previous stage of 'evolution of being,' we are drawn into a consideration of our oneness with the cosmos. In the past, many societies provided us in our waning years on earth with the time and the means to make this journey if we chose to do so. In the present, we must make our own way, and the way is strewn with obstacles. The guru to whom we could once turn is either no longer there, or untrustworthy if he is there, more often than not. So in our time we are left to ourselves to find God, and perhaps that is the way it was meant to be. But how many at this late stage of life still have those Water energies, the foundation of our being, which we have spent wantonly on a lifetime of energic excesses, and which are necessary for the courage to make this lonely journey into the unknown? Prepared or otherwise, it remains true, nevertheless, that those of us who do not at least turn our soul in that direction and seek the 'way' live with a 'depression of the spirit' which finds no peace.

The Unconscious

I should like here to interject some comments about the 'unconscious.' The existence of what Carl Jung called the "other reality,"[12] and Freud the "unconscious," is the subject of a never-ending debate. The irrelevance of this discussion and the heat it generates are about equal.

Those of us who have had the experience, in times of great stress, of having 'another self' perform tasks which we never ordinarily perform know that there is an 'other reality.' For me, this has been a super-rational layer of my being not ordinarily available to me. At other times, remarkable thoughts have appeared, which place the ordinary in a new and excitingly different perspective. At still other times, I have had a 'stream of consciousness,' either awake or asleep, that defied logic but conveyed the truth about myself and others far more clearly than all the reasoning to which I have been exposed. And surely there is some place where my memory goes, as it wishes and not subject to my control, to recall what eludes me.

What this has meant to me is that there are many layers of existence, some more rationally organized than others, that are ordinarily outside of my awareness. It matters little to me what they are called. What this 'other reality' consists of seems to me to be a function of the reporter's own experience, both personal and collective, a matter of revelation not subject to temporal theocracies.

14

THE SYSTEMS MODEL OF DR. SHEN

We have examined the Five Phase system model in terms of the evolution of being. We will now turn our attention to another model. This model, which is termed the 'systems' model, was developed by Dr. John Shen, C.M.D., during a period of over fifty years of practice and study. The foundation for what follows was communicated to me during the eight years of our close association. Its elaboration, based on thirty-five years of psychiatric practice, and seventeen years of Chinese medical clinical practice, is my own. This is especially true of those sections dealing with social and psychological considerations and traditional and alternative Western medicine. Distinguishing among the contributions of Dr. Shen, myself, and Chinese medicine to this model is difficult, but I have attempted to do so, except where it would interfere with the unfolding and flow of the material.[1]

FOUR MAJOR ORGAN SYSTEMS

Dr. Shen came to formulate the systems model when he found patients complaining of symptoms for which he could find, on pulse, tongue, and eye examination, none of the familiar signs that were associated with disease in the traditional Chinese medical system. The complaints were of general discomfort in one or another respect. The symptoms tended to be somewhat vague, and the signs unrevealing of the organ disease usually associated with disharmony according to Chinese medicine.

What Dr. Shen discovered was that, rather than specific organ dysfunction, functional systems in their entirety were disturbed. He reduced these to four major systems, drawing upon the layering of energy, from superficial to deep, as described by Zhang Zhong-Jing in the *Shang Han*

Lun (Discussion of Cold Damage).[2] In this major treatise, written around the third century, Zhang attempted to describe the progress of disease, from the most superficial to the deepest layers, primarily known as 'injury from cold.' Originally, there were six layers or divisions: the outermost was known as Tai Yang, followed by Shao Yang, Yang Ming, Tai Yin, Shao Yin, and finally Jue Yin, the deepest layer. The disease, having reached this level, is in its most serious stage and the person closest to death. At a somewhat later epoch, each of these divisions became associated with particular channels, which, for the purposes of our discussion, are irrelevant. Dr. Shen associated the three most superficial layers with specific systems, and the three deepest layers — Tai Yin, Shao Yin, and Jue Yin — together as one system. Specifically, he identified Tai Yang as the 'nervous system,' Shao Yang as the 'circulatory system,' Yang Ming as the 'digestive system,' and the combination of Tai Yin, Shao Yin, and Jue Yin as the 'organ system.'

In this work, we are principally concerned with the most superficial layer, the Tai Yang, which Dr. Shen equates with the 'nervous system.' However, it will be useful to describe the other systems in a little detail in order to give an overall sense of what we are considering. We will, therefore, consider the other systems first, and then return to Tai Yang for our principal discussion. These systems have a widespread effect on health and disease, in contrast to organ dysfunction, which tends to be more specific in symptomatology, at least in the early and middle stages of the disease process.

CORRELATION BETWEEN FOUR SYSTEMS AND FIVE COMMAND POINTS

There are several interesting correlations between these systems and other concepts in Chinese medicine. For example, we are familiar with the five command points, or antique points, located on each channel, from the toes to the knee, or from the fingers to the elbow. Traditionally, the first was related to the nerves, the second to fevers and heat, the third to muscles and ligaments, the fourth to respiration, and the fifth to digestion. Dr. Shen revised this to some extent in keeping with his systems concept, equating the first and second to the 'nervous system,' the third to the 'circulatory system,' the fourth to the 'digestive system,' and the fifth to the 'organ system.' There is considerable sense to this kind of organization, since, for example, heat, which is normally associated with the second command point, is a very important concern in the treatment of nervous disorders, particularly heat from the Liver and the Heart. The third, or the 'circulatory system,' is, in Chinese medicine, a frequent source of problems in the musculoskeletal system, in the form of migrating pain. In this and other respects, it coincides with the traditional assignment of the third position to the musculoskeletal system. The fourth is traditionally thought of as respiration, but, as Dr. Shen points out, the 'digestive system' consists not only of the Stomach, Intestines, and related organs, but of the Lungs and the Kidneys as well. Whereas mucus is made in the Stomach, it is the Lungs (if they are strong enough) that digest (disperse) it into water, and the Kidneys which digest the water after the Lungs cause it to descend. Within this framework, the Lungs are part of the 'digestive system' and so Dr. Shen's assignment of the 'digestive system' to the fourth position is rational. The fifth position he sees as the 'organ system,' by which he means the function or dysfunction of all of the five yin organs in unison, but especially what he considered to be the most vital of the yin organs, the Heart, Liver, and Kidneys, generally regarded as the most basic functional units of the organism. Shao Yin and Jue Yin encompass these three organs, and, in contrast to the 'digestive system' whose organs are found on the right side, those of the 'organ system' are found on the left. Particularly important, in his view, is the dynamic relationship between these two systems, especially in terms of the stress on the 'digestive system' to support the 'organ system' that is burdened and drained by all of the excesses of modern life.

In addition, the 'nervous system' has been related to the upper burner or to heaven; the 'circulatory system' to the lower burner and to man; and the digestive and organ 'systems' to earth, or the middle. The latter is not of great significance to us here but does play some part in another of Dr. Shen's concepts concerning 'timing' points of the body.

These systems have a very broad physiological function, and their disorder, a very broad effect on the entire organism. Let us examine the systems in greater detail. Our main concern will be with the 'nervous system,' which we will consider last and in the greatest detail. Suffice it to say now that, in terms of ideology, the Tai Yang may, in addition to being affected by life experience, also be predominantly affected by constitution and congenital influences. Likewise, the 'organ system' may be affected by constitutional, congenital, and life considerations, while circulatory and digestive 'system' disorders are primarily influenced by life experience itself.

Shao Yang: The 'Circulatory System'

Let us first consider the 'circulatory system.' Circulation, in Chinese medicine, is either of the qi, which is the moving energy of the body, or of the blood, which, in Chinese medicine, is not exactly the same as our concept of blood but refers to a heavier, more dense form of energy. Traditionally, it is said that the qi moves the blood and that the blood nourishes the qi.

They are, in this sense, interdependent. With qi diseases, there is generally a feeling of weakness and, if there is pain, it tends to come and go, depending on the energy of the person at that particular time. With blood circulatory diseases, there is generally a feeling of coldness in the extremities and, in addition to pain, there will be swelling. This will be persistent and always present. Naturally, one can have a combination of qi and blood stagnation or weakness. Generally speaking, the less serious the problem, the more likely it is to be just a qi disease; the more serious the problem, the more likely it is that there will also be a blood disease.

Life experience is the basic etiology of 'circulatory system' problems. There are two general categories: one in which the circulatory problem is secondary to an energy problem, and one in which the circulatory problem creates the energy problem. In the first situation a person has either over-worked or overexercised, creating a weak body condition and deficient qi. This in turn affects circulation because the qi moves the blood, and the qi is the moving part of the energy. The pulse is generally Slow and Feeble, though in the extremes it may be unbalanced, and one may not be able to get the rate at all.

The second category, in which the circulation has secondarily af-fected the energy, is caused by some kind of relatively strong and sudden experience, such as an accident, emotional trauma, or very severe weather conditions. In this situation, the pulse may at first be either very Fast or very Slow, but later is generally Slow though Tight, rather than Feeble. In general, the pulse tends to be somewhat slower when circulation has been affected by accident, emotion, and weather than when it is affected by the body condition or energy.

When the problem begins with energy, it is the qi, or top portion of the pulse, that tends to be most Feeble. When the circulatory problem has been caused by a traumatic episode, the top portion of the qi will be Feeble; but the middle portion, the blood portion, may also be Feeble, or, in the earlier stages, rather Tight. If the trauma is severe enough, the deepest part of the pulse will also be Robust and Tight, since the circulation in the organs themselves may be affected.

In the situation where the energy has affected the circulation, the tongue will tend to be pale. Where the circulation has affected the en-ergy, due again to some severe trauma, the tongue may have a darker, even purple, coloration. If there has been a severe accident, there will be small, purple eccymosis on the side of the body where the accident occurred.

Another situation affecting circulation is one in which people who are exercising to the extreme for a period of time stop very suddenly. In this situation, there will be vague complaints of tiredness, labile emotions, easy anger, feelings of being 'spaced out,' and, in some way, out of control. Sometimes, when these people lie down they feel that their bodies are floating away or that their arms are floating, and sometimes they can become extremely anxious and terrified by this experience. They are often seen by psychiatrists and receive diagnoses of anxiety neurosis or panic attacks.

Exercise causes the vascular system to expand so as to accommodate the increased volume of blood; the blood vessels are, therefore, wider than ordinary. When it is stopped abruptly, the amount of blood in the vascular system decreases suddenly but the blood vessels themselves tend to remain expanded. The traditional Chinese thought is that blood and energy flow together and that blood is actually a form of energy. It tends to stay toward the center of the blood vessel, while the energy stays more on the outside. The blood is considered yin, and the qi, or energy, is considered more yang. Traditionally, yang wants to expand and yin to contract; the yang is held in check from expanding too much by the yin. When the yin is markedly diminished, as in this case, the yang goes out of control. This is a situation (one of several) in which the Chinese say that the qi is 'wild.'[3] The pulse is Yielding Hollow Full-Overflowing and Rapid. All of the organs are affected. Since the circulation of energy to the organs that maintain function is disrupted, the energy is no longer under control and is completely 'wild.'

In another kind of circulatory problem, less often experienced in our time, the pulse is extremely irregular, so much so that one is unable to actually count the number of beats per minute. Different names have been used to describe this pulse, but I shall call it Interrupted. This kind of pulse would be found in situations where people were overworked at an extremely young age, for example, in children who were forced to work in factories and mines. The Scattered pulse is not continuous, and the Unstable pulse in one position rapidly hits the finger in different places with each beat. These pulses also arise from excessive abuse at a very early age. Both of these pulses are also considered ones in which the qi is 'wild,' and both are considered to be pathognomic of a very short life, unless some very strong intervention takes place. An Empty pulse may also be considered in the same category, but somewhat less serious in terms of the overall body condition; it occurs when there may be less overwork, or overwork may have occurred at a later age in childhood, or there may be a constitutionally deficient Kidney.

All of the above are conditions of the 'circulatory system' in which the entire organism and the entire pulse are involved and which cannot be delineated in terms of a single organ disharmony.

Yang Ming: The Digestive System

The 'digestive system,' in Dr. Shen's terms, includes the Stomach, Intestines (both small and large), the Spleen-Pancreas, the Lungs, and the water function of the Kidneys. The symptomatology includes the following: the appetite is sometimes good, sometimes poor; irregular bowel movements, sometimes constipated, sometimes loose; general discomfort. Frequently, there will also be complaints of a great deal of mucus in the chest and throat. In addition, there may be some complaints of vague pain, in terms of response to heat, pressure, and diet, that do not fit into the usual diagnostic categories.

There are a number of factors that can affect the 'digestive system' as a whole. One is eating irregularly. (Such enduring patterns of congruity between hunger cycles, work, sleep, and play habits develop early in life.) In this situation, all of the organs mentioned above, plus the Liver and Gall-bladder, are affected. Over a period of time, the 'digestive system' becomes weakened because, as with all of the systems of the body, regularity is essential. In other words, the 'digestive system' is ready to work when one is hungry. But the person who, over a period of time, eats when he is not hungry and does not eat when he is hungry disrupts the balance within all of these organs, with consequent overall weakness. One will find that the pulse on the entire right side is extremely Feeble. Depending on the kind of food that the person is eating and the degree of stagnation, there may or may not be coating of varying thickness on the tongue. If the Stomach is considerably overworked, red spots may appear. These will be on the surface if the condition is acute, and deeper if it is chronic.

The second important etiology of 'digestive system' disorders in our society is the habit of eating too fast. Here, the patient tends to complain of feeling bloated, though he or she may also have some pain on occasion due to the fact that eating fast creates heat and affects the nerves of the Stomach and organs of the 'digestive system,' particularly the esophagus. In this situation, the entire right side of the pulse is very Tight, especially at the surface. The tongue, again, may have some coating, depending on other eating habits, as well as the red spots mentioned above.

The third cause is consumption of cold food and drink, which creates stagnation. This is particularly true of people who drink a great many iced beverages or who eat excessive amounts of ice cream. In this situation, stagnation occurs because cold interferes with the circulation throughout the 'digestive system.' Eventually, irregular eating creates weakness, rapid eating creates heat, and eating cold foods creates stagnation. Other factors contributing to digestive problems may be: lifting before and after eating; over-work or returning to work too quickly after eating; emotion; and the habit of sitting bent over after eating. These tend to have more specific rather than broad effects, but may also affect the overall 'digestive system.' The final result here is a slowing down of the digestive process and all the diseases which attend it. This disease process can also be seen as a disruption of the balance of the Triple Burner system. Eating irregularly disrupts the rhyth-mic cycle of enzyme excretion and peristalsis and the normal intervals of rest and activity for all the functioning components of this intricate system, which are included as part of one or another of the Triple Burners. Each of the etiological factors mentioned above creates an imbalanced condition in one of the burners, which removes that burner from the coordinated func-tioning of the system as a whole.

TAI YIN, SHAO YIN, JUE YIN: THE 'ORGAN SYSTEM'

In referring to the 'organ system' we mean, simultaneously, all of the Zang (solid) organs: particularly the Heart, the Kidneys, and the Liver, and, somewhat less so, the Spleen and the Lungs. The Lungs are considered to be the most yang of the yin organs, since it is the yin organ most related to the outside of the body, the one that receives the qi from the atmosphere, and the one located in the upper burner. The Spleen-Stomach, though less immediately than the Lungs, are also relatively yang, relating to the outside through the ingestion of food. By contrast, the Liver through the bile duct and the Kidneys through the urethra are far less connected to the outside world, and the Heart not at all, making them increasingly yin. Dr. Shen's concept of the 'organ system' corresponds to the Tai Yin, Shao Yin, and Jue Yin, as described in the *Shang Han Lun (Discussion of Cold Damage)*. The principal problems related to the 'organ system' fall into three categories, yin deficiency, qi deficiency, and yang deficiency.

Generalized yin deficiency in our time is the result primarily of the overworking of the mind, thinking and worrying excessively, a sign of a white collar society that does less physical and more mental work. An-other cause that is the result of stagnation is often associated with feelings of frustration with other people, and is usually found in the Liver. This has occurred more and more frequently since the onset of the industrial revolution, before which people worked more by themselves or with family members, and since which we work more and more for strangers to whom expression of our frustrations is a threat to our livelihood.

This stagnation, where the 'immovable object meets the irresistible force,' is especially uncongenial to the Liver, which is responsible for moving qi. The Liver attempts to move the qi by bringing metabolic heat to the Liver. If this does not succeed in overcoming the 'immovable object,' the heat accumulates and becomes a toxic substance that we call heat from excess. The body attempts to compensate for this heat by providing water (fluid), and over a long period of time, depending on the constitution, the degree of overwork, and the initial body condition, there will be a depletion of this water. In Chinese medicine, yin represents water in a general sense, so the water, or yin, becomes depleted. This is the condition of yin deficiency. Over a still longer period of time, if there is a continuation of the depletion of water, metabolism at the organ cellular level will slowly lose its ability to function. At this point, the involved organs will be unable to contribute to the overall energy of the body, and a new situation will arise, which, in Chinese medicine, is described as yang deficiency. As the functioning of the organ or the organs together diminishes, their output of energy diminishes, and the concomitant output of usable heat in the body (what the Chinese would call 'strong heat,' metabolic heat, or heat that does positive work) will diminish, leaving the person with a feeling of coldness. The heat produced in the yin deficient condition is known as 'heat from deficiency.' This heat has no positive function in the body. It is the heat of friction, such as we would find in an engine that is overworking, and it needs to be dissipated. When it cannot be correctly dissipated in the urine, feces, or sweat, it is experienced as uncomfortable heat in the palms and soles of the feet, flushing up in the face, and in episodes of hot flashes or hot sweats. Later symptoms of yin deficiency may be irritability, nervous tension, insomnia, low fever later in the day. Other symptoms of yang deficiency are spontaneous sweating, very easily fatigued, frequent urination, dislike of cold and preference for warmth, abdominal pain relieved by pressure and/or heat, diarrhea with undigested food, a wide variety of infections, and a general susceptibility to illness and difficulty in recovering. The yang deficient and qi deficient conditions are almost identical. The former is an extension of the latter and is distinguished from it by the general feelings of cold.

In terms of etiology, 'organ system' problems may be constitutional or from life or both. The life problems involve situations in which there is inappropriate overwork in relation to the person's basic energy or his stage of life. For example, sex at a very early age, particularly in women, may lead to a yin deficient condition, which will have profound effects on the menstrual cycle for their entire lives. This kind of overwork will affect the entire 'organ system' and particularly, of course, the Kidneys, which are most closely related to the sexual and reproductive energies. The condition of yin deficiency itself is generally made worse by sex, a form of work that is one of the more profound depleters of Kidney energy, which stores, creates, and provides the yin. Most people are unable to make a connection with this, because sex will generally relieve the nervous tension that is associated with the condition of heat from deficiency in the body (yin deficiency), and so they associate sex with an improvement in their overall being. However, while they are engaged in this generally favorable experience, this form of work beyond their energy will undo their overall condition and exacerbate the yin deficient situation.

When constitution is the cause, we generally have a more yang deficient condition to begin with. Whereas this person will feel enervated for much of his or her life and be very easily tired by exertion, in certain respects, he will be less vulnerable to severe illness because the energy depletion will stop him from overworking and generally give him a chance to recuperate, thus interrupting the process that could lead to serious disease. These people are exquisitely in touch with the disease process. On the other hand, those who are yin deficient do not connect their symptoms with their activities and tend to continue those activities to the point of exhaustion, which frequently comes about suddenly, with devastating symptomatology and equally severe disease. I am referring now to conditions such as cancer or coronary artery disease with infarction. Here the person has gone from yin deficiency to yang deficiency, which is almost always accompanied by some kind of collapse.

The functioning of the 'organ system' is to be found over the entire pulse on the left side. In yin deficiency, where the yin (or water) of the body is being depleted, all three pulses on the left side will be Thin and Tight to Wiry, like one continuous line. Thinness means blood depletion, and the Tightness and Wiry qualities represent yin depletion. When the 'nervous system' is affecting the 'organ system,' one will find this continuous, very Thin, Tight line in the most superficial part of the pulse. With the yin deficient condition, the tongue has a red to magenta body and possibly a thin, yellow coating. Under the eyelid one will see a loss of the distinction of the separate red lines, which are parallel to each other in normal circumstances, and a certain amount of confluence, depending on the degree of heat from deficiency.

With yang deficiency, the entire pulse on the left side will be Deep and, in the beginning, perhaps a little Wide and Diffuse, while later, extremely Feeble-Absent. The tongue will be pale, possibly with a thin, milky-white coating and some teeth marks. The eyes will tend to show a lack of spirit in the pupils, and under the eyelids there will be paleness. In yang deficiency, the entire face may show pallor.

Tai Yang: The 'Nervous System'

The 'nervous system' is simply another name for what is generally considered Tai Yang, that is, the outermost energy of the body, which in some ways might also be equated with the *wei* qi, or defensive energy of the body. It is this outermost defensive layer of energy that is first affected by 'pernicious influences.' In our time, pernicious influences might also include daily living habits. If the Tai Yang, or 'nervous system,' is vulnerable, eating too fast will more easily affect the nerves of the 'digestive system.' Overexercising will affect the nerves related to the 'circulatory system,' and overwork the nerves of the Zang (solid) organs. It is my personal impression that Dr. Shen's association of the 'nervous system' with Tai Yang, or the outermost, light, and most volatile of all energy (qi), is partially an association with the relative rapidity of the 'nervous system' impulses (electrical) compared with the others (humoral).

The integrity of the 'nervous system' is the primary factor in the etiology of all psychological disorders. No matter what the stress may be, if the 'nervous system' is vulnerable, there will inevitably be some kind of psychological disorder, and these disorders come relatively easily. On the other hand, if this level of energy, which Dr. Shen calls the 'nervous system,' is strong, the stress is more likely to produce a physical illness than one which has psychological components, except, perhaps, as an eventual reaction to the physical illness should it last long enough or be serious enough. For example, a person who suddenly discovers that he has cancer may experience significant emotional shock, though how he ultimately handles this discovery would again depend on the strength of the 'nervous system.' With sufficient stress, even an extraordinarily healthy 'nervous system' may develop severe psychological problems. This is quite clear during war, when people who are otherwise emotionally extremely stable break down due to impossible physical and emotional strain. In other words, everyone has their psychological breaking point, no matter how healthy their 'nervous system' may be to begin with.

Western psychologists have always found it difficult to explain why, under similar circumstances, people who appear relatively equal respond so differently on the psychological level. Why, for example, do people raised in the same family, under very similar conditions, develop different psychological patterns? The concept of systems, according to Dr. Shen, brings some order to this area of confusion. Let us again take a situation of extreme stress, such as war. In my own experience during World War II, I observed responses to severe stress that more or less fit into this notion of the four systems. Some people had mental breakdowns, some fainted, some had gastrointestinal reactions such as vomiting or diarrhea. More rarely, there were people who seemed to simply die of fright, undoubtedly from cardiac arrest. Those who broke down mentally had vulnerable 'nervous systems.' Those who fainted had difficulties with their 'circulatory system.' Those who had reactions of vomiting or diarrhea had difficulty on the level of the 'digestive system,' and those who died suddenly from cardiac arrest, from what seemed like severe shock or fright, undoubtedly had some kind of susceptibility (anomaly, e.g., aneurysm-formen ovale), probably of a constitutional nature (since they were so young), in their 'organ system.'

In addition to these factors which influence the 'nervous system,' there are interactions among the different systems. In the event of more or less equal integrity of these systems, stress, whether it is chemical, physical, or emotional, will move from the most superficial to the deepest very much in the order described in the *Shang Han Lun (Discussion of Cold Damage)* for the progress of cold from superficial to deep. If there is stress and the Tai Yang 'nervous system' is intact, there will be no psychological problems, but nervous innervation of the circulatory, digestive, and organ systems will be affected in that order. In other words, if we have a system that is vulnerable, stress will bypass the systems that are relatively intact and go directly to the weaker system. In that vulnerable system it would again affect the outermost layers first, then progressively move deeper. For example, if some kind of stress bypasses the 'nervous' and 'circulatory' systems and goes directly to the 'digestive system,' the first part of the 'digestive system' to be affected will be its nervous innervation. Later, the circulatory aspects of the 'digestive system,' and finally the parenchyma itself, or the organ, will be affected. In order to tell whether or not the 'nervous system' has played a part in a problem of the 'digestive system,' one may look to the left side of the pulse, which would tend to be Tight and somewhat more Superficial than the right side. The latter will be either Deficient, if one's eating habits are irregular, or Tight, if ingestion is too fast.

Another issue that has always plagued the field of psychology concerns the relationship between different kinds and different degrees of mental illness. For example, there are mental illunesses generally subsumed under the heading of neurosis, those under the heading of psychosis, and those that are considered 'organic.' There are many factors determining the form of an emotional disturbance. Variations in the quality and quantity of the Tai Yang 'nervous system' energy may be one approach to the problem, which may shed some light on these distinctions.

I have mentioned earlier that traditional Western medicine and psychology view psychosomatic illness as a sign of a weak 'nervous system.'

This view holds that psychosomatic symptoms appear when a person is unable to cope with emotional stress.

I repeat for emphasis that quite to the contrary, psychosomatic symptoms occur in a person whose 'nervous system' is, at least at first, relatively intact. Let us consider for a moment a child under great emotional stress. In most situations of this sort, an emotional reaction to the stress would aggravate rather than resolve the problem. The child who reacts emotionally to an abusive parent is in far worse trouble than one who reacts with some kind of physical illness. It is a strong 'nervous system' which, under circumstances adverse to healthy emotional outlet, is able to contain itself to physical symptoms in the service of survival.

If, of course, the conditions are optimal and the 'nervous system' is very strong, one would prefer to deal with stress using the verbal communicative energies of Fire, or the physical expressions of Wood, rather than the defensive restorative maneuver of somatization.

It is our intention here to discuss the 'nervous system' in depth in terms of the many factors that influence its integrity and its relationship to the entire organism. One word first on the more traditional view of the 'mind' in Chinese medicine. The 'nervous system' is one of the five 'singular' organs arising from the ancestral (yuan) energy, akin to Kidney essence (jing), which provides the 'marrow' substance of the 'nervous system'. It is one of two sources of a reservoir of energy for the 'nervous system'. The second is called 'mental energy' and is one of the five 'functional energies' that stem from the 'five tastes', which are stored and distributed by the Spleen energies. Each organ also makes a direct contribution. The distinction between the two is that the former, the marrow, is concerned with Kidney energies and with the material foundation of brain activity. The latter is concerned with Heart energies, with the more ephemeral activity of mind and spirit. Kidney yang provides the yang qi of the body, the heat for basal metabolism which fires the 'nervous system'. Liver blood nourishes the peripheral nervous system. The Metal gives structure, and the Heart 'controls' the mind, which to me means the 'conscious' mind. Little on this subject is available in English.

FACTORS THAT INFLUENCE THE TAI YANG 'NERVOUS SYSTEM': AGE OF ONSET

We will begin our consideration of factors that influence the Tai Yang, or the 'nervous system', with a discussion of the age at which the factor becomes an etiologically significant event. We will consider genetic issues, such as constitution, parturition, delivery, early life from ages zero to ten, pre-adolescence, adolescence, and those factors that affect the growing organism prior to the cessation of physical growth.

{ 313 }

Why is it important to consider the era of life or age of onset? Most people suffering with some kind of problem, whether psychological or physical, are enormously confused about its relationship to their life. The thrust of our society is to pressure people into overcoming their handicaps through force of will. When they are unable to do this, they are not only criticized from the outside, but also generally inwardly as well begin to feel extremely unworthy. A good deal of self-hatred develops in the course of time, due to this kind of conflict. The person who is handicapped attempts to break out of the handicap, or overcome it, and finds that he or she is constantly defeated. Frustration, despair, and depression follow and further poison his existence.

One important value of Chinese diagnosis is that it can differentiate for the patient those things about which he himself can do something, such as current life patterns that he can change, from those things that are intrinsic and inherent, due to constitution, congenital problems, or very early life trauma, which he does not have power to change. When a person becomes clear about what he can and cannot do, energy that had previously gone into irrelevant guilt is now available for the assumption of real responsibility in more productive areas. Some of this misdirected energy can be wholly, or partially, redirected with outside help, and some cannot; but with this information the patient has, for the first time, an opportunity to develop a life plan that is based on reality and minimizes inner suffering.

Needless to say, the skill required to make these distinctions is acquired only over a long period of study and practice. This book is not intended to train people in that skill, which, in my opinion, can come only from following a master, but rather to call attention to the important issues one should consider in making such a diagnosis.

Constitutional and Genetic Factors

Genetic indispositions generate a wide range of imbalanced states, usually of the 'nervous system,' sometimes of the 'organ system' (more often the Heart and the Kidneys), and occasionally of the digestive or circulatory 'systems.' Effects may be so catastrophic as to threaten life itself, as with an encephalic infant. The incidence of these kinds of defects is yet to be fully appreciated by Western medicine. Hampered by a relatively gross diagnostic system, neurophysiologists do not have the tools with which to define genetic defects that produce subtle physical and, particularly, personality changes that physicians observe in their practice and find so resistant to any kind of conventional intervention. Chinese medicine does offer refined diagnostic tools that can be helpful in differentiating constitutional 'nervous system' disorders from those whose etiology occurs at a later date.

Kidney yin essence is the energy system of the body most related to the vicissitudes of the Tai Yang 'nervous system.' Kidney yin essence makes the 'marrow,' which is the counterpart of the Western central nervous system. Chinese medicine considers all constitutional or genetic defects as arising principally from a fundamental fault in this energy system, which, in the post-embryonic years, is referred to as *jing* energy. There are, generally speaking, two kinds of constitutional defects related to the 'nervous system.' The first is called 'nervous system weak' and the second 'nervous system tense.'

'Nervous System Weak'

The symptoms of constitutionally derived 'nervous system weak' begin in early childhood and remain until death. In addition to fatigue, these people will complain throughout their lives that they cannot think clearly. They describe themselves as living in some kind of fog a good deal of the time, though they are often very creative and extremely bright. One such person, with an I.Q. of 159, described his condition as being "not present." They complain of vague pains and discomfort, which shift from one area of the body to another, and dysfunctional episodes in almost all of the systems classified by Western medicine, such as the urogenital, gastrointestinal, endocrine, ophthalmological, gynecological, and pulmonary, as well as neurological. Sleep patterns may be reversed in some, and with others they may be perfectly normal; they may shift within one individual from time to time. In addition to being easily fatigued, there may be palpitations, shortness of breath, and excessive perspiration. Symptoms are constantly changing, and the more often they change, the more serious the defect (probably of constitutional origin). Western medicine is unable to find signs that will lead to specific physical diagnosis. Terms such as neurasthenia were most commonly used in the past to describe the condition, though some people were classified as schizophrenic. These are borderline people, who make their way through life to some extent as shadows, and who may suffer from episodic psychotic breaks that seem to have some kind of rhythm. The individual is shy, emotionally vulnerable to his peers to whom he easily falls victim, is easily disturbed, and unstable from childhood, at which time he sometimes appears sickly and unable to physically compete with children his own age. Some of these people will have been classified according to DSM-II as having "pathological hatred": an enduring, unmitigating hatred for someone all of their life about whom they are also paranoid and by whom they feel threatened. In my experience, they may frequently be free of many of the minor ailments that afflict mankind, such as the common cold; however, they often die relatively young. In the past, it might have been from tuberculosis and, in our time, often from neoplastic disease. More recently, alternative medicines have defined classifications of disease such as hypoglycemia, hypothyroid, candidiasis, food allergies and other ecological diseases, Epstein-Barr virus, and the acquired immune deficiencies in which these people have finally found a medical place.

{315}

Diagnostically, the face is generally pale with a bluish-green color, especially around the chin and mouth, and often around the nose and between the eyes. The depth of the color is a measure of the seriousness of the problem. There may be a single line of varying depth between the eyebrows, and the color within that line will be rather dull. Skin on the entire body may be relatively thin and transparent; and, frequently, the person's overall demeanor suggests strangeness. They often appear ill-at-ease and wear dark glasses. One frequently senses that they are not all completely there, and that if one reached out, one might even be able to put one's hand through them. In other words, there is a suggestion of a ghostlike quality. Therapists in particular have reported feeling the hair on the back of their own necks rise in the presence of such people, which they use as a diagnostic tool. Milder degrees of this condition may have their origins in difficult childhoods, the subject of a psychoanalytic literature too vast to discuss in this context.

According to Dr. Shen, but outside my own experience, in the beginning the entire pulse is a little Floating, since the 'nervous system' is on top. The rate may vary anywhere from 88 to 120. The higher the rate, the more serious the problem. At the same time there may be a very fine Superficial Vibration over the entire pulse and, frequently, the Kidney pulse is weaker than the others. This is related to Kidney essence as a critical factor in the development of the 'nervous system' and as a measure of constitutional weakness, especially when it appears in the younger person. Gradually, the 'organ system' is affected, and especially the left side of the pulse is Deeper with Reduced Substance and Thin, finally Feeble-Absent, with a Tight quality at the surface. Over a longer period of time, the rate may become slower as the 'nervous system' affects the 'circulatory system,' and the pulse may become thinner and weaker on the left side as the 'organ system' is affected.

If the 'organ system' is affecting the 'nervous system,' the left side of the pulse will be more deficient than the rest of the pulse, and the first symptoms will be fatigue rather than nervousness. In most cases where the primary etiology is with the 'nervous system,' the tongue and the eyes will be relatively clear and the most significant complaint will be nervousness.

The Case of the Sick Relation

K. was a fifty-seven-year-old woman who was generally too weak to come to my office, and whom I usually visited in her home. She had had all of the above complaints of severe exhaustion, low blood pressure, shortness of breath, palpitations, migrating pains and discomfort, skin rashes, insomnia, and general malaise. At the time we met, her chief complaint was hyperventilation.

Conventional medical examinations were unremarkable. Chinese diagnosis indicated Kidney, blood, and qi deficiency of the Heart, with a Rapid heart rate, Flatness of the Heart and Lung pulse, and weakness of the rest. Her tongue showed a vertical line and some heat.

Although she had a successful career as a young woman, she had retreated into this maze of physical complaints before she was thirty years old, because, she claimed, she was just too weak. The evidence from history supplied by relatives who cared for her was that she had always been on the fragile side, and, as indicated by the Flatness of the Heart and Lung pulse, had become markedly dysfunctional after a severe disappointment in love many years before. Although she would not acknowledge any serious improvement in her condition, she was last seen as a relatively vigorous hostess to a large party of affluent people. Apparently she was either somewhat better or led a double life. I suspect a little of both. Any admission to herself of being better would have interfered with a lifetime patterned on being the sick relation, which, incidentally, in the sense of having a constitutionally weak 'nervous system,' she certainly was.

'Nervous System Tense'

When the constitutional 'nervous system' dysfunction is 'nervous system tense,' we find a person who throughout his entire life is extremely tense even under the most favorable circumstances when there is little or no stress, even while he is asleep. Often, there is a family history of tension of a very similar nature. It would, of course, be arguable that this tension is the result of living with tense people, that tension is self-perpetuating. Nervous system tense people have a uniformly Tense quality over the entire pulse and moderate Robust Pounding. If the origin is constitutional, the pulse tends to be a little Slow, and if from life experience, a little Rapid. With a constitutional origin the eyebrows will be rather thick and it will be difficult to see the roots; this is accompanied by impulsivity. The tongue and the eyes are clear.

CONGENITAL DISORDERS OCCURRING DURING PREGNANCY

Congenital defects are those that occur either during pregnancy or at birth. Our first concern is with those occurring during pregnancy. Speaking generally, disorders of the 'nervous system' that fall into this category are due to one of six causes: malnutrition, substance abuse, emotional stress, excessive physical activity, serious illness, and noise.

Malnutrition

Malnutrition is found in the Western world primarily in adolescents, especially girls who diet. In other parts of the world, however, malnutrition is still a major cause of lifelong 'nervous system' disturbances in the offspring of those suffering from this condition.

Substance Abuse

A more recent and growing problem is one of substance abuse. This encompasses a wide variety of drugs, including alcohol, nicotine, caffeine. A middle-aged woman in my practice came with a Liver pulse showing the characteristic Thin, hard quality of one who has been exposed to chronic alcohol abuse for a relatively long period of time. Her symptoms were mostly related to defects in the Liver organ system including a general, ongoing angry stance toward life. Although this patient had no significant history of alcohol intake, her mother drank to excess while pregnant with her. It is my conjecture that the Liver problem was congenital and the result of alcohol passing the placental barrier and entering the fetal circulation.

Since the advent of the industrial revolution, the number of teratogens to which pregnant women are exposed is overwhelming. It is suspected that pregnant women who work as computer programmers and sit in front of a computer eight hours a day show a higher incidence of congenital defects in their offspring than occurs in the general population. The problem, as we shall see later, is incalculable.

Emotional Stress

Another area of increasing intensity in our time is emotional stress. Obviously, our ancestors' lives were encumbered with enormous physical stress. We have little information, however, about the kinds of emotional stress to which they were constantly and continually exposed. We do know that the psyche of primitive society operated in a very inflexible mold of mores and taboos designed to evoke the protection of helpful spirits against all of the endless dangers, both material and ethereal, by which they felt threatened. Until recently, our own churches served the same purpose as the "opiate of the masses," as a buffer between stress and the individual. Western society today has nothing but powerful and dangerous chemicals to offer for this purpose, once so well served by tradition, the shaman, and the priest. We have lost our innocence and our peace.

Increased communication has resulted in an ever-increasing pace of life, which, by itself, contains a degree of stress previously nonexistent in this world, and which, in my opinion, is beyond the healing powers of ancient practices. Pregnant women who continue to work are under constant pressures of time and space to produce. Time is money.

More often than not, mothers of children who have some kind of Tai Yang 'nervous system' problem will deny any severe emotional upset during their pregnancy until they are questioned about it in some detail. People tend to forget unpleasant things. For example, parents who I interviewed recently had totally put out of their minds the fact that the wife had become pregnant prior to her marriage, and that, as she was from an extremely conservative family, enormous repercussions of an emotional nature had resulted.

Excessive Physical Activity

Another area that is frequently underrated in terms of its effect on the fetus is the mother's physical activity during pregnancy. For example, pregnant women who sit in very cramped positions while practicing yoga and meditation, or women who continue to do work which necessitates sitting at desks for long periods of time, will adversely affect the respiratory system of the fetus, a condition that will remain throughout life. I had a patient in whom the pulse rate on the two sides of the body was different. This was a woman who had been born a month prematurely and had spent the first month of her life in an incubator. Her mother was a dancer who danced up to the day of delivery. Her daughter has had respiratory problems throughout her entire life.

Serious Illness

I have seen a number of children with 'nervous system' disorders whose mothers have had a history of being severely ill during pregnancy. The most common illness that leads to these kinds of defects is toxemia of pregnancy. This illness involves unremitting and ever-increasing water retention (edema) and consequent hypertension. In Chinese medicine this is known as 'water poison.' The primary defects that result are in the Kidneys and sometimes the Spleen. At our stage of knowledge, we can say little about the direct effect of this condition on the fetus, though recently, fetal anoxia is associated with toxemia of pregnancy (eclampsia). Since circulation is critical to the integrity of the fetus, we can say with some assurance that any change in blood pressure of the mother will compromise the exchange at the placenta. We can also postulate that impurities in the mother's blood that are not being cleared by her Kidneys present a potential danger to the fetus. These would include substances such as renin, which is present in some forms of hypertension and could lead to hypertension in the fetus if passed across the placental barrier. Any severe illness will, of course, have a deleterious effect on circulation in the placenta, and certainly any kind of physical trauma is bound to have a profound effect of this nature and will clearly influence the fetus.

Noise

Another source of stress in our time, which some investigators (such as John Diamond, M.D.[4]) have studied in terms of its effect on the human organism, is noise. For millions of years, humans have lived in a world filled with extremely gentle sounds. Loud noise was usually associated with some kind of danger and usually created fear and panic. The relative stillness of the world was interrupted only by thunder and lightning, and, very occasionally, by the eruption of a volcano or the disruption of an earthquake. The noise to which modern man is subject is incredible. Much of it is by choice. Witness, for example, the astounding increase in the decibel level of music from the waltzes of Johann Strauss through the Big Band era to the cacophony of hard rock.

Congenital Damage Occurring During Delivery

Congenital disorders have either a natural or an iatrogenic etiology. In the realm of natural causes, there is either prolonged labor, improper position of the fetus, excessively narrow outlet, deformation of the placenta, a weak uterus, or a variety of problems with the umbilical cord.

We can assume that any of the above problems, and most of those which will be mentioned under the aegis of iatrogenic, will affect respiration or represent a delay in the onset of normal respiration while, at the same time, creating enormous circulatory distress in the placenta. In Chinese terms, one would say that the qi has been trapped in the Lungs. This may lead to a wide variety of respiratory and allergic disorders in infancy and later in life. All of this is complicated by the common practice of slapping the baby on the back at birth, at which point the qi, trapped in the Lungs, will cause qi stagnation in the Heart. In addition, therefore, to the chronic Lung problems of infancy, childhood, and adulthood, the effect on the Heart, experienced as shock, will cause nervousness, irritability, restless sleep, and low energy in the child.

In this connection, a study published in *The Lancet* conducted by Lee Salk, Ph.D., of the Psychiatry Department of Cornell University Medical College, along with several colleagues,[5] claims to have found a link between respiratory distress for more than one hour at birth and the increased incidence of adolescent suicide. Other factors also related were the absence of prenatal care before the twentieth week of pregnancy and chronic disease in the mother during the pregnancy. All of this would make absolute sense in the Chinese system inasmuch as the Lungs are directly associated with the emotion of sadness.

Any impediment to the complete oxygenation of the blood will have its primary effect on the nervous system, since, as is well known, it is more dependent on oxygenation for its integrity than any other organ of the body. With oxygen deprivation, the brain dies before the rest of the organism. This is another way of looking at Dr. Shen's concept of the Tai Yang 'nervous system' as being the outer perimeter, the most sensitive energy, and the first to be affected by stress from any trauma. Damage during delivery to any of the organs that deal with circulation of oxygen to the central nervous system will, therefore, have a direct effect upon it.

Natural Causes

Let us examine two situations that may occur during delivery which result in relatively clear-cut syndromes that may be discerned in the adult. Both affect the Heart, and both involve prolonged, or delayed, deliveries. The first involves the situation of a delayed delivery during which the head remains inside the birth canal and is called *trapped qi in the Heart* ('Heart full'). In many cases this is due to a breech presentation that cannot be corrected, or labor, induced for the convenience of the obstetrician (a common practice in the 1950s), which does not proceed at the proper pace. The second, called *Heart blood stagnation* ('Heart small)', is due to prolonged delivery in which the head is outside. Usually, this situation involves a cord problem. In between is a discussion of *severe Heart qi deficiency* ('Heart large'), which may be a long-term consequence of the other two disorders.

• Trapped Qi in the Heart ('Heart Full')

This is a condition in which the qi is unable to exit the Heart. There is no known TCM term for this condition, but in quasi-biomedical terms, it would be a very slight energetic enlargement of the heart undetected by x-ray, and might also accompany incipient hypertension.

It manifests on the pulse as an Inflated quality at the left distal position. When the condition is less serious, the left distal position can be a little Yielding Inflated, and the rate Normal or a little Rapid. According to Dr. Shen, but outside my own experience, when the condition is more serious the left distal position will be Deep, Thin, and Tight, and the rate over the entire pulse will be Rapid.

A minor cause is sudden and very profound repressed anger at a time when a person is extremely active. A more serious etiology is a prolonged birth with the head inside (breech delivery), because it begins at such an early age. Other causes are trauma to the chest, prolonged grief, or after one episode of sudden extreme lifting beyond one's energy, the seriousness of which depends on the degree of the event. Uncorrected, 'Heart full' can develop into either an *enlarged heart* ('Heart large') or hypertension, or both.

Such individuals will feel tired their entire lives, have little energy, and can be rather depressed. They are frequently very quick to anger. These symptoms are similar to, but more severe than, those associated with *Heart blood deficiency* ('Heart weak'). The entire body may be uncomfortable. There is more difficulty lying down on the left side. When more advanced, there may be coughing up of blood because frequently the Lungs become secondarily stagnant due to cardiopulmonary insufficiency from diminished heart function.

- Severe Heart Qi Deficiency ('Heart Large')

This is the equivalent of severe Heart qi deficiency bordering on Heart yang deficiency in TCM, and an enlarged heart in Western medical terms, as evidenced by x-ray. Some of the pulse qualities associated with this condition are Changing Intensity or Qualities, and Rough Vibration at the left distal position. There can be a positive response at the Heart Large position in the area between the left distal and left middle positions, which is very Inflated and/or Rough as one moves the finger from distal to proximal, compared to moving from proximal to distal.

Another pulse sign of the 'Heart large' condition is a Deep, Thin, and Feeble quality with a rate in excess of 100 beats per minute. Dr. Shen associates this sign with prolonged overwork in a person with constitutionally deficient Heart qi. An Interrupted or Intermittent quality may also be present, and the Mitral Valve position may be Slippery. A Tense Hollow Full-Overflowing quality at the left distal position with a rate exceeding 100 beats per minute is another combination associated with the 'Heart large' condition. Dr. Shen associates this with suppressed emotion over a long period of time. An Interrupted or Intermittent quality and Slippery quality at the Mitral Valve position can also be found with both of these latter qualities.

The underlying causes are constitutional Heart qi deficiency, any of the above listed Heart conditions, especially *trapped qi in the Heart* ('Heart full') and *Heart blood stagnation* ('Heart small') with coronary occlusion over a long period of time, and rheumatic heart disease. All of these factors may be exacerbated by chronic, repressed, and profound anger that occurs especially while active.

Also, more common before the advent of child labor laws but still prevalent in the underdeveloped world, is child labor with excessive physical work at an early age, together with malnutrition. With this etiology there is usually an Interrupted or Intermittent rhythm and the pulse is Yielding Hollow.

Symptoms include extreme shortness of breath, especially on exertion, difficulty breathing if lying flat on the back or on the left side, and chronic chest discomfort, as well as extensive fatigue. Hypertension is often present.

> E. was referred to me because she had had a headache every day since the age of five. They increased at the age of twelve when her parents separated, again when she was a senior in high school, and reached the most severe state after she worked for three years as a secretary. She had been everywhere for diagnosis and treatment and had tried every medication and other treatment modality.
>
> Examination revealed prominent blue veins in both temples and white around her nose and mouth, indicating some kind of birth trauma. When presented with this possibility, she recalled her mother telling her that she had been a breech presentation and that the delivery was very difficult. It was also of interest that her pulse rate was 110 and the tip of her tongue was very red, indicating some Heart involvement, and possibly the condition *trapped qi in the Heart* ('Heart full'). This could not be ascertained because her pulse was uniformly pounding and individual positions could not be accurately read. I saw her only twice.
>
> She is one of many women whom I have seen who had lifelong headaches with a history of birth trauma. Most of them have also shown some kind of Heart energy deficits. These headaches are very resistant to any intervention, including Chinese medicine. In the course of therapy, many things may improve, but the headaches in these women have been only moderately mitigated.

• Heart Blood Stagnation ('Heart Small')

The closest TCM term for 'Heart small' would be *Heart blood stagnation*, and the closest condition in Western medicine would be coronary artery occlusion. There is a mild and temporary and a serious and enduring form. With the mild and temporary form, this pattern is usually the result of a sudden shock during which the heart contracts, constricting the arteries of the heart. The constriction of these vessels due to shock deprives the Heart of qi and blood, leading to transient blood stagnation in the coronary arteries and capillaries, and an insufficient oxygen supply to the coronary muscle. The cardiac muscles are tense, the coronary arteries are in spasm, and breathing is difficult. In Dr. Shen's words, the Heart is "suffocating." The left distal position can be extremely Flat.

With the more serious form the pulse becomes very Deep, Thin, and Feeble. The rate is Normal, slightly Rapid, or slightly Slow. Less often, a Choppy quality has been observed here in the presence of this condition. The condition of 'Heart small' is permanent unless treated, and is equated by Dr. Shen with what he calls "true heart disease," by which he means coronary artery disease.

The etiology of the more serious 'Heart small' condition is a profound shock at birth when there is prolonged labor and the head has already reached the outside of the birth canal, but is being held back by something like the cord around the neck of the infant.

Prolonged fear and unexpressed anger may also lead to this condition, though these emotions may also be the consequence, since one finds in people with the 'Heart small' condition a lifelong, unexpressed, and unexplained fear, and some anger and tension. Night terrors and being easily startled are common complaints. There is shortness of breath, in which it is easy to expel air and difficult to take it in. There may be chest pain, usually of a needle-like or stabbing quality in one spot, in the left shoulder and/or down the left arm. Other symptoms are palpitations and cold extremities.

Iatrogenic Factors

Iatrogenic factors, such as high forceps, excessive sedation, and premature induction have profound effects on the central nervous system for essentially the same reasons we have already discussed, in terms of nourishment to the nervous system. An increasingly common event is delivery by caesarian section. While it is obvious that much trauma to both mother and child is eliminated through this procedure, there are many unknown factors. We know nothing about the premature separation from the placenta or what the importance of the journey through the birth canal means to the mental and physical evolution of the individual or to the child-mother relationship. How does the absence of the struggle to emerge and separate affect all of the issues of coping with pain, bonding, boundaries, and the expansion of bonds during separation? Throughout my career as a psychiatrist, and particularly as a child psychiatrist, I was impressed by the wide range of soft neurological problems (including most of the learning difficulties) I encountered that I felt could be traced back directly to parturition.

Defects in Abstract Thinking

A group of people who have especially impressed me are those who, from early childhood, and throughout their entire lives, are extraordinarily literal and incapable of abstract thinking. This literalness becomes a severe handicap, particularly in adolescence, when interpersonal relations shift outside of home and become more complex. Subtle shadings in communication are lost, misunderstandings proliferate; a sense of isolation, victimization, and confusion leads to severe emotional and interpersonal problems. Along with this literalness, a sense of humor fails to develop. Gradually, these people feel, for all of these reasons, that the world is a confusing and dangerous place. Other people are seen as the enemy. Ultimately, paranoid states develop, accompanied by unprovoked violence when the person feels very much under siege and as though the danger they feel may escalate at any moment, requiring some kind of self-protective attack.

Learning and Personality Disorders

In the eight years I spent as director of a child guidance clinic, I was overwhelmed by the number of children with very subtle kinds of learning and personality disorders which I did not feel could be accounted for by their home life. My suspicion grew that this problem involved a far greater percentage of the population of the mental health clinic than I originally understood. I attempted to get statistics from the public schools in the district on the number of children who were experienced by their teachers as having some kind of significant learning disability. Schools were extremely reluctant to give out this information. It took me literally eight years to get it; and when I did, there was a record that showed very clearly that over fifty percent of the children in each class had significant learning difficulties, which had existed from the beginning of the educational process. The reasons given for not wanting to reveal this information were, first, that if it were acknowledged, the educational system would not be able to function, and second, that there would not be enough funding available for the rehabilitation of so many children requiring special classes and special teaching methods. Throughout the years I have met other health professionals who shared my impressions. Those children who came to my attention in the clinic and who were investigated all had histories of stress during the mother's pregnancy, and both natural and iatrogenic trauma during the birth process.

It is important to realize that the permutations and combinations of damage to the central nervous system that could occur through the processes we have just discussed are endless and that the results, in terms of function and personality, will, likewise, be endless. I believe it is important for us to begin to recognize more fully than we do this terrible devastation that we are wreaking on future generations.

Chinese medicine offers some hope and can provide both herbs and acupuncture, which may help to ameliorate some of the effects of constitutional and congenital problems. For example, shock and trauma during pregnancy, at birth, and shortly afterwards has been treated retroactively and successfully with the use of such herbs as Yunnan Bai Yo and variations of Sheng Mai San that reverse the effects of shock on the Heart and circulation. Qi gong likewise will help strengthen the Kidneys that are always damaged with such early distress. In addition, constitutional points are used quite routinely by the Japanese and Koreans in the treatment of many diseases. Apart from the general points for treating a disease such as asthma and the specific organ that may be contributing to it, these constitutional points are always included. When the 'nervous system' is 'weak' one would tend to build energy using techniques such as moxa and tonic types of herbs. For the patient whom we have described as 'tense,' treatment would be aimed more towards relaxation and balance, and sedating herbs would be used. Naturally, any other organ or system deficiency or excess should be simultaneously treated. In Chinese medicine, all things are related and interconnected. Treatment of the 'nervous system,' therefore, must be global in approach.

Early Life

Early life experiences that affect the 'nervous system' are relatively serious, inasmuch as this is a time when the 'nervous system' is still extremely vulnerable and rapid growth is occurring. Similar insults to the 'nervous system' after growth has already ceased are less serious until one reaches old age. The Chinese say that youth "lives on energy." From age twenty to forty, energy steadily increases. After fifty, energy declines; old age "lives on constitution"; one might say the same about very young age.

By 'early life' we are referring to the ages between birth and ten. In the first six months, the 'nervous system' is affected by nursing, by the quality and quantity of human contact, by food, loud noise, and pernicious influences such as wind, cold, wet, heat, and dryness. Later, the premature acceleration of the child's development, especially attempts to have the child stand and walk too early and premature intellectual demands to talk, to read, and to perform, are severe stresses to the 'nervous system.' Excessive exercise beyond the child's energy will affect the 'circulatory system' and, secondarily, the 'nervous system.' Where food is concerned, the Chinese recommend regularity and quiet and say that rice is the best early solid food for children. Chinese custom says that if a baby is "cold thirty percent of the time and hungry thirty percent of the time he will never need to see a doctor," especially if, in the early stages, he is wrapped up carefully and laid on his belly. (This refers to overheating and overfeeding.)

Trauma to the 'nervous system' frequently will be expressed in the early months of infancy in the form of digestive problems, particularly in the form of colic. This is not primarily a 'digestive system' problem, but a 'nervous system' problem. When understood as such and treated with Chinese herbs, it can be effectively healed. Concentration on the Stomach and Intestines alone is unavailing in these situations. With regard to nursing, the Chinese recommend that the mother take a combination of Chinese fish known as Jiju and pig's feet, together with the herb Dang Gui.

Emotional Trauma

Emotional trauma in the first ten years of life is of extreme importance in the development of the Tai Yang 'nervous system' and, consequently, the entire organism. For the individual who has suffered thusly, information from the history, the pulse, the tongue, the eyes, and the face can be pieced together to reveal the occurrences and nature of psychological trauma. One can be relatively accurate about the age at which it has occurred. These early emotional wounds are often buried, and confrontation will evoke only denial. Many times, re-evoking memory of the event and overcoming the denial will enhance a person's overall development. This occurred to a man who was referred to me because he had hurt his knee playing tennis and had been unable to walk without pain. He had submitted unsuccessfully to every kind of treatment available. When I saw him, he was still relatively young (in his late thirties) and appeared in good physical condition, so there had to be some explanation as to why all these other modalities were unsuccessful. On the pulse, the upper burner was Flat and somewhat weak, and the Kidney pulse was relatively weak. The color around his mouth was not blue, ruling out a severe shock before the second year. The Flatness of the upper burner pulse would have resulted, therefore, from a significant disappointment or sadness. Flatness at a point on the upper half of the ear and the degree and quality of the Kidney pulse suggested to me that this disappointment occurred before the age of five. My impression, therefore, was that he had experienced a strong disappointment just before the age of five, which had created the Flat wave in the upper burner positions, affecting his Heart and Lungs. Eventually, this led to an overall effect on circulation and to a partial reduction of blood in the Liver, which stores the blood. The blood stored by the Liver nourishes the ligaments and tendons and is essential to the integrity of this system, as well as to the healing of these tissues. His knee had, in my opinion, failed to heal because of impairment to the general circulation and because the Liver could not deliver sufficient nourishment to the injured area.

I asked this man if he had had a disappointment before the age of five, and he simply stared at me and did not respond. His wife, however, who had brought him for treatment, waited for him to reply and when he did not, she said, "Oh, Barry, you know that your mother died when you were four years old." He had forgotten. He was treated successfully with acupuncture, which, in addition to knee points, included an attempt to open the upper burner through the use of such Bladder points as B-17 *(ge shu)*, B-13 *(fei shu)*, B-15 *(xin shu)*, and B-18 *(gan shu)*; Pericardium points such as P-6 *(nei guan)*, and P-7 *(da ling)*; and Heart points H-5 *(tong li)*, and H-7 *(shen men)*. Moxa was used on B-23 *(shen shu)*, an important Kidney point, to support the lower part of the body.

'Qi is Wild'

Most of the severe Tai Yang 'nervous system' problems that begin in the first ten years of life are related to Heart function. The Heart is extremely important to the integrity of that system, due to its importance to the circulation of oxygen and nourishment across the blood-brain barrier. These Heart-related Tai Yang syndromes may be generally summarized as the 'qi is wild,' a situation in which the yin is unable to control the yang. These problems affecting the Heart may begin at birth with severe shocks or may be associated with very severe deprivation in the early years or very heavy work at an early age, such as used to occur with children working in mines, factories, and farms. Individuals in whom the 'qi is wild' will frequently be severely emotionally unstable and will also often have dissociated experiences in their body. They will feel, and may be described by others, as being "spacey" and will periodically experience great degrees of fatigue. Usually their life is in a shambles, because they are unable to concentrate their thoughts and actions into some kind of truly purposeful, consistent behavior. In psychiatric clinics these people are diagnosed as 'borderline personality,' many bordering on, but not quite, psychotic. All of these conditions, therefore, have a very severe effect on psychological functioning.

The conditions just described, in which the pulse rate is always Irregular, are related to traumas during pregnancy, at birth, and up to the age of ten. Those in which the rate is Irregular only some of the time may be due to severe and prolonged traumas that occurred between the ages of ten and fifteen, or even up to the age of twenty, the approximate time when growth ends. Whatever has created an Irregular pulse has usually occurred before growth stopped; and the more constant the finding, the earlier and greater the trauma. The only other time this pulse is found is in terminally ill people, and it is one of the seven pulses of imminent death.

PRE-ADOLESCENCE AND ADOLESCENCE

During pre-adolescence and adolescence, the overriding issues concern separation, bonding, and individuation. These issues are discussed in the chapters on the Earth phase and the Metal phase, and the reader is referred there for an in-depth discussion.

These are ages of rapid growth and development, during which time any excess will tend to leave a significant impact. It is important to remember again that the 'nervous system' is the last system to develop fully.

Exercise and Food

Exercise is one of the more important etiologies of 'nervous system' Tai Yang disorders during adolescence and pre-adolescence. Exercise beyond one's energy during this period has the most profound effects upon women, who, especially if there is excessive exercise during the menarche, will experience stagnation of qi, leading to circulatory disturbances that manifest as the pre-menstrual syndrome (a form of what was once known as hysteria: the word uterus, in Greek, means hysteria) or stagnation of blood, leading to menstrual pain and to menorrhagia. These conditions, which begin at this time and also include irregular menstruation, amenorrhea, and ultimately infertility, last a lifetime and become increasingly worse unless corrected. The issue of excessive exercise is, therefore, crucial to women during this period.

Many of the symptoms we have described in our discussion of the 'circulatory system' are due to excessive exercise at a young age, which, when suddenly stopped, causes the condition of 'qi is wild.' This occurs in both men and women, but especially in men. Feelings of profound depersonalization (the sense that one's body is not real, is floating and not grounded, especially when lying down) creates severe anxiety. This disorder, which is totally misunderstood in Western medicine, will lead to lifelong emotional problems that are compounded by the treatments offered in the form of drugs and shock therapy.

The long range effect of excessive exercise on circulation is to diminish the circulation, thus affecting the Heart, which, in Chinese medicine, "controls the mind" and leads to poor concentration, easy irritability, general restlessness, and easy exhaustion, all signs of Tai Yang 'nervous system' disorder. By excessive I mean beyond one's energy. In addition, the circulatory problem will lead, frequently, to pseudoarthritic migrating pains, a situation in which the person feels pain when he wakes up in the morning and feels better as he gets moving. This equally misunderstood situation again leads to mistaken interventions with medications that are quite powerful, often causing their own form of mental suffering.

> D. was a twenty-six-year-old man who reported that he had not "felt right" for two years. He reported sinus pressure and pain, headaches, loose bowel movements every other day, pain, gas in the lower abdomen, yeast infections, acne, varying sexual potency, circles under his eyes, and, most of all, mental confusion and "spaciness." A significant aspect of his history was an intense athletic schedule from age fourteen, including strenuous calisthenics, weightlifting, and stretching, until he stopped suddenly at age nineteen. He married at age twenty-three, with a marked increase in sexual activity, stopped school, and went to work. His symptoms began as he resumed exercise in the context of increased sex and overwork. His pulse was Slow, Pounding, and totally Empty.

Another factor in adolescence and pre-adolescence has to do with excessive intake of cold beverages and food, such as ice cream. In women in particular, this leads to stagnation of qi and blood in the lower burner, with often profound effects upon the menstrual cycle, including pre-menstrual syndrome, pre-menstrual and menstrual pain, and diminished blood flow or heavy clotting. Menstrual irregularities can cause severe emotional problems. In the male, the effect is more on the digestive system, creating an irritable bowel, which may sometimes lead to various forms of colitis and concomitant emotional disturbance.

Sex

An extremely important issue during these sensitive years is sex. Sex for a woman during the menarche is always a severe shock, a situation in which she can become easily unbalanced, and another cause for the condition described as 'qi is wild,' with all of the attendant signs and symptoms. In addition, there will be qi and blood stagnation from the shock, which will lead to pre-menstrual syndrome and the other menstrual difficulties mentioned above. For the male, sex during and shortly after puberty is less of a shock, but excessive masturbation will cause a depletion of Kidney yin essence, or *jing*. Immoderate ejaculation gradually erodes the Kidney qi, which is a product of Kidney yin and yang. As Kidney qi decreases, and Kidney yin is concomitantly depleted, the balance between Water and Fire will be altered. The Heart Fire will be out of control and, because the Heart controls the mind, symptoms of irritability, insomnia, poor memory, and impaired concentration will result. This is due to the fact that the Kidney organ system in the adolescent male has not matured to the degree to which it can effect a proper balance with the Fire when there is excessive ejaculation. As a result, adolescence, for these people, is turbulent beyond the normal expectation.

For a girl, masturbation is less of a problem. The *jing*, or energy stored as Kidney yin, is made from the blood. The human female, in contrast to the male, has an excess of blood and recovers quickly from orgasm. The male has a less rich blood supply and recovers more slowly. Sexual intercourse, however, is more of a shock, both physically and mentally, to the as yet incompletely developed female than it is to the male.

The Kidney pulse is the best measure of these activities in adolescence. When it is found to be weak in a young adult, one can assume that there has been some kind of trauma of a relatively severe nature before the age of fifteen. If it is found in a person over the age of fifty to sixty, the weakness will occur more normally, due to the fact that life is work, and all work depletes the Kidneys and Liver. The Kidneys are the foundation constantly providing yin (water) for the substance of metabolism and yang (heat) for the energy of metabolism to the ever-working being. Of course, one always has to consider other signs and symptoms in making a diagnosis, as in the case of the gentleman with the knee problem. In a young person with the symptoms I described above, and a relatively weak Kidney pulse, one may be safe in investigating the sexual area as an etiological issue. A Kidney pulse that is Empty usually indicates a constitutional problem.

Drug Abuse

Another important area in pre-adolescence and adolescence in our time is the incidence of drugs. The brief discussion on Liver yang deficient conditions provides some elaboration on the pathology one may expect to find. For a clearer understanding of this problem, one needs to look at the social setting in which it takes place. In passing, let me state that we have a population of over 250 million people. Approximately 50 million of these are young people. Eighty percent are said to have experimented with drugs at one level or another, and this percentage seems to be increasing every year. By the year 2,000, the majority of people under the age of fifty had experience with drugs. Even now they are becoming the establishment, sitting in our seats of power. Captains of industry smoke pot. Presidents, governors, mayors, ministers, and generals will all have shared in this experience. They have a body of knowledge that was never before available to a maturing generation. It is not simple to know whether this will be for better or worse.

I have observed the effects of marijuana on both the pulse and the life of many people over the years and can testify to specific changes that occur generally. With drugs, the Liver pulse gradually becomes Empty, a yang deficient condition observed after mononucleosis, hepatitis, significant exposure to chemical pollutants, and with lymphomas and other neoplasms affecting the Liver. Life gradually loses a clear focus, the gap between fantasy and reality decreases, and finally the two become reversed. Fantasy is perceived as reality, and reality becomes unreal. Alcohol leaves a Liver pulse that feels like a wire. Its damage to lives needs no elaboration here.

Another factor, discussed in greater depth elsewhere, is the effect of television, computers, and "future shock" not only on our young, but on every 'nervous system' on earth. Pulses are becoming increasingly Tense and Tight, as these factors affect almost every man, woman, and child in the Western world.

TOXICITY

In 1972 a friend of mine crossed the Atlantic in a 19-foot boat. Over the course of 57 days he recorded his experiences in a short book, one of which was that every day of that trip when he put his hand in the water deeper than one foot, he came up with sludge.

During the past fifty years, more and more chemicals are being discovered in our blood that were not there before, including even oil derived from hydrocarbons such as rayon and nylon. While we have been aware of the profound desecration of our environment by the widespread use of fossil fuels, it was not until around the year 2000 that signs began to appear regularly on the pulse in increasing numbers of people. The principal change was the appearance of the Choppy quality over the entire pulse, sometimes more highly concentrated in certain organs, especially the Liver. At first, this was confusing since the Choppy quality is generally regarded as a sign of blood stagnation. Then I learned that many poisons kill by creating irreversible coagulation of blood.

This began with the following patients, in quick succession:

> A young 28-year-old woman had her pulse taken during a pulse workshop prior to hearing her history. It was Choppy throughout. She presented with symptoms of increasingly extreme fatigue since her participation as a soldier in the first Gulf war in 1991, a syndrome denoted as the Gulf War Syndrome. She did not respond to any therapy. After many studies and commissions, the government denied responsibility until recently, when chemicals used during that conflict were identified as etiological agents of the illness.
>
> A second young woman, age 24, appeared shortly after the first with extreme fatigue. She too had failed to respond to any treatments. Her pulse was likewise characterized by Choppiness. At the age of 14 her step-father, as a punishment, forced her to swallow something akin to Drano, which required heroic emergency medical intervention to save her life.

From that time until now, the incidence of Choppiness on the pulse has become epidemic. The poisoning of our environment has reached saturation and has created profound health problems.

ORGAN DYSFUNCTION

At this point we are going to turn our attention to the relationship between the Tai Yang 'nervous system' and the individual internal organs. Western psychosomatic medicine addresses only the effect of emotion on vulnerable organs (organ neurosis). Except for the endocrine system, little is said about the effect of organs on emotion. By contrast, Oriental medicine sees the process as working both ways, but not equally. The pathway from organ to emotion is highly predictable, but less so from emotion to the organ. Therapy in the latter case depends on relaxation, and in the former on removing heat and then building energy.

In general, when there is a Tai Yang 'nervous system' problem, the first organ to be affected will be that which is already the weakest, either from constitution or from life, or from both. If all of the organs are approximately equal in strength, the organ first affected will be the Liver.

Initially, it is the qi or yang energy of the organ (or, in Western terms, the nerves of the organ) that is affected and, in a sense, caused to work overtime. Work requires metabolic heat, which becomes a problem only when a person works beyond their capacity. At this point the organism, or a particular organ, will have difficulty dissipating this heat, which accumulates and becomes 'excess' heat. The body responds by trying to cool and balance the heat with fluids (yin), first depleting the yin of the affected organ, and then the yin of the Kidneys that supply yin to organs that require relief from the heat. When the yin is depleted, a new kind of heat develops which we call heat from deficiency. The deficient yin is unable to anchor the yang, which moves aimlessly away and usually rises because it is lighter in nature; this is caused yang rising and is associated with mild symptoms such as headache. This aimless yang will also attack vulnerable organs such as the Stomach (rebellious Stomach qi) or the Lungs (shortness of breath), or even the Bladder (interstitial urethritis), if that is the most vulnerable area. All of this can arise from overworking the 'nervous system.'

When the qi, or nerves, of an organ are active beyond their ordinary function and capacity, this heat from deficiency appears. For example, if the most vulnerable organ is the Heart, there will initially be stagnation, at first causing heat from excess and eventually heat from deficiency. These stages of the early process are referred to as agitated qi of the Heart, or 'Heart tight' in the words of Dr. Shen. If it is the Stomach qi that is vulnerable to the overworked 'nervous system,' the Stomach will become yin deficient, and we will see gastritis with pain and possibly (ultimately) an ulcer. If it is the Intestine whose qi is overworked leading to yin deficiency, we will first see an irritable colon and, later, spastic colitis.

Looking at it from the other direction, if there is a problem in an organ, it will affect the most vulnerable system (nervous, circulatory, digestive, or organ). Should they all be of equal strength, then we have a situation in which the progression of illness will go from the inside out; that is, the organ will first affect the 'organ system,' due to a loss of its energy contribution. This will affect the 'digestive system,' which will in turn affect the 'circulatory system.' The 'nervous system' will be the last to be affected. This is a relatively slow process, occurring over a considerable period of time. It is due to a progressive loss of nourishment in each system, from the one most yin to the one most yang.

On a less protracted time scale, imbalance of an organ can lead to an emotional disturbance only if the 'nervous system' is already compromised.

Otherwise, the imbalance will be on a more physical level. For example, if the Spleen is weak and the 'nervous system' is strong, one will tend to get digestive problems. Naturally, over a longer period of time, the 'nervous system' may ultimately be affected. However, if the 'nervous system' is precarious, one will first find a person who is thinking too much, is obsessed and preoccupied with his own thoughts, and the physical digestive problems will only be secondary and come at a much later period of time. In other words, the conventional relationship between an organ and an emotional state requires an intermediate step. If the Tai Yang 'nervous system' is not vulnerable, then the result of dysfunction in an 'organ system' will not necessarily lead to the emotional symptom that traditionally corresponds to that organ. In those conditions in which a damaged organ and a vulnerable 'nervous system' are constantly recreating an emotional disorder, relief will never be complete through psychological or spiritual means unless the organ and the 'nervous system' are being treated and healed simultaneously. No matter how much we may concentrate on the emotional problems by means of any one of the many varieties of psychotherapy, the continued dysfunction of an organ and the 'nervous system' will endlessly recreate the emotional imbalance which the psychotherapy is trying to resolve. Successful therapy must be an integrated therapy. There have been a number of instances in my experience where people have come with physical symptoms and worked through powerful emotional problems with extraordinary rapidity, as the energetic, physical side of the problem was resolved. Often, there is a tremendous catharsis of emotion, followed by a rather rapid integration through insight and understanding. It is as if a self-fulfilling negative feedback circuit between perception, interpretation, and behavior is broken so that new experiences, new ideas of a corrective nature, may enter into the system.

CASES OF STRONG AND WEAK 'NERVOUS SYSTEMS'

If the 'nervous system' is assailable, then even a minor problem in an organ can lead to psychological disturbance. If, on the other hand, the 'nervous system' is strong, only a severe organ problem can, over a relatively long period of time, lead to significant psychological disturbance. For example, a 28-year-old patient, who came because of panic attacks and an inability to sleep, had awakened one night approximately three years before and found her 27-year-old husband dead. He had had no previous illness, and this was as complete and sudden a shock as anyone could experience. In her case, the shock was to her Heart, to the organ most vulnerable to shock. Approximately a year-and-a-half later, her infant child died relatively suddenly from an intussusception of the bowel, another sudden and severe shock to her Heart. Throughout both these periods she functioned well and had no symptoms. It was only after being in a very stressful situation that involved settling a chronic struggle between her brother and her mother at the Thanksgiving table that she began to develop psychological symptoms. The two shocks to her Heart had weakened that organ. This was able to affect her 'nervous system' only after the repressed anger, which had affected her Liver, caused heat and the qi from the stagnant food to ascend to the Heart and create a condition in that organ that finally overwhelmed the 'nervous system' and led to significant psychological disturbance.

Another patient I saw at the same time was a young man who had been in a continuous panic since he had eaten a small amount of a psychedelic mushroom several years earlier. This brief experience of strange feelings, along with qi stagnation from a large meal eaten shortly thereafter, left a lasting fear in his mind that he was crazy and led to three years of dependence on psychotropic drugs.

The first patient's 'nervous system' was strong initially, and it took much to affect it. The second patient had a weak 'nervous system' and was highly vulnerable to even a minor stress.

The 'Nervous System' Affects the Organs and Vice Versa

If an organ such as the Heart or the Liver is extremely deficient over a very long period of time, the 'nervous system' will eventually be affected. Each of the organs is essential to the overall energy on which the 'nervous system' depends. The essence (*jing*) of the Kidneys is essential to the development and repair of the 'nervous system,' and to will power, drive, and maturity. Liver blood is particularly important to the peripheral nervous system, and, on the mental level, controls the function of planning. The Heart controls circulation and the conscious mind and thus has a special relationship to the 'nervous system.' The Spleen-Pancreas configuration provides the glucose that is so essential to 'nervous system' functioning. And, of course, the Lungs provide the qi, which, driven by Kidney yang, is the force behind all living systems. If, for example, the Spleen is weak, digestion will gradually break down and symptoms of excessive rumination while eating may develop in middle or old age, even though the 'nervous system' was initially strong. The Pericardium is the defender not only of the Heart but of the entire mental-emotional organism and is essential to the defensibility and adaptability of the 'nervous system.'

One needs to differentiate etiologically between the 'nervous system' affecting the organ, and the organ affecting the 'nervous system.' History, of course, will help in terms of whether or not there were symptoms of organ disharmony before or after there were symptoms related to the 'nervous system.' In other words, the one with the earlier symptoms is more likely to be the prime etiological agent. If fatigue preceded the tension, the primary cause is the 'organ system.' If the tension preceded the fatigue, the origin is in the 'nervous system.' If the history is not available or clear but one finds the entire pulse to be Tight and Rapid and the tongue and eyes normal, then it is more likely that the 'nervous system' is affecting the organ. If one finds only one pulse that is compromised and the tongue and the eyes are not normal, then it is more likely that the organ is the primary factor.

Organ disease may be the result of constitutional predispositions; shock, both physical and emotional; overwork; overexercise; poor nutrition; emotional or chemical stresses over a very long time, or too early in life; poisons from pollution and substance abuse, as well as in the workplace or by accident; and physical trauma, either through accident or iatrogenically induced.

We have already discussed the conditions of yin deficiency and yang deficiency. If an organ is yin deficient, generally the effect on the 'nervous system' is to make it tense, leading to agitation and aggression. If the organ is yang deficient, the effect on the 'nervous system' is to make it weak, leading to more passivity and fear.

Another way in which the organs are important to the 'nervous system' is in connection with pernicious influences such as phlegm, fire, and cold. In order for these influences to affect the 'nervous system,' they must always work first through an organ. Phlegm, for example, is sometimes derived from a combination of dampness and heat from the Spleen-Stomach to the 'nervous system,' usually through the Heart. Likewise, fire comes from the Liver, affecting the 'nervous system' through the Heart.

I will now attempt to deal separately with each organ in its relationship to the 'nervous system,' accepting the general principles that have already been laid out. Though I will not be following a strict format, I will be looking at the organs and their effect on the 'nervous system' primarily in terms of their yang deficient and their yin deficient conditions. Yin deficient conditions generate tension in the 'nervous system,' and yang deficiency weakens the 'nervous system.' Although the yin deficient condition will first develop in the weakest organ, as it progresses it will eventually compromise the Kidneys. At this point one will see the full-blown symptoms of the Kidney yin deficiency such as night sweats, hot palms and soles, malar flush, low grade afternoon fever, dry and recurrent sore throat, dry stools and constipation, dark urine, sore and weak lumbar area and knees, vertigo, emission problems, and tinnitus.

HEART

Mild Heart Qi Agitation ('Heart Vibration')

Vibration over the entire pulse or at individual positions is further differentiated by whether it is transient or consistent, superficial or deep, and rough or smooth. Transient, superficial, and smooth characteristics at the left distal position, or even over the entire pulse, indicates a relatively innocuous process involving passing worries or a tendency to worry which I define as mild *Heart qi agitation* (very mild Heart yin deficiency). This sometimes begins with a very mild emotional shock, and often there is background of very mild Heart qi deficiency.

Consistent Smooth Vibration over the entire pulse is a sign that one is highly susceptible to worry, and will find something to worry about even when there is no reason to. Consistent Vibration which is rougher and deeper over the entire pulse is a sign of shock, guilt, or fear, and at individual positions it indicates parenchymal damage (severe Heart qi-yang deficiency).

Moderate Heart Qi Agitation ('Heart Tight')

This condition is equivalent to mild to moderate *Heart qi agitation*. This is initially a condition of heat from excess of the Heart (Heart fire flaring upward), and later one of Heart yin deficiency.

With heat from excess the left distal position will at first feel Tight in the Pericardium position, as if a strong, sharp point is sticking the middle of the finger with each beat. If the heat becomes overwhelming, the entire position can feel Tense with Robust Pounding. This heat usually has its origins in the Liver, Gallbladder, and Stomach.

With heat from deficiency, Tightness is felt over the entire left distal position. If the condition has existed for a short period of time owing to an emotional shock, the pulse is usually relatively Rapid, between 84-90 beats per minute. Over a much longer period of time, the pulse rate will be slower, as this condition weakens the Heart qi and affects overall circulation. There can also be some coincidental transient, superficial Vibration at the left distal position from time to time, reflecting episodes of worry.

A 'Heart tight' pulse can also be associated with heat from yin deficiency due to overwork of the Heart as it tries to balance the heat from excess in the Liver, Gallbladder, and Stomach, or from worry, from shock, Grave's disease and manic phases of bi-polar disease, and from stimulating drugs and herbs such as cocaine and Ma Huang.

The 'Heart tight' condition associated with heat from excess is marked by symptoms of irritability, tension, and difficulty getting to sleep. With the yin-deficient variety, one is more restless and complains of constant worry, a 'racing mind,' and sleep marked by constant awakening through the night. With both there is mild to moderate anxiety.

Occasionally there will be some discomfort in the left side of the chest over a relatively large area. This discomfort is an early form of mild angina, which is due to heat from excess or stagnant qi migrating to the Pericardium from the Liver, Gallbladder, or Stomach, and causing a mild spasm of the coronary arteries. There may also be some shortness of breath during episodes of anxiety.

Severe Heart Qi Agitation and Mild Yin Deficiency ('Heart Nervous')

This is a condition in which the yin of the Heart is deficient and the qi is consequently agitated, erratic, and mildly deficient; I call it *Heart qi agitation.* Often there is a constitutional predisposition toward Heart qi deficiency.

There are two types. The less serious one is due to prolonged worry, either a 'Heart vibration' or a 'Heart tight' condition, in which the pulse rate tends to be somewhat Rapid, between 80-84 beats per minute. With this type, the person will report feeling nervous. With the second, more serious type, which is due to moderate to strong emotional shock, physical trauma, often at birth and sometimes in utero, there is occasional Change in Rate at Rest, with no missed beats. When the change in rate is large, there is a propensity to panic.

A 'Heart weak' condition (see below) can also cause the more serious 'Heart nervous' pattern, in which case the pulse is generally Deep and Thin and the rate on exertion increases by more than 8-12 beats per minute. On the other hand, a 'Heart nervous' disorder can lead to 'Heart weak.' Smooth Vibration at the Neuro-psychological positions accompanies and is another sign of the 'Heart nervous' condition.

The 'Heart nervous' person will complain of being easily fatigued, especially in the morning when waking. Sleep is restless, marked by frequent wakenings, so that one is in and out of an agitated state of sleep throughout the night. Palpitations may occur occasionally. The person will report frequent and disturbing mood swings, changes of mind about others and the chosen course of one's life, and as if they are on a roller coaster and mildly out of control. There will also be increased irritability of a relatively mild nature.

Mild Heart Yin Deficiency ('Push Pulse' [Hesitant Wave])

This is one of two pulses which Dr. Shen referred to as a 'push pulse.' I put Hesitant Wave in parentheses here, since that is my term and describes how it feels. This quality occurs over the entire pulse, and is found in cases of *Heart yin deficiency* with agitated qi. Descriptively, the pulse wave has lost its normal sine wave form, whereby the flow to and from the wave peak becomes sharp and abrupt instead of gradually rising and falling. The term 'Hesitant' is used because some people experience this quality as faltering or balking, yet not missing a beat.

The Hesitant quality is the form of the 'push pulse' associated with a person who pushes herself mentally, in contrast to the Flooding deficient quality, which is the 'push pulse' associated with a person who pushes herself more physically.

In traditional medical terms, the Hesitant Wave 'push pulse' is closest to mild to moderate *Heart yin deficiency*. I have found that this quality occurs when one has a tendency to think incessantly about one subject. The most extreme form is a monomaniacal obsessive preoccupation with some aspect of life, usually work, in which the person's mind never ceases to rest, even when asleep. This is distinguished from a general tendency to worry about almost anything, real or imagined, which is expressed over the entire pulse by a superficial Smooth Vibration at all depths.

In the early stages, except for the symptom of worry or difficulty in getting to sleep, there are no other related signs or symptoms. Later, the person will seek help because of a strong sense of malaise and a feeling that one cannot keep up the pace one has set for oneself. Individuals with this pulse quality often collapse suddenly, physically and/or emotionally.

Heart Qi Stagnation ('Heart Closed')

The closest one can come to this condition in TCM terms is *stagnation of Heart qi*. In this pattern, a moderately Flat pulse quality is a sign that the qi and blood are slightly stagnant in the Pericardium, and cannot freely reach into the Heart. The reason is that the circulation of qi, and to a lesser extent of blood, to the Heart has been blocked from entering the Heart, usually due to shock. This ultimately leads to Heart qi deficiency and diminished peripheral blood circulation. While with 'Heart nervous' the shock affects the nervous innervation of the heart, with 'Heart closed' the substance of the Heart (the parenchyma) is slightly affected, though much less so than in the case of either 'Heart small' or 'Heart full.'

The shock is most often an emotional one experienced during childhood while the body's qi is still quite immature, and usually involves the loss of someone very close, such as a parent. However, it can occur later in life due to a major emotional shock, such as sudden bad news or the sudden breakup of a romance in which the person withdraws their 'heart' feelings. Other causes include a condition of *Heart qi agitation* ('Heart nervous') over a long period of time, or even a physical shock to the chest. The Flat wave associated with a 'Heart closed' pulse usually occurs in a person whose qi is already deficient or undeveloped.

This type of person seems to be in some kind of constant emotional difficulty. By nature the person tends to be vengeful and spiteful. The spirit of the eyes can seem somewhat withdrawn or angry. The person may experience some chest pain in connection with the closing of qi circulation.

Stagnation of Heart Blood ('Heart Small')

The closest TCM term for this condition would be *stagnation of Heart blood*, and in Western medicine, coronary artery occlusion. There is a mild, temporary and a serious, enduring form of this condition.

With the mild and temporary form this pattern is usually the result of a sudden shock during which the heart contracts, constricting the arteries of the heart. The constriction of these vessels due to shock deprives the Heart of qi and blood, leading to transient blood stagnation in the coronary arteries and capillaries, and an insufficient oxygen supply to the coronary muscle. The cardiac muscles are tense, the coronary arteries are in spasm, and breathing in is difficult. In Dr. Shen's terms, the Heart is "suffocating." The left distal position can be extremely Flat.

With the more serious form the pulse becomes very Deep, Thin, and Feeble. The rate is Normal, slightly Rapid, or slightly Slow. Less often a Choppy quality has been observed here in the presence of this condition. 'Heart small' is permanent unless treated, and is equated by Dr. Shen with what he calls "true heart disease," by which he means coronary artery disease. The etiology of the more serious 'Heart small' condition is a profound shock at birth when there is prolonged labor and the head has already reached the outside of the birth canal, but is being held back by something like the cord around the neck of the infant.

Prolonged fear and unexpressed anger may also lead to this condition, though these emotions may also be the consequence, since one finds in people with the 'Heart small' condition a lifelong, unexpressed, and unexplained fear, and some anger and tension. Night terrors and being easily startled are common complaints. There is shortness of breath, in which it is easy to expel air and difficult to take it in. There may be chest pain, usually of a needle-like or stabbing quality in one spot, in the left shoulder and/or down the left arm. Other symptoms are palpitations and cold extremities.

Heart Blood Deficiency ('Heart Weak')

This condition is one in which the blood of the Heart is deficient, with some consequent Heart qi deficiency, both of which render a deficit in Heart function. The pulse shows a Change in Rate on Exertion of more than 20 beats per minute if the Heart is very blood deficient, and a lesser change (12-20 beats) if the Heart is only slightly blood deficient. The rate may be a little Rapid, Normal, or Slow, depending on the chronicity of the condition: the longer the condition, the slower the rate. The left distal position is often Thin when the blood deficiency is more severe, with Reduced Substance if the Heart qi is deficient.

While constitutional *Heart qi deficiency* is sometimes a predisposing factor, *Heart blood deficiency* is most often due to prolonged and severe *Heart qi agitation* ('Heart nervous'). If this condition continues, the pulse will generally be more Tight and the vessels under the eyes will be normal. However, *Heart blood deficiency* can be due to one or any combination of the following: Kidney essence deficiency, Spleen qi deficiency, and gradual blood loss over time. When blood deficiency is the cause, the entire pulse is Thin and a little Feeble and the vessels inside the lower eyelid are pale.

The patient may experience palpitations throughout the day, especially with activity, because there is not enough blood in the Heart. There will also be a general feeling of weakness, depression, poor concentration, and forgetfulness. The sleep pattern is one of steadily sleeping for a few hours and then waking, but able to return to sleep. One will be tired in the morning. A prolonged 'Heart weak' pattern can lead to Heart qi and yang deficiency, serious Heart disease, such as congestive heart failure.

Trapped Qi in the Heart ('Heart Full')

'Heart full' is a condition in which the *qi is trapped in the Heart*. The patient will feel tired his entire life, have little energy, and be rather depressed. These symptoms will be more severe than in the condition of 'Heart weak.' The patient's entire body may be uncomfortable; he may, at times, cough up blood; there will be discomfort when lying down on the right side; and, frequently, this person is very quick to anger. The pulse, in a less serious situation, may be a little full (Inflated) and a little Rapid, somewhat like the Scallion pulse. When the condition is more serious, the pulse is Deep, Thin, Tight, and very Rapid, frequently over 100 beats per minute. The tongue is red and a little swollen on the end, and the eyes show some confluence of blood vessels inside the lower eyelid. The patient may have difficulty breathing out and less difficulty breathing in, and the face is usually very red. The causes are either prolonged birth with the head inside, frequently in a situation such as a breech delivery, or very profound anger at a time when the individual is extremely active and unable to express the anger. This condition may develop into either an enlarged Heart or hypertension or both.

Heart Conditions and Sleep Patterns

All Heart conditions affect sleep. With *agitated qi of the Heart* (early 'Heart tight'), a condition of heat from excess of the Heart brought on by worry, it is hard to fall asleep. The mind is racing, worried, and the person is restless and uptight. The person who suffers from a condition of *Heart yin deficiency* ('Heart nervous' and/or later 'Heart tight') is restless and up and down all night. Those with *Heart blood deficiency* ('Heart weak') sleep four or five hours, awake, and return to sleep relatively easily. Those who awake after four or five hours and cannot return to sleep have *Heart blood stagnation* ('Heart small'). Those with *Heart qi stagnation* ('Heart closed') cannot sleep at all some nights, being preoccupied with imagined hurts and thoughts of vengeance. Those with *trapped qi in the Heart* ('Heart full') find their bodies to be uncomfortable because they cannot lie flat and wake up to find a more comfortable position. *Heart qi deficiency* finds people up and down all night but not agitated, as with *Heart yin deficiency*. With all of these Heart conditions, people wake up tired, even on nights when they sleep all night.

LIVER

We will examine several conditions of the Liver including qi stagnation, Liver yin deficiency, uprising of the yang, Liver fire, and Liver wind, as well as the yang deficient conditions. All of the ensuing disharmony is the result of stagnation, usually from emotion, overwork, and toxicity. The more severe conditions are due to longer and more profound stagnation.

The Liver is the first line of defense against stress: emotional, physical, and chemical. Constitutionally it is the strongest organ, capable of more work (four-hundred-and-fifty separate chemical actions at any one moment) and of absorbing more abuse (alcohol, drugs, pollution, chemically altered foods) than any other organ. Its strength lies in its capacity to 'store the blood,' which renders it capable of restoring itself, the rest of the body, as well as mind and spirit. When an emotion is a stimulus to the nervous system, Kidney yang (adrenal and thyroid) are alerted, causing the Liver to move the qi and release the blood (stored glycogen to glucose), thereby mobilizing both the mind (Spleen qi goes up) and body (blood nourishes ligaments, tendons, muscles, and nerves). The Liver mediates emotional response released through physical activity, the Lungs through breathing, and the Heart through speech.

If an emotional response is not possible through these normal channels, and the Pericardium energies are called upon for another solution, one of the many restorative maneuvers mentioned in our discussion of the Peridardium will go into action. These strategies range from the most primitive, such as regression, to the most ecologically effective, such as sublimation. Whichever it may be, some sort of suppression or repression of emotion and energy is involved, setting off in the Liver (which moves the qi) the process of 'stagnation.'

Liver Fire Rising

Very severe qi stagnation will eventually lead to a condition known as Liver fire rising, in which we have heat in the blood and an Overflowing pulse. If the nervous system is strong, one will get symptoms such as conjunctivitis, severe headache, portal vein hypertension, general hypertension, and maybe hematemasis, epistaxis, constipation, and a bitter taste in the mouth. If the nervous system is compromised, this condition of fire will reach to the Heart and the mind to create a somewhat irascible personality. If the fire is very strong, a mild, intermittent madness will ensue, such that one day the person seems perfectly normal, and the next day he is clearly mentally disturbed.

Liver Yin Deficiency

Restorative strategies are additional work for the nervous system, as is the tension caused by lack of release for the musculoskeletal system, both of which then call for more nourishment (blood) from the Liver. The Liver is gradually depleted, rendering it unable to promote a free flow of qi, to move the blood, and recover the energy. Circulation of qi and blood is impeded by both the depletion of the Liver and the increased tension in the muscles. This leads to a buildup of 'noxious' or unmoving qi, and to a heating of the blood stored in the Liver which is caused by the 'friction' of two opposing forces: one for free and easy movement, and the other for repression.

If the nervous system is normal, the 'noxious' qi will manifest on a physical level and cause an inability to recover energy and to nourish the ligaments and tendons. The result will be increasing fatigue; musculoskeletal problems, which occur more easily and are more difficult to heal; and easy infection. Menstrual difficulties, such as irregularity, distention, headaches, cramping, and abnormal flows, may occur. Digestion may gradually be affected. The 'noxious' qi may migrate around the body causing one type of arthritis (wind *bi*) or go to one vulnerable area, such as the Heart, and cause palpitations (sino-auricular node) or labile high blood pressure (the carotid sinus). Gradually, the body tends to become weaker, especially if the person continues to overwork.

If the nervous system is vulnerable, first the heat from excess and later the yin deficiency of the Liver will increase tension in the nervous system, creating a situation in which a person is very easily angered and irritated, usually without significant provocation. There may be a stimulus that leads to this, but the reaction is usually distorted. Planning, decision making and judgment, the principal ego function of the Liver-Gallbladder, may be difficult and distorted by lack of patience.

Uprising of the Yang

After a considerable period of yin deficiency (that is, lack of water), the Liver yin cannot control the Liver yang, and the two separate. The Liver yang, now out of control and aimless, and being a lighter substance, tends to rise, creating the condition of uprising of the yang. The following symptoms are noted: the person is easily angered, but more so by real events; he complains of headache, in which the head feels throbbing and distended; vertigo; tinnitus; insomnia; a great deal of dreaming; and tremor and numbness of the extremities.

Liver Wind

The final outcome of Liver stagnation is Liver wind. There are three etiologies of Liver wind, each leading to a different neurological condition. One is due to Liver yang rising (yin deficiency). Conventionally, the associated condition is wind in the channels, or 'little strokes.' In my experience, if these are unchecked, they progress to the blood clot type of cardio-vascular accidents (stroke).

A second type of Liver wind is Liver (Heart) fire, which is akin to the tremendous hot winds that blow out of the Sahara desert and across the Mediterranean to southern France. Liver fire is usually associated with what the Chinese call 'utmost heat,' which is the equivalent of meningitis-encephalitis type symptoms, with delirium and opisthostonos, coma, and death. In my experience it is also responsible for the more serious type of stroke that is due to cerebral hemorrhage (heat in the blood), and is often preceded by life-saving nosebleeds.

The third type of wind is less serious and is due to blood deficiency associated with neurological diseases such as epilepsy and Parkinson's disease.

Liver Yang Deficiency

The principal onset of a yang deficient condition of the Liver is heat from deficiency over a long period of time, such as that caused by over-work, alcohol, or direct damage by hepatitis, mononucleosis, drugs, and (more rarely) insults during pregnancy such as heroin, LSD, and marijuana use. Overlooked is a long-term chronic infection associated with mono-nucleosis. The most common complaint is malaise of varying degrees, and those whose nervous systems are not intact will find themselves relatively aimless and indecisive.

Yang deficient conditions of the Liver lead, in those whose 'nervous systems' that are fairly intact, to diseases such as lymphomas. These are, of course, ultimately fatal, some moving very rapidly, some very slowly. In certain kinds of yang deficient conditions—those that, in my experience, have been caused by the prolonged use of marijuana—people tend to lose their ability to make decisions and plans that are realistic for their own lives and gradually become extremely passive, almost totally indolent, and out of touch with the real world. They live in a world of unrealized dreams; and their judgment, for example of their own creative work, becomes ex-traordinarily distorted. The pulse is Deep, with Reduced Substance and/or Pounding, and Diffuse or Empty, similar to the pulse of a person who has recovered from hepatitis or mononucleosis. The excessive use of these so-called recreational drugs occurs, to begin with, because the Tai Yang 'ner-vous system' is precarious; the inescapable result is its deterioration. I have observed this process all too often.

KIDNEYS

Kidney essence *(jing)* is the energy responsible for the development of the central nervous system. Any deficiency in this essence, especially on the genetic and congenital level, will manifest in some kind of central nervous system defect from either the most subtle personality disorder to the most gross mental or neurological incapacity. It is my impression, after fifty-one years of clinical experience, that the majority of psychological problems we encounter in our daily lives are, to some extent, determined by damage oc-curring to Kidney essence before birth or shortly thereafter. Handicaps that occur at such an early age on a psychological level interfere with the solu-tion of every developmental challenge, escalating and magnifying their im-pact on the 'evolution of being' at each stage. No psychiatric or neurological diagnosis escapes this influence.

Kidney Yang Deficiency

Yang deficient conditions of the Kidneys are usually of a constitutional etiology. They generally weaken the nervous system and tend to make the person susceptible to lifelong endogenous depression and unexplained low self-esteem. Since the Kidney yang is the source of the Spleen yang (the digestive energy), these patients frequently have severe ecological disease with incapacitating allergies to both food and inhalants, further complicating their emotional existence.

Kidney Yin Deficiency

Yin deficient conditions of the Kidneys that develop after birth can generally be attributed to overwork of the central nervous system, especially overuse of the mind (thinking, rumination, worry), a nervous system that may be vulnerable due to earlier insults during pregnancy and at birth. Kidney yin deficiency will lead to a very tense nervous system, a situation in which the person literally appears to be 'wired,' or in a generally agitated state. The person is jittery and fearful, especially of the unknown. In more severe conditions, he may experience terror. The fearfulness develops slowly, in contrast to that which develops after sudden shocks that affect the Heart.

Fear of the unknown triggers, in those who have the capacity, the primitive solution of projecting oneself onto the frightening world, which then becomes more familiar. In addition, this projection contains elements of the 'dark' side of ourselves, which we also know but always wish to expunge. So the best and the worst go out together, and though we may deny one, we really know both. Projection, which manifests itself in what we call paranoia, is the paradox that at once renders the world both more and less frightening, with the fear of the unknown being the greater of the evils to be averted.

STOMACH AND SPLEEN

Stomach Yin Deficiency

Yin deficient conditions of the Earth phase (Spleen and Stomach) generally are of the Stomach and are usually due to eating bad food or eating too fast over a long period of time. This is equivalent to overwork. Again, the yin deficient condition creates tension in the nervous system, as well as tightness in the general upper abdominal epigastric area. The nervous system is impaired in its ability to digest and assimilate ideas. Since the nervous system is tense, these undigested thoughts also tend to have a certain excitement associated with them, making them even more difficult to organize and assimilate properly. Information is stored unevenly, in part because it is incompletely absorbed. It does not 'stick to the gut,' as the saying goes. The incomplete digestion also leads to the absorption of incomplete molecules and to the myriad of slow-acting (IGA) allergies, including those referred to as 'brain allergies.' Since they cannot properly digest thoughts, these people feel empty on a certain level, crave frequent mental stimulation, and need to be constantly intellectually fed. This, of course, has its physical counterpart in the form of food cravings.

Spleen Yang Deficiency

Earth yang deficient conditions generally involve the Spleen. If the nervous system is strong, physical conditions such as loss of appetite, anorexia nervosa, or colitis may ensue. The long-term effect upon the nervous system is generally related to obsessive types of thinking (ruminating), the preoccupation being with food in a negative sense. Ruminating is most harmful to the Spleen when it occurs during mealtime. If the Tai Yang 'nervous system' is vulnerable, people tend to be overly sympathetic and to suffer exceptionally in situations where there is emotional pain. These people are naturally drawn to the helping professions, especially social work, where they tend to 'burn out' rather quickly. The exposure to endless misery drains their yang energies, leaving them vulnerable to many illnesses associated with enervation, such as Chronic Fatigue Syndrome.

Many complain that they feel as if they are in a fog; their heads are heavy, and they are "not all there." They tend to fall asleep easily, especially after meals, when Spleen qi is not available to perform its normal task of moving the qi upward to the head. Another Spleen related mental problem is psychosis and epilepsy, which in Chinese medicine is attributed to phlegm-fire obstructing the openings of the Heart. Since eighty percent of food is water, and since it is the function of Spleen qi to move the water, and Spleen yang to 'mist' it, failure of these energies results in exceptional dampness in the body, which, over a period of time and in conjunction with heat from the Liver, congeals to form phlegm. This phlegm will go to the most vulnerable area of the body. If that area is the Heart, and if the nervous system is compromised, insanity or epilepsy (more severe phlegm-fire) will follow. Spleen yang deficient conditions at a very early age may be associated with problems with bonding and boundaries and difficulties with separation, leading to the general condition of dependent personality. This subject is covered more specifically in the chapter on the Earth phase.

LUNGS

Lung Yang Deficiency

A yang deficient condition of the Lungs generally leads to what could be described as an endogenous sadness, one that is very deeply hidden in the person and can be seen only by looking deeply into their eyes. For it is a sadness with which, unlike Pericardium pain, the person is usually not consciously in touch, until it is evoked by somebody who observes it. These are people who tend to be inexplicably easily injured and hurt emotionally; sometimes they want to cry but do not know why. They cover this and a persistent pessimism with a superficial lightheartedness. Their energy is low, their spirit worn, and they are rarely ever truly happy, without, however, being obviously depressed. Their appearance may, as I have said, be deceptive and this unhappiness may not be easy to read, except very deeply in their eyes.

Frequently, these people will have a great deal of mucus and may possibly be asthmatic or allergic, because the Lungs are weak and cannot perform their job of 'digesting' the dampness and moving it down to the Kidneys. The cause may be constitutional or congenital, severe Lung disease or chest trauma at a very early age, or being forced, at a very young age, to control the natural tendency to cry. Very deep disappointments, without an emotional catharsis and working through the grief, such as the loss of a parent at a very early age when the child is too young for such a process, may also hurt the Lungs by 'killing the qi' in the chest. These are hurts that are very rarely remembered, but which play a significant part in physiology and psychology throughout the person's life. Difficulties with separation and the expansion of bonds (as discussed in the chapter on the Metal phase) are one possibility. The 'killing of the qi' in the chest can interfere with deep breathing and result in poor oxygenation of the blood and mental staleness.

Lung Yin Deficiency

Lung yin deficiency is the result of stagnation of Lung qi due to a cold external pathogenic factor that interferes with the movement of qi in the Lungs. The Lungs attempt to move the stagnant qi and cold by bringing metabolic heat to the Lungs. If they are strong, this metabolic heat will resolve the stagnation. But if the Lungs are not strong enough to overcome the qi stagnation, the heat will accumulate and become heat from excess, which is experienced by the organism as toxic. Dampness (yin) is brought to cool the heat, leading eventually to a condition of damp-heat, a perfect culture medium with vulnerability to deep infections with a productive cough. Eventually, the Lung yin is depleted, ending with a condition of Lung yin heat from deficiency. This is marked by a dry, unproductive cough.

These people tend to be somewhat self-indulgent and attention-seeking. This is often associated with a good deal of jealousy toward those who seem to be getting the attention they want. All of this leads to considerable bonding problems in adolescence, during which time there are also many problems in separating from family and making new relationships with peers. This may result in an adolescent breakdown, which, if poorly handled, may lead to a lifetime of mental illness.

Hollow (Fu) Organs and Ego Functions

Disharmony in the hollow (Fu) organs is generally a reflection of disharmony in the solid (Zang) organs. While recognizing the importance of their functions as conveyors of nutrients to the solid organs, in my view of their more important role in physiology and pathology, the hollow organs function as conduits to the outside world for excesses of heat, dryness, dampness, cold, wind, and fire in their partner solid organs. If the system is functioning, the direction of the elimination of these excesses is downward. Should it fail, the excess will stay put or go up and appear as signs in the head, eyes, ears, mouth, skin, and upper gastrointestinal tract. For example, if the Heart has excess heat, it will be removed by the Small Intestine to the Bladder and excreted in the urine. If the Small Intestine fails, the heat will go to the tongue and face. If there is an excess in the Lungs, it will go to the Large Intestine and leave with the bowel movement. If this fails, it will stay and become bronchitis or asthma, or rise to become a sore throat, sinus problem, or hemoptysis. The Liver excretes bile to the Gallbladder and then through the gastro-intestinal tract to the outside world, partly through the bowel movement and partly through the blood and urine. If these systems fail, the excess rises to become hematemosis or epistaxis, or to become stagnant in the Liver and lead to cirrhosis, or in the Gallbladder and become stones. The Kidney excretes heat through the Bladder to the urine. If this fails, we have stagnation and stones. Spleen excesses go to the Stomach and out by the bowel movement. Failure leads to nausea and vomiting. On the level of the Tai Yang 'nervous system', those organs may be seen as playing a major role in ego orientation. The following discussions assume an already precarious 'nervous system.'

Stomach

One natural ego function of the Stomach energies is to digest and assimilate ideas. Disharmony occurs from ingesting bad food over a long period of time, eating rapidly or irregularly, and leads to stagnation in the Stomach, tightness, a yin deficient condition of heat from deficiency, eventual dryness (no hydrochloric acid), and excitable states in which thoughts become difficult to refine, organize, and process. In other words, these people are unable to break down information into smaller components ('chunking down,' in NLP terms) in order for there to be complete absorption. As mentioned above, these people have great difficulty in having information 'stick to their gut,' leading ultimately to a feeling of emptiness, a craving for stimulation, and, interestingly enough, a craving or compulsion for food. For a discussion of the Stomach in connection with the issues of bonding and boundaries, see Chapter 11.

Large Intestine

The natural function of the Large Intestine is to eliminate impure energy and useless wastes. The ego disharmony here is an inability to eliminate unneeded and unwanted thoughts, leading to stagnation and long-term contamination of the mind with noxious feelings and ideas. These are the people who can never forgive or forget and for whom any ill fate becomes a lifetime preoccupation. They compensate with perfectionist and compulsively clean behavior, are extremists, proselytizers, and stubborn. Their personalities are often described as toxic. For a discussion of the Large Intestine (Lung yang) in connection with the issues of the transformation of bonds, see Chapter 12.

Small Intestine

The Small Intestine's function is partly to eliminate heat from the Heart. In this way alone, it plays an important part in disturbances of the Spirit, where heat alone, or in combination with phlegm, obstructs the Heart orifices causing serious mental illness. Its basic natural function is to separate the pure from the impure: pure ideas from impure ideas. Disharmony here takes the form of confusion in a person who is unable, because he cannot separate the pure from the impure, to find clarity and to establish priorities in his life. (These issues are discussed in the chapter on the Fire phase.) For a discussion of the Small Intestine in connection with issues of the transformation of creative ideas into creations, see Chapter 10. The metaphor is that of the Heart as the creator who imagines a form within a large rock that the Small Intestine transforms into a sculpture.

Gallbladder

The natural function of the Gallbladder in relationship to its solid (Zang) organ, the Liver, is the elimination of toxic wastes, as well as 'evil' influences, from that organ. On a psychological level, its main function is decision making. However, its ability to make decisions depends, to a very large extent, upon the ability of the Stomach to properly digest and assimilate ideas, the ability of the Small Intestine to properly separate them, and the ability of the Large Intestine to eliminate impure ideas. Only after all of this has been done can the Gallbladder, if it is healthy, make its decisions. When the Gallbladder is unhealthy, its effect upon the nervous system and the mind is to create paralyzing ambivalence and, in combination with Heart deficiency, a form of anxiety and insomnia characterized by being easily startled. For a discussion of the Gallbladder (Liver yang) in connection with the issues of advance and retreat, see Chapter 9.

{351}

Triple Burner

The natural function of the Triple Burner on a psychological level is balance, orientation, and socialization. Its function, on the one hand, is to balance the two sides of the brain, and, on the other, to balance the spirit, the soul, and the body. It is responsible for harmony and for family ties. Disharmony results in a disorientation in terms of relationships, broken social and family ties, suspiciousness, and a lack of balance, in which a person may be literally carried away by an idea and unable to place it in its proper context. For a discussion of the Triple Burner in connection with the issue of its control of the thermostat in bi-polar disease, see Chapter 10. It is important to note again the central role that the Triple Burner plays in the entire metabolic cycle, the creation of qi and blood from the ancestral qi to the *ying* (nourishing) and *wei* (protective); the separation of the pure from the impure in the Lungs, Spleen, Stomach, Intestines, and Kidneys as a function of the internal duct; in the control of water metabolism; and its basic function with respect to distributing the source qi to the source points at birth.

Bladder

The Bladder is said to be the keeper of the archives and the energy related to memory. Some say that it "stores the overflow," acting as a reservoir of energy, including mental energy. Disharmony would imply collapse under stress, an inability to cope, and a fear of being submerged and overwhelmed. This sense of inadequacy may make the person overly self-involved to the point of neglecting the care of others.

I have no clinical experience with this phase on a psychological level except for the fact that I use the outside *shu* ("associated") points, along the outer line of the Bladder channel, for the treatment of emotional disorders, as these points correspond to different aspects of the spirit. Pohu, outside of the Lung *shu* point, is the Animal Soul, which is known as 'soul door' and is used in the treatment of anxiety. Each point outside of a *shu* point makes a direct connection with a solid (Zang) organ and has a particular emotional, mental, or spiritual significance.

EMOTION

To reiterate some general principles: if the 'nervous system' is strong, the organism will respond to stress at first through expression, either verbally (Fire) or physically (Wood); and if these fail, through physical symptoms. If the 'nervous system' is highly vulnerable, we will observe psychological symptoms; if the 'nervous system' is only partially defective, physical and psychological problems will appear, more or less simultaneously. In general, the energy condition of the 'nervous system' and the energy condition of the body will determine the ultimate outcome.

Many other factors are important in considering the relationship between stress and the Tai Yang 'nervous system'. These include the age of onset, the activity at the time of the stress, whether the stress is large or small, whether it is sudden or gradual, the predilections of the specific organs, and whether or not the stress is internal and endogenously generated or external.

A basic principle, which belies the traditional concept, is that, whereas organ dysfunction will predispose a person to a specific emotion (as outlined in the system of correspondences of the Five Phases), a specific emotion does not always follow those correspondences in terms of its effect upon the organs of the body. However, these issues fall into two general categories: stress and terrain. The terrain is the condition of the organism and the stress to which the terrain is subject. In other words, anger does not always affect the Liver; fear does not always affect the Kidneys; sadness does not always affect the Lungs; thinking does not always affect the Spleen; and joy does not always affect the Heart, as stated in the Five Phase laws. The organ affected is the most dysfunctional. Partial exceptions to this rule are the conditions of sadness and excessive thinking, which affect both the weakest as well as their corresponding organs. The factors mentioned in the previous paragraph alter these correspondences, as we will observe. If all organs are of approximately equal strength, the traditional emotion-organ relationship continues to apply.

The ultimate effect of sudden emotion on the 'nervous system' is through the organ; the organ that is affected will tend to create emotions that correspond to it and gradually erode even a strong 'nervous system'. For example, if a sudden fright affects the Heart, it in turn will make a person even more susceptible to fright or shock. A vicious cycle is established, which is broken only by dealing with the emotion (with some form of psychotherapy), and with the 'nervous system' and 'organ system' (with acupuncture and herbs). An emotion is an energy configuration that, if it cannot be naturally and constructively expressed by the person experiencing it, will appear as excess energy in its target organ. The organ, already too weak to resist, will attempt to transform the excess energy into the particular work of that organ. For example, if the organ in question should be the Heart, it will beat harder in order to increase circulation and dissipate the excess energy. The organ and the entire system with which it is associated will soon show the wear and tear of work beyond its innate ability, and disease will follow.

{353}

Especially in the same burner, emotions that affect one organ will have an impact on the other over time. Sadness that creates stagnation in the Lungs will diminish circulation from the Heart that must then work harder to maintain that circulation. Stagnation of Liver qi due to repressed emotions will deprive the Stomach of one of the forces that enhances peristalsis, leading to a form of constipation, while stagnation in the Stomach, for example, due to cold, or to over-thinking while eating, will call upon the Liver to work harder and become qi deficient more quickly.

There are five general categories of emotion. There are the tense emotions, such as chronic anger, frustration, and disappointment, which work slowly on organs such as the Liver and Kidneys. Second, there is shock, caused by sudden anger, fright, or sudden disappointment, which most often affects the Heart, Lungs, and Kidneys. There are the sad emotions, such as sadness, grief, and anguish, which work slowly on primarily the Lungs and Kidneys. There are ruminating types of emotions, such as worry, guilt, and excessive thinking, which work slowly on the Heart, Spleen, and Kidneys. Lastly, there are the fearful emotions such as anxiety, which work slowly on the Heart, Kidneys, and Lungs. Though there are exceptions, generally speaking, emotions that develop suddenly tend to affect the Heart and the Lungs, and those that develop slowly tend to affect the Liver, Spleen, and Kidneys.

GRADUAL EMOTIONAL STRESS

Let us first consider the effects of gradual stress. If the nervous system is constitutionally 'weak,' the result, over a period of time, will fall into the category of neurasthenia, with symptoms such as vulnerability, fragility, easy fear, and difficulty in steady, consistent functioning. The overall picture will be one of instability and frailty. In later stages, as the energy difficulties work their way through the other systems (circulatory, digestive, and organ), the nerves, or qi, of vulnerable organs will be affected, leading to a variety of physical illnesses, including immune diseases and carcinoma.

If the 'nervous system' is constitutionally 'tense,' the direction will go toward hypertensive states with symptoms such as ulcer, hematemasis, constipation, menstrual cramps and pre-menstrual difficulties, headache, and high blood pressure. The terminal conditions would be cardiovascular accidents, coronary occlusions, stroke, and other illnesses in which heat, especially in the blood, and the ensuing blood stagnation, is an essential factor. The following thoughts concerning the effects of specific, slowly-developing emotional states of stress on organs are predicated on the assumption that the nervous system is compromised and therefore inadequate to protect these organs from stress. Disappointment, anger, fear, thinking, worry, tension, grief, frustration, and sadness are all examples of stress that occurs gradually.

Repressed Anger

Repressed anger, and the repression of any emotion, is generally associated with the Liver, and we have discussed the physiology and pathology of those energy pathways in an earlier chapter. Any vulnerable organ can be involved. The principal effect is a gradual increase in the stagnation of the circulation of energy in the organ that is affected. Repressed anger carries with it a considerably greater heat factor than other emotions because anger itself is a hot emotion struggling to find expression against a strong counterforce. Therefore, the signs and symptoms connected with repressed anger will always involve, in the early and middle stages of the process, various heat manifestations. Initially, the heat may be classified as excessive in nature because it is the direct result of the organ's attempt to move the stagnation, and because the organ is still powerful. Symptoms such as costo-chondral and chest pain would be significant evidence that the Liver still has the strength to push against the stagnation.

If the anger went to the Heart, for example, we would get the condition of 'Heart tight,' and, while the cause might be repressed anger, the result will be an increased tendency on the part of the person to worry. In such a condition as 'Heart tight,' the Small Intestine will drain the heat from excess from the Heart and transmit it to the Bladder by absorbing fluid through the gastrointestinal wall by way of the blood. Should the Small Intestine fail, the heat will rise and the signs appear as ulcers on the tongue. If the effect is upon the Kidneys, the signs and symptoms of heat will appear in the lower burner and might include apparent inflammations and infections in the genital organs and in the Bladder. These are signs of heat from excess. This type of heat in any part of the body may be related to repressed anger, affecting that particular organ, if it is the one that is vulnerable. The presence of heat from excess over any relatively long period of time will damage an organ and interfere significantly with its function. The heat from excess requires the organ to do extra work in order to reduce or remove it and restore harmony, and that overwork will slowly weaken the organ and result in another condition of heat known as heat from deficiency, or yin deficiency.

[355]

Whereas heat from excess has a profound vulcanizing effect upon the blood vessels of an organ, making them relatively inflexible, both heat from excess and heat from deficiency affect the nerves innervating an organ, leading to irritability, which, in the case of the Heart for example, might lead to various forms of arrhythmias. The metabolism of the organ and its overall ability to contribute to the general energy will be significantly impaired and the indirect effect upon the nervous system will he felt. However, in the intermediate stages, the effect upon the nervous system will be related to the factor of increased heat from excess and heat from deficiency in terms of its vicissitudes within the organ and on the rest of the body, which is trying to eliminate it. So, when we find an irritable bowel or an irritable bladder, we must always consider the possibility that heat coming from repressed anger is affecting these organs generally through the effect of the heat upon the solid (Zang) partner organ. In other words, if we find an irritable bowel, we must think of heat in the Lungs; or an irritable Bladder, heat in the Heart or in the Kidneys, from repressed anger. Initially there will be a fullness (Inflated quality) in the pulse, later turning to a Tightness in the pulse for that particular organ. In addition, heat signs will show on that part of the tongue corresponding to the particular organ we are discussing.

Chronic Fear

As anger creates heat, interferes with circulation, and tends to make the nerves more irritable in a particular organ, chronic fear seems to have a more destabilizing effect upon the nervous innervation, both of the nervous system and of the nerves of any particular organ. Chronic fear in its various forms, from minor fear in the form of worry to its most severe form of terror, is characterized on the pulse by Vibration, Spinning Bean, and other qualities. It must be considered in terms of the number of organs that are affected, the depth, and the fineness or coarseness of the vibration. For example, transient, superficial Vibrations on the Heart position usually indicate a temporary condition of worry; however, as the Vibration spreads to other organs, particularly on the left side of the pulse (such as the Liver and the Kidneys), we are involved with a more chronic situation. For example, if the Liver is included, the likelihood is that the worry has been there for at least one year, and if both Liver and the Kidneys are involved, it may have been present for five years. Should the entire pulse be involved, the likelihood is that this condition has existed for at least ten years. If the Vibration is found over the entire pulse at all depths, we probably have a person who is a 'worrier', one who will create worry even when there is nothing to worry about. In addition to the length of time, the number of organs involved may also indicate something about the origin of the fear. Chronic fear may be something that is generated by constitutionally deficient Kidneys. Fear for a person's life usually involves some kind of interpersonal situation. It may be the result of what another person is doing or the result of what one is doing to another person or to other people. Again, the result depends on the terrain, the Kidney qi, and the stress on the terrain, the life situation. Both must be considered, but ultmately the terrain is the important treatment consideration, since we cannot always control life. (Chronic fear is also a sign of Heart blood stagnation ['Heart small'], as described in our discussion of the Heart.)

One form of chronic fear is guilt, an unspoken fear of punishment. Sometimes the guilt is imagined and sometimes it is real. When it pervades the entire pulse, the guilt is more likely to be related to a real event, usually to some kind of major crime. On the other hand, when the Vibration is found, for example, just on the Heart and the Liver positions, the likelihood is that this fear is internally generated and, perhaps, largely imaginary. An example is a patient whose entire pulse showed this Vibration at our first meeting. Confronted with this, she attributed it to her past dependence on drugs. When we knew each other better, she told of being a sexual slave to her brother-in-law since the age of twelve. Later, she admitted to having had an affair with her best friend's husband.

Chronic fear is more often the product of Kidney energy dysfunction than the cause of it; however, if the Kidney is vulnerable, chronic fear will usually affect the Kidney yang. This is because fear descends and is more likely to affect the major organ in the lower burner, the Kidneys, involved with courage. Also, chronic emotional states call more upon the slow adaptational mechanisms associated with the endocrine system and especially the adrenals. The adrenal glands are, of course, in close proximity to the Kidneys and would be included in the broad purview of the Kidney organ system, with the emphasis on the term 'system'. In fact, many observers have compared adrenal gland functions with those of Kidney yang. The fire of *ming men*[6] ("gate of vitality") is ascribed the task of providing the rest of the organism with the 'burning' drive and push necessary for each of the other systems to fulfill its special energy function. The adrenal gland consists of a cortex and a medulla. The part of the adrenal gland involved in this discussion of Kidney yang would be the medulla, the producer of epinephrine. The cortex would be more involved in water metabolism functions of Kidney qi and Kidney yin. Both are involved with chronic fear: the yang and yin respectively with the endlessly recurring syndrome of 'fight or flight' ("a coward dies a thousand deaths"), and the yin with the heat from deficiency generated by a chronically overworked mind.

[357]

Excessive Thinking

Since the mind consumes more energy than any other process in the organism, excessive thinking has the effect of depriving organs of the quantity and quality of energy necessary to their optimum productivity. In the short run, excessive thinking tends to speed up the nervous innervation of the organs, which will cause them to consume extra energy to perform their functions. In the long run, all organs must sacrifice their energy to the mind, which has first call on it. Those organs that are most vulnerable will suffer the most apparent dysfunction and will produce the most immediate and severe symptoms. Excessive thinking drains yin, especially of the Heart and Kidneys, with one exception: when the thinking occurs while eating, which we will discuss below. However, since thinking requires an energy that is entirely reliant upon a supply of glucose, there is also a greater likelihood of it having an effect upon the 'digestive system' (especially the Spleen-Pancreas, the Stomach, and the Liver, which stores glycogen) than on any other system besides the Heart and Kidneys, however vulnerable that other system may be.

The Chinese consider the entire process of eating to be sacred, both the food itself and the social atmosphere. Food is supposed to be eaten regularly, to be eaten slowly, and to be shared. It is a social event, and not something to be done in solitude. This would tend to preclude thinking during mealtime, the time when thinking has its greatest effect upon the 'digestive system'. The person who eats alone, and whose eyes seem turned up to the ceiling, lost in thought upon some internal preoccupation rather than on the meal in front of him, diverts energy from the digestive process. At first, in an attempt to compensate for that loss, the digestive process speeds up, creating spasm and pain, first in the esophagus and later in the upper part of the Stomach. The stagnation may be felt, on the pulse, as an Inflated quality between the Lung and Stomach positions. Translated into Western terms, we might see the same event as competition between the brain and the gastro-intestinal system for circulation, the latter losing to the former during mealtime. The gastro-intestinal system will soon be working beyond its energy. The process of overwork, over a longer period of time, will lead to a situation of yin deficiency in the Stomach; and over a very long period of time, to a condition of yang deficiency in the Spleen. In order to avoid this, the Chinese say that one must concentrate on one's food, and that one must take the time to enjoy it.

Worry

The effect of worry on the body resembles a combination of both fear and thinking. In other words, worry is excessive thinking, tinged with fear. Worry involves the process of rehearsing, mentioned by Freud, and is a talisman whose message is "as long as I worry, I am safe." Thinking causes an initial speeding up of function in an organ and later an energy deprivation, and fear has a destabilizing effect upon the nervous innervation of that organ. Worry, therefore, does both. It accelerates an organ's work while, at the same time, depriving it of energy, deharmonizing the smooth nervous innervation of that organ, and leading to a degree of chaos rather than smoothness of operation.

We have already looked at the effect of worry upon the Heart in our discussion of fear, creating not only the Superficial Vibration pulse quality that comes with fear, but also an increase in the rate and, possibly, some irregularity of a transient nature in the rate. Chronic worry affecting the Heart will lead to the conditions of *Heart qi agitation* ('Heart tight'), mild heat from excess to mild heat from deficiency of the Heart, and later, to *Heart yin deficiency* ('Heart nervous') and *Heart blood deficiency* ('Heart weak'), if it is sufficiently longstanding. One sign of this may be seen in the color of the face and the hands. Normally, they should be of the same color, but, in this instance, one will find that the face is redder than the hands, especially between the eyebrows (*yin tang*). The tongue will often have a little red on the end. *Heart qi agitation* ('Heart tight') is a condition that stimulates worry, creating another vicious cycle.

Susceptibility to the thinking aspect could come from a deficient Spleen, and the fear from deficient Kidney energies. With regard to thinking, the consequences may be qi stagnation in the Stomach, leading eventually to heat from excess and finally heat from deficiency, using up the HCl in that organ, poor digestion and absorption, and thus increased hunger and craving for food.

Tension

Although the basic formulations still provide a valid, useful foundation for a psychological medicine, the original Chinese system requires some expansion to take account of the difference in lifestyles between China and industrialized Western society. Even today, China is eighty percent rural. The tensions and stresses of modern living (or "modern times," as Charlie Chaplin put it) are all but unaccounted for by Chinese medicine.

There is nothing in this system of emotions that expresses the 'tension' experienced by people since the industrial revolution, and especially noticeable since World War I. The world has changed remarkably, and life for most people has shifted decisively away from a predominantly pastoral, religious ambience featuring individual manual or craft labor. The slow pace of individual labor has been galvanized into the violently-paced mass labor of the factory by the profit motive of absentee investors. Added to these pressures is the anxiety engendered by the isolation attendant upon the loss of the extended family and the 'anonymity' that attends this isolation in depersonalized population density centers. These stresses are compounded by the general tension of living in an industrial, competitive society in which people overwork, eat devitalized food, have poor eating habits, are inundated with pollution, and where the education and family systems are aimed pretty much at seeing that the individual becomes a machine rather than a person.

{359}

Perhaps even more devastating is the accelerating rate of change to which we have become subject. Civilizations and all of their practices were relatively enduring in the past. People knew their place and what to expect for hundreds of years at a time with no alteration except natural disasters and, after the fifth millennium B.C., the ravages of war and enslavement. The shift from the Stone Age to the Bronze Age to the Iron Age took several thousand years. Today an entire transformation of technology may occur within a few years, even months; from the time of the first American rocket launch it took less than ten years to put a man on the moon.

Modern medicine is a product of the industrial civilization with which the gentler medicines could not entirely cope. The ancient medicines were meant for a life where there were elaborate, shared, protective rituals for each of the predictable chronic stresses, both chemical and emotional. They were slow and aimed at underlying causes as well as acute symptoms. Our market society does not reward the practices that are not cost-effective and symptom-removing. We now require powerful substances that act quickly so that we may rapidly return to productivity.

A commercial fisherman friend of mine once recounted to me a story of his uncle as a young man. The uncle hitched his horses to his fish wagon, climbed in, and went to sleep while the horses slowly took him down to the dock where his boat was moored. He awoke whenever the mood and his biorhythms moved him, and he fished. When he returned, he loaded his fish on his wagon and went to sleep again, while the horses took him home. As an old man, his uncle would fish with my friend, who then owned an old Model T; and the old man kept asking him what his hurry was as they sped toward the dock at twenty miles an hour!

The chemical and emotional stresses of the industrial revolution have adversely affected human physiology as never before. Tobacco, coffee, refined foods, pollution with the most toxic substances everywhere, all of the time, in the air and water, have weakened and poisoned the human animal almost beyond endurance, leading to the prevalence of the most widespread, life-threatening chronic diseases: cancer, cardiovascular disease, congenital anomalies. Recent reports list between 50 and 150 chemicals in our blood that were not there 50 years ago, including long-chain oil-derived hydrocarbons from industrial products such as nylon and rayon. The prospects are terrifying, yet people have gradually gotten so used to this state of affairs that they do not even know that it is abnormal.

Life has always been a struggle, which some aspects of modern life have softened and eased. This is especially true of public health practices and civil engineering for larger population centers. Some aspects of the softening have been counterproductive, leaving us with a sizable population able to cope with the pain of living only through escape, either psychologically, through severe mental illness, or through pain-relieving drugs.

According to the opening passages of *The Yellow Emperor's Classic of Internal Medicine*, ancient physicians were already struggling five thousand years ago with lifestyles out of harmony with nature. In ancient times when the Yellow Emperor was born, "He was endowed with divine talents; while yet in early infancy, he could speak; while still very young, he was quick of apprehension and penetrating; when he was grown up, he was sincere and comprehending; when he became perfect, he ascended to Heaven."

The Yellow Emperor once addressed Chi Po, the divinely-inspired teacher: "I have heard that in ancient times the people lived [through the years] to be over a hundred years, and yet they remained active and did not become decrepit in their activities. But nowadays people reach only half of that age and yet become decrepit and failing. Is it because the world changes from generation to generation? Or is it that mankind is becoming negligent [of the laws of nature]?"

Chi Po answered: "In ancient times, those people who understood Tao [the way of self-cultivation] patterned themselves upon the yin and the yang... and they lived in harmony with the arts of divination. There was temperance in eating and drinking. Their hours of rising and retiring were regular and not disorderly and wild. By these means, the ancients kept their bodies united with their souls, so as to fulfill their allotted span completely, measuring unto a hundred years before they passed away. Nowadays people are not like this; they use wine as beverage, and they adopt recklessness as usual behavior. They enter the chamber [of love] in an intoxicated condition; their passions exhaust their vital forces; their cravings dissipate their true [essence]; they do not know how to find contentment within them-selves; they are not skilled in the control of their spirits. They devote all their attention to the amusement of their minds, thus cutting themselves off from the joys of long [life]. Their rising and retiring is without regularity. For these reasons, they reach only one half of the hundred years; and then they degenerate."

"In the most ancient times, the teachings of the sages were followed by those beneath them; they said that weakness and noxious influences and injurious winds should be avoided at specific times. They... were tranquilly content in nothingness, and the true vital force accompanied them always; their vital [original] spirit was preserved within; thus, how could illness come to them? They exercised restraint of their wills and reduced their desires; their hearts were at peace and without any fear; their bodies toiled and yet did not become weary. Their spirit followed in harmony and obedi-ence; everything was satisfactory to their wishes, and they could achieve whatever they wished. Any kind of food was beautiful [to them]; and any kind of clothing was satisfactory. They felt happy under any condition. To them, it did not matter whether a man held a high or a low position in life. These men can be called pure at heart. No kind of desire can tempt the eyes of those pure people, and their mind cannot be misled by excessiveness and evil."

"[In such a society] no matter whether men are wise or foolish, virtu-ous or bad, they are without fear of anything; they are in harmony with Tao, the Right Way. Thus, they could live more than one-hundred years and remain active without becoming decrepit, because their virtue was perfect and never imperiled."[7]

It seems to me that it would be too much to expect the ancient physi-cian, with all of his remarkable skill and wisdom, to have anticipated the incredible onslaught of stress and stimuli to which modern man is subject, or to have anticipated every detail of the medicine he might require.

There is nothing in the annals of Chinese medicine that tells us very much about the effects of the kind of tension I have just described on the human body, since it has not, even up to the present time, existed within the framework of the Chinese civilization. As previously noted, eighty percent of China is a rural country, and almost a billion people still live a relatively simple life in the countryside where the pace of life is still within the time framework that was the only one known to man for thousands and thousands of years.

It would seem that, for some people, tension has its most direct effect upon the autonomic nervous system, and most particularly on that part of the autonomic nervous system that affects smooth muscle, whether it be in the intestinal tract, in the eyes, in blood vessels, or even in the skin. Diseases as seemingly unrelated to each other as colitis, angina, glaucoma, asthma, and migraine headache are all diseases of the autonomic nervous system, and particularly its innervation of smooth muscle. The function of any organ that is vulnerable can be further compromised by the effect of tension on its autonomic functions. I have observed this in people with chronic disease of any organ and have observed rapid deterioration of that organ under the influence of tension from which the person was unable to escape. Likewise, I have seen totally unexplained episodes of diseases such as tuberculosis in very low-risk populations under similar circumstances where there was, in their minds at least, no solution to their problem.

I recall, as an intern in 1952, admitting a middle-aged Jewish woman from a middle-class neighborhood, with massive, sudden tuberculosis. With considerable effort, it was learned that her daughter had married a man who, in addition to being from a Puerto Rican background, was also a drug addict, was living in her house, was supported by her, and was seducing her younger son into a homosexual relationship and drug addiction. This woman also cared for a sister who was a chronic invalid and lived in the neighborhood. The straw that broke the camel's back, her son's seduction, enervated her immune system. If her 'nervous system' had been weak, un-doubtedly this woman would have had a psychotic break, such as I have observed in other hospitalized patients enduring similar circumstances.

Another group of people seem to be affected by tension primarily through the peripheral nervous system, affecting striated muscle. For these people, tension in the larger and smaller voluntary muscles leads to extreme discomfort. A common finding in our time is the temporal mandibular joint syndrome (TMJ), which seems to be a direct, or one-to-one, response to tension. Some muscle groups are more vulnerable than others, especially those around the hinge joints, such as the jaw, and the hip. In my own prac-tice, one of the most common complaints is low back pain and sciatica, which is related to a shifting of the pelvis due to tension in the muscles in this area.

From a Chinese point of view, the organ most affected by tension is the Liver. When all the other organs are more or less intact, the Liver is, ap-parently, not only the detoxifier of chemical stresses, but also of emotional stress in the form of tension and frustration. The pathway, most likely, is through the nervous system to the Liver. It is said that Liver yang is associ-ated with the functioning of the nervous system and, therefore, would be in a state of hyperactivity as an expression of the effect of the tension on the nervous system and its effect on the Liver. As previously noted, Liver yang moves and seeks productive resolution of the tension either through its own energies and those of Liver yin and blood (nourishing ligaments and tendons), in the form of physical action, or through other organs such as the Heart, in the form of verbal expression. The failure to achieve such a solution will lead to stagnation and hyperactivity of the Liver in its attempt to overcome this stagnation. A hyperactive Liver is associated with an increase in heat, which, as part of a vicious cycle, will then increase the excitability of the nervous system, on the one hand, and, on the other, heat the blood in the Liver. Liver blood-yin will then be unable to nourish the muscles, ligaments, and tendons, which is its job, exacerbating the already tense condition of the musculoskeletal system. The Liver will also be less able to clear the blood of toxins, leading to other problems such as eczema, allergies, and sinus problems.

Frustration

By definition, frustration is a situation in which something is prevented from being attained. An energy force is thwarted and unable to move in its intended direction toward its chosen goal and may be altogether blocked or diverted in another direction not chosen by the originator of the drive.

If the essence (*jing*), or 'nervous system,' is strong, the person will adjust in a positive way to the bad fortune. If the frustration cannot be resolved in a constructive fashion, the weakest organ will begin to show the effects of the cathexis of the blocked energy by overworking to dissipate it. If the nervous system is compromised and the organs are of approximately equal strength, the frustration, acting like any other significant interference with assertion, will cause stagnation in the Liver and will create all the problems associated with the blockage of energy in that organ, leading eventually to Liver exhaustion. Once the assertion is rendered ineffectual and nullified, and unless total acceptance is achieved, stagnation develops on the energy level and impotent rage on the psychological. If the frustration comes from an outside, ongoing, identifiable source, the impotent rage that follows will be thus directed and have energy effects very similar to that of blocked anger, including passive-aggressive personality patterns. If, on the other hand, the frustration is internally-generated, the anger and the energy will more likely be turned inward, on one's self, in the form of self-destructive behavior and self-hatred. If it is the result of bad fortune, such as an accident, disease, or loss of a parent, partner, child, or one's career, it may be turned outward against God, whose studied indifference to this approach will not mitigate the frustration.

If the frustration is sudden, the organ most affected would depend on the activity state. During a period of quiescence, it will be the Liver; during activity, most likely the Heart; if the person is eating, it could lead to stagnation in the esophagus and Stomach. In this kind of situation, the energy is trapped inside the organ and creates, on the pulse, a fullness (Inflated quality), which is translated into symptoms of choking if it is in the esophagus; of distention in the hypochondriac area if it is in the Liver; difficulty in catching one's breath and sense of fullness in the chest if it is the Lungs or Heart that is affected. In the latter case, hyperventilation and/or palpitations might follow, or sudden redness in the face and elevation of blood pressure.

Grief and Anguish

Grief is a normal response to loss and separation, characterized by wailing and crying and the "rending of garments" as an expression of pain and anger. If the wailing and rending knows no end, we are dealing with a non-functional psychosis, a form of melancholia, which will deplete the yin (water) of the body and result in a state of inner dryness and heat from deficiency (yin deficiency). This occurs in people whose 'nervous systems' are already at risk and who, during this period, engage in too much sex and/or who push themselves too hard in work. Sex and overwork play a part here because the Kidney energies are thought to play a role in the resolution of grief.

When the grief is felt and continued beyond the 'normal' time parameters in a subdued and controlled fashion, it is called anguish. Anguish is audibly distinguished from grief and sadness by the frequent occurrence of little groans without tears. It is said that grief that does not dissipate naturally is a grave and heavy energy that sinks to the deepest part of the body, which is how the Chinese view the Kidney organ system. Together with the suppression of tears, this heaviness stagnates Kidney function, inhibiting the water control mechanism superintended by Kidney yin energies, causing both the Kidneys and other organs to become dry.

Dryness is therefore a consequence of either outcome for different reasons. Without too much stretch of the imagination, one could see impaired electrolyte imbalance and depletion of the neuro-humeral system by such a sequence of events. Dryness, especially of the Kidneys, that creates and supports the central nervous system, will cause the system to become more easily inflamed and irritable. Chronic fear will, as we have already stated, damage the Kidney yang; chronic deep-seated grief and anguish will damage the Kidney yin.

Sadness

Repressed grief, which we will arbitrarily call sadness for the sake of discussion, is a most important source of deep-seated and lifelong personality problems. With anguish, one knows and remembers, and with sadness, one forgets. With disappointment we have a person who could not speak, but who may have eventually cried; with true sadness we have a child who may have spoken but could not feel or cry. On the energy level, we have stagnation deep inside the Lungs where the feeling and crying is hidden and blocked. The Lung pulse is Deep and the wave is either Flat or Weak. Though chronic sadness may affect one or more vulnerable organs, it tends to affect the Lungs for the following reason. The posture of the sad person is common knowledge. With the head down and eyes focused on the ground, the back is bent forward and the chest depressed, gradually 'killing' the qi circulation in the chest. Sadness also involves holding back crying. This holding causes further stagnation and 'killing of the qi' in the Lungs. Since the Lungs draw in the qi, which is the driving force of energy and blood circulation throughout the body, it has to work harder and is slowly weakened. For this reason, sadness is more likely to affect the Lungs before any other organ, even if another organ is more vulnerable to stress.

In terms of its effect, there is a distinction between unresolved grief that originates in childhood and that which originates in later life. The earlier and more severe the loss, the greater the effect upon Lung function on both a physical and emotional level. Anaclytic grief (the loss of a parent in infancy), for example, despite being initially accompanied by poignant and profuse crying, which is later repressed, is a profound state of defeat that will have greater repercussions than the loss of a parent at the age of twelve. Many of the adults I have treated with repressed sadness, and whose 'nervous systems' were not strong to begin with, tended to be schizoid personalities. However, those who lived with fantasies of the lost person as still being available to them, or who on some mystical level actually did maintain such contact, did not develop physical Lung problems. One, whom I recall vividly from my early days as a psychiatrist, was actually a successful opera singer, though severely disturbed emotionally.

Those who do not weave this loss into a separate fantasy life hold the loss more completely out of awareness and may develop Lung problems, in which case the Special Lung pulse is Inflated and/or Tight and/or Slippery. The tongue may be swollen just before the tip, and, in the most serious Lung disharmony, may show a total loss of tongue body color just behind the tip. The physical effect of this stagnation may express itself as asthma, chronic bronchitis, recurrent upper respiratory infections, allergies, pneumonia, and even tuberculosis, depending on other factors. On an emotional and spiritual level, there will be problems with bonding and separation at any time and especially adolescence, with freely giving and taking, and with a sense of inner emptiness and worthlessness that may be compensated for by compulsive perfectionism. There may also be some confusion in the area of ethics and values, since the Metal phase (the Lungs) is concerned with the 'right way of living.' More specifically, and most importantly, there is a 'hole' in the personality where repression inhibited the growth and development of feelings of attachment and/or its expansion. The result is, among other things, a profound grief for one's lost self, which perpetuates the original scenario until one finds it in conscious experience, and there, finds oneself. (The relationship of the Metal phase to personality is more completely explored in Chapter 12.)

Unexpressed sadness that begins later in life evolves differently and has less profound effects upon the personality, body, and 'nervous system' than the sadness we have described above. A Cotton quality is accessed on the pulse from the surface to the impulse and is measured in terms of the resistance to the finger. Dr. Shen calls this a 'sad' pulse, and it translates to a form of energy stagnation in the organ or organs affected. I refer to this pulse as the 'resignation' pulse because it is found in people who have resigned themselves to a life situation that is barely tenable, but in their opinion beyond their ability to change. Thoreau referred to this situation in his well-known statement that "Most men lead lives of quiet desperation." It is the failure to overcome the stagnation in their lives and fulfill their destiny that creates this sadness.

If the sadness (or resignation) has occurred for only a short time, the Heart (and, more rarely, the Lungs) will show this kind of pulse. If it is found also on the Liver, the duration is usually at least one year and involves a more gradual and prolonged interpersonal problem involving rejection. Sometimes this pulse is found only on the Liver and Kidney positions, in which case the problem is of two or three years' duration. If the entire left side is involved, the problem is at least five years old; and if over the entire pulse, at least ten years. Usually it is found over the entire pulse. One finds most often a general decrease of qi and blood circulation, with lassitude and easy fatigue and/or vague pains and discomfort. More significantly, according to Dr. Shen, if uncorrected over many years the outcome can be cancer. If found in only one position, such as the left middle position, it is by itself a sign of mild qi deficiency of the organ associated with that position, in this case the Liver.

Another form of sadness is that associated with a lack of joy. This is associated with the depletion of the 'fire' in the Fire phase, either constitutionally, from rejection by a partner, the depressed phase of a bi-polar condition, or because of dampening of the spirit from excess dampness associated with Kidney yang deficiency. The left distal position is often Muffled.[8] We see this in the oral character of the deflated phase of the bi-polar inflation-deflation cycle, and, less profoundly, in the 'hysteric' when he fails to win approval.

Disappointment

Disappointment, though sometimes occurring relatively suddenly, is more often an emotion that results from a slow erosion of faith and trust during which process a person clings as long as possible to the hope that his expectations will be gratified. It is also a much less profound experience than sadness or an emotional shock, with a more gradual effect on a person.

While the consequences described below are similar, they are less severe in adults than in children. For this reason, we are especially concerned with the kind of disappointment that occurs earlier in life, when consciousness is not fully developed, as, for example, the loss of a parent by a very young child. The lifetime consequences are often complicated and perplexing. At the time of the loss, the Heart and Lungs are affected by a contraction of the muscles of the chest and a closing down of the qi circulation in the upper burner, leaving us with the familiar Flat wave in the left distal position of the pulse. The mechanism here is a suppression of hurt and anger by the holding back of words, of verbal expression, but an ability to cry within a reasonable period after the disappointment. Though out of awareness, the hurt is not as profoundly repressed as in sadness, where consciousness of the pain at the time of its occurrence is a greater threat to life. Disappointment is therefore more easily recalled than sadness. For example, the man I discussed earlier with a bad knee whose upper burner position had a Flat wave had forgotten that his mother died when he was four years old, but remembered it immediately when it was brought to his attention. While he could not vocalize upon first hearing the news of his mother's death, he must have been able to cry and mourn shortly afterward.

The long-range symptoms will be a decrease in overall energy circulation, a tendency toward slow healing, and a sense of a weight in the chest. There will be little or no awareness of the disappointment, the memory of which may only be reawakened when the patient is questioned as a result of the findings of the examination. The pulse will show a Flat wave in the upper burner. The rate may be normal or slightly lower, due to the effect on circulation. The tongue will rarely reveal anything of significance, except some swelling at the end, unless there are other problems. Herbal and acupuncture treatment may be necessary in order to open up the circulation in the upper burner. The new awareness of a connection between that early experience and current life problems is sometimes of great importance to the patient in terms of expanding self-knowledge and self-awareness. I saw a young woman who was beset with physical and emotional problems. Her examination revealed the Flat wave and some problems around the age of ten. The focus of her emotional life was her conflicts with her father, with whom she lived alone, and later, during her teen years, with a stepmother. Until this examination, she had completely forgotten about her mother's death when she was ten, and had blocked the grief and anger of that event, which she could handle less well at the time than the struggle with her father.

Sudden Emotional Stress

In general, a sudden stress will tend first to affect a vulnerable organ. If none is particularly vulnerable, it will affect the organ that corresponds, according to Chinese medicine, to that particular emotion; and, ultimately, through that organ, it will affect the 'nervous system' if it is vulnerable. So the pathway is first to the organ and then to the 'nervous system.' For example, if the Heart is vulnerable, and if the 'nervous system' is also vulnerable, the stress will affect the mind, which is controlled by the Heart, and there will be mental symptoms such as anxiety, nightmares, phobias, and restlessness. If the 'nervous system' is strong, then the effect may be physical and remain in the involved organ or move, on a physical basis, to some other organ, depending on other factors. With a shock to the Heart, one would get palpitations with activity, insomnia, shortness of breath, and fatigue.

Sudden, strong emotion blocks and stimulates the circulation of qi and blood simultaneously. The shock inhibits circulation, and the Heart responds by beating harder and faster. Consequently, the blood and energy, which are trying to move faster and cannot, will become hot; the vessels of that organ, and the organ itself, will expand rapidly; and the pulse will feel Hollow Full-Overflowing. An important factor in determining the outcome of sudden emotion is the activity in which the person is engaged at the time of the sudden emotional stress. For example, if a person has a great anger and happens to be quiet, physically, at the time, it will affect the Liver. There will be a big change in the Liver pulse, which will become Inflated. If the person is active, the anger will affect the Heart, and the Heart pulse will become Inflated. If the person is eating, it will affect the esophagus and Stomach and, of course, the digestion; one will find an Inflated pulse, frequently on the upper part of the Stomach or between the Lung and the Stomach positions, on the right side. If a person receives bad news or is involved with somebody he dislikes, the pain will be most severe if this occurs during the meal. If it occurs before the meal, the pain will be moderate; and if it occurs after the meal, the pain will be mild. Sudden emotional stress that causes qi and food stagnation in the middle burner, especially if combined with mucus and fire (from the Liver), can have profound effects on the 'nervous system.' (We shall examine these in more detail in our discussion of 'pernicious influences.') If the person is urinating (as during toilet training), it will affect the Bladder, leading to either reduced or increased frequency, and the stagnation will show itself on the pulse in the form of a Tight wave. If the person is engaged in sex, there will be a similar effect upon the uterus and the prostate.

Sudden, powerful emotional experiences have a potent impact upon the autonomic nervous system. The most immediate autonomic nervous system response to sudden, overwhelming emotion is a massive increase in circulation, placing upon the Heart an enormous, often cataclysmic demand for pumping action, which may overwhelm its own blood supply if that supply is already compromised. We are all too familiar with the scenario of people dying of fright, or even from unexpected good news (such as winning the lottery). Rapid excitation is mediated by way of the Small Intestine to the Heart — from the outside (Fu/hollow organ) to the inside (Zang/solid organ) — bypassing the defending Pericardium. The Heart is, therefore, always the organ most immediately affected by sudden and rapid emotional stress.

Effects on the Heart

Each of the acute emotions has a different effect upon the Heart. Sudden sadness will cause stagnation, a dampening of the circulation of blood and energy, and a Flat quality at the left distal position. Joy and anger will cause a sudden filling of the Heart ('trapped qi') when these emotions are ones that a person may not wish to reveal at that time. The Heart will, therefore, hold the qi and the blood and become Inflated.

Most serious is fright, which will cause an emptying of the Heart in its attempt to maintain the circulation, causing a state of shock and an inability of the body to get blood into and through the Heart. Apparently, this drains the Heart yin.

According to Chinese medicine, once the state of shock has occurred, especially if the person is very young or very old, circulation is, to one extent or another, permanently altered until adequately treated. If the yin and blood supply to the nervous innervation of the Heart is permanently reduced, a nervous instability of the Heart will ensue and remain throughout life until some form of therapy intervenes. If the Heart condition is good, the residue of the shock will only be a Rapid pulse condition, which is known as *Heart qi agitation* ('Heart tight'). If the Heart energy is weak, there will be variations in the rate, in addition to its being Rapid. With *Heart qi agitation* ('Heart tight') and *Heart yin deficiency* ('Heart nervous'), the pulse may be a little Rapid and there may be Change in Rate at Rest; *Heart blood deficiency* ('Heart weak') will involve a large Change in Rate on Movement.

Emotional shock depletes the yin of the Heart, and the ability of qi and blood to either enter or leave the Heart. The most important consequence of this draining of the Heart yin is the *separation of yin and yang* of the Heart and the loss of control of yin over the yang. Yang represents function and when function is out of control, chaos is the consequence. This chaos is both physical and mental. Physically the manifestation is in the circulation of blood, discussed elsewhere. Mentally the effect is emotional instability, forms of neurosis, or even psychosis if the 'nervous system' is vulnerable and especially if phlegm is misting the orifices. Mentation can also be impaired.

Persistent stagnation for a long period of time can generate the condition known as *Heart qi stagnation* ('Heart closed'), in its less severe form, or *Heart blood stagnation* ('Heart small'), in the more severe condition. *Trapped qi in the Heart* (Inflation at the left distal position) can lead to various degrees of Heart enlargement over a period of time. If the emotional stress develops gradually, the effect will first be on the nervous system and, through the nervous system, eventually to vulnerable organs. If none are particularly vulnerable, it will affect the organ that corresponds to the emotion, according to the system of correspondences in Chinese medicine. The pathway, therefore, with gradual stress, is first to the nervous system and then to the individual organs. With gradual stress, the stress alone will not be sufficient to cause symptoms. The Chinese say that "You cannot make a sound with one ball," meaning that one pathogenic factor is rarely sufficient to create obvious disease. Two or more factors, such as gradual emotional stress and overwork, are necessary to produce clinical pathology. Another factor, a constitutional weakness of the nervous system, was discussed above as leading, with gradual stress, to a neurasthenic condition.

Age

Age is another important factor in the outcome of a sudden emotional stress, which we have already discussed at some length above. Speaking more broadly, the effect of stress on the 'nervous system' is, of course, much greater in the very young, where it is still highly undeveloped, and, again, in the very old, where the essence (*jing*) is greatly diminished, affecting the viability of the 'nervous system.' Constitutional and congenital vulnerability plays a key role in the effect of any emotional stress on an organism. The impact of an emotion on the 'nervous system' varies directly with its strength, so that a strong emotion has a greater effect, whether or not it is gradual or sudden, in the young and old, before birth or after.

On the other end of the spectrum, a strong overall body condition (terrain) will protect even a vulnerable 'nervous system.' Here again is the usual paradox. People with a weaker body condition tend to be more sensitive to changes both within themselves and without. They complain more and seek help sooner and avoid serious disease more often than those with a better body condition, who ignore the subtle changes in themselves until disease is far developed.

PERNICIOUS INFLUENCES

Pernicious influences are another important factor in the vicissitudes of the nervous system. I am referring here to internal influences that represent an excess of some normal physiologic function, such as an excess of qi, water (dampness), blood, heat and fire, cold, dryness, or phlegm (mucus). These excesses, either alone or in combination with each other, and with any of the other factors considered in this book, account for the most serious derangements of the nervous system, which we call psychosis.

All psychoses involve the stagnation of qi, especially in the middle burner. They all involve another factor in addition to the pernicious influence, such as shock, grief, shame, fatigue, or unrelenting fear (as during war). They all work through the Heart, which controls the 'mind,' and the Kidneys, which control the *jing* (central nervous system), and they are most influential if the nervous system is already compromised, though under cataclysmic stress even the strongest nervous system can collapse. Broadly speaking, those psychoses whose origins include heat and fire are more agitated than those whose origins do not.

QI STAGNATION

Qi stagnation in the middle burner (Spleen-Stomach) occurs most often when the qi in the Liver becomes stagnant. Whereas this may be the result of chemical stress, such as alcohol, or trauma, it is most often the result of suppressed feelings, especially unexpressed anger. Liver qi stagnation causes stagnation in the entire middle burner and is eventually accompanied by some heat, which may be likened to the heat of friction from two strongly opposing forces. The qi is unable to move down to the lower burner (Intestines) and may either stay in the middle, causing physical discomfort, or, if the Heart is vulnerable, will rise with the heat and go to the Heart; because the Heart controls the mind, mental symptoms will occur.

These symptoms include mental confusion that occurs periodically, clearing and clouding on and off throughout the day. There may even be days when the person is entirely well, interspersed with days when these symptoms appear. Qi problems generally tend to come and go, depending on whether the qi is stronger or weaker at any one time. And since qi is relatively so insubstantial, so ephemeral, its strength, and therefore stagnation, responds to influences much more readily than blood or water stagnation. This process can be likened to a fire in a house in which the windows are closed. The smoke will be unable to escape and will tend to rise with the heat to the attic.

Food Stagnation

Food stagnation is our second consideration. This occurs most often as the result of a severe emotional shock while eating, or just after, sharply curtailing digestion. The stagnation is of both food and qi and occurs actually in the esophogeal area and is an upper burner chest distress problem. The pulse is stagnant in the form of a right diaphragm position that is more Inflated and often Rough, as one rolls the finger between the middle position and right distal position, than when one rolls the finger from the distal toward the middle position; and the tongue coating is thick and 'dirty.' The symptoms are the same as those mentioned under qi stagnation, except that the periods of confusion are more frequent, last longer, and are more severe.

Phlegm-fire

Phlegm-fire congestion is the result of stagnant dampness from poor digestion (Spleen qi deficiency or poor food habits), which accumulates into mucus, combined with excessive heat from Liver qi stagnation. Since food is eighty percent water, a deficient Spleen or excess food that is difficult to digest can leave the digestive tract with more dampness (water) than it can handle. Chinese medicine states that this dampness normally ascends to the Lungs with Spleen energy to be 'digested' or, more accurately, 'misted.' If, in addition to poor digestion, the Lungs are weak and cannot digest this dampness that is normally dispersed through sweat or sent to the Kidneys, the dampness accumulates into mucus. Long-standing heat from Liver qi stagnation turns into fire and combines with the mucus to become the more viscous substance referred to as phlegm-fire, which goes to the Heart where it blocks the orifices. Especially if the 'nervous system' is already compromised, we have mental confusion that is continuous and unabating. These are the severe, long-term psychoses that, according to Chinese medicine, are on a continuum with epilepsy, which is thought to represent an even greater aggregate of phlegm-fire in the Heart orifices. The pulse is Slippery, and the tongue has some coating and mucus threads.

[373]

A Case of Mental Confusion

F. was a 63-year-old woman who had been in and out of mental hospitals for about 16 years. During this period of time, she had every type of diagnostic workup, but to no avail, and her treatment included many drugs and several courses of electric shock therapy, which did not help. Her hospital diagnosis was chronic schizophrenia. At the time that I first saw F., she walked around the room in circles at considerable speed, collapsing suddenly, and frequently breaking bones in the course of the fall. Her explanation for her behavior was that someone was controlling her mind and forcing her to do this. The "someone" was not clear at first. It was known that she had lived a life of service to her family and to her husband, who controlled her throughout the marriage.

At our first meeting, F. was running and falling as described above. I managed to take her pulse briefly when she fell, and noted clear-cut Slipperiness on her Heart pulse and observed a thick coating on her tongue. I prescribed an herbal formula (Niu Huang Qing Xin Wan) to remove mucus and heat from the Heart and open the Heart 'orifices.' Within three days she stopped the running and falling, and within a week she reported that she was no longer being controlled. The Slipperiness on the pulse disappeared and the tongue coating diminished. She was placed on a diet that minimized mucus-producing foods, and her gastrointestinal function was treated with herbs. She received acupuncture after she stopped running. She was well for one-and-a-half years until she stopped taking the herbs. Shortly thereafter, she was in an airport, about to visit a relative in another part of the country, when she suddenly attacked her husband. At this point she felt possessed again and reported that it had always been he who controlled her. He, in turn, was controlled by the devil. F. belonged to a religious sect in which the devil played a prominent and literal role. Reinstitution of the herbs and acupuncture had no effect. While she no longer ran around the room and functioned better than she had in the past, she tried to kill her husband any time she could. They were separated. Attempts at some kind of insight therapy were to no avail, especially since her husband would not cooperate; her sister, who was a religious fanatic, blocked changes that might have helped.

An important principle of herbalism, of which I was unaware at the time (until a personal communication from Miles Roberts, an American authority on Kanpo, or Japanese herbalism), is that often an herb that helped the first time will not be effective the second time.[9] I was told of the importance of continuing a formula, even in small amounts, without interruption in treating difficult chronic situations like this.

Mental conditions associated with 'blood' problems are limited, I believe, to the grandiose delusions and paresis associated with the third stage of syphilis. Western diagnosis and treatment have supplanted Oriental medicine in this area, and have largely eliminated the disease as a clinical challenge. Porphoria is another possibility.

IATROGENIC ILLNESSES

Iatrogenic (physician-caused) illnesses constitute at least fifty percent of all those that I see in a practice consisting largely of seriously and chronically ill people. Any statements by industry, government, and individual investigators on the long and short range effects of the panoply of medications in use are totally unreliable. If our knowledge of biochemistry has increased at least 100 percent in the past five years (according to Jeffrey Bland, Ph.D., a noted biochemist-nutritionist), how little we must still know about ourselves! Tests conducted prior to this could tell us nothing about these areas of our physiology, and yet authoritative reports reassured us that the long-term effects of thousands of powerful chemicals were safe. And how limited are the meaning of those tests we conduct today to evaluate the impact of the never-ending cascade of new chemicals on a body and mind that we barely begin to understand? Those tests of the harmful effects of the chemicals with which we are inundating the world tell us nothing about what is happening because we do not know enough ourselves to construct a meaningful inquiry.

One indicator of the powerful impact these substances have is their effect on the pulse and tongue, as interpreted by the Chinese. The former is a sensitive and effective purveyor of information about the mind, the body, and even the spirit. Modern chemicals eliminate all of the subtleties of this remarkable instrument that universally conveys the message that our entire physiology is being put under the utmost stress. In Chinese terms, there is overwhelming heat from excess in the blood and throughout the system. The tongue that becomes heavily coated and red tells us that we are witnessing extreme toxicity. These signs develop quickly.

Other signs of toxicity, iatrogenic and otherwise, on the pulse are 'Blood unclear,' a very Deep and very Slow pulse, and, as mentioned above, more recently the Choppy quality over large sections of the pulse, which is associated with the cascade of more recent chemical assault alluded to in the discussion on toxicity.

A Case of Iatrogenesis

A typical example from my practice is that of J., a retired musician employed as the superintendent of a large school where he was very happy. During a routine physical examination in his new job, the patient, who was now 60 years old and had known little illness in his life and no mental-emotional difficulty, was found by his physician to have an elevated blood pressure for the first time. He had no complaints or any other signs of illness. His father died at the age of 90 and his mother died suddenly at the age of 74. Eight brothers and sisters were all well.

J. was placed on Tenormin for hypertension, which caused him shortness of breath and wheezing. Rather than remove the medication, his physician put him in the hospital and put him on Slobid, which led to further side effects, prompting this physician to put J. on Prednisone. By this time he required oxygen and was told by his physician that he had just had a heart attack. He was then placed on Peritrate, Theodore, Capitane (which caused dizzy spells), potassium (which caused a skin rash), and Moduretic.

When I saw J. he had leg cramps, dizzy spells, impotence, severe fatigue, was unable to work, and suffered from profound depression. According to his daughter, who was a nurse, J. spent his days crying, something she had never see him do in her entire life. Another Western medical examination of his heart revealed no previous heart attack. Over the period of a few weeks we eliminated most of his medications and reduced the rest to a fraction of what they had been. J. went back to work, and recovered completely from all of his symptoms, including the depression.

MEDICATION INTERFERES WITH HOMEOSTATIC INTELLIGENCE

In the beginning, illness is an attempt on the part of the body to restore itself, to correct the mistakes that the owner of this body is making. These are the acute diseases. As time passes, and the mistakes are not corrected, illness becomes an expression of the body's fatigue from the extended restorative process. These are the chronic debilitating diseases.

The restorative process, both in mental and physical areas, is an expression of the body's basic homeostatic intelligence. In 99 percent of all illness the matter is settled internally, and we never know about it or are aware only of mild discomfort. The constitutionally healthy who abuse this heritage may never know until it is too late. The constitutionally weak, the complainers, whom we all decry, all seem to live to ripe old ages. "The meek," it is said, "shall inherit the earth." Despite the evidence, we never get the message.

When restorative intelligence is unable by itself to reestablish function, we have symptoms, and often they are unpleasant and even painful. Since the medical profession and the multitude it educates are not trained to regard the symptom as an important message about the person's life, and since both are committed to avoid pain at any cost, one of two things occur. A drug is prescribed to suppress the symptom and/or a battery of tests is ordered to find a name for the symptoms.

The connection between a positive test result on any of the battery of tests and the person's life is unlikely to be clear to the physician, and even less likely to be clear to the patient. If the tests are negative or the symptoms persist despite medication, the patient is referred to a psychiatrist.

Homeostatic intelligence is so strong, especially in the young, that often the alleviation of the symptom, even without getting to the root cause, will allow the body a chance to re-group its forces and bring itself into balance until the next assault on its integrity. This is, however, not science, only chance.

Synthetic medication suppresses the symptom and the message, and with them the body's intelligence. With each successive round of medication, that intelligence is slightly more impaired. Generally, symptoms represent an attempt in the earliest stages to eliminate an impediment to the free circulation of qi, blood, and fluid, especially qi. Some activity on the part of the patient is impeding this flow and the body is pushing to break the block. Medication is working against physiology, in league with the destructive force in the patient's life. Chronic disease is the corruption of this living intelligence, over time.

CONCLUSION

Dr. Shen has made a valuable statement about the existence of 'systems' [377] beyond the organ energy systems, or 'orbs', with which Chinese medicine is primarily concerned. His insights into the effects of development, lifestyle, organ system states, and other factors on the 'nervous system', or what we roughly allude to as 'mind' and 'emotion', are significant, as are his contributions to the effects of emotion on these energies. The organization and elaboration of these ideas in terms familiar to Western psychology is a liberty I have taken in the service of my own enlightenment, which I hope will also prove useful to others.

15

A Medical Model

Humanistic psychology seeks a congenial medical model within which it can function without conflict. It has never been able to find a comfortable place within the traditional Western medical model that has emerged since the Industrial Revolution. I believe that Chinese medicine is a medical system with which Western psychology is highly congruent. In light of this, it is worthwhile to reexamine the principal features of this model, keeping in mind the expanded role it could play in the Western medical paradigm.

Chinese medicine is a medicine-philosophy. In ideology and methodology, it considers the total man in dynamic interplay with his total environment. As a form of medicine, it reflects, and then contributes to, a unified concept of human life, within each man, and with the entire universe.

In the West, the race between technology and spirituality for possession of the human soul is gathering momentum. Chinese medicine embodies a remarkable union of technical competence and spiritual force. This unity has eluded us in the Western world, where the increasing and desperately felt need for it has reached endemic proportion. Indeed, there is an element of panic in the way we have turned our gaze toward the East, as if we sense, individually and collectively, the rising tide of a cultural catastrophe.

Because it is also a successful method of alleviating suffering, Chinese medicine may succeed in bringing popular attention to the unifying concepts of the East more quickly and completely than any other manifestation of Oriental thought. Where gurus, religion, and philosophy alone have failed to capture the mass of people, Chinese medicine may bring a deeper and more lasting comprehension of what the others were trying to say. People are turning to this medicine in increasing numbers, and accepting it as a legitimate institution in their lives more readily than one could ever have predicted, and against much established opposition. It is conceivable that, having once realized its efficacy, people will at least consider the spiritual foundations on which this efficacy rests.

Whereas in the East, Chinese medicine is a child of spiritual philosophy, in the West it may be its parent. The revival of this ancient form of healing may help lead us from a path of increasing fragmentation and disintegration toward internal unification. Let us explore the attributes of Oriental medicine that distinguish it from Western medicine and which lend themselves to unity and harmony in human affairs and spirit.

I wish to make one point painfully clear. The statements that are about to appear are stereotypes of West and East. In the East there is now and has always been conflict. In the West we have Jesus and many before and since who have preached and practiced harmony. I have no personal illusions about the superiority of the Oriental over the Occidental, which may be inferred from these pages. My principal objective is to explain how the presence of energy concepts and adherence to their philosophical precedents contribute to a more coherent and comprehensive medicine. The forces in the East countermanding this influence in both daily life and the practice of medicine have always existed in China since the beginning of its history, as they do at this very moment. And in the West these ideas are, paradoxically, steadily growing.

THE TIE THAT BINDS

Western medicine has no unifying matrix. In the West, some token homage is paid to the unity of man with the universe by academic theologians, theoretical physicists, and a few science fiction writers. Medicine, with all its accomplishments, remains an uncoordinated accumulation of anatomical, physiological, pathological, and biochemical information. No one part is connected to another part. There is no whole, living thread of cohesiveness. This leaves us in a major state of chaos, which, in the absence of some potential solution, no one in Western medicine has the courage to face. Each organ system in the body is an entity unto itself, unrelated to any other organ system or to the general function of the whole. From this comes a proliferation of specialists, each of whom regards his area of the body as a separate, living system. No Western medical text addresses the absence of the concordances and relationships within its physiological model. The question is not even raised. How could it be, for example, that the eye and the liver could function with such complete independence in the same body? Even if such a connection were inconsequential, one would expect someone to ask the question.

Furthermore, the human body is known as an entity unto itself, with little or no connection to the outside world, to the gravitational field of the earth, or to the rhythmic movements of the other celestial systems. Yet we know that these systems function with extreme consistency, are highly predictable, and, most important of all, are rhythmically related to each other's cycles. We know of the relationship among bodies in the universe. All are moving together and affecting each other, yet it is inconceivable to Western science that the movements of living things and inanimate things may be slightly or profoundly affected by unseen, but in some cases identifiable, forces such as cosmic energies.

{ 381 }

All aspects of the Chinese medical system are intimately connected to each other in an observable, predictable fashion. Intervention in one area has a broad spectrum effect on the others. For example, the Kidney energy transmits genetic material, or the 'fire of life,' from one generation to another. Kidney energy assists the Lungs to receive the qi. It is responsible for the development of the central nervous system and of the bone marrow, controls growth and development as well as the urogenital system and sexual energy. It is related to the inner ear and the retina of the eye, and also controls the lower half of the body. On a psychological and spiritual level, I have discussed this energy in some detail in the chapter on the Water phase, in which I talked about the will, divine spirit, divine power, divine love, and the balance between fear and courage. This Water energy is the mother of the Liver energies, controller of the Heart Fire energies, and is itself controlled by the Earth and nourished by the Lung Metal energies.

There is a similar confluence of functions on a musculoskeletal level. Repressed chronic anger may express as muscular tension and spasm, referred to metaphorically as 'holding back.' In the upper back, repression can manifest as an inhibition to 'strike out' with one's arms, and in the lower back, an inability to 'kick out.' This anger can be released by treating spasm in these areas and balancing the energy that is released. As it is released, it is rapidly worked through by its own momentum on the levels of past, present, and future character, and total personality. This aspect of Chinese medicine has been a most amazing and awesome experience for me as an analyst. Its only limitation has been the limitation of my own understanding, in any one situation. We have, therefore, the unity, not only in the largest sense of philosophy, religion, and universal laws, but also in the smallest details of microcosmic phenomena.

It has been said that in the future, information will be power, and that the nation which can most efficiently harness that power through computers will inherit the earth. What value is all of this information when these correspondences, so necessary to the understanding and maintenance of health, are largely ignored, or left in a state of informational chaos? What will bring us out of this anarchy of knowledge and give coherence to our medical existence? In an age of increasing fragmentation, the medical model we will be looking for must be a unifying force by being itself the model of unity.

Oriental philosophy, and its medicine, teaches that all of life may be understood as a function of a single force, an invisible energy called qi by the Chinese, and prana by the Hindus. All of us, and all existence, is a manifestation of this one unifying force, obeying the universal laws of nature in a variety of forms, essences, and movements. The form and substance of the universe is the materialization of this force. Man lives in this sea of force, greater than his own. When this force moves and changes, man must also move and change.

Energy is the essential factor in life and, therefore, the prime consideration in sickness and health. Whatever other forces may be at work in a given instance, the distinction between health and illness is predominantly determined by the vicissitudes of that energy in the body it inhabits. This is a unifying concept, emphasizing the powerful single tie that binds us rather than the less significant forces which divide us. The energy that causes disease is the one that cures it. Sickness is only a variation of, and not a state separate from, health. We are essentially one with nature.

The ancients observed and recorded in detail the rhythmic movements of this energy in the most cosmic and most minute structures. Out of this came the Laws of Nature. Only man has a choice to follow or defy these laws. Disease follows deviation from these laws. If they are followed, the energy forces within men are free and flowing, and there is no problem. If, however, this system is in any way impaired, blocked, weak, or unbalanced, the changes of energy in the cosmos will be resisted, and the result will be a conflict of forces. This conflict between a moving energy against another resisting force in the human body results in pain or emotional disturbance.

Western medicine exists within the same philosophical framework that produced industrialization, sharing with it the aim of controlling and defeating nature and the universe. It reflects the resentment of Western man toward any control over his fate, other than by his own ego, which is, I believe, the deepest source of his impressive, compensatory, obsessive (and, therefore, never-ending) struggle for power and his escalating alienation and loneliness.

By contrast, Oriental medicine subscribes to the axiom that "Man helps, and nature cures." The Chinese believe that 'good manners' toward the natural world are contiguous and continuous with good manners in society. Respect for nature is at the core of all Oriental philosophy. Health is, therefore, not conceived as an endless struggle against nature, but instead a welcome return to nature. Yin and yang, for example, are not simply opposing forces. They are two contrasting aspects of one energy. Yin and yang are also interdependent, interconsuming, and interchangeable. They may transform one into the other. They are simply two contrasting aspects of one energy. This congeniality with the natural order is in sharp contrast to the discordant philosophy in the West, which views nature as an enemy to be conquered.

Minimization of conflict with the world in which we live has a far-reaching effect on the tone of healing. The underlying philosophy of harmony, balance, rhythm, moderation, gentleness, unity, and non-judgment in the support of nature lends itself to ease and relaxation, to the reduction of tension; that is, toward all the things that people in the Western world say they desire but which are inherently inconsistent with their conflictual philosophy of life. The West believes in conflict for its own sake and in overwhelming nature rather than respecting it.

MEDICINE AND LIFE ARE ONE

I have mentioned that in the West we have an increasing accumulation of unrelated facts, born of analytic research, and resulting in the fragmentation of medicine into specialties without an appreciation of the relationship between these fragments. We have the concept of disease, which is basically the germ theory inherited from Pasteur, and the concept of an outside force attacking, which is a reflection of Western industrial society and the ambiance of struggle of man against nature. In this model of conflict and disunity, the search has been for the 'magic bullet' with which to destroy the alien forces causing disease.

The reason for these problems is the lack of a coherent theory of health. Such a theory is necessary to tie together all the massive accumulation of disparate facts. What, in essence, is a theory of health? Essentially, a theory of health is a reflection of a theory of life.

In Chinese medicine we have a theory of health based on the knowledge (through the use of the pulse, the tongue, the eyes, color, sound, emotion, smell, and other parameters) of the healthy movement, balance, rhythm, and amount of energy. Using this body of knowledge to define health, we are able to detect and describe the smallest deviations from that observable standard. This standard is an energy physiology, described in intricate detail, encompassing the correspondences and interrelationships among all parts of our material and spiritual being, and between that being and the environment in its entirety and at all stages of maturation.

This medical model is thus capable of correlating the incipient stages of a deviation from this testable standard of health with the patient's lifestyle. Diagnostically, we are able to answer the question, "How is the patient, through his daily life, creating his own illness?" We can bring the medicine back to the simplest facts of life, so that the issue of responsibility is easily understood and, therefore, the steps to health more clearly within the patient's grasp. In speaking of lifestyles, I am referring to eating habits, working habits, environmental stress (both chemical and physical), weather, climate, social habits, sexual habits, trauma, exercise, emotion, and recreational habits such as drugs, television, and, more recently, computers. The Chinese medical model has the capacity to relate the smallest changes in function to excesses in any one of these parameters of everyday existence, to judge how long they have occurred, how heavily indulged in, and how significant to the person's life.

Using the signs and symptoms of disordered energy, we are capable, in the Chinese model, of distinguishing constitutional and congenital disorders. Identifying problems coming from these two sources early in life is useful for parents and physicians, so that they may, early on, offer support in those areas that require it and may alter habits and patterns of living and emotional development, thus minimizing the impact of these problems. When parents have realistic, rather than inflated, expectations of their child's abilities from the early stages of development, enormous conflict and pain in people can be avoided.

Without a concept of the process of disease based on the theory of health and life, and without a set of correspondences between living conditions and health, we are in no position to discuss prevention. In Western medicine, we know little or nothing about the disease process. So, despite the voluminous compilation of scientific research, there is no true preventive medicine in our culture. To be truly preventive, intervention in disease has to begin before it becomes a clinical, pathological entity. Today it costs several million dollars to build a prevention clinic, which at best can tell us that we are already afflicted with a fatal disease in its early stages. As yet, we are unable to detect disease on a sub-cellular level.

Chinese medicine, on the other hand, has traditionally been a preventive medicine. It has the ability to pick up the process of disease prior to its manifestations as morphological pathology, and it can relate these early signs and symptoms to lifestyle. Thus the patient's attention can, early on, be brought to how he or she is creating his or her own illness, and to what is needed to prevent its more serious manifestation. In a sense, medicine and life are essentially one. If we follow the basic laws of our nature and the limits of our own constitution, we will, barring bad fortune, enjoy good health.

{385}

INTERNAL DEVILS

Consequently, Chinese medicine views illness as an expression of the personal violation of a person's own nature and calls upon the person to become aware of how he or she is interfering with the flow of nature, both within and without. People are encouraged to examine how they live, think, feel, and to evaluate their habits and values in order to understand their illness. The focus is, therefore, on an inner, rather than an outer, alien cause; one is ill because of something innate in oneself or in one's way of life. Chinese medicine studies the human process as a standard against which to evaluate the dynamic phenomena called disease. Recognizing the existence of external pathogenic factors leaves responsibility for health or illness primarily with the individual. Rather than being attacked from the outside by 'germs' and defended on the inside by extrinsic forces such as drugs, this medicine sees the person as being attacked by himself and defended by himself.

It is only recently, and hesitatingly, that Western medicine has begun to acknowledge that mechanisms in the human body designed for its own protection are as important as the 'germ,' and to see disease as an alteration in those defenses. With the acknowledged epidemic proportions of diseases, such as Acquired Immune Deficiency Syndrome (AIDS) and AIDS-related diseases, the acceptance of this view has necessarily accelerated. Yet, the concepts of "milieu interior"[1] as outlined by Claude Bernard in 1868, or of "homeostasis," as described by Cannon,[2] are still not a significant guiding force in Western medicine.

There are many areas of life for which we must take responsibility, including work, our environment, nutrition, exercise, and emotion. The ones that have received the least attention in our society are iatrogenic etiologies and the relationship of the disease process to sexual function.

With regard to the iatrogenic causes of illness, I would estimate that approximately 50 percent of the patients whom I have treated over the years have been ill primarily as the result of the medical treatments that they have received. I have described one such history in a previous chapter. Chemicals are introduced into our environment, into our bodies, with no knowledge of the long-range effects. Furthermore, even the available tests of short-range effects are too gross and inadequate to inform us of the subtle changes in the organ systems. Liver function tests are positive only when a large percentage of the organ is in a serious state of dysfunction. These tests tell us nothing about the process of disease or the process of damage as a result of the introduction of these artificial substances into our lives in the air we breathe, in the water we drink, in the food we eat, and in the form of medications.

The process of isolating the 'active agent' and concentrating it into a medication destroys the balance that exists in the natural form from which it was taken. One need only observe the effects of the herb Ephedra (Ma Huang) and its so-called active ingredient, Ephedrine. The latter has an effect analagous to a sledge hammer on a penny nail. Even the Ephedra itself is an herb that is used with caution and combined with others to counteract its stimulating side effects.

Used judiciously and with great restraint, these concentrated chemicals are of enormous use temporarily in extreme conditions; however, they were not meant to be used for more than a short period of time. The side effects are numerous and debilitating. Many complain of simply feeling "not alive."

The ubiquitous distribution of these basically toxic substances as medicinals is a consequence of the concept of sickness as an extraneous force. The emphasis is placed on powerful, synthetic drugs foreign to our life system to combat the 'foreign invader.' The thrust is to detach ourselves from the struggle. The price for this detachment is incalculable and is measured only partially by the remarkable list of adverse, and often fatal, side effects of allopathic medicines, many of which are overlooked and denied by its practitioners. Oriental medicine adheres to the Hippocratic Oath that "I will give no deadly medicine to anyone." It generally uses a gentle, slow-acting medicine whose focus is to restore physiology.

Symptomatology is viewed by Chinese medicine as a signal of poor living habits and an attempt by the body's intelligence to restitute, or restore, health. The symptom is, therefore, not our enemy; it is our friend, and we wish to find a way to do its work more efficiently in order to achieve a true and lasting restoration. The principal work is to restore function. The elimination of symptoms may sometimes be an important, immediate goal of treatment; but it is not its fundamental, or ultimate, goal. If it is the physician's role to restore physiology, it is the patient's responsibility to maintain it.

In terms of the lifestyle of our patients, and, in fact, our society, little is understood by Western medicine of all of the factors listed above, including the effects of weather and trauma. Each of these is discussed in terms of its psychological effects in the previous chapter on the 'systems model' of Dr. John Shen. These discussions could be greatly expanded. The consequences of inappropriate sexual activity, nutrition, and exercise would each in itself deserve the attention of an entire chapter. All of these factors have been studied extensively in Chinese medicine in terms of their impact on energy function and energy systems. It has a great deal of information for patients in terms of how they, as individuals, should behave in these areas of life so as to maintain health. In contrast to Western medicine, education of the patient has substance, meaning, and detail not available to Western practitioners.

The allopathic treatment principle is one that combats disease by the use of remedies which produce effects the opposite of those produced by the disease. It is basically antagonistic and suppressive. For example, in the treatment of catecholamines deficiency in relation to depression, the tricyclic medications block the reception of serotonin and nor-epinephrine by nerve endings. The MAO medications inhibit the oxidative deamination by the body's amine oxidases. In schizophrenia, where there is an increase in dopamine, the object is to inhibit the dopamine with the major tranquilizers.

The other physiological approach is replacement rather than repression. In this approach, an attempt would be made to find systems that make serotonin or nor-epinephrine and to discover the basic defect that creates the increase in dopamine and correct the defect. Replacement, or 'constitutional therapy,' is the therapeutic approach of Chinese medicine.

PROPER LIVING

I am saying, essentially, that a further, unifying aspect of Chinese medicine consists in our studying and treating a person rather than a disease, which is the opposite of our approach in the West. The diagnosis made by Chinese evaluative tools reads the inner state of the individual in terms of energy balance. Each individual is treated for his own special imbalance, notwithstanding the nature of the symptoms. The treatment is generally of the unique and total person, and not simply of alien signs and symptoms. As Osler said, "Don't tell me what type of disease the patient has, tell me what type of patient has the disease."[3]

The fact is that we are not all made, nor do we all develop, equally. As a general approach to life, it would be a great contribution on the part of any medicine if it could lend its authority to the understanding and treatment of people, especially during their developmental years, in terms of their inherent deficits. Countless lives would become worth living with a little more of this understanding and acceptance. One person I know, born in China, was identified by his mother as having weak Lung energy at birth. In distinction to his eight siblings, his mother never allowed him to go to a regular school, to dress himself until age 16, or to participate in strenuous activities. This person is now in his 70s, still with weak lungs, having had two pneumothoraxes in his 60s under circumstances of stress, but still well and functioning as long as he observes the limits set down by his basic deficit.

Based on such a precept, any person's life could be organized rationally on an individual basis from the beginning, emphasizing the positive. Struggle and conflict that ensues from the ignorance of deficits could be minimized. On a strictly medical level, those diseases to which a person might be more prone could be prevented by proper living; and with a knowledge of correspondences, those organs that ordinarily support others in the physiological state could be enhanced to back up those that are recognized to be deficient from birth, or from life. It is extremely important for people to know in what way their lifestyle creates significant stress on areas of constitutional vulnerability.

A dichotomy has existed in the West between mind and body since the Middle Ages, when the church permitted dissection of the body by the laity but reserved the mind for the church. A significant gesture toward unity, which this book has hoped to demonstrate, is the fact that in Chinese medicine there is no distinction between mind and body. An imbalance of energy may show itself as a disturbance in the highest functions or in the so-called lower functions, or both. Corrective medicine concerns itself with the disturbance in the balance of energy, and not with whether the symptom is emotional or physical.

Today in the West, if the patient has complaints that cannot be identified by our diagnostic tools, he is considered to have a disease of the mind. The profession seems to have forgotten that germs did not exist until the microscope came along. The fact is that something very real is occurring on an energy level that affects both mind and body while both of these are having a corresponding effect on energy. This two-way system, described here and elsewhere, enables Chinese medicine to offer the patient an opportunity for self-discovery, rather than the opportunity to be an observer of a gigantic struggle for dominance between the physician and the disease. Indeed, if there is a tension in this model, it is not one of conflict but rather one of harmony, man in harmony with himself and the world around him. Disease is not an abstract, detached phenomenon, but a maladaptive restoration, an attempt to heal that miscarries, a retreat from intolerable or unsolvable problems with the object of staying both 'intact' and in 'contact.'

The emphasis on self-responsibility makes it incumbent for a medical model to deal with the struggle between what Karen Horney described as the "ego ideal" and reality. The person who is confronted with abuses of his constitution by his lifestyle may not find such confrontation congenial. Often, it is a blow to the ego to concede an innate defect or to acknowledge the self-destructiveness of one's favorite pastime, addiction, or habituation. There is, therefore, in this model a very relevant place for a variety of therapeutic tools, which are subsumed under the heading of psychotherapy. Ultimately these ego issues are expressions of the more fundamental polarizations of love and power. A medicine must be prepared to deal with people in this most crucial variable in the equation of health and disease. If there is no resolution here, there is no resolution anywhere; and this model of medicine must be capable of engaging people on this terrain.

The Energy of the Physician

In Western medicine it is anathema for the physician's subjective being to be critical to the practice of his medicine. The validity of his practice is his intellectual ability to choose the correct drug and procedure, which consequently also gives him personal satisfaction and respect among his colleagues. Should the patient recover without this objective, reproducible documentation, the profession and the doctor question whether the patient was sick to begin with. This creates a natural authoritarian gulf between healer and healed. It creates conflict rather than harmony in the therapeutic milieu. It also raises the question of how we define disease.

If we require a medicine that encourages and allows the physician, through its very practice, to maintain his own humanity, this medicine would impel a physician to exercise all his senses in his contact with patients. To a large extent today, the physician is a robot, operated by a pharmaceutical company. There is no way that he could avoid conceding that he could not be better replaced by a computer. When, however, physicians constantly use their eyes, ears, taste, smell, and touch as their principal tools of communication, they do not have the high incidence of suicide and early death from disease that physicians now suffer. Alienation is the Greek word for insanity.

The humanity and the health of the physician as well as the patient, therefore, depends very much on a more human, personal contact between the two. The laying on of hands has important overtones, in terms of healing, as the transmission of the sense of caring from one person to another. This is a form of love, and love is ultimately the great healer. In this model of medicine, therefore, the element of what is popularly referred to as suggestion, ineffable power that passes from one human being to another, will gain a new level of respect. Osteopathic physicians have demonstrated rotation and side-bending of vertebrae due entirely to emotional stress. If emotion can rotate vertebrae, then surely the loving relationship can rotate them as well. In such a relationship, all are enhanced. Physician and patient are mutually nourished. We denigrate this enriching process as 'suggestion.' Yet it was said of Jesus that "No miracle could He work here, because of lack of faith."[4]

The diagnostic system itself is the sense, mind, heart, and spirit of the physician. There are no machines. The key to this system is the personal awareness of the physician and his faith in that awareness and himself, rather than in a machine. In the West, reality must be captured by shape and form. It is real only if it is reducible to a material object or a statistically-significant number. By doing this, we are eliminating only the element of chance, for that is the true meaning of statistical significance. It does not mean, however, that whatever is not statistically significant is not true. It is only that it could have happened by chance.

Pursuit of knowledge in this fashion would, therefore, eliminate most of the important medical discoveries of the past 50 years, which have been primarily the result of serendipity. The Amine-Oxidase Inhibitors were originally a treatment for tuberculosis. Thorazine was developed as a treatment for nausea. Penicillin and more recent antibiotics that have been discovered in the skin of frogs came to Western medicine from non-medical investigations, having nothing to do with statistical significance or double-blind studies. Nevertheless, we are, by design, ruled by machines; and with the advent of the computer, we will become less respectful of innate human worth as a reliable source of important information.

In the beginning, science was the art of observation, as opposed to the art of speculation. Chinese medicine is scientific by that standard. The trained Chinese doctor, like the trained Western physician of yesteryear, is a keen observer of phenomena. Whereas in Western medicine we are now alienated from the power and value of our senses, in Chinese medicine the training and value of these senses is retained. By its original definition, Chinese medicine is far more faithful to the basic tenets of science than modern Western medicine.

In Chinese medicine, the physician is objective but not alienated. His energy, indeed, is an accepted part of the healing process. It does not mean that his herbs and his needles are not meaningful; it means only that he, also, is meaningful. Approximately 15 years ago, there was a physician in the Long Island Jewish Hospital who was the only one anywhere in the metropolitan area who could use streptomycin without creating any side effects, primarily hearing loss, for which this medicine is so infamous. In his hands, this medication had no side effects.

The model of medicine congruent with modern humanistic psychology would embrace philosophy beyond the concept of a double-blind study and statistical significance. Oriental medicine takes a positive, rather than negative, approach to human processes. It examines symptoms as restorative, rather than destructive; as educational, rather than adverse; and a hopeful indication that the body still has the strength to attempt to heal itself. The restoration of balance and respect for natural rhythms are its fundamental guides. Philosophically, the thrust of Oriental medicine is to replace conflict with homeostasis and to return physiology to normal. This model embraces opposites and seeks for the mean. It values gentleness and moderation. If it does not help, it will do no harm.

Oriental medicine is syntonic with a universal model of existence, a cosmology that unifies man with his universe and with all phenomena. It is prepared to include the spiritual, as well as the material aspects of life as factors in health and in the etiology of dysfunction. Within this framework, spiritual life is not dissociated from the physical, mental, and emotional. This model is capable, therefore, of assessing the spirit as readily as any other basic function of life. It is committed to helping people search for their own free and independent spiritual growth when they signal their readiness.

I have observed that acupuncture is a medicine-philosophy. The laws that govern its concept of sickness and health, diagnosis and treatment, are the laws that govern all of Daoist life. Medicine, diet, art, government, family life, education, agriculture, and astronomy are guided by the same principles inherent in the laws of the Five Phases. Medicine and science are in a consonance with life as a whole and contribute to its stability. Highest and lowest levels of functioning cohere. No one part of the total picture is ignored without compromising the remainder. A medicine that enhances a unified concept of existence is a countervailing force to the profound and deadly alienation and fragmentation which characterizes the 21st century.

CHINESE MEDICINE IN THE WEST

How will acupuncture actually fare in the Western world? What can we say about this in advance of its main thrust into Occidental culture?

The first problem I foresee is related to the absence in Western medicine of a concept of energy comparable to that in Oriental medicine, and on which the latter rests so heavily. Energy enters our thinking in disconnected ways as a metabolic concept. The energy force described in Oriental medicine has no counterpart in our system, with the exception of the relatively undeveloped work of Reich,[5] and Alexander Lowen, and John Pierrakos.[6]

These ideas have been rejected by all but a few in the Western world. In the West we will, therefore, have considerable difficulty in seriously entertaining a medicine built around something we cannot measure with our tools and devices.

This conceptual block has inspired many in the People's Republic of China and in the West to abandon the energy concepts defined by ancient law and to Westernize acupuncture. Explanations of its mechanism have involved colloidal solutions, the autonomic nervous system, neuro-inhibition, pain walls, and endorphins. In pursuit of a modern explanation for the effectiveness of Chinese medicine, there is currently a frontal assault on every measurable human chemical and physical unit by clinical, experimental laboratory science, especially in the People's Republic of China. The concept of energy that has given acupuncture its internal consistency, and all of life a meaningful core, is being quickly and quietly expunged.

The law of the Five Phases and universal laws of the Tao concepts of yin and yang and most of the acupuncture points are quickly following 'qi energy' into obscurity. We are obliged, by the prestige and power of Western science, to confirm the validity of phenomena according to its specific standards and techniques. In the West, we know only what registers on our machines. If we cannot measure, we cannot know. We have limited the parameters of our knowledge to the sensitivity of our mechanical devices.

Chinese medicine faces several other conceptual barriers in the West. One is the basic conflict between technology and art in the healing process. Technology insists that the healer must not be important to the healing process as a test of the validity of the healing system. However, in a healing system in which the movement and balance of energy is the critical factor in sickness and health, the energy of the healer enters significantly into the system as a positive or negative force. Lawson-Wood stated: "It is therapeutically significant what is going on in the practitioner's mind. In other words, the practitioner's intention has great influence upon the quality and polarity treatment he will, in fact, administer."[7]

The importance of the healer to the medicine bespeaks of acupuncture as an art. As such, there will be little of the verifiable data so indispensable to the scientific model. The spirit of man, the energy of nature, and the knowledge of its ways are the healing powers of Oriental medicine. The modern scientific institution will test and apply what is verifiable by reproducible and statistically-significant experiment. For this reason, I believe that Chinese medicine will pass again on its long historical journey through a period of great difficulty and devaluation by the establishment. Oriental medicine is at a crossroads, as is mankind. One way leads to extinction, the other, which I believe is being increasingly chosen by the people who use medicine, if not by the people who practice it, leads to a new and profound spiritual reunion of man with heaven and earth.

MEDICINE AND SOCIETY

With all of their potential to solve the most difficult medical dilemmas, why are these models relatively obscure in our part of the world and missing their mark even in their countries of origin? What seems most obvious is that we cannot change medicine without changing society, without a significant alteration in values in which ecology takes precedence over economics, and love balances power. A world in which our senses and sensibilities are violently assaulted is syntonic with a violent medicine. Each of the values I have mentioned as being desirable for the ideal medicine applies equally to the ideal society in which it must exist. One will never flourish without the other.

The endeavor to practice an ideal medicine will be an endless struggle against superior odds, until each individual member of that society desires it and, through his or her own quest, arrives at those values upon which it rests. In order to have a medicine that is more sensitive to our humanity, we must take responsibility for it. Changing governments and ideologies avails little. I wish to end with the message that less demanding solutions than internal growth are dangerously misleading and endlessly frustrating. The hope and the courage we need along our separate paths toward a loving society and a compassionate medicine, which enhance health, depend on our clear perception of that principle. The kingdom of heaven lies within.

16

A Recapitulation

The most consequential intention of this book is to present the mental, emotional, and spiritual roles of the Five Phases and organ system energies as positive natural functions in the service of the survival and fulfillment of 'being.' The negative emotions that are customarily associated with these organ system energies are artifacts of a distortion of the natural function and not the function itself. They are restorative, not basic attributes. Chronic anger is seen as a failure of the dynamic need to assert, mediated by Wood energies. Chronic fear is the response to a breakdown in the natural function of Kidney qi energies to balance awe, reverence, faith, and courage. It is imperative to our use of Chinese medicine in spiritual, mental, and emotional areas that we associate each organ system with special functions which, in their totality, account for all important human attributes.

These natural functions in the areas of mentation, emotion, and spirituality embody and express the growth and development of potential 'being'; I have attempted to examine these natural energy functions in the context of an evolutionary model of stages of development. The purpose here is to see these energies as essential to human growth through all of its epochs, from birth to death, and to see them in terms of the familiar and everyday experiences of life. The consequences of failures in the unfolding of these energy functions at each evolutionary step have been explored. These are the disharmonies of personality, the discussion of which is instructive but by no means exhaustive. The personality sketches that we have observed as possible outcomes are illustrative and at no time to be taken as an attempt to establish a hard and fast diagnostic typology.

A related issue open to further consideration is the correctness of viewing enduring personality traits as the most reliable indicator of fundamental energy disequilibriums. This is an area calling for considerable study over a relatively long period by many practitioners.

I have attempted to illustrate the dynamic interplay of organ systems in relationship to emotion, mind, and spirit, and to demonstrate how the Ko ('control') cycle of the Five Phase system operates as a corrective system similar in concept to the 'reaction formation' described by Freud. I have tried to impart the concept of all pathology as a natural function of the organism in its attempt to restitute itself for survival, that is, to "maintain 'contact' while staying 'intact.'"

Most Western bioenergetic therapies, emphasizing direct attack on defensive energies and breaking down 'resistance,' wrongly assume that healing automatically will follow therefrom. Chinese medicine offers the possibility of providing the deeper nourishing energies, unavailable in the Western modalities, that enhance healing and permit many people the luxury of feeling internally stronger and in less need of defensive postures. Resistance and the breaking down of defensive energies retreats to the background as an issue, and, instead of engaging the negative aspects of a resistance, we are working with the intent.

Acupuncture also provides an opening to the unconscious and a break in maladaptive feedback loops. The growth that may follow depends, in my opinion, on the coincidence of this opening to areas of unfilled or distorted life-force with the opportunity for a 'new experience' with that energy. That new experience may begin when the practitioner recognizes the positive intention of the patient's restorative maneuvers (defenses).

When practiced at its best, acupuncture promotes and enhances awareness. The growing awareness is often painful as well as gratifying, since awareness is the antithesis of denial as well as a detoxifier of all that deadens the feelings and senses. From the first encounter with the needles, that side of a person that wants most to feel fully alive is engaged in unraveling the enigma of an avoidance of one's own life.

Dr. John Shen's concept of an intact 'nervous system' as a bulwark against emotional stress allows us to re-examine our traditional view of the psychosomatic patient as less than emotionally competent. To the contrary, we can see, from Dr. Shen's perspective, that it is only with a strong 'nervous system' that the organism breaks physically rather than mentally.

The basic principles of Chinese medicine, which, in my opinion, render it the most completely holistic medicine, are reviewed in several parts of this book, especially in Chapter 15. Here, special attention is paid to the unifying role of the concept of energy, or qi. The dynamic interactions of organ system and emotion and the influence of constitution, life experience, and lifestyle are discussed in Chapter 14.

[397]

Lastly, I have tried to impart the flavor of Chinese medicine as an evolving one in the hands of Westerners, one which provides the suitable, unifying medical context so long sought by Western humanistic psychology, with which it is remarkably congenial in principle and practice.

CHINESE MEDICINE IS 'ROUND'

I have not attempted to cover the subject of treatment in this book. I have not presented acupuncture points, formulae, or strategies specific to emotional, mental, and spiritual dysfunction, except by way of example. These are relevant and will be presented in a different context. I have omitted them here in order to emphasize that the fundamental approach to psychological problems is best reached by staying true to those principles of energy transformations that have been tested by the centuries. I have an entire notebook filled with formulae for every psychological condition, culled from numerous sources. While these are valuable, they are no substitute for those laws that govern the manipulation of energy in all of its manifestations.

I am also stating categorically that each of us has the privilege to explore the outer frontiers of Chinese medicine and report our impressions. Only time will tell which of these investigations have universal application. In the early years of the 21st century, conditions exist which the human race has not encountered in its recorded history. The medicine conceived by cultures who faced none of the physical, chemical, and mental vicissitudes of the industrial and communications revolutions cannot without amendment be sufficient to cope with the world in which we live today. The violence of Western medications is syntonic with the ecologic violence impinging on the innate survival mechanisms of the human organism. Chinese medicine must stay true to its principles of harmony and gentleness, yet meet the challenges of an industrial society.

Although it must change, we will increasingly need Chinese medicine as a unifying concept that allows us to examine and understand ourselves as one, to collate and correlate massive amounts of disparate facts into one integrated system, and to preserve our integrity within the framework of inevitable chaos. We will need a medicine in which the force that occasions disease is the same one that cures; in which a person and his disease are joined by responsibility; in which mind and body are an indistinguishable single entity, and healer and healed converge; in which man is one with nature, and united with God.

Chinese philosophy has managed to create order where it is required, while living comfortably with chaos as an ineluctable fact of life. It accommodates chaos by acknowledging that beyond constitution, and what we do with it, there is the third, overriding principle of existence: fate. This is why Dr. Shen always referred to Chinese medicine as "round." Reflecting the trends of Chinese society to evolve as a closed system, much of the flavor of this flexibility is not present in the available writings, but only in the association with a particular 'master.'

Chinese medicine is changing to meet the challenge. It must do this by absorbing ideas from other disciplines that do not inherently demand the medicine to succumb to a fragmenting reality and lose its lasting quality of unity. I have tried to show that humanistic Western psychology is one body of knowledge congruous in principle to the axioms of Chinese medicine. There are two general approaches to mental illness. We may concentrate first on intellectual and emotional insight and behavioral alterations, as we do in psychotherapy, hoping that blocks to life flow will dissolve in the process; or we may first open energy blocks and let awareness and insight follow the flow of the life force. There is now, in my experience, ample reason to believe that we have a choice, and that insight and being are realized at least as much, or even more fully, by the latter approach as by the former. By combining dynamic psychotherapy with Chinese medicine we have an opportunity to embrace both approaches in a simultaneous and integrated fashion. Together they are greater than the sum of their parts.

My own thesis delineates an evolutionary approach to energetics reflecting developmental psychology. Distortions in the natural functions of energies at the different eras of life leave us with general personality configurations that may be among the earliest indicators of energy disharmony. Whether this will further illuminate the mysteries of the 'rising dragon,' or the flight of the 'red bird,' is a story in the making of this book and, I hope, of those who are inspired to go beyond.

Endnotes

PRELIMINARY DISTINCTIONS

1. Lu Xun, *Selected Works* (Beijing: Foreign Language Press, 1956).

2. Bo Yang, *The Ugly Chinaman* (Taipei, Taiwan: Lin Bai, 1985).

3. Joseph Campbell, *The Masks of God: Oriental Mythology* (New York: Penguin Books, 1976), 418, 422.

4. Ilsa Veith, *The Yellow Emperor's Classic of Internal Medicine* (Berkeley: University of California Press, 1972), 215-216.

CHARTER ONE

1. Ilsa Veith, *The Yellow Emperor's Classic of Internal Medicine* (Berkeley: University of California Press, 1972), 118, 120.

2. Rodger Williams, *Biochemical Individuality* (Austin: University of Texas, 1956).

3. Leon I. Hammer, "Psychotherapy and Growth," *Contemporary Psychoanalysis*, Vol. 10, No. 3, 1974.

4. Joseph Campbell, *The Masks of God: Primitive Mythology* (New York: Penguin Books, 1986), 60-62.

5. Roberto Assagioli, *Psychosynthesis: A Manual of Principles and Techniques* (New York: Viking/Compass, 1971). See also Assagioli, *The Act of Will* (New York: Penguin Books, 1974).

6. Carl Jung, *Memories, Dreams, Reflections* (New York: Vintage Books, 1965).

7. Selah Chamberlain, "Shen & Ling," *The Journal of Traditional Acupuncture*, Vol. 4, No. l, summer, 1980:16.

8. "Thus Hun is Yang in relation to P'o, yet Yin (structive) in relation to its determinant Shen. P'o is Yin in relation to Hun, yet-because it represents the

substantive aspect or even the substantiation within the individual of Shen, the active configurative force -is Yang in relation to *Ching (Qing). Ching* is but a metaphor for the individually specific function of P'o within an organism." Manfred Porkert, *The Theoretical Foundations of Chinese Medicine: Systems of Correspondence* (Cambridge: The MIT Press, 1974), 184.

9. Richard Wilhelm, *I Ching: The Book of Changes* (London: Routledge and Kegan, Paul, 1951).

10. See Sigmund Freud, "Psychotherapy of Hysteria," *The Standard Edition of the Complete Psychological Works of Sigmund Freud*, Vol. 2 (London: Hogarth Press, 1955), 302; Freud, "Transference in the Analytic Therapy," *General Introduction to Psychoanalysis* (Garden City, New York: Garden City Publishing, 1943); and Freud, "Analysis Terminable and Interminable," *The Standard Edition of the Complete Psychological Works of Sigmund Freud*, Vol. 5 (London: Hogarth Press, 1953), 316.

11. Ralph Waldo Emerson, "Self-Reliance," *Essays: 1st & 2d Series* (Boston: Houghton Mifflin Company, 1929), 45.

12. See Alfred North Whitehead, *Field Theory Process and Reality* (New York: Mac-Millan, 1929); Kurt Lewin, *Field Theory in Social Science: Selected Theoretical Papers*, ed. Dorwin Cartright (New York: Harper, 1951).

13. Veith, *Classic of Internal Medicine*, 97-98.

14. Hans Selye, *The Stress of Life: General Adaption* (New York: McGraw-Hill, 1956).

15. John Shen, personal communication.

16. Albert Einstein, *Relativity: The Special and General Theory* (New York: Crown Publishers, 1961), 45.

17. Veith, *Classic of Internal Medicine*, 104.

18. Freud, " The Anxiety Neurosis," *The Standard Edition of the Complete Psychological Works of Sigmund Freud*, Vol. 3 (London: Hogarth Press, 1962), 107-111.

19. Jung, *Memories, Dreams, Reflections*, 138.

20. Wilhelm Reich, *The Discovery of the Orgone*, Vol. 1 (New York: Orgone Institute Press, 1942).

21. For the theories developed by Alexander Lowen and John Pierrakos, see Alexander Lowen, *Physical Dynamics of Character Structure* (New York: Grune and Stratton, 1958).

22. Harry Stack Sullivan, "The Interpersonal Theory of Psychiatry," *Collected Works of Harry Stack Sullivan* (New York: W. W. Norton and Company, 1953), 36.

23. Arthur Waley, *The Three Ways of Thought in Ancient China* (London: G. Allen and Unwin, 1963).

24. While I agree with the view that individuality is an illusion, it is also my opinion that the only valid achievement of oneness comes through and from a phase of authentic individuation. Those societies in which the individual is subordinate to the group (such as China and Japan) are not representative of an egoless condition. I see them as an organized group ego, possibly one step behind us on the path. One cannot lose an ego one does not have.

CHAPTER TWO

1. Dennis and Joyce Lawson-Wood, *Five Elements of Acupuncture and Chinese Massage* (Northamptonshire, Great Britain: Health Science Press, 1973), 90.

2. Ibid, 88-89.

3. Leon I. Hammer, "Psychotherapy and Growth," *Contemporary Psychoanalysis,* Vol. 10, No. 3, 1974:389.

4. Harry Stack Sullivan, *Clinical Studies in Psychiatry* (New York: W. W Norton and Company, 1956), 5, 103.

5. Sullivan, "The Interpersonal Theory of Psychiatry," *Collected Works of Henry Stack Sullivan* (New York: W. W. Norton and Company, 1953), 36.

6. Hammer, "Integrated Acupuncture Therapy for Body and Mind," *American Journal of Acupuncture,* Vol. 8, No. 2, April-June, 1980.

CHAPTER THREE

1. Joseph Campbell, *The Masks of God: Primitive Mythology* (New York: Penguin Books. 1986), 404.

2. *The Centennial of Von Stradonitz's Work* (Washington, D.C.: American Chemical Society, 1966).

3. Matthew 7:20.

4. If medical technology succeeds in pursuing this direction far enough, it will find itself in the world of quantum physics where many of the mechanical and materialistic aspects of reality give way.

   An article in *Science News* which concerns itself with small particle physics, entitled "Axion Hunt: Getting Something Out of Nothing," traces the quest for the smallest particle of matter: "Instantons are solutions to the mathematical equations that describe the forces of chromodynamic field, but, unlike field quanta, they have no materiality. They are not particles and have no direct physical interpretation." Prof. Dodd writes further, "They are properties of the vacuum; and since a vacuum is defined as a state of zero energy, there is no question of material objects there. Instantons are mathematical but they have a physical effect. In their presence the gluons feel force, so, nothing can affect something. The vacuum thus contains mathematical beings that teeter on the edge of reality and affect the behavior of material objects, starting with the gluons and working outward until, quite literally, the green grass grows all around.

Furthermore, the introduction of instantons requires the existence of a new particle that should be quite material, the axion. While instantons seem to solve a number of important difficulties in quantum chromodynamics, including the tantalizing question of why the quarks seem to always remain bound inside the particles they build and never go free, they raise other problems." (James Dodd, "Axion Hunt: Getting Something Out of Nothing," *Science News,* Vol. 113, No. 15, April 15, 1978:228.)

5. Dennis and Joyce Lawson-Wood, *Five Elements of Acupuncture and Chinese Massage* (Northamptonshire, Great Britain: Health Science Press, 1973), 72.

CHAPTER FOUR

1. Leland Hinsie and Robert Campbell, *The Psychiatric Dictionary* (New York: Oxford University Press, 1960), 613.

2. Georg Groddeck, *The Book of the It* (New York: A Mentor Book, 1961).

3. Franz Alexander, *Psychosomatic Medicine: Its Principles and Applications* (New York: W. W. Norton and Company, 1950).

4. Otto Fennichel, *The Psychoanalytic Theory of Neurosis* (New York: W. W. Norton and Company, 1945), 236.

5. Stewart Wolf and Harold G. Wolff, "Life Situations, Emotions and Gastric Function," *American Practitioner,* Vols. 3 and 4, 1948-1949:1-14.

6. Robert Ader, "A Historical Account of Conditioned Immunobiologic Responses," *Psychoneuro-Immunology,* ed. Robert Ader (California: University Academic Press, 1981).

7. George F. Solomon, "Immunologic Abnormalities in Mental Illness," *Psychoneuro-immunology,* ed. Robert Ader (California: University Academic Press, 1981).

8. Sir William Osler, *Counsels and Ideals from the Writings of Wm. Osler* (New York: Houghton Mifflin Company, 1921).

9. Mark Seem and Joan Kaplan, *Bodymind Energetics* (Rochester, Vermont: Thorsons Publishers, 1988).

10. *Diagnostical Statistical Manual of Mental Disorders,* III-R (DSM-III-R) (Washington, D.C.: American Psychiatric Association, 1987).

11. Ted J. Kaptchuk, *The Web that Has No Weaver* (New York: Congdon and Weed, 1983), 118-129.

12. Dennis and Joyce Lawson-Wood, *Five Elements of Acupuncture and Chinese Massage* (Northamptonshire, Great Britain: Health Science Press, 1973), 91.

13. Ibid., 91-96.

14. Anna Freud, *The Ego and the Mechanisms of Defense* (New York: International University Press, 1946).

ENDNOTES

CHAPTER FIVE

1. Ted J. Kaptchuk, *The Web that Has No Weaver* (New York: Congdon and Weed), 60.

2. Ibid.

3. Ibid., 61.

4. Ibid.

5. Manfred Porkert, *The Theoretical Foundations of Chinese Medicine: Systems of Correspondence* (Cambridge: The MIT Press, 1974), 107-196.

6. Kaptchuk, *The Web*, 60.

7. Ibid.

8. Ibid., 61.

9. *Essentials of Chinese Acupuncture*, (Beijing: Foreign Language Press, 1980), 68.

CHAPTER SIX

1. Leon I. Hammer, "Activity: An Immutable and Indispensible Element of the Therapist's Participation in Human Growth," *The Neurosis of Our Time: Acting Out*, George D. Goldman and Donald S. Milman, eds. (Springfield, Illinois: Charles C. Thomas, 1973), 281. See also Hammer, "Psychotherapy and Growth," *Contemporary Psychoanalysis*, Vol. 10, No. 3, 1974:389.

2. Dennis and Joyce Lawson-Wood, *Five Elements of Acupuncture and Chinese Massage* (Northamptonshire, Great Britain: Health Science Press, 1973), 91.

3. Ibid., 95.

4. Sigmund Freud, "Introductory Lectures on Psychoanalysis: Lecture XXVII," in *The Standard Edition of the Complete Psychological Works of Sigmund Freud*, Vol. 16, Part 3 (London: Hogarth Press, 1963), 436.

5. Wilhelm Reich, *Character Analysis* (New York: Farrar, Strauss, and Giroux, 1972).

CHAPTER SEVEN

I. Personal communications at the Traditional Acupuncture Institute in Columbia, Maryland.

2. Gordon Allport, *Becoming* (New Haven: Yale University, 1955), 31-33.

3. For an explanation of the work done by Alexander Lowen and John Pierrakos, see Alexander Lowen, *Physical Dynamics of Character Structure* (New York: Grune and Stratton, 1958).

4. Harry Stack Sullivan, "Interpersonal Theory of Psychiatry," in *Collected Works of Harry Stack Sullivan* (New York: W. W. Norton and Company, 1953), xviii.

5. Stella Chess, Thomas Alexander, and H. G. Birch, *Temperament and Behavior Disorders in Children* (New York: New York University Press, 1968).

6. Allport, *Becoming,* 7.

CHAPTER EIGHT

1. Matthew 6:12.

2. Man has long asked himself "Who am I?" The answer has been our scientific, mythological, literary, and religious heritage. The answer has never been completely satisfactory. We are better at saying who we are not. On the one hand, science has differentiated us with great precision from the animal, mineral, and plant world, and even from our predecesors on Earth. On the other hand, theology has been less precise about our distiction from the angels, devils, and gods.

3. Gerald Green, *The Last Angry Man* (New York: Scribner, 1956).

4. Manfred Porkert, *The Theoretical Foundations of Chinese Medicine: Systems of Correspondence* (Cambridge: The MIT Press, 1974), 166-196.

5. This forward motion in time and space is not only a talent, but, for some, also an actual state of mind. Those of us who are concerned about the future consequences of the impulsive, easy, and profitable practices of the present are generally known as conservationists. What we have is too highly valued to be squandered with abandon; and the standards generally acceptable to the majority are rarely sufficient for those whose sensitivities about the future are highly developed. Modern conservationists have fared less well than modern prophets of science, with whom they may, paradoxically, often be at odds. The misuse of science has narrowed the time-space gap between the present and the future. Their virtual coincidence has created the modern psychological catastrophe of *Future Shock.* (Alvin Toffler, *Future Shock* [New York: Random House, 1970].)

6. John Bunyan. *The Water of Life* (Swengel: Reiner, 1967).

7. Joen Fagan and Irma Lee Shepard, *Gestalt Therapy Now* (New York: Harper Colophon Books, 1970), 49.

8. Lee Salk, Lewis Lipsitt, William Sturner, Bernice Reilly, and Robin Leavat, "Relationship of Maternal and Perinatal Conditions to Eventual Adolescent Suicide," *The Lancet,* March 1985:624-627.

9. George Bernard Shaw, *The Complete Bernard Shaw Prefaces* (London: Paul Hamlyn, 1965), 189.

CHAPTER NINE

1. See "The Liver in Chinese Medicine," *Medical Acupuncture*, September 2009, Vol. 21, No. 3, September 2009: 173-178.

2. Stella Chess, Alexander Thomas, and H. G. Birch, *Temperament and Behavior Disorders in Children* (New York: New York University Press, 1968).

3. Alexander Lowen, *Physical Dynamics of Character Structure* (New York: Grune and Stratton. 1958), 204.

4. Ibid., 190.

5. Stephen M. Johnson, *Characterological Transformation* (New York: W. W Norton and Company, 1985), 35.

6. Lao Tzu, *The Tao Te Ching* (New York: Vintage Books, 1972).

7. Matthew 5:39 and also Luke 6:29.

8. Leo Tolstoy, *War and Peace* (New York: Simon and Schuster, 1942).

9. Matthew 5:39 and also Luke 6:29.

10. Henry David Thoreau, *Walden and Other Writings.* (NY: The Modern Library, 1965).

11. Ted J. Kaptchuk, lecture on depression, given in 1986 in New York.

12. Lowen, *Physical Dynamics,* 190.

CHAPTER TEN

1. Dennis and Joyce Lawson-Wood, *Five Elements of Acupuncture and Chinese Massage* (Northamptonshire, Great Britain: Health Science Press, 1973), 92.

2. Ibid.

3. Joseph Campbell states, "Neither is it clear why the myth of Elohim should ever have been thought to be one of creation *ex nihilo,* 'out of nothing,' when it describes creation from the power of the word, which in primitive thought is far from 'nothing,' but on the contrary is the essence of its thing." Joseph Campbell, *The Masks of God: Occidental Mythology* (New York: Penguin Books, 1976), 112. As early as 2850 B.C. there was an Egyptian myth of creation by the power of the word. And as recently as the 1920s, a youngster, six-and-a-half years old, said to the Swiss psychologist Dr. Jean Piaget, "If there weren't any words it would be very bad; you couldn't make anything. How could things have been made?" Jean Piaget, *The Child's Conception of the World* (New York: Harcourt Brace and Company, 1929), 72. Divine Intelligence has elaborated "The Word" into "The Law," the divinely inspired codes of ethics that characterize the transformation of the creative spirit into organized religion, the language of the Gods into the language of man. In the Orient, these "Laws" tend to be universal and apply to all phenomena. In the Occident, they apply only to man. The Developed Spirit of Man is the profound formulation of Divine Revelation glorified in language by Divine Intelligence.

4. Gordon Allport, *Becoming* (New Haven: Yale University, 1955), 31-33.

5. *Diagnostical Statistical Manual of Mental Disorders-III* (DSM-III) (Washington, D.C.: American Psychiatric Association, 1980), 219.

6. Ibid., 217.

7. Esteban Lucas Bridges, *The Uttermost Part of the Earth* (London: Hodder and Stoughton, 1948), 264.

8. John Donne, "Devotions Upon Emergent Occasions", Meditation XVII. *Norton Anthology of English Literature* (New York City: 1968), 528.

9. Alexander Lowen, *Physical Dynamics of Character Structure* (New York: Grune and Stratton, 1958), 231.

10. Ibid., 238.

11. Ibid., 258.

12. Ibid., 254.

13. Leon I. Hammer, "Psychotherapy and Growth," *Contemporary Psychoanalysis*, Vol. 10, No. 3, 1974:389.

14. Carl Jung, *Memories, Dreams, Reflections* (New York: Vintage Books, 1965), 45.

15. Ilsa Veith, *The Yellow Emperor's Classic of Internal Medicine* (Berkeley: University of California Press, 1972), 208.

16. Donald W. Winnicott, *The Maturational Processes and the Facilitating Environment* (Madison: International University Press, 1968), 140.

17. Veith, *Classic of Internal Medicine*, 208.

18. Anna Freud, *The Ego and the Mechanisms of Defense* (New York: International University Press, 1946).

19. Alan H. Francis, "Kidney Fire: Philosophy and Practice," *Journal of Traditional Acupuncture*, Vol. 3, Spring 1984:18.

20. Herman Melville, *Moby Dick* (New York: W. W. Norton and Company, 1967), 394.

21. Max Long, *The Secret Science Behind Miracles* (Marina del Ray, California: Book Graphics, 1948).

22. Frank Stass, personal communication based on work by Leslie Cameron Bandler.

23. Giacomo Puccini, *Turandot*.

24. Alan Jay Lerner and Frederick Loewe, *My Fair Lady* (Coward-McCann, 1956).

25. Fritz Perls, personal communication at a workshop.

26. Herman Wouk, *War and Remembrance* (Boston: Little, Brown, 1978).

27. George Bernard Shaw, *The Complete Bernard Shaw Prefaces* (London: Paul Hamlyn, 1965), 189.

CHAPTER ELEVEN

1. Theron Randolf, *Human Ecology and Susceptibility to the Chemical Environment* (Illinois: Charles C. Thomas, 1962).

2. *Diagnostical Statistical Manual of Mental Disorders, II* (DSM-II) (Washington, D.C.: American Psychiatric Association, 1952).

3. Donald W. Winnicott, *The Maturational Processes and the Facilitating Environment* (Madison: International University Press, 1968).

4. William H. Philpott and Dwight Kalita, *Brain Allergies* (New Canaan, Connecticut: Keats Publishing, 1980).

5. Leon Hammer, "Terrain, Stress, Root and Vulnerability," *Chinese Medicine Times,* Vol. 5, Issue 1, Spring 2010.

6. John Shen, personal communication.

7. Stella Chess, Alexander Thomas, and H. G. Birch, *Temperament and Behavior Disorders in Children* (New York: New York University Press, 1968).

8. Gordon Allport, *Becoming* (New Haven: Yale University Press, 1955), 7.

9. Bertolt Brecht and Kurt Weill, *The Threepenny Opera.*

CHAPTER TWELVE

1. Harry Stack Sullivan, "Interpersonal Theory of Psychiatry," *Collected Works of Harry Stack Sullivan* (New York: W. W. Norton and Company, 1953), 245.

2. Ibid., xviii.

3. Max Long, *The Secret Science Behind Miracles* (Marina del Ray, California: Book Graphics, 1948).

4. Joseph Campbell, *The Masks of God: Primitive Mythology* (New York: Penguin Books, 1986), 60-62.

5. Krishna Murti, *The First & Last Freedom* (London: Victor Gollanez, 1969), 12, 32.

6. Luke 17:21.

7. Matthew 10:37.

8. Eric Fromm, *Escape from Freedom* (New York: Farrar and Rinehart, 1941).

9. Walter Evans-Wentz, *The Tibetan Book of the Dead* (New York: Oxford University Press, 1960).

10. Tad James and Wyatt Woodsmall, *Time Line Therapy and the Basis of Personality* (Cupertino, California: Meta Publications, 1988), 23-26.

11. Burton Lane and E. Y. Harburg, *Finnian's Rainbow.*

CHAPTER THIRTEEN

1. Leland Hinsie and Robert Campbell, *The Psychiatric Dictionary* (New York: Oxford University Press, 1960), 50.

2. Hans Selye, *The Stress of Life* (New York: McGraw-Hill, 1956).

3. Dennis and Joyce Lawson-Wood, *Five Elements of Acupuncture and Chinese Massage* (Northamptonshire, Great Britain: Health Science Press, 1973), 89.

4. Sigmund Freud, "The Interpretation of Dreams" in *The Standard Edition of the Complete Psychological Works of Sigmund Freud,* Vols. 4 and 5 (London: Hogarth Press, 1900), 261.

5. Harry Stack Sullivan, "Interpersonal Theory of Psychiatry," in *Collected Works of Harry Stack Sullivan* (New York: W. W. Norton and Company, 1953), 245.

6. Walter Evans-Wentz, *The Tibetan Book of the Dead* (New York: Oxford University Press, 1960).

7. Joen Fagan and Irma Lee Shepard, *Gestalt Therapy Now* (New York: Harper Colophon Books, 1970), 31-32.

8. Joseph Breuer and Sigmund Freud, "Case Histories II: Frau Emmy Von N.," in *The Standard Edition of the Complete Psychological Works of Sigmund Freud,* Vol. 2 (London: Hogarth Press, 1955), 101.

9. Donald W. Winnicott, movie about anaclitic depression at the Tavistock Clinic in 1971.

10. Frank Stass, Personal communication based on work by Leslie Cameron Bandler.

11. John 1:1.

12. Carl Jung, *Memories, Dreams, Reflections* (New York: Vintage Books, 1965), 45

CHAPTER FOURTEEN

1. There is considerable discussion of specific pulse qualities and characteristics in this chapter which will be unfamiliar to the general reader, and even to many who have studied Chinese medicine. For more information, see Leon I. Hammer, *Chinese Pulse Diagnosis: A Contemporary Approach* (Seattle: Eastland Press, 2001).

2. Chang Chung Ching, *Shang Han Lun (Discussion of Cold Damage)* (California: Oriental Healing Arts Institute, 1981). The author's name is also rendered as Zhang Zhong-Jing.

3. There are three degrees of the 'qi is wild.' The least serious is one which comes from lifting beyond a person's energy over a relatively long time. Here the entire pulse is very light on top, hollow in the middle, and stronger below. The second and more serious is one in which the entire pulse is Empty, where something can be felt above and nothing felt below. This is due to excessive exercise in adolescence and sudden stopping, as described in the text. The most serious, also described in the text, is when the rate is so irregular that it cannot be accurately determined. This is usually due to severe deprivation at an early age, before ten. In recent years I have found the two latter conditions in those people who are now considered to have severely compromised immune systems.

4. John Diamond, *Your Body Doesn't Lie* (New York: Harper and Row, 1980).

5. Lee Salk et al., "Relationship of Maternal and Perinatal Conditions to Eventual Adolescent Suicide," *The Lancet,* March 1985.

6. Leon I. Hammer, *American Journal of Acupuncture*, Vol. 27, No. 3 (1999): 179.

7. Ilsa Veith, *The Yellow Emperor's Classic of Internal Medicine* (Berkeley: University of California Press, 1972), 97-98.

8. Leon I. Hammer, *Chinese Pulse Diagnosis: A Contemporary Approach* (Seattle: Eastland Press, 2001), 397.

9. Miles Roberts, personal communication.

CHAPTER FIFTEEN

1. Bernard Claude, *Rapport sur le Progrés et la Marche de la Physiologie Générale en France* (Lincoln: University of Nebraska Press, 1960), 81.

2. Walter Cannon, *The Wisdom of the Body* (New York: W. W. Norton and Company, 1939), 21.

3. Sir William Osler, *Counsels and Ideals from the Writings of Wm. Osler* (New York: Houghton Mifflin Company, 1921).

4. Matthew 5:7-8.

5. Wilhelm Reich, *The Function of Orgasm* (New York: Bantam Books, 1967), 52.

6. Alexander Lowen, *Physical Dynamics of Character Structure* (New York: Grune and Stratton, 1958), 31.

7. Dennis and Joyce Lawson-Wood, *Five Elements of Acupuncture and Chinese Massage* (Northamptonshire, Great Britain: Health Science Press, 1973), 72.

BIBLIOGRAPHY

Ader, Robert. "A Historical Account of Conditioned Immunobiologic Responses," in *Psychoneuro-immunology,* ed. Robert Ader (California: University Academic Press, 1981).

Alexander, Franz. *Psychosomatic Medicine: Its Principles and Applications* (New York: W. W. Norton and Company, 1950).

Allport, Gordon. *Becoming* (New Haven: Yale University, 1955).

Andreas, Connirae and Steve. *Change Your Mind and Keep the Change* (Moab: Real People Press, 1987).

Assagioli, Roberto. *The Act of Will* (New York: Penguin Books, 1974).

—. *Psychosynthesis: A Manual of Principles and Techniques* (New York: Viking/ Compass, 1971).

Austin, Mary. *Acupuncture Therapy* (New York: ASI Publishers, 1972).

Bensky, Dan, and O'Connor, John, trans. *Acupuncture: A Comprehensive Text* (Chicago: Eastland Press, 1981).

Bernard, Claude. *Rapport sur le Progrés et la Marche de la Physiologie Générale en France* (Lincoln: University of Nebraska Press, 1960).

Bo Yang, *The Ugly Chinaman* (Taipei, Taiwan: Lin Bai, 1985).

Brecht, Bertolt, and Weill, Kurt. *The Threepenny Opera.*

Breuer, Joseph, and Freud, Sigmund. "Case Histories II. Frau Emmy Von N.," in *The Standard Edition of the Complete Psychological Works of Sigmund Freud,* Vol. 2 (London: Hogarth Press, 1955).

Bridges, Esteban Lucas. *The Uttermost Part of the Earth* (London: Hodder and Stoughton, 1948).

Bunyan, John. *The Water of Life* (Swengel: Reiner, 1967).

Campbell, Joseph. *The Masks of God: Occidental Mythology* (New York: Penguin Books, 1976).

—. *The Masks of God: Oriental Mythology* (New York: Penguin Books, 1976).

—. *The Masks of God: Primitive Mythology* (New York: Penguin Books, 1986).

Cannon, Walter. *The Wisdom of the Body* (New York: W. W. Norton and Company, 1939).

The Centennial of Von Stradonitz's Work (Washington, D.C.: American Chemical Society, 1966).

Chamberlain, Selah. "Shen & Ling," *The Journal of Traditional Acupuncture,* Vol. 4, No. 1, Summer 1980.

Chess, Stella; Thomas, Alexander; and Birch, H. G. *Temperament and Behavior Disorders in Children* (New York: New York University Press, 1968).

Ching, Chang Chung. *Shang Han Lun (Discussion of Cold Damage)* (California: Oriental Healing Arts Institute, 1981).

Connelly, Dianne. *All Sickness is Home Sickness* (Columbia, Maryland: The Center for Traditional Acupuncture, 1986).

—. *Traditional Acupuncture: The Law of Five Elements* (Columbia, Maryland: The Center for Traditional Acupuncture, 1975).

Diagnostical Statistical Manual of Mental Disorders, II [DSM-II] (Washington, D.C.: American Psychiatric Association, 1952).

Diagnostical Statistical Manual of Mental Disorders, III [DSM-III] (Washington, D.C.: American Psychiatric Association, 1980).

Diagnostical Statistical Manual of Mental Disorders, III-R [DSM-III-R] (Washington, D.C.: American Psychiatric Association, 1987).

Diamond, John. *Your Body Doesn't Lie* (New York: Harper and Row, 1980).

Dodd, James. "Axion Hunt: Getting Something Out of Nothing," *Science News,* Vol. 113, No. 15, April 15, 1978.

Einstein, Albert. *Relativity: The Special and General Theory* (New York: Crown Publishers, 1961).

Eisenberg, David. *Encounters With Qi* (New York: W. W. Norton and Company, 1985).

Emerson, Ralph Waldo. "Self-Reliance," in *Essays: 1st & 2d Series* (Boston: Houghton Mifflin Company, 1929).

Essentials of Chinese Acupuncture (Beijing: Foreign Language Press, 1980).

Evans-Wentz, Walter. *The Tibetan Book of the Dead* (New York: Oxford University Press, 1960).

Fagan, Joen and Shepard, Irma Lee. *Gestalt Therapy Now* (New York: Harper Colophon Books, 1970).

Fennichel, Otto. *The Psychoanalytic Theory of Neurosis* (New York: W. W. Norton and Company, 1945).

Francis, Alan H. "Kidney Fire: Philosophy and Practice," *Journal of Traditional Acupuncture*, Vol. 3, Spring 1984.

Freud, Anna. *The Ego and the Mechanisms of Defense* (New York: International University Press, 1946).

Freud, Sigmund. "Analysis Terminable and Interminable," in *The Standard Edition of the Complete Psychological Works of Sigmund Freud*, Vol. 5 (London: Hogarth Press, 1953)

—. "The Anxiety Neurosis," in *The Standard Edition of the Complete Psychological Works of Sigmund Freud*, Vol. 3 (London: Hogarth Press, 1962).

—. " The Interpretation of Dreams," in *The Standard Edition of the Complete Psychological Works of Sigmund Freud*, Vols. 4 and 5 (London: Hogarth Press, 1953).

—. "Introductory Lectures on Psychoanalysis: Lecture XXVII," in *The Standard Edition of the Complete Psychological Works of Sigmund Freud*, Vol. 16, Part 3 (London: Hogarth Press, 1963).

—. "Papers on Techniques," in *The Standard Edition of the Complete Psychological Works of Sigmund Freud*, Vol. 2 (London: Hogarth Press, 1924).

—. "Psychotherapy of Hysteria," in *The Standard Edition of the Complete Psychological Works of Sigmund Freud*, Vol. 2 (London: Hogarth Press, 1955).

—. " Transference in the Analytic Therapy," in *General Introduction to Psychoanalysis* (Garden City, New York: Garden City Publishing, 1943).

Fromm, Eric. *Escape from Freedom* (New York: Farrar and Rinehart, 1941).

Green, Gerald. *The Last Angry Man* (New York: Scribner, 1956).

Groddeck, Georg. *The Book of the It* (New York: A Mentor Book, 1961).

[414]

Hammer, Leon I. "Activity: An Immutable and Indispensible Element of the Therapist's Participation in Human Growth," in *The Neurosis of Our Time: Acting Out,* George D. Goldman and Donald S. Milman, eds. (Springfield, Illinois: Charles C. Thomas, 1973).

—. *Chinese Pulse Diagnosis: A Contemporary Approach.* (Seattle: Eastland Press, 2001).

—. "Integrated Acupuncture Therapy for Body and Mind," *American Journal of Acupuncture,* Vol. 8, No. 2, April-June 1980.

—. "Psychotherapy and Growth," *Contemporary Psychoanalysis*, Vol. 10, No. 3, 1974.

—. "The Liver in Chinese Medicine," *Medical Acupuncture*, September 2009, Vol. 21, No. 3, September 2009: 173-178.

—. "Terrain, Stress, Root and Vulnerability," *Chinese Medicine Times,* Vol. 5, Issue 1, Spring 2010.

Hinsie, Leland, and Campbell, Robert. *The Psychiatric Dictionary* (New York: Oxford University Press, 1960).

The Holy Bible, New International Version (Canada: International Bible Publisher, 1984).

James, Tad, and Woodsmall, Wyatt. *Time Line Therapy and the Basis of Personality* (Cupertino, California: Meta Publications, 1988).

Johnson, Stephen M. *Characterological Transformation* (New York: W. W. Norton and Company, 1985).

Jung, Carl. *Memories, Dreams, Reflections* (New York: Vintage Books, 1965).

Kaptchuk, Ted J. *The Web that Has No Weaver* (New York: Congdon and Weed, 1983).

Lane, Burton, and Harburg, E. Y. *Finnian's Rainbow*

Lao Tzu, *The Tao Te Ching* (New York: Vintage Books, 1972).

Lawson-Wood, Dennis and Joyce. *Five Elements of Acupuncture and Chinese Massage* (Northamptonshire, Great Britain: Health Science Press, 1973).

Lerner, Alan Jay, and Loewe, Frederick. *My Fair Lady* (Coward-McCann, 1956).

Lewin, Kurt. *Field Theory in Social Science: Selected Theoretical Papers,* Dorwin Cartright, ed. (New York: Harper, 1951).

Long, Max. *The Secret Science Behind Miracles* (Marina del Ray, California: Book
  Graphics, 1948).

Lowen, Alexander. *Physical Dynamics of Character Structure* (New York: Grune
  and Stratton, 1958).

Lu Xun. *Selected Works* (Beijing: Foreign Language Press, 1956).

Mann, Felix. *Acupuncture: Ancient Art of Healing* (London: William Heinemann
  Medical Books, 1971).

Matsumoto, Kiiko, and Birch, Stephen. *Extraordinary Vessels* (Brookline, MA:
  Paradigm Publications, 1986).

—. *Five Elements & Ten Stems* (Brookline, MA: Paradigm Publications, 1983).

Melville, Herman. *Moby Dick* (New York: W. W. Norton and Company, 1967).

Murti, Krishna. *The First & Last Freedom* (London: Victor Gollanez, 1969).

Osler, Sir William. *Counsels and Ideals from the Writings of Wm. Osler* (New York:
  Houghton Mifflin Company, 1921).

Philpott, William H., and Kalita, Dwight. *Brain Allergies* (New Canaan, CT: Keats
  Publishing, 1980).

Piaget, Jean. *The Child's Conception of the World* (New York: Harcourt Brace and
  Company, 1929).

Porkert, Manfred. *The Theoretical Foundations of Chinese Medicine: Systems of
  Correspondence* (Cambridge: The MIT Press, 1974).

Puccini, Giacomo. *Turandot.*

Randolf, Theron. *Human Ecology and Susceptibility to the Chemical Environment*
  (Illinois: Charles C. Thomas, 1962).

Reich, Wilhelm. *Character Analysis* (New York: Farrar, Strauss, and Giroux, 1972).

—. *The Discovery of the Orgone,* Vol. 1 (New York: Orgone Institute Press, 1942).

—. *The Function of Orgasm* (New York: Bantam Books, 1967).

Salk, Lee; Lipsitt, Lewis; Sturner, William; Reilly, Bernice; and Leavat, Robin.
  "Relationship of Maternal and Perinatal Conditions to Eventual Adolescent
  Suicide," *The Lancet,* March 1985.

Seem, Mark. *Acupuncture Energetics: Workbook* (Rochester, Vermont: Thorsons
  Publishers, 1987).

Seem, Mark, and Kaplan, Joan. *Bodymind Energetics* (Rochester, Vermont: Thorsons Publishers, 1988).

Selye, Hans. "General Adaptation," in *The Stress of Life* (New York: McGraw-Hill, 1956).

Shaw, George Bernard. *The Complete Bernard Shaw Prefaces* (London: Paul Hamlyn, 1965).

Solomon, George E. "Immunological Abnormalities in Mental Illness," in *Psychoneuro-immunology,* Robert Ader, ed. (California: University Academic Press, 1981).

Sullivan, Harry Stack. *Clinical Studies in Psychiatry* (New York: W. W. Norton and Company, 1956).

—. "Interpersonal Theory of Psychiatry," *Collected Works of Harry Stack Sullivan* (New York: W. W. Norton and Company, 1953).

Thoreau, Henry David. *Walden and Other Writings* (New York: The Modern Library, 1965).

Toffler, Alvin. *Future Shock* (New York: Random House, 1970).

Tolstoy, Leo. *War and Peace* (New York: Simon and Schuster, 1942).

Veith, Ilsa. *The Yellow Emperor's Classic of Internal Medicine* (Berkeley: University of California Press, 1972).

Waley, Arthur. *The Three Ways of Thought in Ancient China* (London: G. Allen and Unwin, 1963).

Whitehead, Alfred North. *Field Theory Process and Reality* (New York: MacMillan, 1929).

Wilhelm, Richard. *The I Ching* (London: Routledge & Kegan Paul, 1951).

Williams, Rodger. *Biochemical Individuality* (Austin: University of Texas, 1956).

Winnicott, Donald W. *The Maturational Processes and the Facilitating Environment* (Madison: International University Press, 1968).

—. Movie on anaclitic depression at Tavistock Clinic in 1971.

Wolf, Stewart, and Wolff, Harold G. "Life Situations, Emotions and Gastric Function," *American Practitioner,* Vols. 3 and 4, 1948-1949.

Wouk, Herman. *War and Remembrance* (Boston: Little, Brown, 1978).

Index

[417]

─── E

——— **M**

About the Author

Leon Hammer, M.D., is a graduate of Cornell University, Cornell Medical College, and the William A. White Institute of Psychoanalysis and Psychiatry. Until 1971, he practiced psychiatry and psychoanalysis, directed a child guidance clinic and drug abuse council on the southeast shore of Long Island, taught at Adelphi University, and was psychiatric consultant and associate professor at Southampton College in Southampton, New York.

After working with Fritz Perls and Alexander Lowen over a period of eight years, he began the study of Chinese medicine in England during 1971–1974. He then continued his studies with a Chinese Master, Dr. John Shen, in New York City for eight years followed by several months in Beijing. Dr. Hammer has been a certified acupuncturist in New York since 1975, and in Maryland since 1988, where he studied and taught at the Traditional Acupuncture Institute. In 1985 he was granted honorary Diplomate in Acupuncture status by the NCCA. He actively practiced Chinese medicine from 1975 until 1990.

Dr. Hammer has lectured and taught in places as diverse as Poland, Italy, Germany, England, Australia, Japan and throughout the United States. In 1984 he served on the Commission for Evaluation of Acupuncture Schools, and in 1995 was appointed to the National Blue Ribbon Committee for Initiation of the Herbal Examination. From 1991 to 1998, he was a member of the New York State Board of Acupuncture.

In addition to this book, Dr. Hammer published *Chinese Pulse Diagnosis: A Contemporary Approach* in 2001, and in the same year was selected "Educator of the Year" by the American Association of Oriental Medicine for participation and contribution to excellence in education. In 2002, he received an award from the Traditional Chinese Medicine Foundation for "Building Bridges of Integration" between Oriental and Western medicine.

In 2001 Dr. Hammer helped found the Dragon Rises College of Oriental Medicine in Gainesville, Florida, where he now serves as a member of its faculty and Board chair. The school emphasizes diagnosis, especially the pulse, and its curriculum focuses on psychology and the integration of various models of Chinese medicine, including TCM and Five Element (Phase).